Racing & Football Outlook
FLAT RACING
GUIDE 2008
Previews • Training centre reports

A **RACING POST** COMPANY

Contributors: Amy Bennett, Neil Clark, Nick Deacon, Steffan Edwards, Dylan Hill, Mark Howard, Tony Jakobson, Kel Mansfield, Steve Mellish, Mark Nelson, Dave Nevison, Ben Osborne, Graham Wheldon, Richard Williams.

Designed and edited by Nick Watts and Dylan Hill

Published in 2008 by Raceform,
Compton, Newbury, Berkshire RG20 6NL

A catalogue record for this book is available from the British Library.

ISBN 978-1-905153-73-2

Printed in Wales by Creative Print and Design

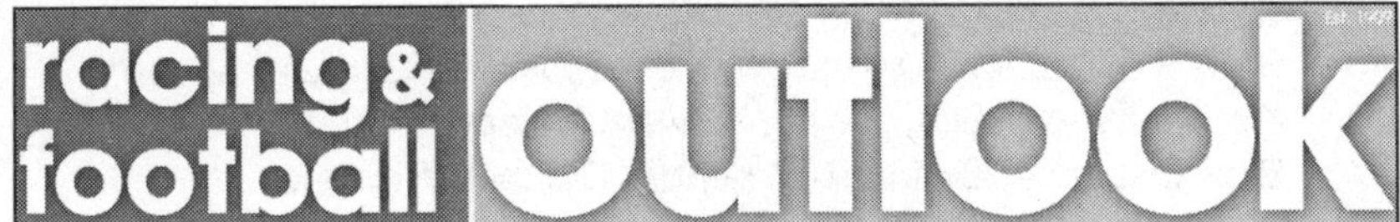

Contents

Introduction ... 4
Profiles for punters   Clive Cox ... 7
                       Ann Duffield ... 12

2008 Preview

Ante-post ... 17
Racing & Football Outlook's 30 horses to follow ... 31
Pedigrees for punters with Amy Bennett ... 39
Aborigine ... 43
Jerry M ... 48
Downsman ... 52
Borderer ... 57
Hastings ... 61
Southerner ... 64
John Bull ... 67
Steve Mellish ... 70
Dave Nevison ... 74
Time Test with Mark Nelson ... 76

2007 Review

News Diary ... 79
Group 1 Review ... 87
Two-year-old Review ... 96

Statistics, Races and Racecourses

Three-year stats for ten top trainers ... 113
Jockey & trainer stats ... 154
Group 1 records ... 161
Big handicap records ... 171
Fixtures ... 178
Big-race dates ... 184
Track facts for all Britain's Flat courses ... 187
Sprintline with Graham Wheldon ... 225

Final furlong

Picture quiz ... 232
Betting guide & Rule 4 deductions ... 236
Horse index ... 238

Editor's introduction

IF ever a year typified the drama and unpredictability of racing, then 2007 was that year. And here at the RFO we were caught out the same as everyone.

Twelve months ago this very guide was published with a front-cover shot of Teofilo beating Holy Roman Emperor in the National Stakes at the Curragh, surely the first of several thrilling battles between the two great juveniles.

Yet, after just one more epic head-to-head in the Dewhurst at Newmarket, neither ever saw the racecourse again.

Teofilo retired to stud after a couple of injury setbacks, while Holy Roman Emperor went the same way in controversial circumstances as he was drafted in as a stallion replacement for the ill-fated George Washington.

While that was bitterly disappointing, it says a lot for the magic of the racing world that back at Newmarket little over a month later a new and unexpected set of heroes forced their way into the sport's folklore.

Cockney Rebel, written off after being twice beaten as a two-year-old, produced a devastating performance in the 2,000 Guineas, proving every bit as good as his enigmatic trainer Geoff Huffer had promised.

And rock legend Steve Harley, after whose band the horse was named, was even in the horse's corner to add another remarkable twist.

Not surprisingly, Aidan O'Brien had a rich back-up to Holy Roman Emperor, producing a pair of brilliant multiple Group 1 winners in Dylan Thomas and Peeping Fawn.

More astonishingly, however, Jim Bolger also had another Teofilo in waiting.

He sent out New Approach to win the exact same five races as Teofilo did, arguably even more impressively, and once again he starts the year with the hot favourite for both the Guineas and the Derby.

The main opposition to New Approach is likely to come from a rejuvenated Godolphin challenge.

Racing Post Trophy winner Ibn Khaldun is exactly the sort of horse Sheikh Mohammed's operation promised to produce when it first came into existence, while there could also be plenty to come from fellow Group 1 winner Rio de la Plata and new purchase Fast Company, narrowly beaten by New Approach in the Dewhurst.

Three of last season's Classic winners, Finsceal Beo, Light Shift, and Lucarno, have stayed in training as well as two other special three-year-olds, runaway Irish Derby winner Soldier Of Fortune and the new 'Iron Lady' Peeping Fawn.

News-wise, it is to be hoped the sport hits the front pages as much as it did in 2007 because, for all the furore over the Old Bailey race-fixing trial, more often that not racing made the headlines for the right reasons.

There was Frankie Dettori 12 years on from being caught in the dying strides when Lammtarra pipped Tamure, finally winning his first Derby on Authorized, and then going on to secure a Group 1 hat-trick on Ramonti to ensure his famous flying dismount became a familiar sight once more.

And Jamie Spencer and Seb Sanders produced the most thrilling battle for the jockeys' championship in living memory, with Spencer winning the last race of the season to secure a tie after the race had swung backwards and forwards almost every day in the closing weeks.

Fingers crossed 2008 will produce more of the same, and the following pages should give you a good idea of just what to expect.

Our reporters have been around all the yards in their region to bring you the latest from the top trainers, with in-depth analysis of the Ballydoyle and Godolphin strings, the sure-fire winning machines of Mark Johnston and Richard Hannon, and many more.

We also have in-depth interviews with two improving and potentially underrated stables, those of Clive Cox and Ann Duffield, in a bid to sniff out more winners.

Steffan Edwards studies the ante-post markets for the four Classics to find the early value, there are the expert views of Steve Mellish, professional punter Dave Nevison and Time Test guru Mark Nelson, and using all our experts' views we have identified the 30 horses we reckon most likely to make a major mark on the campaign in our horses to follow section.

Amy Bennett looks at the latest batch of first-crop sires who could have an impact in Pedigrees For Punters, and the first half of this book finishes with a form guide to the last year, examining those performances which may have slipped under the radar.

If you like stats, then the second half of the book is for you as we bring you the most comprehensive analysis imaginable.

We have looked at the ten winningmost trainers of last year to find when and where their horses are most backable, as well as which age group, type of race and jockey you should look out for.

We have examined all of Britain's racecourses to see which trainers and jockeys have the best strike-rates, accompanied by unrivalled draw analysis from Sprintline expert Graham Wheldon.

And, of course, you need to know exactly when they will be racing at your local track in the next year, together with a guide to all the big-race dates.

All in all, we have every base covered in order to bring you a profit-filled 2008, and don't forget to buy your copy of the RFO every week for the very latest news and tips. Happy punting!

AT LAST! after a long wait, Frankie Dettori finally lands the Derby on Authorized

Trainer Files
by Neil Clark

Clive Cox

CLIVE COX: sharing a joke with John Francome, owner of Beechdown Farm Stables

IT must be something in the air. The county of Somerset has a habit of producing successful racehorse trainers or being the base of successful racing stables – think Paul Nicholls, Martin and David Pipe and Philip Hobbs.

And although Clive Cox trains in Berkshire, the talented handler is very much a Somerset man. The son of a West Country farmer, Cox did not enter the racing game through the traditional farmer's son's route of point-to-pointing, but by becoming a jockey on the Flat.

"I was quite light so I went for the Flat," Cox recalls. "I had a dozen rides before I rode my first winner, for Peter Cundell on the last race of the last day of the season in 1981. I beat John Lowe on a horse called Swift Palm."

At that time, Cundell's yard was one of the strongest in the country, saddling plenty of winners under both codes.

"He had some very good horses, like King of Spain and Aqareem. He also had all of Peter Harris' horses."

Cox then switched to riding exclusively over jumps, becoming second jockey to Oliver Sherwood, again a yard at the peak of its powers.

Cox forged a successful partnership with the staying chaser Sacred Path, but unfortunately only got as far as the first fence when the gelding started favourite for the 1988 Grand National – "my only ride in the race".

A highlight of Cox's riding career, in which he rode almost 100 winners, was winning the Frogmore Chase on Fred Winter's Admiral's Cup. "It was great to ride some really good horses and ride for some top stables," he says.

In 1991 Cox retired from the saddle and took out a licence as a dual-purpose trainer in partnership. But things didn't work out and a year later he became assistant trainer to

Mikey Heaton-Ellis. "It was a very enjoyable time of my life. From Mikey I learned a lot about life and how to train horses."

Sadly, Heaton-Ellis died in 1999, and a year later Cox once again set out on his own, making the John Francome-owned Beechdown Farm Stables at Lambourn his new base.

And every year since then he has made progress. Cox's tally of winners over the last five seasons speak for themselves. In 2003 he saddled 14 winners, since when it has risen to 16, 23, 25 and, last year, 33.

Make no mistake, this is a stable seriously on the up, not just in terms of the number of winners, but in the sort of races that are being won.

Consistent 1m2f specialist handicapper Ionian Spring was one of the first horses that put Cox on the map, and in 2003 he saddled his first Royal Ascot winner when New Seeker landed the Britannia Handicap.

Under Cox's expert care, New Seeker climbed through the ranks from handicapper to Listed winner, and last year the trainer won the Group 3 Horris Hill Stakes at Newbury with Beacon Lodge, Listed races at Goodwood and Ascot with Dunelight and Perfect Star, the Great St Wilfrid Handicap at Ripon with Kostar and the Old Newton Cup at Haydock with Dansili Dancer.

Cox has shown that he is adept at getting sprinters ready for valuable handicaps and handling two-year-olds to win Group races.

"I am extremely ambitious and I'm always looking to improve things," he says, "without overlooking tried and tested methods. You never stop learning in this game – if you believe you know everything, that's when you trip over. Everyone makes mistakes, but the most important thing is to learn from then and not make the same mistake twice."

Cox has his own grass gallops as well as a 7f all-weather gallop and two American barns. Having private gallops allows him to exercise his horses in the peace and quiet of beautiful downland countryside, without having to wait his turn.

The trainer will have around 60 horses on the go for the new campaign, including 27 two-year-olds, with Philip Robinson and Adam Kirby again riding most of them.

"I'm hopeful that with the formula we've got, we'll have another good season", Cox says. And with the talent he has assembled, few would bet against it.

NEW SEEKER: one of the horses who helped to put Clive Cox on the map

BEACON LODGE: lands his maiden at Newbury under Adam Kirby

Cox's charges

Amylee
3yo bay filly
Danehill Dancer - Igreja (Southern Halo)
Ran very well to finish fifth, just behind a Group 2 winner, in the Goffs Fillies Million at The Curragh in her final start. She wasn't over-raced at two (she only ran four times) and I would hope she will continue to progress.

Beacon Lodge
3yo bay colt
Clodovil - Royal House (Royal Academy)
Did very well for us last season, winning the Horris Hill at Newbury in October. He's wintered well and looks tremendous. He will be entered in the 2,000 Guineas and I'd like to be as positive as possible. I hope he has progressed. He'll probably run in the Greenham at Newbury in April and we'll see how we go from there. I've little doubt that he'll get the mile.

Dansili Dancer
6yo bay gelding
Dansili - Magic Slipper (Habitat)
Proved worthy for the step up in trip by winning the Old Newton Cup over 1m4f at Haydock in August and then ran well again off his revised mark when stepped up to 1m6f in the Old Borough Cup, in which he finished third. He loves top of the ground and will be campaigned with the ground in mind. I'd hope he'd carry on progressing and the race I have in mind for him is the Ebor.

Den's Gift
4yo grey gelding
City On A Hill - Romanylei (Blues Traveller)
He had a problem last year which is why he didn't race on turf. He won on his first run for over a year over 7f at Lingfield in November and followed up a couple of weeks later over a mile at Kempton. I've entered him in the Lincoln, I think he'll probably get

DUNELIGHT: grabs another win at Goodwood, his favourite track

into the reserve race off his rating of 80. I hope he will continue to improve.

Don't Forget Faith
3yo bay filly
Victory Gallop - Contredance (Danzig)
Won her maiden very pleasingly, beating Sir Michael Stoute's Visit, who went on to win a Group 3 at Ascot on her next start. We've always held her in high regard and she showed a lot of class to win over 6f, which was plenty sharp enough. She didn't handle the quicker ground on her next two starts at Newmarket and Doncaster, unusually for an American filly, but she finished off with a very good run in the Marcel Boussac at Longchamp, staying on very nicely to finish fifth. She's entered in the Irish Oaks and I think she'll stay. She is better with a bit of cut and I'll be looking to run her where the ground is suitable. She has a lot of ability.

Drifting Gold
4yo chestnut filly
Bold Edge - Driftholme (Safawan)
Won three times for us last year, once at Wolverhampton and twice on turf. She's a real 5f specialist. She's a recent winner on the all-weather and although she'll be starting on a higher mark this time round (currently rated 75), I'm sure she'll be scoring again this summer.

Dunelight
5yo chestnut horse
Desert Sun - Badee'a (Marju)
A Listed race winner last year who also ran wonderfully well in defeat. I thought he'd won the Lennox Stakes at Glorious Goodwood, but he ran a great race (finished a close third behind Tariq). I'm hopeful he can achieve Group race success. He needs top of the ground and I'm sure Goodwood will feature in his programme as he loves it there.

Electrolyser
3yo grey colt
Daylami - Iviza (Sadler's Wells)
Had a setback and didn't run as a two-year-old but finished second on his racecourse debut behind Pacifism at Lingfield over 1m2f. He then won a maiden on his second start, over the same course and distance in February. A cheaply-bought yearling, his family pedigree warranted an entry in the Derby and the way he has run at Lingfield indicate

Sponsored by Stan James

that he'd have no problem with getting further than 1m2f.

Highland Daughter
3yo bay filly
Kyllachy - Raysiza (Alzao)
Won first time out at Leicester and then finished third in the Empress Stakes. She signed off by finishing third in a Group 3 race at Ayr. She's very gutsy and determined. She has got taller during the winter. It's likely she will stay 7f but, if not, it doesn't much matter as she's very good over 6f. She's full of class.

Jimmy Styles
4yo chestnut gelding
Inchinor - Inya Lake (Whittingham)
Didn't run as a two-year-old due to injury but made up for lost time last year. Won his maiden at Windsor in August and then won a 6f handicap very nicely at Newbury. The handicapper put him up 11lb to a mark of 89 but he still ran respectably off his revised mark at Doncaster on his final run of the campaign. He has plenty of gears and I still hope he can improve further.

Kostar
7yo chestnut gelding
Komaite - Black And Amber (Weldnaas)
A late foal, he has improved every year. Last season he won the Great St Wilfrid Handicap at Ripon. Once again, he's come back bigger and stronger. He has his own way of doing things – he has a few habits we'd rather he lose! He prefers to be loaded first in the stalls. He loves top of the ground and will be aimed at all the top 6f handicaps again.

Miracle Seeker
3yo brown filly
Rainbow Quest - Miracle (Ezzoud)
Just touched off when making a very pleasing racecourse debut at Haydock in September and then finished third in a very hot Doncaster maiden. She is very well-bred – she's a half-sister to Katchit and 1m2f winner Prince Erik. She's done very well during the winter and is full of promise. She holds an entry in the Irish Oaks.

Pearly Wey
5yo bay gelding
Lujain - Dunkellin (Irish River)
Won the Silver Stewards' Cup last year and I'm really pleased we've got him. Although

KOSTAR: wins at Lingfield in 2006

he won first time up at Newmarket as a two-year-old, he's taken a bit of time to really come to his own and he needs to learn how to relax in a race. He's come back bigger and stronger. His target will be the top sprints. He prefers top of the ground.

Perfect Act
3yo bay filly
Act One - Markova's Daughter
(Mark Of Esteem)
Won first time out over 7f at Newbury in August and then ran a super race at Newmarket over a trip shorter than her best. At Newbury on her last run, when she finished fourth, she probably hit the front too soon. She's a very flighty filly, quite small but real dynamite. I still think she'll get a mile.

Perfect Star
4yo filly
Act One - Granted (Cadeaux Genereux)
She signed off with a very pleasing Listed win at Ascot in September. Her form stands up really very well, at Salisbury, in the race before Ascot, she beat Barry Hills' Miss Lucifer, who went on to win a Group 2 at Newmarket. For a Listed winner she's potentially still well-handicapped (she's currently rated 96) and we've entered her in the Lincoln. She's a very gutsy, gritty filly and although she's won on good-to-firm, she would appreciate a bit of juice and I really don't fear the ground at Doncaster.

Ann Duffield

LOST IN CONVERSATION: Ann Duffield talks to jockey Royston Ffrench

IT was Ralph Waldo Emerson who once said, "Nothing great was ever achieved without enthusiasm". If the American sage could come back to life today and make his way up to Sun Hill Farm, at Constable Burton in North Yorkshire, he would find ample evidence of the truth of his old adage.

Trainer Ann Duffield brims with enthusiasm for her job. "My work is my hobby," she says. "The Chinese say that if you find a job that you love you will never work for the rest of your life, and that's what I've done. I love building the place up and I love training. I never wake up thinking 'Oh no, here we go again'."

But, of course, while enthusiasm is essential for success it is not the only ingredient. Skill and hard work are also necessary and when someone possesses all three, like Duffield, the results inevitably follow.

Last year, for the second season running, Duffield saddled 30 winners, capped with a win in the valuable two-year-old Watership Down Sales race at Ascot, with a horse, Lady Rangali, that had cost just 11,000 gns at the Newmarket Yearling Sales.

Just six years earlier Duffield's yard only had eight horses, so there are few stables progressing at such a rate and it means a lot more is likely to be heard of her in the years to come.

Although she has spent the last 20 years living and working in the White Rose county, Ann is a born-and-bred Lancastrian, raised in Merseyside, the daughter of a bookmaker.

On moving across the Pennines in 1988, she began buying and selling horses, hunting (which remains a great passion) and eventing. It was in the late 1980s that she went to the Ascot sales and bought a horse to go point-to-pointing.

"He won three times and I sold him for a profit at Doncaster and thought 'this is easy!'"

LADY RANGALI: winning a valuable prize at Ascot last season

recalls Duffield. Her first winner under Rules was a hunter chaser named Jaaez, who won the Garthorpe Maiden Hunters' Chase at Leicester on 2 March 1992 at 33-1.

In August that year she took out a full training licence and just two months later she had winners on successive days – White Diamond won a bumper at Carlisle at 20-1 and Jupiter Moon won at 14-1 at Bangor.

Duffield claims her metamorphosis into a Flat trainer "just happened", though it seems likely husband George Duffield, legendary stable jockey to Sir Mark Prescott, may have had a bit to do with it.

The pair bought the 50-acre Sun Hill Farm in 1999 and over a period of time, and after much hard work, converted it into the top-class training centre it is today.

"The facilities here are great," the trainer says. "It's all been purpose-built. We've got three horse walkers, three American barns, our own parade ring in an area to the front of the yard as well as a small 'play pen'.

"We've also got an exceptionally good 6f uphill All-Weather gallop. George, who helped with the design, maintains it is as good as any he has ridden on. The gradual but stiff 250ft climb helps to get the horses race fit without them realising just how hard they are working. It gets them fitter, quicker, but with less stress on their joints."

Duffield is also keen to stress the role her staff play in the success of the operation. "They are a fantastic bunch and without doubt the best staff I have ever employed," she says.

Husband George is not only assistant trainer, but also chief work rider, where his years of experience in the saddle is invaluable. And when he's not on duty, George loves nothing better than landscaping the gardens at Sun Hill Farm, his hobby featuring in the Racing Post's 'My Other Life' series.

Duffield's training philosophy is a simple one: to get the very best out of every horse in her yard.

"It's important not to confuse geese with swans. If it's clear that the horse is not going to make the grade, then we move them on. It's best to be honest with owners rather than keep stringing them along.

"Sometimes, though, you get very attached to horses who have been with you a long time and you want to keep them for longer. For example, Pauvic won for us as a two-year-old, and although he is only ordinary, it would be nice to win a couple of races on the All-Weather with him before we let him go."

Buying yearlings is also a key part of Duffield's strategy. "Ordinary owners can't afford to buy horses with form in the book, so that's why we've started buying yearlings. It's the only way we'll be able to get really top-class horses."

An analysis of Duffield's statistics over the past five years shows that she does exceptionally well when sending her charges on long trips to southern venues.

At Brighton she has saddled four winners from just six runners, a phenomenal strike-rate of 67%, while on the All-Weather at leafy Lingfield her strike-rate is a healthy 36%.

But she also has great records at Carlisle, where one in four of her runners wins; Haydock, where she has saddled seven winners from just twenty runners, and nearby Catterick, where anyone betting £1 on all of her runners would have made profits of £39.33.

The stable does very well in apprentice races – around one in four of Duffield's runners in such events win – and the strike-rate rises to one in three if only her older horses are considered.

Regarding jockey arrangements, Royston Ffrench, who had been riding Duffield's horses regularly for three years, formally became stable jockey in 2007.

Meanwhile, apprentice rider Andrew Mullen, who has ridden 80 winners and who currently has a 3lb claim, has recently joined the team.

So what are Ann Duffield's ambitions for 2008? "To continue to train an increasing number of winners, to carry on enjoying the job, to get the best out of each and every horse in our care and to raise the standard of all aspects of our operation."

Seeing the progress Duffield has made over the past few years, only a fool would bet against her achieving her targets.

Duffield's diamonds

Bonjour Allure
3yo bay filly
Hawk Wing - Exact Replica (Darshaan)
After a good debut at Thirsk, where she finished second, she then impressively beat Dubai Times, who was later sold for £250,000 at Ayr. At Doncaster on her final run, she disappointed, (finished last), but she had a poor draw and saw too much daylight. 1m2f might be her best trip.

Falcon's Fire
4yo bay gelding
Orpen - Tres Chic (Northern Fashion)
Won a maiden at Catterick in May, but we felt he wasn't really putting it all in on the Flat. We schooled him over hurdles and he was a revelation. He won on his first start over hurdles at Bangor and later on won a good race at Market Rasen. We took him to Cheltenham for a race at the Open meeting, but it was one run too many – he'd been kept on the go a long time and he'd just gone over the top. He's quite well handicapped on the Flat, (his current rating is 57, compared to 133 over hurdles!) and if he wants to do well, he will do. He's a strong, impressive sort.

Just Lille
5yo bay mare
Mull Of Kintyre - Tamasriya (Doyoun)
Did very well for us last year, winning four on the bounce in May/June. I wouldn't say she'll be able to win four times again this year as she's obviously risen in the weights (she's now rated 83), but I do think that on her day she'll be able to win a decent little 10/15K handicap. My philosophy is to win what you can with them on the Flat and then when the handicapper's got them, to send them jumping – and that's where she'll go in the autumn.

Lady Rangali
3yo bay filly
Danehill Dancer - Promising Lady
(Thunder Gulch)
Bought on spec for only 11, 000gns from the Newmarket Yearling Sales, she did really well for us last year with four wins, finishing off by winning the valuable Class 2 Watership Down Stud Sales race at Ascot, which was worth £134,000. Some have said that the race wasn't a good one, but the form has actually worked out very well. The third, Sophies Girl finished a close-up fourth in a

Listed race at Newmarket, the fourth, Insaaf, won on his next start and the fifth, Anosti, was beaten a neck in an ultra-competitive Newmarket maiden. I'm sure if we'd have been a fashionable southern yard, she'd have been hailed as the next Indian Ink, who won the race the year before. Physically, she's done very well over the winter, she's really filled out. She's got a handicap rating of 82, so well start her off in handicaps, but the aim will be to get some black type. She's as tough as old boots and goes on any ground.

Prince Namid
6yo bay gelding
Namid - Fen Princess (Trojan Fen)
Has a lot of ability but has been in the grip of the handicapper for a long while now. He's a real spring horse, and we'll be trying to win early with him. He always runs well in the 6f Sprint at Epsom on Derby Day (he's finished second the past two years) and we'll certainly be taking him there again. He's very genuine.

San Silvestro
3yo colt
Fayruz - Skehana (Mukaddamah)
A great big tall leggy colt, bought at the Breeze Up sales, he won a maiden at Catterick on his only start of last season. He's still very green, but if he trains on, he could be anything. We're very hopeful. We've got no specific targets – we'll just take it step by step with him.

Shandlelight
4yo bay filly
Dilshaan - By Candelight (Roi Danzig)
She's only ordinary (currently rated 51) but she did run some good races last summer on the All-Weather and on turf and finished the season finishing a good second in a 1m4f handicap at Thirsk. I think she will win and the plan is to win a couple of races with her and then sell her to go jumping.

GALILEO: sired the classy Lady Luachmer

The Real Guru
3yo bay colt
Ishiguru - Aloma's Reality (Proper Reality)
Won his maiden at Pontefract in July but then lost his way after that and has been castrated. I think the handicapper over-reacted by giving him a rating of 81, and even though he's dropped now, I think his current rating of 72 is still too high. He's a fast horse and when he does fall to a more realistic handicap mark, I think he can win again.

Toboggan Lady
4yo bay filly
Tobougg - Northbend (Shirley Heights)
She was a very weak two-year-old, shaped like a razor blade with hardly any meat on her, but did tremendously well last year to win three times, at distances between 1m4f and 2m2f. Her form is very decent – she was only beaten a quarter of a length by Franchoek at Nottingham in August. In her last seven runs she has only been out of the first two once, at Redcar where she didn't like the firm ground and ran as if something was amiss. On her last run she won a 2m2f handicap at Pontefract and now we know she acts on the track I'd be keen to bring her back there for more long-distance races.

In addition, Ann singles out the following two-year-olds from her team for RFO readers to follow. "HELS ANGEL is a very tough racey filly by first season sire Pyrus, she is the double of Lady Rangali, I hope she goes as fast! We like her a lot. STREVELYN is a Namid colt who we've had castrated. He's a lovely horse who wouldn't be out too early. LADY LUACHMER is by Galileo and out of a staying mare. She's a lovely, classy filly. She won't be seen out until the backend and we'll probably see more of her as three-year-old. I've also got a nice filly called CAMELOT COMMUNION by first season sire Elusive City out of Second Prayer, a Singspiel mare.

2008 Preview

Ante-Post

with Steffan Edwards

2,000 Guineas

IT'S very much a case of deja vu in the first colts Classic, with the ante-post favourite an unbeaten Galileo colt trained by Jim Bolger.

New Approach won the same five races at two as Teofilo did the previous year and tops the betting at a very similar price.

Teofilo never made the racecourse at three, which goes to show the perils of backing Classic prospects at short prices over the winter, but while I always thought that Teofilo was more of a Derby horse than a Guineas prospect, I think that New Approach has more speed.

He should be fully effective over a mile this year, as well as stay further as the season progresses, and the stiff finish at Newmarket suits him ideally, as we saw in the Dewhurst.

He'll be a tough nut to crack, but a top price of 5-2 makes little appeal and there are a number of potential improvers further down the lists.

FAST COMPANY was one of the least experienced in the Dewhurst and so the fact that he got within half a length of the winner having been forced to challenge wide suggests that he could well turn the tables with a winter on his back.

Just as at York when he won the Acomb, he was finishing his race strongly, and the extra furlong of the Guineas looks sure to suit this Godolphin recruit.

His pedigree also strongly suggests that he'll be a miler this term, which is encouraging, and at over three times the price of the favourite he looks a sound bet to im-

prove past him.

Raven's Pass travelled like the winner into the dip but was outstayed in the softish ground on the climb to the line.

He'd previously been an impressive winner of the Solario Stakes on quick ground, bolting up by 7l from subsequent Royal Lodge winner City Leader, so if the ground came up fast he would be a strong contender.

However, he'll have to prove his stamina, and his pedigree isn't entirely convincing on that front. Indeed, it wouldn't surprise me to see him end up sprinting this year.

Rio De La Plata won an average renewal of the Prix Jean-Luc Lagardere in between being put in his place by New Approach at The Curragh and at Newmarket, where he'd have finished close to Raven's Pass with a clear run.

He might well fall between two stools this season and turn out to be a 1m2f horse, which brings in the French Derby as a possible target, and perhaps the French Guineas will be used as a stepping stone beforehand.

Ibn Khaldun is another possible Godolphin representative.

Highly progressive last autumn, he won a nursery off 85 at the end of September but improved over the next four weeks to bag a Group 3 race and then follow up with a 3l success in the Racing Post Trophy.

There are question marks over the value of that form, with a pair of 66-1 shots finishing third and fourth, but he still beat the

HENRYTHENAVIGATOR (foreground): beats Luck Money (far side) in the Coventry Stakes

Royal Lodge winner comfortably into second.

He showed a useful turn of foot on more than one occasion last season and, one thing's for sure, he's certainly bred to be a Guineas horse, being by top-class miler Dubai Destination out of Irish 1,000 Guineas winner Gossamer.

At first glance Aidan O'Brien doesn't seem to hold much of a hand in the race, but it's never wise to write him off in a race he's won four times in the last ten years.

HENRYTHENAVIGATOR is the forgotten horse of the race.

He was an early favourite for the Guineas after winning the Coventry Stakes at Royal Ascot, but he got turned over at odds-on in the Phoenix Stakes next time and was then beaten under a penalty by New Approach in the Futurity.

The very testing conditions he encountered in both those races didn't suit him at all and there's every chance he'll bounce back into the Guineas picture on quicker ground.

He's bred to make a better three-year-old as well, and the 20-1 some bookmakers are quoting underestimates his chance.

There are also a couple of less exposed types from the Ballydolyle stable who have the potential to improve into Guineas contenders.

Jupiter Pluvius won the Killavullan Stakes on his second start and, while not overly impressive (2l covered the first six home) he always looked like winning and has the scope to go on to better things this year.

However, at a best price of 16-1 that's already been taken into account, and he looks short enough for what he's achieved.

The race that followed the Killavullan was a maiden over the same trip, and it was won in impressive fashion by **Plan**, who recorded similar sectionals, and a final time only marginally slower than his more highly touted stable-companion.

The quality of the opposition was obviously not as high as in the Group 3 race, but it was an eye-catching performance.

A son of Storm Cat out of Breeders' Cup Distaff winner Spain, he's bred to be something special, and hopefully he'll get his chance to earn his place in the big one by taking in a Guineas trial.

Winker Watson looked a precocious two-

Sponsored by Stan James

year-old last season and there has to be a doubt as to whether he'll maintain his advantage over later-developing rivals this year.

His pedigree screams that he'll be a sprinter, although surprisingly he's a half-brother, by another sprinter, to a dual 1m2f winner, so perhaps we shouldn't be too hasty in assuming he won't stay a mile this year.

McCartney, who won a steadily-run Champagne Stakes from Alexander Castle, has already shown his effectiveness over a mile, and quicker ground than he encountered in the Dewhurst should help him.

Luck Money, who was found out by the step up in class at Newmarket, had previously earned his connections a nice few quid by winning the Goffs Million, but it's open to debate whether he'll get a mile this year.

His stable, however, might have a more interesting candidate in the shape of **Moynahan**, who was supplemented for the Dewhurst but pulled out on the eve of the race after catching an infection.

The vibes were that he was the more fancied of the pair, and his maiden win over Iguazu Falls at York certainly looks sound form in the light of the Godolphin colt's form in Group company since.

Gothenburg bolted up in a Newbury nursery off 87 in August and was promptly switched to the Godolphin stable.

He's clearly a Group horse, but with so many other possible runners for the race, it's difficult to know where he'll fit into the stable's plans.

An unraced Gone West colt named **Amaakin**, trained by Peter Chapple-Hyam and available at a best price of 33-1, is of curiosity value but no more at this stage.

Confront looks a nice type and is sure to progress from two to three. He should be fully effective over a mile in the early part of the campaign, and it wouldn't be a surprise to see him given a prep run in the Craven, to give him a bit more experience, before the Guineas.

Promising maiden winners who have the potential to improve over the winter and possibly enter the Guineas picture include Newbury winner **Cat Junior** and **Forgotten Voice**, who overcame greenness to win on his debut on the Polytrack in October.

A big shell of a horse, he can only improve, and the same can be said of Godolphin's **Calming Influence**, who won impressively at York the same month.

Bruges is two from two in Ireland but his level of form leaves him a long way short of the principals at the moment.

Criterium International winner **Thewayyouare** looks a top-class prospect for this season, but his first big target is the French Guineas, where he could well be joined by **Young Pretender**. John Gosden's colt was below form when beaten into fifth in the Prix Jean-Luc Lagardere but remains a smart colt in the making.

It'll be a surprise if Horris Hill winner **Beacon Lodge** is up to the task, while **Tajdeef** looks like the type to pick up a trial race somewhere over 7f, but then struggle to get home in the Guineas itself.

2,000 Guineas

Newmarket, 5 May

	Bet365	Bl Sq	Coral	Hills	Lads	PPower	SJames	VC
New Approach	7-4	**5-2**	**5-2**	7-4	2	2	2	9-4
Raven's Pass	**7**	**7**	6	6	**7**	**7**	13-2	**7**
Fast Company	**8**	7	6	**8**	**8**	6	7	7
Ibn Khaldun	**10**	8	**10**	**10**	**10**	**10**	8	**10**
Rio de la Plata	10	**12**	**12**	**12**	10	8	**12**	**12**
Winker Watson	12	12	12	12	**14**	12	12	12
Jupiter Pluvius	14	14	**16**	14	12	**16**	14	14
Henrythenavigator	16	16	14	14	14	14	**20**	14
Myboycharlie	16	16	16	14	14	14	**20**	14
Amaakin	20	16	20	**33**	**33**	20	20	25
McCartney	28	25	25	**33**	**33**	25	**33**	**33**
Luck Money	**33**	**33**	**33**	**33**	**33**	25	**33**	**33**
Skadrak	**33**	25	-	**33**	**33**	**33**	**33**	**33**
Gothenburg	**33**	**33**	**33**	**33**	**33**	**33**	**33**	**33**

each-way 1/4 odds, 1-2-3

Others on application, prices correct at time of going to press

1,000 Guineas

THEY go 7-1 the field in the 1,000 Guineas and it's difficult to argue that it's an open heat at this stage.

The highest-rated filly in last year's International Classifications was **Zarkava**, and on the back of her scintillating win in the Marcel Boussac she would undoubtedly be the one to beat were she to line up at Newmarket.

It would be something of a surprise, however, if she doesn't go for the French version, as her connections initially indicated, for as a rule her trainer favours running his charges in the Classics at home rather than in England.

As a result of Zarkava's likely absence, the general favourite is Fillies' Mile winner **Listen**.

Her victory over Proviso at Ascot in a quicker time than the colts recorded in the Royal Lodge marked her down as a leading candidate, and although she's by Sadler's Wells, there's no doubting that she has the speed to be fully effective over a mile this year.

In fact, her sister Sequoyah, who was similarly highly-rated at two having won the Moyglare, was fourth in the Irish 1000 Guineas.

Proviso was sent off a warm favourite at Ascot but lacked the pace of the Irish filly in the straight.

It's true that she didn't enjoy the best of runs, but at the end of the day she looked like a filly who will benefit from another couple of furlongs this year, and the Prix de Diane is likely to be more her cup of tea.

Saoirse Abu finished back in third in the Fillies' Mile but had previously won two Group 1 races in Ireland.

A tough sort, she was heavily campaigned at two, perhaps as a result of her being on the small side and having less scope than some of her rivals. I expect we've seen the best of her already.

Natagora was another who had plenty of racing at two, and exclusively over sprint distances.

Her win in the Cheveley Park was a tremendous effort as she had a strong rival in Flying Childers winner Fleeting Spirit, but fought her off to win a shade cosily, in a time quicker than the colts managed in the Middle Park later the same day.

Her rider's immediate reaction after the race was to suggest that she had so much

LOOK AT ME: Lush Lashes happy after winning the Goffs Fillies Million on her debut

Sponsored by Stan James

	Bet365	Bl Sq	Coral	Hills	Lads	PPower	SJames	VC
Listen	7	6	6	5	7	7	6	7
Zarkava	7	8	9	8	8	8	15-2	8
Proviso	8	7	9	8	8	7	10	8
Natagora	12	12	8	12	12	12	14	12
Spacious	14	14	12	12	14	14	14	12
Lush Lashes	16	14	12	14	14	16	12	16
Sense Of Joy	16	12	16	12	14	16	16	16
Laureldean Gale	16	16	16	12	16	20	20	16
Nahoodh	20	20	14	20	16	16	20	16
Saoirse Abu	20	16	16	20	16	20	14	16
Savethisdanceforme	20	16	16	-	20	20	20	-
You'resothrilling	16	20	16	16	-	16	25	16
Visit	25	20	20	20	25	20	25	-
Kitty Matcham	20	25	25	25	-	25	25	-

each-way 1/4 odds, 1-2-3
Others on application, prices correct at time of going to press

speed that she'd struggle to get a mile at three, but her trainer was a bit more optimistic. Her breeding certainly offers hope that she'll stay, but her racing style suggests otherwise.

The disappointment of the Cheveley Park was the favourite **Visit**, who made a bright start to her career, winning a Group 3 at Ascot second time out before finishing runner-up in the Lowther.

She was subsequently found to have tested positive for a tranquilliser at York, so perhaps she deserves extra credit for that effort.

It's easy to forgive her one disappointing effort in the Cheveley Park, especially as the Lowther Stakes form was upheld, with the York third and fifth finishing second and third respectively at Newmarket.

Her sire Oasis Dream seems to be imparting his progeny with more stamina than he had, and there's plenty of stamina on the dam's side, so a mile should suit her well this year.

The Lowther winner **Nahoodh** returned from York sore and wasn't seen out again, but she created a good impression that day and should progress this season.

Her stablemate **Nijoom Dubai** coughed after winning the Albany Stakes at Royal Ascot and her trainer couldn't get her back in time for a backend campaign.

It wouldn't be a surprise to see both stake a claim for a place in the Guineas line-up in either the Nell Gwyn or Fred Darling, and we should learn more then.

Giant's Causeway's sister **You'resothrilling** couldn't hold her position in the Lowther and that was the main reason she got hampered next to the rail. She was crying out for a step up in trip last summer and a mile will be perfect for her this season.

SAVETHISDANCEFORME took a while to show what she was capable of last season, but she really progressed towards the end of the year, winning a maiden on the Polytrack at Dundalk before being stepped up in class in the Marcel Boussac and performing above expectations in fourth.

She built on that back in Ireland on her final start, absolutely running away with a Listed race at The Curragh.

She showed an incredible burst of speed that day, a real whoosh moment, and left some useful rivals for dead.

On pedigree she'll be at her best between one mile and 1m2f this year, and given the pace at which she was progressing last autumn the 20-1 currently available for the Guineas looks big.

Lush Lashes is an interesting filly. Jim Bolger compared her to Finsceal Beo when she won the Goffs Fillies Million on her debut in September, and she certainly had some very useful rivals behind her that day.

She's short on experience, though, and will be trying to win the Guineas on the back of a juvenile campaign lacking Group-race form, something which hasn't been done for over a quarter of a century.

She'll surely benefit experience-wise from running in a trial race in Ireland before being thrown into Group 1 company.

Unbeaten in two starts, **Sense Of Joy** recorded a wide-margin maiden win at Newmarket and then followed up with a cosy success in a steadily run Prestige Stakes.

A setback ruled her out of her autumn target, the Marcel Boussac, and she remains something of an unknown quantity.

She's a half-sister to Day Flight by Dansili and ought to make up into a middle-distance filly this year, but it wouldn't be a surprise if she was a player over a mile in the early part of the campaign.

It's possible that James Fanshawe may have found a replacement for Soviet Song in the shape of **SPACIOUS**, who impressed greatly in winning on her debut, and again in following up in the May Hill.

A strong traveller, she was given a very confident ride by Jamie Spencer at Doncaster, who came from last to first on her to win far more easily than the margin suggests.

She was still green and idled in front at Town Moor, and her trainer, who sees her very much as a Guineas filly, was happy to put her away for the year after that.

By Nayef, she's sure to make up into a better three-year-old, and her turn of foot should ensure she's a serious contender come the first week of May.

Laureldean Gale looked a promising filly going into the Marcel Boussac as she'd run Proviso close in a Group 3 race earlier in the year, but she disappointed on Arc day, getting upset beforehand and racing with the choke out.

It's probably best to ignore that run, but she has something to prove now, and wintering in Dubai has not always proven to be a good preparation for the Guineas in recent years.

Since being granted Group 2 status in 1998 the Rockfel Stakes has become the key trial, producing five winners of the 1,000 Guineas and three seconds, in addition to four Irish 1,000 Guineas winners and two winners of the Oaks.

Even when the form looks fairly ordinary, the race has come up trumps in the past, and it would be wise not to underestimate last year's winner **Kitty Matcham**, as she was progressing fast last autumn.

Reappearing just six days after breaking her maiden tag at Naas at the fourth time of asking, she stepped up massively on that form to win at Newmarket, and being by Rock Of Gibraltar out of Oaks and Irish 1,000 Guineas winner Imagine, she's bred to win a Classic.

Given the incredible record of the Rockfel, she has to be respected, but she's a late May foal and there's a chance that the English Guineas will come too soon for her.

Psalm should have beaten Kitty Matcham first time up despite racing over an inadequate trip, but she was given a very tender ride.

However, along with her stablemate **Halfway To Heaven**, she probably lacks the experience to play a part in the English Guineas, which comes so soon in the season.

Makaaseb was sent off a well-backed favourite for the Rockfel and, while she was disappointing, the softish ground was probably against her. She remains a very promising filly.

Campfire Glow seemingly needs plenty of dig to show her form. She beat Listen in a Group 2 race at The Curragh when getting her ground, but ran way below that level when beaten into fifth behind Lush Lashes on good to firm.

Rinterval and **Festoso** look likely types for Guineas trials, but will probably find a few too good on the big day itself, while **Conference Call** looks set to stay on the French side of the English Channel for the Poule d'Essai des Pouliches.

Francesca D'Gorgio, meanwhile, has done nothing to deserve quotes as short as 25-1 for the Guineas.

SPACIOUS: replacement for Soviet Song

Oaks

THE top two in the betting for the Oaks are the same two who head the market for the 1000 Guineas, but neither makes much appeal at the prices.

Zarkava is once again more than likely to be an absentee, with the Prix de Diane surely a more attractive target to her connections.

Listen, on the other hand, will almost certainly be aimed at the race, and she'll also have a good chance of getting the trip.

By Sadler's Wells, she's a sister to Sequoyah, who like Listen wasn't short of pace but was still able to finish fourth in an Irish Oaks on her only start over 1m4f.

Johnny Murtagh, who rode Sequoyah that day, suggested that she might not have quite got home, so there's likely to be some doubt about her younger sister's stamina, too.

Listen deserves to be favourite based on her two-year-old form, but to take 8-1 now I would want to know she'll definitely stay, not just that she'll probably stay.

As a half-sister to Day Flight by Dansili, sire of Arc winner Rail Link, **Sense Of Joy** looks likely to get the trip, and her two efforts last season left the impression that she'll develop into a very smart filly this year. Her preference for a decent surface is a plus and she has a solid chance, but that's already reflected in her current price of 14-1.

Lush Lashes, who beat a big field in a valuable sales race at The Curragh on her debut, is seen as a Classic filly by her trainer, and being by Galileo one would expect her to get at least 1m2f this year.

However, there's a fair amount of speed on the dam's side and it wouldn't be a surprise to me if she didn't stay as well as some people expect.

Mad About You placed in a couple of Group 1s last term while all the time looking the type to improve for a winter on her back and a step up in trip.

She should get 1m2f this year but 1m4f might be stretching things, and her trainer Dermot Weld, who had a cracking season with his two-year-olds in Ireland last year,

SENSE OF JOY (near side): win at Goodwood marked her out as a very smart filly

looks to have a stronger candidate in the shape of **CHINESE WHITE**.

She looks a serious player on the evidence of her win in a Leopardstown maiden in September.

She won it impressively by a wide margin, beating among others, the subsequent Rockfel winner Kitty Matcham, and her breeding allows little doubt that she'll relish the Oaks trip.

By Arc winner Dalakhani out of a Sadler's Wells mare who won a Group 3 race for Aidan O'Brien over 1m3f, there are fewer doubts about her than many of her opponents, which makes her a decent bet at 20-1.

Kitty Matcham obviously improved quite a bit after being beaten by Chinese White, and she is out of an Oaks winner in Imagine, by Rock Of Gibraltar, sire of last year's Derby runner-up Eagle Mountain, so it wouldn't be a surprise to see her line up with a real chance, too.

Her stablemate **Savethisdanceforme** also holds claims on her two-year-old form, but her chances of getting the trip are not as convincing.

While the dam's side of her pedigree provides plenty of encouragement, her sire Danehill Dancer is very much an influence for speed. She did improve dramatically for a step up to a mile last term and certainly shapes as though she'll have no trouble getting 1m2f this year, but the Oaks trip will probably be beyond her.

Cape Amber did it well on her debut, beating a big field of rivals by 3l, and she should make up into an even better three-year-old, but the bare form is nothing to get carried away with, and it's easy to resist a top price of 25-1.

KATIYRA won a hot maiden at Leopardstown in August on her debut and wasn't seen afterwards, but the form worked out well with the next four home all winning on their next start in maiden company.

CHINESE WHITE: breeding suggests the Oaks trip will be right up her street

Epsom, 1 June

	Bet365	Bl Sq	Coral	Hills	Lads	PPower	SJames	VC
Listen	7	8	8	7	7	7	7	7
Zarkava	8	8	8	8	12	8	8	10
Sense Of Joy	14	10	10	12	12	14	12	12
Lush Lashes	16	16	-	16	16	16	16	16
Chinese White	16	14	14	16	20	16	16	20
Savethisdanceforme	20	14	16	20	-	16	20	-
Kitty Matcham	20	16	16	20	20	20	20	20
Mad About You	-	16	-	20	25	20	20	-
Cape Amber	20	20	25	-	-	20	20	-
Katiyra	20	20	20	-	20	25	20	25
Spacious	20	25	16	-	25	25	25	25
Cruel Sea	-	25	25	-	-	25	25	-
Look Here	-	-	-	-	25	25	25	25
Makaaseb	25	25	20	-	20	25	33	20

each-way 1/4 odds, 1-2-3
Others on application, prices correct at time of going to press

She made a strong impression that day and looks a high-class filly in the making.

With the Oaks in mind, stamina won't be an issue at all, as she's by Peintre Celebre out of a Darshaan mare who won over as far as 1m6f, but she isn't short of pace either, and 25-1 about her Oaks prospects looks a very fair price.

Despite winning the May Hill over a mile at two, I suspect that Spacious won't be wanting to go any further than 1m2f this term.

She's a keen-going filly with a lot of pace, and the Guineas looks a more attractive target for her.

On the other hand, **Kotsi**, who finished runner-up to her on Town Moor, shapes as though she'll appreciate at least 1m2f.

Her effort in the Fillies' Mile was a bit disappointing, but she's bred to make a better three-year-old.

Albabilia's dam won over 1m6f, but her sire looks to have passed on plenty of speed to her, evidenced by the fact that she was able to win over 6f at two, and her prospects of getting the trip look limited.

It'll also be a surprise if **Screen Star** wants further than 1m2f this year.

Simawa, a half-sister to Sinndar, won't be having any trouble with the Oaks trip, but her form to date doesn't read as well as that of her stablemate Katiyra, and of more interest from the Oxx stable might be **Masiyma**, who chased home Kingdom Of Naples on her debut.

Look Here has plenty of stamina in her pedigree, but the form of her maiden win at Salisbury doesn't look too hot at the moment, while **Cruel Sea** might be the sort to take one of the trials en route to Epsom.

Laughter, an attractively bred daughter of Sadler's Wells owned by the Highclere Thoroughbred syndicate, overcame greenness to win on her debut at Leicester.

It was the same maiden in which Petrushka, who raced in the same colours, made a winning debut back in 1999, and while she obviously has a long way to go to match that filly's achievements, she's certainly bred to make up into an Oaks filly.

The French Oaks, run over a furlong and a half shorter trip than the Epsom version, is probably a likelier target for the Andre Fabre-trained **Proviso** as 1m4f might just stretch her, while **Makaaseb** doesn't strike me as a likely stayer either. She makes more appeal as a lively outsider for the Guineas rather than the Oaks.

There would have to be big question marks over the stamina of both **Muthabara** and **Laureldean Gale**, while **Celtic Slipper** lacks that touch of class required at the top level.

The same can probably be said of **Queen Of Naples**, who is still a maiden, albeit after three runs in good company, and **Rosa Grace**, whose pedigree is very much a mix of speed and stamina.

Dar Re Mi is bred for the job but the form of her debut effort at Newmarket needs improving on considerably.

Derby

THE Guineas favourite **New Approach** is also the Derby favourite and it's difficult to argue with his credentials for the race, considering that he's by Galileo and often appeared to win his races at two by stretching his rivals and testing their stamina, rather than by beating them for speed.

It may be misleading, however, to assume that that means he'll definitely get the Derby trip.

His pedigree raises some doubts and perhaps of more concern is that he'll be running in the Guineas first. Since Generous in 1991, Sir Percy is the only Derby winner to have run in the Guineas, so it's far from an ideal route to take.

At just 9-1 for the race, **Twice Over** is a poor price considering what he's actually achieved.

Two from two last year, he followed up his maiden win with success in the 1m2f Zetland Stakes.

Often contested by future stayers, last year's renewal lacked serious opposition and Twice Over was able to outclass his rivals, beating them for a turn of foot at the finish.

Essentially he didn't need to improve on his maiden form to win that day and, having initially been available at 25-1 for the Derby soon after that race, it's somewhat surprising to see him now quoted in single figures.

Indeed, he's not even sure to get 1m4f, for while there's stamina on the dam's side, he's by a miler in Observatory, and I wouldn't at all be surprised if 1m2f turned

CITY LEADER: useful at two, but being by Fasliyev, will he have the stamina for the Derby?

IBN KHALDUN (left): won the Racing Post Trophy but stamina doubts persist

out to be his best trip.

One who looks sure to fail on stamina grounds is **Ibn Khaldun**, winner of the Racing Post Trophy.

Both parents were high-class milers and, while he might get 1m2f, it's another thing getting 1m4f against stouter stayers.

City Leader, whom he beat at Doncaster, is another likely to fall short, being by sprinting two-year-old Fasliyev.

Having already won the Prix Jean-Luc Lagardere, I can see **Rio De La Plata** going back across the Channel for the French Classics. The shorter trip of the Prix du Jockey Club should be more up his street than the 1m4f distance at Epsom as well.

Thewayyouare would be of major interest were it confirmed that he was being aimed at the race, but at the moment it remains up in the air whether the Andre Fabre-trained colt will go for the Prix du Jockey Club or the Derby after running in the French Guineas.

A half-brother to Peeping Fawn, he recorded a cosy win in the Group 1 Criterium International on his final start at two, and the form reads well.

A mile and a half should be within his compass and at this stage he looks like being one of the stars of 2008.

Hello Morning gave him a real race in the Criterium International and also looks a top-class prospect for this season.

A rematch in the Poule d'Essai des Poulains is his first big target, but were he to suffer defeat again his trainer may well consider bringing him over to Epsom to avoid running into Thewayyouare in the Prix du Jockey Club. She did run American Post in the Derby in 2004, so it's not out of the question.

The shortest-priced Ballydoyle runner is currently **Washington Irving**, despite having been beaten into fourth in his one and only start at two.

He's clearly well regarded, though, and

as a half-brother to Alexandrova, he'll get the Derby trip standing on his head.

However, he might just be this year's Macarthur, in that his form so far doesn't live up to the hype.

Of more interest from Aidan O'Brien's stable is **KINGDOM OF NAPLES**, who despite running green, quickened up and ran out a very comfortable winner of a well-contested fast-ground 1m maiden at Navan on his debut.

His pedigree suggests he won't have too much trouble getting the Derby trip, either, and while he's a son of Sadler's Wells, he's already shown that he acts perfectly well on a firm surface, which is reassuring with Epsom in June in mind.

Given that his stable's juveniles are rarely wound up first time these days, it's even more encouraging that he was able to win in such impressive fashion, and I expect him to develop into Ballydoyle's main Derby hope this year.

Achill Island has solid form in the book, including placed efforts in the Royal Lodge and Breeders' Cup Juvenile Turf, and there's every reason to believe he can do better at three, but he lacks star quality.

Neither **Frozen Fire** nor **King Of Rome** enhanced their reputations in the Racing Post Trophy, while **Alessandro Volta**, a Listed winner towards the backend, doesn't look one of the stable's leading lights at the moment.

It's not out of the question that **Henry-thenavigator** will get the Derby trip this year, despite the fact that he had the speed to win the Coventry Stakes at two.

His sister Queen Cleopatra ran her best race when third over an extended 1m2f in

CURTAIN CALL: impressive winner of the Beresford and now with Luca Cumani

Derby

	Bet365	Bl Sq	Coral	Hills	Lads	PPower	SJames	VC
New Approach	3	4	7-2	3	3	7-2	3	3
Twice Over	9	8	8	8	8	9	8	8
Ibn Khaldun	12	12	-	14	-	12	16	14
Thewayyouare	16	16	16	14	16	16	14	14
Rio de la Plata	16	16	-	-	-	16	16	-
Washington Irving	16	-	25	16	-	16	20	-
City Leader	20	25	-	-	25	-	25	25
Curtain Call	25	25	33	33	25	25	20	25
Alessandro Volta	25	33	-	-	20	25	33	-
Kandahar Run	33	25	-	-	33	20	33	-
Confront	-	25	20	33	-	25	33	-
McCartney	25	25	33	33	25	25	33	25
Bruges	25	25	-	33	25	33	33	33
Kingdom Of Naples	20	25	25	33	40	33	25	-

each-way 1/4 odds, 1-2-3

Others on application, prices correct at time of going to press

the Prix de Diane, which was the longest trip she ever tried.

Curtain Call, who impressed in winning the Beresford Stakes on soft ground but flopped in the Racing Post Trophy afterwards, has since changed stables and joined Luca Cumani.

Whether the Doncaster run was just one race too many at the end of a long campaign, or whether it was the quick ground that got him beaten, remains to be seen, but if he bounces back to his best he has every right to be considered a genuine contender.

McCartney shaped like a middle-distance horse in the making last season, and could well end up being Godolphin's main representative in the race, so on that basis 33-1 could prove to be a big price.

Alexander Castle, who followed him home in the Champagne Stakes on only his second start, is open to improvement, but stamina might be a greater issue for him.

Kandahar Run isn't bred to get further than 1m2f, while Calming Influence looks like a miler on pedigree.

Bruges may also prove himself best over shorter than the Derby trip, and there's little chance that **Fast Company**, **Jupiter Pluvius** or **Plan** will stay 1m4f, while **Domestic Fund** doesn't look good enough.

Foolin Myself, who's out of a half-sister to User Friendly, won a backend Newmarket maiden and is certainly bred to make up into a Derby contender, but of more interest is **TARTAN BEARER**, the horse he beat at HQ.

A brother to Golan, he would undoubtedly have made a winning debut, just as his Classic-winning sibling did, had he not been badly hampered a furlong from home.

Having his momentum checked at such a crucial time cost him the race, but he rallied well to finish on the heels of the more experienced winner.

Given that Jamie Spencer told the winning connections to enter their horse for the Dante, there's reason to believe that Tartan Bearer will be well worth his place in a Classic trial, too.

He's sure to get the Derby trip and is from a family that improves a good deal from two to three, so a speculative punt at a price for the main event is tempting.

Sir Michael Stoute has a few other interesting candidates, too, of which **Confront** is the shortest-priced.

He should get 1m2f without any trouble and, being out of a half-sister to Oaks winner Reams Of Verse, will have a good chance of seeing out 1m4f.

Tajaaweed disappointed in the Racing Post Trophy after winning his maiden nicely, and has a bit to prove now, but **French Riviera** is quite interesting.

He ran with promise on his debut and is related to that decent handicapper Midas Way.

Patkai, whose dam is a sister to Islington and Greek Dance, also has the pedigree, but his form to date doesn't stand out.

Gothenburg, who clocked a fast time when running away with a Newbury nursery on his third start at two, was soon transferred from Mark Johnston's yard to Godolphin and wasn't seen afterwards.

He looks a class act not short on pace, but he has prospects of getting 1m4f as well.

Centennial is a smart middle-distance colt in the making.

There was absolutely no disgrace in getting beaten by the classy Thewayyouare in the Prix Thomas Bryon on his final start at two, and it'll be interesting to see if he reappears in a Classic trial this spring.

The Prix du Jockey Club is the likelier target for Criterium de Saint-Cloud winner **Full Of Gold**, and the same could be true for **Young Pretender**, who has already shown that he travels well.

First Avenue, **Collection** and **King Of Queens** are promising maiden winners with the potential of being effective over the Derby trip, but their credentials are not as strong as some at the moment.

Recommended Bets

2,000 Guineas

1pt Fast Company 8-1   *NR*
(generally)
1pt Henrythenavigator 20-1   *1st*
(Stan James, Bet Direct)

1,000 Guineas

2pts Savethisdanceforme 20-1   *unp*
(Hills, Ladbrokes, Sean Graham)
1pt Spacious 14-1   *2nd*
(generally)

Oaks

1pt Chinese White 20-1   *unp.*
(Ladbrokes, Totesport, VCBet)
1pt Katiyra 25-1   *3rd*
(Boylesports, Hills, Paddy Power, VCBet)

Derby

2pts Kingdom Of Naples 40-1   *NR*
(Ladbrokes)
1pt Tartan Bearer 50-1   *2nd*
(Blue Square, Hills, Totesport, VCBet)

Prices correct at time of going to press.

CENTENNIAL: a smart middle-distance colt in the making for John Gosden

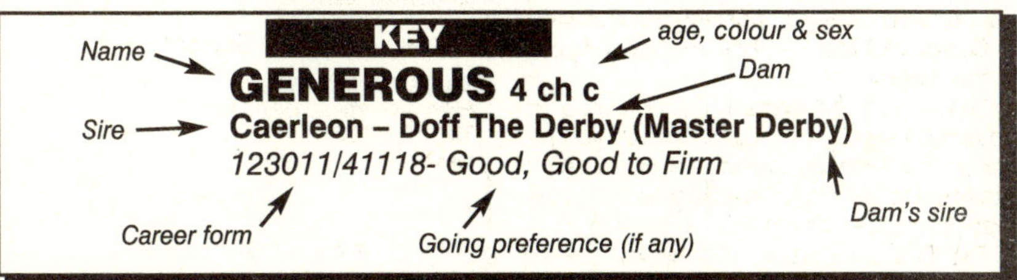

ALESSANDRO VOLTA 3 b c
Montjeu – Ventura Highway (Machiavellian)
831-

This colt's career has been all about steady progress, from the time he came eighth of 17 in a Curragh maiden to his winning a Listed contest at Leopardstown. That race was the Eyrefield Stakes over 1m1f at the beginning of November, and Alessandro Volta gave Aidan O'Brien his seventh victory in it from the last nine runnings. The previous season O'Brien won it with Anton Chekhov who went on to win the Prix Hocquart. Alessandro Volta was late-maturing as a two-year-old but he may well reappear early on and run in a Derby trial.

Aidan O'Brien, Ballydoyle

ARTIMINO 4 b c
Medicean – Palatial (Green Desert)
414240-

Cheveley Park Stud have decided to persevere with Artimino, who didn't quite live up to the potential he showed as a two-year-old. He won a 1m handicap at Newmarket in May and came close on several other occasions. He's on the verge of Group class, though, and James Fanshawe, who trained the the dam, the granddam and two of the dam's half-sisters, is the right man for the job.

James Fanshawe, Newmarket

BABY STRANGE 4 gr c
Superior Premium – The Manx Touch (Petardia)
11041/

A decent two-year-old when with Paul Blockley, he got loose on the gallops and met with such a serious accident he couldn't race at three. He's now with Derek Shaw who hopes he has retained all his ability. As a two-year-old he was beaten 5l in the Coventry, won a Listed race at York by 6l and came second to Captain Marvelous in the Group 2 Criterium de Maisons-Laffitte. Shaw is likely to start him off in handicaps and take things from there. However, judged on his previous form, he could do well and take high rank.

Derek Shaw, Newark

BANKABLE 4 b c
Medicean – Dance To The Top (Sadler's Wells)
811-

Unraced as a two-year-old, Bankable made his first appearance in a Newmarket maiden in August last year, missing the break but then running on to finish mid-division. He knew a lot more about the game next time at Newcastle, beating four others. He then won a 1m handicap at Ascot in late September on good to soft off a mark of 77. Luca Cumani has treated this one with kid gloves and it would no surprise if the Italian maestro hasn't already lined up a big handicap, probably at Royal Ascot or later on the Cambridgeshire.

Luca Cumani, Newmarket

COLLECTION 3 b c
Peintre Celebre – Lasting Chance (American Chance)
21-

Made his debut in October at Salisbury where he was unlucky to run into a good one of Roger Charlton's, Fifteen Love. He then won a 7f Newcastle maiden by three and a half lengths on good to soft ground looking different class to a pretty average bunch. There's no reason to suppose that Collection requires cut in the ground (his Arc-winning sire didn't) and entries in the Derby and Irish Derby suggest that he should be effective up to 1m4f. Highclere Thoroughbred Racing have a knack of coming up with classy colts for their syndicates and Collection could be yet another.

Willie Haggas, Newmarket

CONFRONT 3 b c
Nayef – Contiguous (Danzig)
21-

Sent off 15-8 for his debut at Newbury, he came 4l second to Fool's Wildcat with Ryan Moore never using the whip. The stable's two-year-olds usually need their debut runs and it was no surprise when he won the 7f Hyperion Stakes at Ascot next time out, beating Stimulation by a length with the third horse 9l back in third. The runner-up would have won the Horris Hill Stakes next time if he hadn't been trapped on the rails. Confront has all the hallmarks of a Group horse.

Sir Michael Stoute, Newmarket

CURTAIN CALL 3 b c
Sadler's Wells – Aspara (Darshaan)
62215-

A 4l winner of the Group 2 Beresford Stakes over a mile at The Curragh in September, Curtain Call had previously come second to New Approach in the Group 2 Futurity Stakes at the same track. He beat a really good field in the Beresford, striding out well from the turn so that the others could never catch him. Admittedly he ran flat in the Racing Post Trophy but that is a funny race, coming as it does at the end of October. During the winter he left Jessica Harrington to join Luca Cumani who hopes to start him off in a Derby trial. If he progresses, then he could become a big player in the Epsom extravaganza itself. His trainer won the Derby in 1988 and 1998, could he make it three in 2008?

Luca Cumani, Newmarket

Sponsored by Stan James

DOCOFTHEBAY 4 ch c
Docksider – Baize (Efisio)
22132112326-

Did nothing but improve last season, starting off on a mark of 74 and finishing on 103. He won three handicaps but his moment of fame was in defeat, going down by a length to Pipedreamer in the Cambridgeshire in receipt of 4lb. It was an extraordinary performance because he was tackling 1m1f for the first time and he was stopped in his tracks when he came to make a run. His sixth in the Group 3 Darley Stakes should be forgiven because it came at the end of a long season.

Jamie Osborne, Upper Lambourn

FAMOUS NAME 3 b c
Dansili – Fame At Last (Quest For Fame)
162-

Was a wide-margin winner on his debut at Naas but was thrashed by New Approach in the Group 1 National Stakes on his next start. He was thrown in the deep end that day but he went close the time after when second to Jupiter Pluvius in the Group 3 Killavullan Stakes. With just a little improvement, he will hold his own in the best races.

Dermot Weld, The Curragh

FIRESIDE 3 b c
Dr Fong – Al Hasnaa (Zafonic)
61-

Made his debut in the Parknasilla Hotel Goffs Million at The Curragh, one of the most valuable two-year-old races in Europe. It was a tall order for a newcomer but he paid for his expenses by collecting £6,081 in sixth-place prize-money behind Paul Cole's smart Luck Money. Next stop was the 7f NGK Spark Plugs EBF Maiden (formerly the Westley Maiden), a race that always attracts a classy field. He won it in a fast time to justify odds-on favouritism and Peter Chapple-Hyam will be looking at some of the better 7f prizes, such as the Jersey Stakes over 7f at Royal Ascot in June.

Peter Chapple-Hyam, Newmarket

JACK DAWKINS 3 b c
Fantastic Light – Do The Mambo (Kingmambo)
58411-

After three runs in maidens, one of them an eighth to Raven's Pass at Yarmouth, Jack Dawkins landed a Doncaster nursery over a mile. It was a hot nursery with 19 runners and had gone the way of Bollin Eric and Anna Pavlova in the past. Jack Dawkins was suited by the fast pace and came through strongly to be in front near the line, beating Stubbs Art by half a length. The second horse won a Newmarket nursery next time by 4l. Jack Dawkins subsequently won another nursery over course and distance, looking, if anything, even more impressive. He beat Sir Michael Stoute's Determind Stand by a length and a half, with solid yardstick The Betchworth Kid back in third. He should be a Group colt over middle distances this year, and might even stay a Leger trip.

Henry Cecil, Newmarket

HARADASUN 4 b c
Fusaichi Pegasus – Circles Of Gold (Marscay)
1124112222331-

Possibly the most intriguing development at Ballydoyle this winter was the arrival of this fellow from Australia. In his second season he collected two Group 1s over a mile at Rosehill. He then went on to be runner-up in four Group races at distances ranging from 6f to 1m2f. His last three races were over 1m2f so Aidan O'Brien might stick with that trip. On the other hand the lure of races such as the 1m Queen Anne Stakes might prove tempting.

Aidan O'Brien, Ballydoyle

JUPITER PLUVIUS 3 b c
Johannesburg – Saratoga Honey (Boundary)
11-

Here's a 2,000 Guineas prospect if ever we saw one. He's from the right stable, has the right breeding, won both his races a shade comfortably and is progressive. Reportedly not more than 80 per cent fit for his Curragh debut in October, he beat the Aga Khan's Dahindar by a neck. Next stop was a Group 3 at Leopardstown over 7f in which he beat Famous Name, again narrowly. His sire was a brilliant two-year-old who won the 6f Middle Park Stakes and the Breeders' Cup Juvenile over 1m110yds within the space of three weeks. His dam was a sprinter but Jupiter Pluvius shapes as if the Rowley Mile will be up his street. He could carry on the fine recent tradition of Ballydoyle Guineas winners.

Aidan O'Brien, Ballydoyle

KATIYRA 3 b f
Peintre Celebre – Katiykha (Darshaan)
1-

The once-raced filly won a 7f maiden at Leopardstown in August beating Jim Bolger's Toirneach by two and a half lengths. She took it up at the distance and nothing could catch her. The second and third (Graceful Star) both won next time out. Her dam won five races at middle distances, including the Duke Of Edinburgh Handicap at Royal Ascot. Her sire, the brilliant Peintre Celebre, won the Arc among other races, so Katiykha looks Irish Oaks material, and if not up to that, then definitely the Ribblesdale at Ascot.

John Oxx, Currabeg

KITTY MATCHAM 3 b f
Rock Of Gibraltar – Imagine (Sadler's Wells)
44911-

The illustriously-bred daughter of Oaks winner Imagine and multiple Group 1 winner Rock Of Gibraltar made a quiet start to her two-year-old season. But by October she showed that she was every bit as good as her breeding suggested by winning the 7f Rockfel Stakes, a race Finsceal Beo and Speciosa won in the two previous renewals. It didn't look the hottest of Rockfel renewals and Kitty Matcham is not the biggest of fillies (she takes after her dam in that respect) but she should turn out to be high-class.

Aidan O'Brien, Ballydoyle

LITTLE WHITE LIE 4 b g
Orpen – Miss Informed (Danehill)
1253-

British racegoers saw this Irish handicapper when he was runner-up to Vitznau over 7f in at Epsom's Derby meeting, and they may see him again in the Lincoln at Doncaster. He would have a good chance in that race, especially if the ground was soft or heavy. Although he handles good ground, he likes to get his toe in and it was the good to soft going at Epsom that almost enabled him to defy top weight.

Ger Lyons, Dunsany

LUCARNO 4 b c
Dynaformer – Vignette (Diesis)
2114211-

It's great that last year's St Leger winner Lucarno remains in training and he could well pick up more Group 1s this year. With three other victories – a Kempton maiden on Polytrack, a Newmarket Listed event and the Great Voltigeur at York – he had a great 2007. What John Gosden has in mind for him is hard to say because Lucarno has the versatility for races ranging from 1m4f to 2m4f and handles most types of ground. He always look so relaxed in his races and always finds something when asked. It'll be fascinating to see how Gosden campaigns him and keep him on your side.

John Gosden, Newmarket

LUSH LASHES 3 b f
Galileo – Dance For Fun (Anabaa)
1-

She only raced once and what a big pot she collected. First prize for the Parknasilla Hotel Goffs Fillies Million, run over The Curragh's 7f, was £665,540. The Galileo filly was trained to the minute and came home one and a half lengths clear of a strong field. It would be extraordinary if Jim Bolger saddled the 1,000 Guineas winner two years in a row following the exploits of Finsceal Beo, but it is not impossible. She's got plenty of size and should train on.

Jim Bolger, Coolcullen

MARJALINA 3 b/br f
Marju – Atalina (Linamix)
1-

Marjalina couldn't have impressed more on her debut which took place at Leopardstown in November when the ground was, unusually for the time of year, good to firm. The race was a 1m maiden and she beat 13 others convincingly, putting two and a half lengths between herself and the runner-up Song In My Heart who had previously been second to Kingofrome in another maiden. If she matures and trains on, she could be Group class. Her dam, Atalina, has already produce a winner in Ireland called Australia Day, and as she is by Linamix, you would expect cut in the ground to suit Marjalina. Marju has been a great sire of fillies down the years, with her progeny including Sil Sila, My Emma and Soviet Song. This filly has the potential to be another great one.

Kevin Prendergast, Friarstown

MASIYMA 3 ch f
Dalakhani – Masilia (Kayhasi)
2-

By an Arc winner out of a mare by a Derby winner, the Aga Khan's filly is bred for top honours and she showed promise aplenty on her only run. That came at Navan in late October when she was beaten 3l by Aidan O'Brien's Kingdom Of Naples in a 1m maiden. With only one horse behind her turning for home, she swept through the field to take second place. She holds entries in the Irish 1,000 Guineas and Irish Oaks.

John Oxx, Currabeg

MYBOYCHARLIE 3 b c
Danetime – Dulceata (Rousillon)
1113-

Three times a winner over 6f on soft, heavy and soft, Myboycharlie had his unbeaten record put to the sword by New Approach and Rio De La Plata in the Group 1 National Stakes over 7f at The Curragh in what was arguably the best two-year-old race of the season. The extra furlong and the good to firm ground proved too much for him but don't go thinking he is not a Group 1 colt. He's already had the Group 1 Prix Morny in the bag (beat the subsequent Cheveley Park Stakes winner Natagora by 2l) and big sprinting prizes should come his way.

Tommy Stack, Tipperary

NOWNOWNOW 3 b c
Whywhywhy – Here And Now (Exit To Nowhere)
4121-

This top American juvenile is set to join David Wachman following the suspension of trainer Patrick Biancone in the US. Although he made his debut on dirt, Nownownow proved a class act when switched to turf. He signed off for the season by winning the inaugural running of the Breeders' Cup Juvenile Turf at a soggy Monmouth Park, beating Aidan O'Brien's Achill Island by half a length.

David Wachman, Tipperary

PEEPING FAWN 4 b f
Danehill – Maryinsky (Sadler's Wells)
332132111-

The surprise package of last season. Unraced as a two-year-old and none too promising on her first three starts as a three-year-old, she was placed in two Classics and swept all before her at Group 1 level in the second half of the season. After her second to Light Shift in the Oaks, she took four Group 1s in a row before a setback curtailed her campaign. The plan is to start her off in midsummer. If she can maintain anything like the form she showed in the latter half of the last campaign, then anything is possible and an Arc bid, which was thought about this year before being shelved, must come into the equation. She is thoroughly deserving of the title 'Iron Lady'.

Aidan O'Brien, Ballydoyle

PHOENIX TOWER 4 b c
Chester House – Bionic (Zafonic)
11-

It's quite an event when Henry Cecil runs one on the sand but that is what happened in October 2006 when he sent Phoenix Tower to Wolverhampton. The colt rose to the occasion by scoring cosily. Last season he won both his races, a Newbury handicap and a Windsor conditions stakes, with the minimum of fuss and further progress is assured. Cecil trained his sire Chester House to win a Group 3 here before he transferred to America and won the Arlington Million back in 2000. If Phoenix Tower proves anything like as good he will give Cecil a lot of fun.

Henry Cecil, Newmarket

PROMISING LEAD 4 b f
Danehill – Arrive (Kayhasi)
12412-

Sir Michael Stoute has long been recognised as a great trainer of older horses so anything he keeps in training from three to four has to be looked at. Promising Lead, who never ran as a juvenile, had such a tall home reputation that she was sent off 100-30 favourite for her debut at Newbury in the prestigious 7f Bridget Maiden Fillies' Stakes. She justified market support and went on to run well for the rest of the season, signing off with a head second in the Group 1 Prix de l'Opera over 1m2f. She is a cousin to Banks Hill and Dansili on her dam's side and she could turn out to be classy.

Sir Michael Stoute, Newmarket

SKADRAK 3 ch c
Forest Camp – Occhi Verdi (Mujtahid)
2-

He was beaten a short-head in the prestigious 6f maiden run at Ascot's King George meeting and though the race hasn't been the launchpad of any stars in recent years, Skadrak looked useful. He was switched from Peter Chapple-Hyam to Brian Meehan over the winter and has settled in well at Manton. He looks the proverbial formality for a maiden.

Brian Meehan, Manton

SOLDIER OF FORTUNE 3 b c
Galileo – Affianced (Erins Isle)
115115-

Beat Arabian Gulf a short-head in the Chester Vase and then ran fifth in the Derby, marking him a smart if not brilliant colt. That impression had to be revised when he came home 9l clear of stablemate Alexander Of Hales in the Irish Derby on soft to heavy ground. Next stop was the Prix Niel in which he beat Sagara by one and a half lengths. Sent off 100-30 for the Arc, he had to settle for fifth behind Dylan Thomas and third-placed Sagara. That was surely not his true form and it's possible that he could turn out as good as Dylan Thomas, who also won the Irish Derby.

Aidan O'Brien, Ballydoyle

TARTAN BEARER 3 ch c
Spectrum – Highland Gift (Generous)
2-

It wasn't until November that Tartan Bearer saw a racecourse but he was well worth waiting for. It was a 7f maiden at Newmarket, and he beat all bar Barry Hills' Foolin Myself. A good-looking, strong chestnut, he finished best of all having been blocked early on. The form has since been franked by the seventh home, Pacifism. It was an excellent run for a debutant and this brother to 2,000 Guineas and King George winner Golan should become a class act as befits a produce of the Ballymacoll Stud. He certainly should have no problem in winning his maiden.

Sir Michael Stoute, Newmarket

THE FIST OF GOD 3 b g
Sadler's Wells – Hula Angel (Woodman)
74612-

Noel Meade doesn't train too many Flat horses but that shouldn't put you off this son of Sadler's Wells. He ran with promise in three maidens and then, fitted with blinkers for the first time, obliterated a large nursery field at Navan, streaking home 7l clear. The time was decent, less than a second above standard. On his final run he was runner-up to Alessandro Volta in a Listed race and the winner is in the Derby betting. Valuable handicaps and Listed races await.

Noel Meade, Castletown

UNBREAK MY HEART 3 ch c
Bahamian Bounty – Golden Heart (Salse)
9311-

After two promising runs in maidens, he was sent off 5-2 favourite for a 6f Windsor nursery at the beginning of October and duly obliged despite slipping on a plastic path that crossed the course. He then followed up two weeks later at Goodwood over a furlong further. He looked even stronger than at Windsor and won with something in hand despite being topweight. If he can keep up the progress, he should make into a decent handicap miler or better.

Roger Charlton, Beckhampton

RFO's top 10 to follow

Curtain Call	**Promising Lead**
Docofthebay	**Skadrak**
Famous Name	**Tartan Bearer**
Lush Lashes	**The Fist Of God**
Masiyma	**Unbreak My Heart**
Peeping Fawn	

Outlook

Pedigrees for punters with Amy Bennett

WHEN backing the progeny of first-season sires, it is important to bear in mind not all sires are capable of getting the fast, early two-year-olds who will clock up plenty of wins, and therefore plenty of profit.

The most profitable way of following first-crop sires can therefore often be to consider quantity as well as quality, particularly early on in the season. Six of the top ten leading freshman sires last year sired 20 or more individual winners, while nine of them got to double figures. Although large numbers of runners do not necessarily make a good stallion in the long term, it certainly means more chances of winners.

A typically strong batch of stallions will have their first runners this season, including four 2,000 Guineas winners – Bachelor Duke, Haafhd, Indian Haven, and Refuse To Bend – as well as Group 1 winners such as Exceed And Excel, Falbrav and Sulamani.

The six stallions below all fit the criteria for first-season sire success, boasting plenty of speed and the precocity to win as juveniles, and, perhaps most importantly, plenty of firepower.

BACHELOR DUKE
Miswaki – Gossamer (Seattle Slew)

Bachelor Duke has fewer progeny to represent him than some of his rivals, but those that passed through the sales ring last autumn were met with enthusiasm by trainers and agents alike.

It is also worth noting two shrewd operators in Dermot Weld and Jim Bolger were among those to snap up several Bachelor Duke yearlings last year.

The son of Miswaki has a deceptive race record in that he won only one of his six starts.

However, that victory came in the Irish 2,000 Guineas in which he beat the future triple Group 1 winner Azamour with the Irish Derby winner Grey Swallow back in third.

He was also a smart performer at two, only narrowly beaten in the Group 3 Somerville Tattersall Stakes by the subsequent Dewhurst winner Milk It Mick.

Miswaki doesn't have much of a track record as a sire of sires, although Bachelor Duke does feature such luminaries as Sadler's Wells and Nureyev in his further family.

EXCEED AND EXCEL
Danehill – Patrona (Lomond)

Although Darley's top-class Australian sprinter showed little on his only start in Britain, finishing well beaten in the July Cup, Exceed And Excel was a serious performer down under, netting two Group 1 victories over 6f and three further Group 2 wins.

His progeny can be expected to be similar types to him – sprinters with a serious turn of foot, and more than a touch of class.

Since retiring to stud, he has covered large books in both hemispheres, and his southern hemisphere runners have already touted their sire's ability, with his first two runners both landing Listed contests.

He is currently heading the list of first-crop Australian sires with five individual winners.

Tellingly, Exceed And Excel's progeny were very popular with trainers and bloodstock agents alike at the yearlings sale last autumn.

Bryan Smart bought five, while trainers such as Dermot Weld, Marcus Tregoning, John Gosden and Sylvester Kirk also invested.

HAAFHD
Alhaarth – Al Bahathri
(Blushing Groom)

Haafhd is one of four 2,000 Guineas winners who will have their first runners in 2008, and must be considered a likely candidate for success.

While progeny of Alhaarth have tended to improve with age, Phoenix Reach and Bandari being obvious examples, Haafhd should prove a good source of precocious talent, given his own race record, while his progeny are also likely to train on.

The good-looking chestnut was a very smart juvenile, easily landing the Listed Washington Singer, and finishing a good third in both the Champagne and Dewhurst Stakes.

Better was to come at three when he won the Craven Stakes and 2,000 Guineas , and he later proved his ability over 1m2f when landing the Champion Stakes.

Out of the top-class miler Al Bahathri, Haafhd comes from an excellent family, including half-brother Munir who has done well at stud in Italy from very limited chances.

Haafhd's progeny also brought some eye-catching prices at the yearling sales.

KHELEYF
Green Desert – Society Lady
(Mr Prospector)

Sprinting sons of Green Desert have enjoyed great success with their first crops in recent years, with Invincible Spirit setting a new

HAAFHD: the Rowley Mile specialist storms to victory in the 2,000 Guineas in 2004

KHELEYF: en route to one of his two victories as a juvenile five years ago

record for the most individual winners in 2006, and Oasis Dream siring four stakes winners in his first crop last season.

Kheleyf, who is another with a large crop of almost 100 foals, cannot boast such an illustrious race record as those two Group 1 winners, but he was a sturdy performer, winning twice as a two-year-old and later landing the Jersey Stakes and finishing second in the Group 2 Lennox Stakes.

A full brother to the very speedy juvenile filly Bint Allayl, Kheleyf is from the top-class family of the Canadian champion Fanfreluche, and as such is related to the top Australian stallions Flying Spur and Encosta de Lago, as well as the 'super sub' Holy Roman Emperor who took the place of George Washington at stud last year.

NEEDWOOD BLADE
Pivotal – Finlaggan
(Be My Chief)

Needwood Blade may not exactly fit the criteria given above, having not won at two and lacking the weight of numbers of some of his rivals, but he could be just the type to sire the sort of juveniles capable of winning early in the season.

Tellingly, just under half of the 37 Needwood Blade yearlings sold last autumn went through the ring at Doncaster's two flagship yearling sales, which have a reputation for selling sharp sprinting juveniles.

Needwood Blade himself was well beaten in two starts at two but improved significantly with age, winning the Palace House Stakes at five and a Grade 3 contest in the US at six. Clearly the son of Pivotal had both speed and durability in abundance.

Pivotal has risen to the top of the tree of British stallions the hard way, starting out at a bargain basement fee covering moderate mares.

His fee has rocketed along with his plethora of talented performers, and his son Kyllachy has already proved himself a smart sire capable of getting good two-year-olds. There is every chance of Needwood Blade continuing the family tradition.

ONE COOL CAT
Storm Cat – Tacha (Mr Prospector)

If firepower is one of the keys to being a successful first-season sire then One Cool Cat should be primed for success, with a first crop of over 120 foals ready to debut this year.

Having been purchased for $3.1m as a yearling, One Cool Cat lived up to his steep price tag at two, scoring Group 1 victories in the Phoenix and National Stakes, as well as the Group 3 Anglesey.

Rather disappointing at three, he did manage to add a Group 3 sprint to his tally, and finished third in the Nunthorpe.

Storm Cat's record as a sire of sires is somewhat patchy, although he did produce Giant's Causeway, who was leading first-crop sire in Britain and Ireland in 2004.

However, One Cool Cat, like that illustrious performer, was also a top turf performer and can transfer his own precocious talent to his plethora of runners who are now in the hands of such trainers as Richard Hannon, Brian Meehan, Jeremy Noseda, Peter Chapple-Hyam and Mick Channon.

Other Sires to Note

Refuse To Bend – precocious enough to win the National Stakes at two, the 2,000 Guineas at three, and good enough to step up in trip to land the Eclipse at four. Likely to get smart types who improve with age.

Elusive City - the Prix Morny winner should be capable of siring juvenile winners.
Monsieur Bond - another leading sprinter who has plenty of his progeny in the hands of trainers renowned for their juveniles.

ONE COOL CAT: the dual Group 1 winner pictured at Coolmore

TWICE OVER: Henry Cecil's colt has been the subject of ante-post support for the Derby

Newmarket
by Aborigine

HENRY CECIL came back in from the Classic cold with his Oaks winner Light Shift last year and **Twice Over** and **Kandahar Run** will give him a chance of further Epsom success in the Derby this year.

Much has been made about a big hitter having a substantial ante-post wager on Twice Over for the Derby during the winter following his promising efforts as a juvenile.

There was certainly a lot to like about the Observatory colt's second and final run when he came with a powerful late burst to win over a mile and a quarter on our Rowley Mile.

Cecil hopes that 1m4f might be within his powers but having missed the long odds about him an each-way interest in stable companion Kandahar Run for the Guineas and the Derby might be a worthwhile alternative investment.

Cecil has always told me how much he liked the Rock Of Gibraltar colt before he won his final two starts in fine style.

The feeling is that he could turn out to be Cecil's No 1 gun for the 2,000 Guineas.

As there is stamina on his dam's side the Derby could also come into the picture.

Another Observatory colt **Time Table** could be another star waiting in the wings even though he was beaten into second place behind Redesignation over 7f on the

July Course.

He was then sidelined because of a cracked cannonbone but has recovered and is going sweetly in his building up work.

Among the older Cecil horses **Multidimensional** stands out and provided he does not suffer further injuries will hold his own in the top middle-distance races.

The four-year-old **Phoenix Tower** is one to consider for lists of Horses To Follow as this lightly-raced individual has won each of his three starts over his two and three-year-old seasons.

A winner at Newbury and Windsor last year, the early indications are that he will start making up for lost time in a big way.

PETER CHAPPLE-HYAM did this column proud last year with his Derby winner Authorized but at this stage of proceedings it is hard to see a third Derby winner for the affable Chapple-Hyam emerging.

Winker Watson attracted plenty of support for the 2,000 Guineas after his Norfolk and July Stakes wins before suffering from a sore knee in the autumn.

All is well with him now, though the speed he showed suggests he will ply his trade sprinting rather than around the mile mark.

It could be that Chapple-Hyam makes most impact on the fillies' front and **Cape Amber** clearly has a bright future ahead of her.

By the dual Classic winner Ouija Board's sire Cape Cross she made an immediate impact as a juvenile going in by 3l in a hot maiden at Newmarket on her debut.

She has clearly thrived during the winter and should use either the Nell Gwyn or the Fred Darling Stakes as a stepping-stone to a bid for the 1,000 Guineas and then on to the Oaks.

At a lower level, the progressive **Don't Panic** will be picking up a big handicap or two and strikes me as Royal Hunt Cup material.

Last year he won a couple of handicaps at Goodwood but looks like missing the cut for the Lincoln as he still figures on an extremely lenient rating.

Even though he won that first race on fast ground at Goodwood he is a far better horse when there is plenty of give in the ground.

MARK TOMPKINS enjoyed yet another good year in 2007 and this consummate professional has another powerful team at his Flint Cottage Stables.

The Yorkshireman used to have a hurdler or two including dual purpose horses like the Magnet Cup winner, Champion Hurdle third and Bula winner Halkopous on the move during the winter, so it is significant that he was not prepared to risk **Gee Dee Nen** over the sticks.

WINKER WATSON: could turn out to be a sprinter rather than a 2,000 Guineas hope

ALLEGRETTO (nearside): will still be racing this season as a five-year-old

We will be hearing a lot of him this season in races like the Chester Cup and the Cesarewitch. A bit of cut underfoot does his chances no harm at all.

Tompkins likes a tilt at the Lincoln having won with the 20-1 shot **Babodana** in 2003, though that horse struggled in Pattern company last year. He is beginning to feel his age but should contribute towards his keep in a handicap with some give underfoot.

It is a bit of juice in the ground that will also give stable-companion **Smokey Oakey**, owned by Dame Judi Dench, a chance of picking up some good prize money in mile handicaps.

MICHAEL JARVIS is one of the most respected trainers in town and **Pressing** could spread his fame further abroad as he races in the colours of the jetsetting Gary Tanaka.

Originally trained in Italy, he joined the Jarvis team last spring and returned to Italy to plunder their prize-money with a couple of Group race wins at the backend.

Jarvis again plans a high-profile international campaign for him with the Prince Of Wales's Stakes at Royal Ascot figuring high on his list of earlier priorities.

SIR MICHAEL STOUTE has always done well for Cheveley Park Stud and the staying mare **Allegretto** will reward her owners' decision to keep her in training as a five-year-old, while on the three-year-old front their lightly-raced **Quotation** is a filly with a future.

JEREMY NOSEDA has his usual large string full of potential winners, among whom the Breeders' Cup Juvenile Turf fourth **Strike The Deal** has a bright future.

PAUL HOWLING has been sending out a steady stream of winners since he started renting the Oh So Sharp yard at Henry Cecil's elegant Warren Place training complex.

GENEROUS THOUGHT: won for Jamie Spencer at Doncaster last November

Though he is best known as an All-Weather trainer, he has been upgrading his string and has a really bright prospect in **Generous Thought**.

Bought for 95,000 guineas at the two-year-old in training sales, he rounded his year off by recouping some of that outlay with impressive wins under Jamie Spencer at Pontefract and Doncaster.

Howling feels he is Pattern race material but will start down the handicap route as he reckons he will prove to be ahead of the ball game.

WILLIAM HAGGAS, who won the Derby in 1996 with Shaamit, was back on the trail of big-race winners last year when Very Wise claimed the Lincoln, and Haggas feels there are more races to be won with him.

He is again entered in the big Doncaster handicap but the early vibes are that the classy **Mutajarred** is the pick of his entries along with Heaven Knows.

All three should pay their way and one of them could win the Royal Hunt Cup.

JANE CHAPPLE-HYAM has quickly made her mark in the Newmarket training ranks and **Mighty** looks like being her flag-bearer this year.

Her talents were revealed as she improved him from three modest All-Weather wins early in the year to finish third to Maraahel in Royal Ascot's Hardwicke Stakes.

He looks a picture out on the heath and the plan is to reintroduce him in the Jockey Club Stakes at our Guineas meeting early in May.

Former jockey PAUL D'ARCY holds out high hopes for **Kylayne**.

The Kyllachy filly did not win till her final start last year but has strengthened appreciably over the winter.

The plan is to gain some valuable black type in the Masaka Stakes at Kempton over Easter before having her sights raised.

GEOFF WRAGG is the doyen of the Newmarket trainers and do not desert his 2006 Derby runner-up **Dragon Dancer**.

It is well documented that he has won only

a maiden race since the Derby but his work at home suggests there is a rich vein of gold still to be tapped.

His lead horse **Hotel Du Cap** might have started at 20-1 when winning a Listed race at Newbury in the autumn but was well fancied by the Abington Place team!

There is no doubt that he will prove that was a launching pad to better things rather than a flash in the pan.

JOHN GOSDEN will be looking to **Pipedreamer** to carry the Cheveley Park colours to victory at the highest level as his Cambridgeshire win was planned many months ahead.

The good-looking Selkirk horse could be another improver like Gosden's 1994 Cambridgeshire winner Halling, who went on to complete an unprecedented Eclipse and Juddmonte International double the following two years.

Hot off the Heath

Cape Amber
Generous Thought
Hotel Du Cap

DESPITE Teofilo and Holy Roman Emperor never seeing the racecourse, last season was another brilliant year for Irish racing, led as ever by the incomparable *AIDAN O'BRIEN*.

The Ballydoyle maestro trained the first three home in the St James's Palace Stakes and the Irish Champion Stakes as part of a haul of 12 Group One wins in Britain and Ireland, before Dylan Thomas added the Prix de l'Arc de Triomphe to boot.

Such astonishing feats underline two seemingly paradoxical truths about O'Brien.

Firstly, his wealth of talent allows him to dominate races at the top level tactically, to the extent that very few Ballydoyle runners are ever said to be unlucky in running. Yet still, for all the stick the yard received over Scorpion's running in the King George, nearly every horse runs on its own merits – think back to how many supposed pacemakers made the frame in Group One races last year.

Therefore the following horses should again go from strength to strength in the forthcoming campaign.

One blot on the copybook last year was the failure to land an English Classic (Eagle Mountain, Peeping Fawn and Mahler all came second), and O'Brien will be all out to put that right with a team led by **Listen**.

The one Ballydoyle juvenile to prove herself at the top level last year, Listen was regarded highly enough to start her career in Listed company when winning well at the Curragh.

Two subsequent second-place finishes confirmed her among the best and she left her previous form behind last time out at Ascot, storming to victory in a hot Fillies' Mile as she saw off Proviso.

Having beaten the French once, Listen certainly has prospects of doing so again at Newmarket at the start of May, but her best chance of Classic glory could well come in the Oaks.

She clearly benefited from stepping up

LISTEN: bolts up in the Fillies' Mile at Ascot to mark herself out as Ballydoyle's No. 1

in distance at Ascot and saw out the mile strongly enough to suggest middle distances are well within her capacity, while as a daughter of Sadler's Wells she is bred to be an Epsom winner.

In addition, her full sister Sequoyah, winner of the Moyglare Stud Stakes in 2000, was campaigned largely as a miler the following year but in fact ran her best race at three when a close fourth in the Irish Oaks.

Another who could form part of O'Brien's team for both races is **Savethisdanceforme**, who improved steadily throughout the campaign before exploding into the picture with a devastating 9l win in a Listed race at The Curragh in October. If that form can be taken literally, she could be a star.

It was a quiet year for O'Brien's juvenile colts, particularly with **Henrythenavigator** disappointing after Royal Ascot.

He looked superb when winning the Coventry Stakes but found a softer surface not to his liking when beaten subsequently by Saoirse Abu and New Approach. He could still be worth following back on decent ground, however.

Nonetheless, his top spot in the pecking order has been taken by **Jupiter Pluvius**, who has all the makings of a Group 1 colt this season.

He had his problems last year and didn't see the racecourse until October, but he more than made up for lost time, winning twice in the space of eight days, including a well-contested Group 3 at Leopardstown on his second start.

A son of Johannesburg, he has a pedigree full of speed but looks like he will have no problems staying 1m and looks a strong contender for all the top races over that trip.

It might be too early to identify who will end up as Ballydoyle's leading Derby hope, as even the trainer seemed as in the dark as anyone in the early stages of last season, but at this stage hopes are high for **Washington Irving**.

A major talking horse ahead of his racecourse debut in October, he was sent off the 2-1 favourite but was never seriously put in the race, running on late into fourth.

However, several O'Brien juveniles weren't at their best first time out and he continues to make a massive impression at home, while his pedigree – he is a half-brother to Alexandrova – points the way to Epsom.

Kingdom Of Naples, who wasn't so strongly fancied but certainly caught the eye with a maiden win at Navan the same month, is another expected to come firmly into the equation.

The retirement of Dylan Thomas leaves a gaping hole in the older department, but O'Brien has a superstar in the wings in quadruple Group 1 winner **Peeping Fawn**.

She proved utterly peerless among her own sex last season, improving at a rate of knots from missing out in three maidens in April to having pulled off her awesome four-timer by August, taking in two Classic-placed efforts along the way.

After that she entered the betting for the Arc, but she suffered a slight setback and it was soon decided that 2008 would be the year for the Longchamp showpiece.

Her season will be geared around emulating Dylan Thomas's triumph, taking in some top middle-distance prizes en route.

Soldier Of Fortune could join her in some of those races and looks to have the potential to rack up a sequence as well.

He looked exposed as just below the very best when scrambling home in the Chester Vase and finishing fifth in the Derby, but he then romped home in the Irish version by 9l and proved that was no soft-ground fluke by following up by in the Prix Niel on good ground.

That form would have put him in the frame for the Arc – the second, Sagara, finished third in that race – but he under-performed in fifth. He is clearly better than that and, while he may not be the most versatile in terms of distance, there are few better over 1m4f.

Hopefully readers of this column won't have forgotten the esteem in which **Mount Nelson** was held at this time last year.

He then had a season to forget, a string of niggling problems keeping him off the racecourse until October, when he made the running in the Champion Stakes and tired in the closing stages.

That return proved nothing, but he was a serious Derby contender 12 months ago and connections are hopeful he can fulfil his potential at last.

Excellent Art should perhaps have been crowned champion miler last year, but a string of unlucky defeats meant he had to settle for just one Group 1 win in the St

SEPTIMUS: going to post before a spectacular win in the Doncaster Cup

James's Palace Stakes.

For once good fortune was on his side that day as Cockney Rebel broke down in the final furlong, but there's no guarantee he would have beaten Excellent Art anyway.

The four-year-old then lost out in the Sussex Stakes and Queen Elizabeth II Stakes to Ramonti, both times reeling in the winner too late having been given plenty to do.

On top of his fourth place in the French 2,000 Guineas – when he was clearly the best horse in the race – it suggests Excellent Art is a tough horse to win with, but hopefully Ballydoyle's new No. 1 Johnny Murtagh will get on well with him as he has the ability to prove himself the best around this time.

The leading mile races may also be where O'Brien sends Australian recruit **Haradasun** into battle.

A dual Group 1 winner down under, he has shown top form from 6f to 1m2f, but the Queen Anne Stakes is his main early-season target and connections will know where they stand with him after that.

Dual Ascot Gold Cup winner **Yeats** leads a strong team of stayers, and in fact the only danger to an Ascot treble will probably come from his own yard.

Septimus, like Yeats a leading Derby hope at three, found his form over longer trips last season when he won the Lonsdale Cup and the Doncaster Cup, his performance in the latter, when he beat Geordieland far more easily than Yeats had at Ascot, really making people sit up and take notice.

Previously regarded as better with cut in the ground, he coped brilliantly with the good to firm surface and romped away from a high-class field, suggesting he is right up there with his magnificent stable-companion – or potentially even better.

O'Brien also trained two of the first three home in the St Leger, with **Mahler** and **Honolulu** likely to make their mark at four.

There are no obvious Ballydoyle contenders for the top sprinting prizes, but it seems likely that **US Ranger** will be campaigned at 6f and Michael Tabor also has **Myboycharlie**, who could well end up in dropping back in trip as well, with *TOMMY STACK*.

US Ranger was a warm order for the 2,000 Guineas when trained by Jean-Christophe Rouget and ran with great credit both there in seventh and when second in the Jersey Stakes before switching to O'Brien. He was a brilliant winner of a 6f Listed race at the Curragh before flopping at the Arc meeting, but he is hugely talented on his day and looks a decent sort for the July Cup.

Myboycharlie notched a hat-trick over 6f in the early part of the season, looking something special on each occasion, before losing his unbeaten record when third to New Approach in the National Stakes.

However, he had to be held up to get the trip that day and couldn't match the principals in the final quarter-mile having travelled beautifully, and having proved he can handle all types of ground he could take high issue as a sprinter.

JIM BOLGER's hopes of a Guineas double last year bit the dust early with Teofilo's injury, but remarkable he produced arguably an even better juvenile in **New Approach**, who won the same five races in spectacular fashion to earn winter favouritism for both the Guineas and the Derby.

His last two wins were what really marked him out as something special as he made all the running to tear apart Rio de la Plata and Myboycharlie at the Curragh before winning the Dewhurst under very different circumstances, having been forced to do things the hard way when missing the break.

He sets a very high standard for the 2,000 Guineas and will take all the beating, though it remains to be seen whether he will stay the 1m4f of the Derby. Though he is by Galileo, his dam, a high-class horse over 8-10f, has had several speedy types, a trait New Approach has certainly inherited.

Bolger could also have a say in the fillies' Classics with more expected from **Lush Lashes**, who made only one racecourse appearance last year but certainly made it count when running away with the Goffs Million at the Curragh.

That was an astonishing debut and Bolger said later that he rated her in the same bracket as **Finsceal Beo**. If that is the case, he has another potential superstar on his hands.

On the subject of Finsceal Beo, she remains in training and not even her trainer probably knows what to expect. She was wretched in the second half of the season, but that shouldn't detract from her previous efforts in chasing an unprecedented Guineas treble and if she gets back to that sort of form there is probably no better filly on the planet – Peeping Fawn included.

DERMOT WELD matched O'Brien with 67 winners last year and he has the usual strong team assembled, led by **Chinese White**.

She won a hot 7f maiden at Leopardstown on her only start, making all and quickly storming 6l clear of a field which included the subsequent Rockfel winner Kitty Matcham in fourth. She should come into her own when upped to 10-12f, particularly with some cut in the ground, and looks a real Oaks filly.

Mad About You is another filly who could end up heading for Epsom. She was highly tried last year, but twice came third at Group 1 level and there may be more to come.

Others to note from the Weld yard are **Famous Name**, a brilliant maiden winner who found only Jupiter Pluvius too good on his final start, and **Campfire Glow**, who lowered Listen's colours at the Curragh last year.

KEVIN PRENDERGAST landed a coup in the winter when the Breeders' Cup Juvenile Turf winner **Nownownow** came into his care.

We are lucky to have a solid line to the form with the Ballydoyle colt Achill Island having finished second to him that day. Achill Island had previously come second to City Leader in the Royal Lodge Stakes at Ascot, so it would be wrong to go overboard about the American import, but he clearly still has the ability to win his fair share of races.

Prendergast should also enjoy plenty of success with **Haatef**, who didn't quite make the grade as a Guineas contender last year but hit back to win the Group 2 Diadem at Ascot. He didn't quite get a mile last year but will be interesting given another chance and will be hard to beat over 7f.

JOHN OXX always has some high-class fillies in his yard – **Arch Swing** will be one shining example this year – and **Katiyra** may be another to follow.

She is another who just got the one outing last year, trotting up in a Leopardstown maiden over 7f, and again she is bred for middle distances, being by Peintre Celebre out of a Darshaan mare.

Invincible Irish

Jupiter Pluvius
New Approach
Septimus

IT is a rare feat for a three-year-old sprinter to take the prize for the star performer for the Lambourn area, but there was really only one contender for that title from midway through the 2007 season.

In what was largely a disappointing campaign for the area over the longer distances, **Sakhee's Secret** more than compensated by emerging as the most exciting sprinter since Oasis Dream carried all before him five years ago.

Like Oasis Dream's trainer John Gosden, *HUGHIE MORRISON* banished any thought of a tilt at the 2,000 Guineas and made the July Cup the primary target for the colt even before the turn of last year.

Having landed one of the gambles of the season in a relatively low-key handicap at Newmarket on his return, he quickly asserted his Pattern quality with victories at Newbury and Salisbury on his next two starts.

He still had some way to go to confirm he was a Group 1 performer, but connections approached the July Cup full of confidence and they were not to be disappointed as, despite finding some trouble in running, Sakhee's Secret produced a turn of foot of rare quality in the final quarter-mile and readily held the late challenge of Dutch Art, the juvenile champion sprinter of 2006.

Although he flopped behind old rival Red Clubs on his final appearance of the season, that performance can be put down to the ground and it is with real enthusiasm that connections look forward to his four-year-old campaign.

He has pleased during his winter break at Redenham Stud and a stronger individual will be lining up for what looks sure to be all the top sprinting events.

SAKHEE'S SECRET (second left): completes a meteoric rise by winning the July Cup

Sponsored by Stan James

MICK CHANNON: strong team of fillies

Whilst Sakhee's Secret's comeback win was the bet to remember, the Morrison team landed one or two notable punts with a good crop of two-year-olds.

The standout was **Stimulation**, who landed a fair old gamble first time up before finishing second on his last two starts.

His third appearance was arguably the best. He went down in a photo to the highly-rated Beacon Lodge and might well have won had he not found serious interference in trying to deliver his challenge.

A big, imposing type, he could well have a crack at a Guineas trial and connections hold out high hopes for him.

Rock Peak, who had problems after making a highly promising debut at Sandown, is another sure to win another race or two. So too is **Red Twist**, who could exploit Morrison's mastery at bringing three-year-olds steadily by winning a few handicaps, while **Wing Play** is another likely to improve during the course of the season.

However, perhaps the most interesting member of the second-season crop is **Palace Moon**.

A son of Fantastic Light, he is a half-brother to Sakhee's Secret and seems back on course after a troubled first campaign.

He failed to step out in public because of his training problems, but he showed plenty of potential on the home gallops and is definitely a name for everyone's short-list.

Morrison's neighbour *MICK CHANNON* enjoyed another cracking season, despite not quite picking up one of the very top juvenile prizes.

Consequently, a number of his best three-year-olds face being stepped up from Group 2 class to a tilt at Classic glory, but Channon is nothing if not a trier and there will be plenty of races to win even if they fail to reach the required standard.

Atlantic Sport could just be the colt to attain the very highest level.

Very highly regarded, he started his career in a hot maiden at Ascot and produced a cracking effort to beat Peter Chapple-Hyam's heavily-backed newcomer Skadrak by a short-head.

Channon wasted no time upping him in class and he was well supported in the Group 2 Champagne Stakes on his only subsequent start, but ran well below expectations and there was clearly something amiss. It will be interesting if he can make the Classic grade and a trial looks sure to be on his agenda.

In truth, the fillies were largely better than the colts at West Ilsley last season, boasting a number of smart performers including **Nijoom Dubai**, **Nahoodh** and **Missit**.

Nijoom Dubai looked the pick of the trio, even though her win at Royal Ascot was eclipsed by Nahoodh's success in the Lowther at York.

Neither filly ran after their respective Pattern wins, but they are back in top form and probably heading for the Guineas trials.

Channon is never a trainer to boast a large number of three-year-old maidens, but keep an eye out for unraced pair **Deer Daylami** and **Dream Desert**, and **Madame Hoy**, who was placed in two of her three starts as a juvenile.

The Valley was shaken to its roots when gossip spread during the depths of Winter that *BARRY HILLS* would be shortly announcing his retirement, but the rumours were soon crushed and the great man has another top team assembled.

Always keen to make as good a start as possible to the turf campaign, Hills will be looking to win the Lincoln, one of his very favourite races, and **Zaahid** looks set to take his chance in the contest.

He improved steadily as a three-year-old and has continued on the upward curve during the winter.

Giganticus served Hills well in handicaps last season and he has also continued to thrive, with a wind operation working wonders for him.

The third member of the older brigade to merit a mention is the smart sprinter **Prime Defender**.

He was outclassed by Sakhee's Secret last season, but connections are hoping for much better things this term.

Stamina limitations prevented **Tajdeef** from reaching the highest level as a juvenile, but he could well do well in sprints this term and the July Cup could beckon if all goes well.

Conversely, **Feared In Flight**, who remained a pretty consistent performer at Pattern level in his first season, could be seen to best advantage over longer distances. The Derby and even the St Leger could enter his equation.

Yankadi was another member of Hills' top team and was highly tried after winning his maiden at Newmarket in August.

A bit more backward than some, he should be seen to best advantage in the second half of the campaign.

If there is a surprise package, it could well be **Tharawaat**. Still a maiden after three outings and a beaten favourite on his last start, he has delighted the Faringdon Place team with his progress during the winter.

Slam, who finished in front of Tharawaat at Newbury on his third run, proved a little frustrating, but is also a much stronger individual and is sure to win a good race before the season is too old, a remark which also applies to **Tourist**, a very big, imposing son of Oasis Dream.

Janina looked set for a cracking first season when landing her first two races, but she flopped behind Nijoom Dubai at Royal Ascot and was not seen again.

A knee problem was diagnosed when her legs were scanned and she has taken the subsequent corrective operation very well.

There seems no reason to things why her three-year-old career will be affected and if she continues to progress a Guineas trial will be placed firmly on her agenda.

Spinning Lucy, who seemed to improve towards the backend, and the maiden **Sugar Mint** could well expect the same.

The latter is better than her sixth in the Group 1 Fillies' Mile at Ascot on her final appearance of 2007 suggests.

Many shrewd observers, however, offer **Cruel Sea**'s name as the one they are most looking forward to seeing step out as a three-year-old.

She won her only outing as a juvenile at Doncaster in the closing weeks of the season, and what was striking about the performance was the fact that she pulled hard on the way to post, and again during the race, yet still managed to win emphatically.

It may be too early to say she will be a leading contender for the Guineas, or perhaps her more realistic option, the Oaks, but she does look exciting.

BRIAN MEEHAN is the only trainer to match Channon and Hills for numbers and he will have another 150-plus team for 2008.

Unfortunately, he lost arguably his best chance of Classic glory when the Dewhurst runner-up Fast Company was sold to carry the Godolphin banner in 2008, but the yard may have managed to even out the loss with the winter acquisition of **Skadrak** from the Chapple-Hyam yard.

He was only short-headed by Atlantic Sport at Ascot and Meehan is absolutely delighted to have taken charge of a colt who has oceans of scope and was firmly among the cream of Chapple-Hyam's high-class crop of two-year-olds last term.

Sharp Nephew and **City Leader** were not too far behind Fast Company in the pecking order at Manton last season and City Leader won a big one when landing the Royal Lodge Stakes at Ascot in September.

He relished the cut in the ground that day, unlike his stablemate Sharp Nephew, who started favourite for the race after his excellent win at Newbury but trailed in a well-beaten eleventh.

Both horses have to step up to make Classic grade, but they have scope and give their trainer a good hand with their liking for opposing surfaces.

Polmailly was capable of working well with the best of the juveniles throughout the season and he was rate one of Meehan's leading maidens after two placed efforts, a remark which would also apply to **Austintatious**.

Double Duty is a name to note from the list of maiden fillies and **Exclamation** will be looking to add to his valuable win in the sales race at Newmarket's Cesarewitch meeting.

Of the older horses, **Red Rocks**, one of

SKADRAK (near side): short-headed by Atlantic Sport at Ascot but could be a star

the stars of Meehan's epic first season at Manton, remains and he will be looking to recapture the same form that saw him win the 2006 Breeders Cup Turf.

He failed to attain that level last term, but there were excuses and expect a good show from him at the Dubai World Cup meeting.

The same destination is on the agenda for **Diamond Tycoon**, a most impressive winner of a mile maiden at Newbury in April.

Inevitably, the victory prompted a tilt at the 2,000 Guineas, but he could only finish ninth and was found to be wrong afterwards.

He failed to see the racecourse again, which was most disappointing given the fact that the form of his Newbury win worked out very well, but his trainer reports him back in great nick again and he will be looking for a big run in the desert.

ROGER CHARLTON has a handy bunch of three-year-olds for the new season without, perhaps, a real star for the opening weeks.

The one exception may be **Prime Exhibit**, who could not have been more impressive when landing his maiden at Leicester in October. He does, however, pull too hard for his own good and will have to settle to fulfil his enormous potential.

Cuban Missile was another to create a good impression when landing his backend maiden at Nottingham and he will stay a trip.

A less exposed name is **Barricado**. The son of Anabaa travelled to Leicester on the same day Prime Exhibit won his maiden and produced a good performance to finish third.

The race did not look the best that day, but he had plenty to learn and stayed on well in the closing stages, and he has always been regarded as a three-year-old.

The same can be said of **Oarsman**, a fair second to the smart Iguazu Falls on his only outing as a juvenile on the All-Weather at Kempton.

Few fillies made their mark from Beckhampton last season, but **Trianon** was one when landing her maiden at Newbury.

On the same day, the very well-bred **Scuffle** made her first appearance and delighted connections with her third place in what looked a better class event. Much is anticipated from her this season and she should uphold her proud family tradition.

Clowance is a filly with a bit of stamina in her pedigree and she should mark her mark over middle distances after yet another promising debut effort at Newbury towards the backend.

IL WARRD: shows a smart turn of foot to win on his second two-year-old start at Ascot

MARCUS TREGONING could not repeat the exploits of the Derby-winning 2006 campaign but looks forward to the new year with optimism and will be looking for good things from **Shabiba**.

Beaten a neck on her debut at Goodwood, she stepped up on that performance to see off Elizabeth Swann and Spinning Lucy in what looked a good maiden at Newmarket.

Her trainer reports her in fine nick after her winter break and he is readying her for a trial before a crack at the Guineas.

Lille Ida is another filly sure to win some good races after making it third time lucky in her first season.

She only won a weak maiden on the All-Weather at Wolverhampton, but she fairly hacked up and her form on the Farncombe gallops suggest there is a lot more to come.

Il Warrd was arguably the best of the juvenile colts last season, and he showed a smart turn of foot when landing his second start at Ascot.

A trip to Doncaster for the Group 2 Champagne Stakes followed, but he saw too much daylight and was altogether too immature for such a tough task.

He will be much more the finished article this season, however, and his mettle could also be tested early in one of the Classic preliminaries.

Massalek is the most unexposed of the quartet of juveniles mentioned.

He did not see the light of day again after going down by an unlucky half-length to the smart Coasting at Newbury in May, but he is now back in top shape and will be a much stronger individual in his second season.

The North by Borderer

MARK JOHNSTON had another terrific season with 163 winners during 2007 and while Kingsley House had been dealt the blow of losing the likes of Boscobel and McCartney to Godolphin, there is still plenty to look forward to for the Middleham handler.

Zaham developed in a high-class performer winning five of his ten starts. Unraced as juvenile, the son of Silver Hawk more than made up for lost time winning valuable handicaps at Epsom and Newbury and, of course, the Hampton Court Stakes at Royal Ascot.

He rounded off his season when chasing home Ask in the Cumberland Lodge Stakes and remains unexposed over 1m4f. It will be disappointing if he cannot add to his already impressive CV.

Johnston may not have an obvious Classic contender but he still appears to have a smart team of three-year-olds for the season.

Endless Luck built on a promising racecourse debut at Leicester by routing nine opponents at Musselburgh by upwards of 5l. A colt by Giant's Causeway, he has been granted a provisional handicap mark of 90 but he looks to possess the potential to overcome such a rating.

Robby Bobby boasts an almost identical profile. A colt by Selkirk, he was narrowly denied on his debut at Yarmouth before putting the record straight at Newbury in October when beating Brexca by 3l. This half-brother to the useful Foxhaven looks just the sort to make a decent three-year-old handicapper, if not better, and looks one to follow.

We almost certainly haven't seen the best of **Planetarium** yet either. A striking son of Fantastic Light, he relished the step up to

ZAHAM (near side): gets on top of Al Shemali to land the Hampton Court at Royal Ascot

TURBO LINN: assumed the mantle of stable star at Alan Swinbank's yard

1m2f as a juvenile when grinding his rivals into the ground at Pontefract in the autumn.

It was significant that Johnston let him take his chance in the Listed Zetland Stakes at Newmarket only to find Epsom Derby hope Twice Over a length and a half too good. He starts the season well treated off 88.

ALAN SWINBANK sent out 42 winners in 2007 and he starts the new campaign optimistic he can better that total. Plans to send **Alfie Flits** jumping were aborted as his trainer feels there is more to come on the Flat.

Despite not registering a victory last season, the six-year-old came so close in a Listed contest at Musselburgh and ran well behind Peppertree Lane at the Curragh in a similar event.

He won't be burdened with penalties this year and can regain the winning thread.

Turbo Linn, of course, assumed the mantle of stable star following the retirement of Collier Hill and she enjoyed a memorable season, winning three times, including the rerouted Lancashire Oaks at Newmarket during the summer.

The mare will be campaigned in Group races over middle distances and she has reportedly made good progress during the winter.

There is a host of promising three year old talent at Thorndale Stables and Swinbank has particularly high hopes for **Louis Seffens**, who finished second on his sole outing at Doncaster in October.

A son of Elusive Quality, he looked a sure-fire winner at Town Moor and is expected to make a decent handicapper.

Sheekey is another name to note having lost his maiden at the second attempt at Musselburgh. Third next time in a nursery at Ayr's Western meeting, he may be at his best on a lively surface.

KEVIN RYAN must be looking forward to unleashing his exciting three-year-old **Alexander Castle**.

A colt by Lemon Drop Kid, he barely came off the bridle when making a winning start at Newcastle in August.

Stepped up in class next time, he covered himself in glory when a two-and-a-half-length second to McCartney in the Group 2 Champagne Stakes at Doncaster's St Leger meeting.

Ryan feels he will be even better this year and one would expect to see him targeted at the 2,000 Guineas.

The Hambleton trainer has always been strong in the sprinting division as Advanced's victory in the Ayr Gold Cup proved last term and he will be hoping **Wi Dud** is a force in the top races this summer.

Sponsored by Stan James

Despite not winning in six starts last year, the four-year-old ran some good races, notably when a half-length second to Hoh Mike in a Group 3 at Sandown.

Tiger Dream may be a maiden after three juvenile starts but he remains a horse to follow. The son of Oasis Dream, who cost 150,000gns, was runner-up on all three outings.

Suited by fast ground, his best performance came first time out when he made Henry Cecil's Kandahar Run pull out all the stops at Doncaster's Leger meeting. It shouldn't be long before he sheds his maiden tag.

RICHARD FAHEY plundered some of the biggest handicaps of the season with the Chester Cup, John Smith's Cup and Ayr Silver Cup all going the way of the Malton trainer.

Utmost Respect produced a stunning display to win at Ayr in September.

The lightly-raced four-year-old had been denied the opportunity to win York's William Hill Handicap in June due to the floods but he more than made amends at the Scottish track.

Beaten next time over 7f at Ascot a week later, that run should be forgotten and he can win another big prize during 2008 given cut in the ground.

Another Musley Bank inmate who enjoys plenty of give underfoot is **Anna Pavlova**.

The filly won three times last season, including a Group 2 at Longchamp's Arc meeting under a fine ride from Frankie Dettori.

The five-year-old was tried over 2m in the Lonsdale Stakes at York's Ebor meeting but is arguably at her very best over 1m4f.

Provided the mud is flying she will continue to be a danger to all in Pattern races.

Smart Instinct failed to record a win last year but he ran some cracking races in defeat notably when fifth in the John Smith's Cup behind stablemate Charlie Tokyo.

Fahey feels he took time to recover from

UTMOST RESPECT (right): can win a big prize this year given cut in the ground

CAPTAIN GERRARD: won the Roses Stakes as well as the Cornwallis last season

a gelding operation and we didn't see the best of him last season. It could be a different story with a winter's break behind him.

BRYAN SMART, who also operates from Hambleton, sent out 43 winners last season with **Captain Gerrard** doing more than his fair share by winning five times.

The son of Oasis Dream collected the Roses Stakes at York and, of course, the Group 3 Cornwallis at Ascot in October.

A speedy sort, he won't find it easy this year but his trainer will be disappointed if he cannot hold his own in the top sprints.

Finally, *JOHN QUINN* continues to impress as one of the best dual-purpose trainers on either side of the Irish Sea.

It will be fascinating to see how his new recruit **Solent** fares. Bought for 155,000gns at the Newmarket October Sales, he dead-heated in Listed grade at Ascot in the autumn with Distinction. The ex-Richard Hannon-trained gelding couldn't be in better hands.

SOLENT (left): trained by John Quinn

RICHARD HANNON'S powerful Wiltshire outfit continued to lead the way among those based in the West last season.

The prolific East Everleigh handler enjoyed a typically strong 2007, amassing no fewer than 148 winners on grass and All-Weather combined, while maintaining a near one-in-seven strike-rate along the way.

With stable star Indian Ink sold to join Hamdan Al Maktoum's broodmare band, it's left to another top-class inmate **Major Cadeaux** to fly the flag among the older generation this summer.

He was picked out for the 2,000 Guineas in these pages a year ago and was far from disgraced in the Newmarket Classic, finishing a gallant sixth to Cockney Rebel.

Although the ready Greenham hero wasn't seen much later in the campaign, he was in good heart when only just worried out of it in a Group 3 on a return to Headquarters.

And last time he once again demonstrated an ability to compete at the highest level when a closing fifth in the prestigious Prix Maurice de Gheest at Deauville.

He possesses plenty of size and scope to improve with age and his relaxed attitude will be a major plus in the championship races. Regarding ideal trip, the way he finished over 7f in France suggests he'll be a major force as a miler this summer and is definitely one to have on your side.

Expectations are also sky-high for Hannon's ace **Scintillo**, who looks a must-pick for any ten to follow list.

As a juvenile, he just got better and better as the campaign unfolded. Having netted a Sandown maiden in July, connections wasted little time in upping him in grade.

He certainly didn't look out of place when finishing up with the pace in Listed races at Newbury and Salisbury in August.

With those positive experiences to draw upon, he managed to conjure a sustained run against the far rail to finish on the coat-tails of subsequent Racing Post Trophy runner-up City Leader on softer-than-ideal ground in the Royal Lodge at Ascot.

If that wasn't enough, he signed off a wonderfully consistent campaign with a game defeat of Italian win-machine Glatiatorus in the Group 1 Gran Criterium at San Siro.

He acts on all types of ground and is expected to continue charting an upward path on his second season, picking up more than his share of black-type along the way.

Although Classic contenders are a bit thin on the ground among the Hannon ranks this year, there's a solid each-way case to be made about **Reel Gift** for the 1,000 Guineas.

The well-related filly wasted no time in getting off the mark when making a winning debut on Polytrack at Kempton.

The impressive manner of that introduction led connections to have a crack at Group 3 company next time and she duly rose to the occasion by filling a likeable second to Visit over 6f at Ascot in July.

It was a remarkable effort and, while she failed to quite replicate that level after a return from a summer break, her fourth in a valuable sales race at Doncaster in September provides another reminder of her considerable ability.

She shouldn't have any trouble staying 1m on her second season and she could well emerge as a lively outsider for the fillies' Classic at Newmarket.

Another speculative bet that might yield handsome returns is Hannon's **Latin Lad** in the Epsom Derby as it's hard to pick holes in his juvenile form.

He belied inexperience plus negative market vibes when popping up at 33-1 in a competitive Goodwood maiden over 7f in August.

He then arrived with a storming late run to get within inches of shading out Sharp Nephew in a Listed contest at Newbury just a fortnight later. Next time, he was again just worn down at a similar level at Pontefract, seeing out 1m well that day.

There's even better to come once he's sent over middle-distances on his second term, so Classic aspirations are by no means pie in the sky.

King Supreme could well pay his way as a handicapper on turf for Hannon this summer. Having shown potential in maidens under wildly varying ground conditions on grass, it came as no surprise to see him making a winning handicap debut over 1m at Kempton.

Refreshed by a winter break, he should return raring to go and can fully exploit a lenient turf mark of 65.

Another potential money-spinner among the handicappers is **Talk Of Saafend**, who capped a fine first campaign with a brave head win in a fairly valuable 7f nursery at Newmarket last backend.

The filly is bred to raise her game with age and, with plenty of experience already under her belt, she can pick up as she left off by winning her share early on in 2008.

Hannon's **Firestreak** showed a touch of quality when making a winning debut for the Queen in a 7f maiden at Sandown in June.

He overcame slight mid-race interference that day and has gone on to compete effectively in much stronger company since, including when fifth to the smart Raven's Pass in a Listed race at Ascot.

Although he might not make an impression at the top level, there are a few valuable prizes to be had with the son of Green Desert this year. He ought to stay beyond 1m and handles good or faster.

Watch out for **Chartist** in sprints this summer. Being a half-brother to the yard's speedster Black Moma by Aussie ace Choisir, he's bred to be fast and left a forgettable debut performance behind when relishing the livelier conditions in a 5f maiden win at Nottingham in late October.

He made most before asserting that day and is destined for bigger things as he continues to mature both in mind and body.

Another Choisir progeny to follow closely this year is Hannon's **Hustle**, who can bag a valuable handicap before long.

He possessed the early dash to grab the box-seat against the nearside rail before making all in a 7f maiden on fast ground at Lingfield in September.

He possibly wasn't suited by Newmarket when passed by three rivals off a 79 rating last time, and there's tremendous room for improvement as he strengthens from two to three. He'll probably enjoy most success at up to 1m.

Positives can be gleaned from all of **Berbice**'s juvenile sightings.

Despite lacking sufficient experience,

FIRESTREAK: makes a winning debut in a 7f maiden at Sandown in June

RON HODGES: trains Red Somerset

Hannon's classy grey managed to excel himself by finishing fourth in the Woodcote at the Epsom Derby meeting.

Subsequent prominent finishes behind Dark Angel, including in the Group 2 Mill Reef at Newbury, go some way to highlighting his class. Connections can expect more of the same as a three-year-old and it will be a shock if he's not gracing the winner's enclosure again soon.

Gypsy Baby is bred to be useful and certainly came up trumps as a youngster.

Outside of Listed company, the half-sister to the smart Embossed managed to finish in the front two on all occasions.

Had she enjoyed a clearer passage through, she might well have defied a lofty mark at Ascot and reproduced that sort of level when runner-up to the classy hotpot Dark Angel in the St Leger Yearlings Sales race at York.

She'll be a force in some of the big handicaps in the months ahead and is very much one for Hannon to look forward to.

An unraced three-year-old to look out for is the Epsom Derby entry **Montevetro**, who is a half-brother to French 2000 Guineas winner Victory Note, plus a couple of multiple winners.

He also boasts some excellent female bloodlines to his pedigree and has been given time to fill his frame.

BRYN PALLING has a lot to look forward to with **Edge Of Gold**. She conjured much of the speed of close relation Bright Edge when showing her rivals a clean set of heels to land a 5f Chepstow contest on lively ground.

A greater test of stamina against stronger opposition failed to prevent her following up in a Sales race at Newmarket soon after and she'd had enough for the campaign when running well below market expectations in a nursery when last seen in October, an effort worth putting a line through.

Raquel White has proved a valuable servant to Bridgend dual purpose handler *JOHN FLINT*, best known for training top-class jumper Fair Along earlier in his career.

The David Evans cast-off enjoyed a consistent 2007 and once again showed how dangerous she can be on her day when running away with a 1m4f handicap at Beverley in June.

She's been kept busy on All-Weather over the winter, accruing solid placed form in the process, and will be fighting fit for her return to grass in the spring.

A *RICHARD PRICE*-trained handicapper expected to bag more than his share of prizes this year is **Hoh Hoh Hoh**, who's done well since arriving from Andrew Balding.

Since netting a Chester handicap in June, the tactically versatile chestnut has finished on the podium on a number of occasions in some well-contested races, including when just shaded out by Ayr Gold Cup winner Fonthill Road at York in October.

RON HODGES is a master at placing his horses to best effect and he looks set for another fruitful campaign with **Red Somerset**, who was in the form of his life when last seen.

He was bred to be smart, but lost his way after initially showing considerable promise shown on track.

As a result, his handicap mark dipped to a very attractive level, prompting a welcome revival in fortunes last autumn. He was particularly impressive when effortlessly pulling clear at Nottingham on his final outing of 2007, an effort that strongly suggests he's a horse very much on the upward curve again.

Best of the West

Gypsy Baby
Major Cadeaux
Scintillo

The South by Southerner

JOHN DUNLOP has a big yard stocked with choicely bred individuals and he will again be one of the busiest trainers in the country.

The three-year-olds should be the mainstay for Dunlop this season as there are, as usual, a host of promising types among the Classic generation at Castle Stables.

Elmaleeha is one of the big hopes for the coming months and, if everything goes well with her, she could end up having a crack at either the English or Irish Oaks.

The daughter of Galileo, who is closely related to former stable stars Bahri and Bahhare, made a very encouraging start to her career when second to the well-regarded John Gosden-trained filly Infallible in a 7f maiden at Newmarket in November.

She was given plenty of time to find her feet at HQ and came through strongly at the finish without being at all knocked about by her jockey Richard Hills.

Elmaleeha's dam won over 1m4f and her sire has quickly established himself as a potent source of high class middle-distance performers.

Dona Alba needs to improve if she is to fulfil her Irish Oaks entry but she was highly progressive last year and hails from a family than get better with age.

The Peintre Celebre filly surprised and delighted her connections when a running on fourth to Celtic Slipper at odds of 66-1 for her debut in a 7f maiden at Glorious Goodwood in August.

Dona Alba won a 7f maiden at Folkestone

MOUNTAIN PRIDE: one of John Dunlop's most promising three-year-old colts

a month later on her second outing and was then a length second to Jazz Jam, who was receiving 10lb from her, in a mile nursery at Pontefract in late September.

That form received a massive boost when her conqueror was beaten just a short-head in a Listed event at Newmarket on her next start.

Star Of Gibraltar also needs to step up considerably on her juvenile form if she is to justify her Irish Oaks entry but she too is from a family that improve as they mature, and her two runs at Newmarket last year suggested she possesses considerable latent ability.

She was a never-nearer seventh in a 7f maiden in August and a staying on fourth in a mile maiden in September.

Irish 1,000 Guineas entry **Festivale** is already a winner and therefore worth a fortune as a prospective broodmare.

The well-related Invincible Spirit filly got off the mark at the second attempt in a 6f maiden at Lingfield in June when she powered home 3l clear of a field that contained several subsequent scorers.

She didn't reappear until November when she finished fifth to Spinning Lucy in a 6f Listed contest at Newmarket where she travelled supremely well until her lack of a recent outing found her out in the closing stages.

Having shown so much speed over 6f, Festivale may well prove best at sprint trips but she will be give the opportunity to stay a mile as there is enough stamina in her pedigree.

Mountain Pride is one of Dunlop's most promising three-year-old colts.

The son of Derby winner High Chaparral, who has been entered in both the Epsom and Irish Derbies, progressed really well last year and there should be plenty more to come this time around.

He began his career when finishing well to be third in a 7f maiden at Newmarket in August. Next time he was only fifth in a similar event at Newbury but he was beaten only a length and was again doing all his best work at the death.

Stepped up to an extended mile for his final outing in a Leicester maiden in October, he strode home two and a half lengths in front of Cuban Missile, who franked the form when winning his subsequent start.

Mountain Pride acts very well on easy going and he should have no trouble staying 1m4f.

As a half-brother to the Group 1 winner and highly successful sire Invincible Spirit, whom Dunlop trained, **By Command** has plenty to live up to.

The Red Ransom colt showed plenty of promise on his debut when a running on fourth in a 7f Sandown maiden in June but he was a shade disappointing when only fifth in another 7f maiden at Salisbury in July after which he was put away to mature and strengthen.

Sakhee's half-brother **Yathreb** should do well last year. The Kingmambo colt was very green and backward last year but he still managed to reveal considerable talent when finishing close up in well-contested maidens at Ascot and Sandown.

Goodwood Starlight gave his enthusiastic owners, the Goodwood Racehorse Owners Group, plenty to cheer last year and there should be more for them to enjoy this term.

The Mtoto colt made a winning debut in a 7f maiden at Salisbury in August and the following month sparked wild scenes of celebration when he got up on the line to dead-heat with Townkab for a mile nursery at Goodwood.

Goodwood Starlight should stay at least 1m2f and, no doubt, his trainer will be looking for suitable opportunities back at his local track again

Alwaabel is unlucky to still be a maiden. Following a promising running on sixth to subsequent Goffs Million winner Luck Money in a 6f maiden at Newmarket in May, he finished second to a couple of decent types in Midships and Lord Sandicliffe in similar races at Newbury and Leicester.

Then he was in the process of running another good race when badly hampered and having to settle for fourth in another 6f maiden at Doncaster's closing meeting of the season in November.

The Green Desert colt should put the record straight this time and could develop into a useful handicapper.

Perks should also pay his way in handicaps this season.

The Selkirk gelding, who is owned by Benny Andersson of Abba fame, ran well in decent maiden at Ascot and Newmarket last year and should not prove hard to place. His best form came on easy ground.

Dalhaan had just one outing as a juvenile but the American-bred hinted at plenty of potential when making late headway to be beaten just over 5l in ninth place in the 7f maiden won by Latin Lad at Glorious Goodwood.

Pulborough trainer *AMANDA PERRETT* has plenty to look forward to this season including the promising **Foresight**.

The three-year-old Observatory colt is related to several useful winners and he finished a very encouraging third in a mile maiden at Newbury in October on his only start as a juvenile.

King's General finished second to Sweepstake, who raced on the opposite side of the track, on his only outing last year in a 5f maiden at Salisbury in May.

The chestnut is part-owned by the trainer's father, Guy Harwood, so there is considerable incentive to do well with the colt.

Regal Best was another Perrett inmate to have just one start last year as a juvenile.

Not a great deal was expected of the King's Best colt in a 7f Leicester maiden in October and he was sent off at 66-1.

His fourth place was a real bonus and gave his connections great encouragement for the future.

The Forestry colt **Gaia Prince** didn't manage to finish in the frame on his sole juvenile outing but he still ran a race chock full of promise when making good late headway after being slowly away to finish fifth to Cat Junior in a 6f maiden at Newbury in August

Gaia Prince will have no trouble staying a mile and there should be some decent races to be won with him this season.

Lobby made it to the racecourse twice last season and showed promise both times.

The Dr Fong colt finished fifth in a 7f maiden at Salisbury in July and two weeks later was only beaten around 7l when 11th to subsequent Group 2 winner and Racing Post Trophy runner-up City Leader in a 7f maiden at Ascot.

Midships had been going well at home and made all the running for an impressive victory in a 6f maiden at Newbury on his introduction in June.

The grey son of American stallion Mizzen Mast wasn't able to add to that victory in two subsequent starts in good company but he was far from disgraced on either occasion.

He should have no problem regaining winning ways this season.

Mystery Sail is also by Mizzen Mast and she too made a successful start to her career in a maiden at Newbury.

The filly produced a storming late run to catch next time out winner Lord Peter Flint at the end of the 7f contest run on good to firm going in September on her only appearance last term. She is one of the most exciting prospects in the yard.

Appointment shouldn't test Perrett's placement skills too severely.

The Where Or When filly improved steadily in three starts last year and signed off with a fourth, beaten less than a length, in a mile maiden on the Polytrack at Kempton in October.

Kent trainer *JOHN BEST* broke through the glass ceiling last season when his two-year-old **Kingsgate Native** beat the older sprinters in the 5f Group1 Victor Chandler Nunthorpe Stakes at York's Ebor meeting in August.

Best missed the moment when Jimmy Quinn steered the colt to victory on the Knavesmire as he was in America at the Florida Sales looking for the next star.

The youngster went on to finish second to the six-year-old Benbaun in the Prix de l'Abbaye at Longchamp on Arc day.

The Cheveley Park Stud have bought the breeding rights to Kingsgate Native but he will continue to race in the colours of his owner, John Mayne, and he remains under Best's care.

Meydan Dubai was a close up in all four of his starts last term and should do well for the stable this season.

While not in the same league as his illustrious stable-companion, the three-year-old has plenty of speed.

The Midlands by John Bull

AS he embarks on his fourth season as a trainer since taking over the reins from his father Bryan, Staffordshire handler *ED McMAHON* has good reason to feel proud of the progress he has made.

McMahon's strike-rate has increased for each of the last three year, rising to 14% last year with 56% finishing in the first four, and it could have been even better as the yard was hit by injuries to two of its best horses.

Cartimandua, who ran with great credit in the 2,000 Guineas, lost her maiden tag with embarrassing ease at Salisbury on her next start.

McMahon then aimed her at the Class 1 Listed Timeform Silver Salver Stakes at Haydock, where she made a mockery of odds of 11-1, routing a competitive field of older horses. I have never seen a more impressive winner of a Listed race, with Cartimandua even looking all over the winner at the 3f pole.

After that remarkable victory, it seemed that the filly would be all set for Group success, but sadly that was the last we saw of her as she subsequently chipped a bone in her knee. But the good news is that this highly talented performer should be back in action this season.

"She's a bit like Barry Hills' Nunthorpe-winning filly La Cucaracha in that she's very big and full of muscle but her bones aren't really up to carrying it," said McMahon.

"We've got to be very careful with her. We can't chance her on fast ground and we've got to be going with the ground.

"She'll be out early while there's still some cut in the ground and be aimed at Group 2 or 3 events. If we're lucky and she stays sound, I'm sure she'll win again."

The ultra-consistent **Pivotal Flame**, third in the 2006 Nunthorpe and a winner of over £114,000 in prize-money, missed nearly all of last season. But he's now back in full training and will kick off his campaign in the Cammidge Trophy at Doncaster, a race in which he finished fourth in 2006.

PIVOTAL FLAME: back in full training

"He's six now and although we've said this before, as long as he stays sound, he should pick up some races," the trainer commented.

"Despite his age he's still quite lightly raced. It's good to have him back."

The third of McMahon's big guns for the new campaign is sprinter **Terentia**.

"She'll be my yardstick. The aim will be to win some black type with her. She'll probably start off in the same conditions race at Nottingham which she ran in last year, and then head to York for the 0-100 handicap she won at the Dante meeting 12 months ago."

A lesser-known McMahon inmate who should make good progress in 2008 is **Hyde Lea Flyer**. Formerly with Alan King, the colt was a staying-on second behind Sir Michael Stoute's Derby entry Tajaaweed over a mile on his first run for McMahon at Nottingham in October.

"He was green and backward as a two-year-old but he's grown a lot over the winter. He's a nice horse who could turn out to be a Triumph Hurdle winner. He's got quite a good action. He'll go on most types of ground but wont like extremes of going."

Judging by the evidence of his runs to date

and breeding (by Hernando out of a Slip Anchor mare), this promising performer will have no trouble in going beyond 1m.

In 6f handicaps in the 0-80/0-85 range, McMahon will again be well represented by the consistent **Bahamian Ballet**, a winner of 25% of his races on turf.

After recording his second win of the campaign at Catterick in July, the handicapper harshly and inexplicably raised the gelding 7lb, from a mark of 77 to 84, which proved an obstacle to further success. Once the six-year-old drops down into the 70s (he's currently on 80), expect him to win again.

As for younger horses, McMahon advises *RFO* readers to watch out for **Chain Of Gold**, who has only run once but is a nice prospect, and a two-year-old son of Halling, who is a full-brother to Mark Johnston's highly promising performer Age Of Reason.

While connections paid £200,000 for Age of Reason, McMahon only paid £15,000 for his unnamed full-brother and may have got a great bargain. Expect to see the colt out towards the back-end of the season.

MARK BRISBOURNE enjoyed another great campaign in 2007, the indefatigable Shropshire handler reaching his 50th winner of the year just after Christmas.

Highlights were saddling the first three home in a lady riders' handicap at Chester in June, and a poignant victory in the final of the Bollinger Amateur Riders series at Ascot in late September, 12 months after the yard's promising gelding Brief Statement had broken a leg in the final furlong with the race at his mercy.

Although the winner that day, Elopement, who won on five other occasions as well, has been sold to race in Australia, Brisbourne has no shortage of decent ammunition for the new season.

"One of my best hopes is **Secret Asset**," said the trainer, who gave the horse as his two-year-old to follow last year.

"He won twice last season – beating a Godolphin hotpot at Haydock and following up off top weight in a nursery at Beverley.

SAMARINDA (right): useful sort for Pam Sly who could start off in the Lincoln

He was placed in two other races.

"He's currently rated 94 and I'm hoping he's got a big sprint handicap in him. He'll be out at the back end of April. He's a fast ground horse; if it's good or softer, then he's best left in his box."

Brisbourne believes stable stalwart **Roman Maze** is in for a good campaign if the weather comes right – he was a victim of last year's wet summer. **Just Oscar** has also improved over the winter and should get off the mark after three seconds.

Brisbourne always does well with his Green Desert progeny and the five-year-old **Grafty Green** could be the latest to follow the likes of Adobe and Summer Shades.

"He's better than his form looks on paper. I think he can improve and move up the grades this year. He'll be running in races over 1m2f."

Another Green Desert offspring who looks set for a profitable season is the promising **New Star**, who won a decent handicap at Chester in August.

That win was over the extended 1m2f and Brisbourne believes the colt will get further.

One of Brisbourne's stars last year was **Cheshire Prince**, who chalked up two victories including an impressive 5l success at Chester in August.

The Desert Prince gelding unfortunately picked up a knock in that race and wasn't seen again. But he'll be back this summer and Brisbourne is aiming him at the Chester May meeting.

With her Classic-winning heroine Speciosa retired, it's unlikely *PAM SLY* will be checking the Group 1 programme book this year. But the popular Peterborough handler has assembled a useful team of performers who should pay their way.

Samarinda was a winner four times on Polytrack and failed narrowly to land the final of the valuable London Mile series at Kempton in September.

But the five-year-old is a useful performer on grass too as he showed with a close-up third in a competitive handicap at Ascot in the autumn.

Expect Sly to take advantage of his lower turf rating this summer with the colt possibly kicking off his year in the Lincoln.

The three-year-old **Ovthenight** shaped with promise when fourth at odds of 40-1 on his final start of the campaign in a com-

petitive 1m2f nursery at Nottingham and looks a useful prospect.

And in handicaps around the 2m distance, Sly will also be well-served by her talented dual-purpose performer **Dhehdaah**, twice a winner on the level last year. Despite those victories, the Alhaarth gelding is still rated over 50lb lower on the Flat than he is over hurdles.

Sly has also got some well-bred two-year-olds to go into battle with, details of which will be found in a future edition of the *RFO*. Who knows, there may be a new Speciosa among them.

JOHN SPEARING once again proved his tremendous versatility with another good Flat season. Although his total of 18 winners was three down on his 2006 tally, his strike-rate rose to a highly respectable 12%.

Old favourites Pintle and Cashel Mead have gone off to stud, but Spearing is not short of talented replacements.

Useful hurdler **Rajeh**, who ran a blinder to finish third at 66-1 in a hot 1m4f York handicap behind subsequent Listed winner Galactic Star at the Ebor meeting in August, will again be in action on the level, and Spearing believes he's got a good Flat handicap in him. "I'm sure there will be something suitable for him at York," he said.

The Knavesmire also seems to bring out the best in **Kayf Aramis**, who has won the staying handicap at the Dante meeting for the last two years.

The son of Ascot Gold Cup winner Kayf Tara loves cut in the ground and provided he gets his favoured conditions, he'll be the one they all have to beat if he bids for the hat-trick in May.

Promising fillies **Whiteoak Lady** and **Sawpit Sunshine** both won as juveniles last season and Spearing informs that both will be out early as they like cut in the ground. They are both worth following.

<table>
<tr><td>**Midlands magic**</td></tr>
<tr><td>*Cartimandua*
Rajeh
Samarinda</td></tr>
</table>

Morning Mole

by
Steve Mellish

Godolphin to do better this year

THE Classic roll of honour shows 2007 to have been a very different sort of year.

Look at the winning trainers: Jim Bolger, Geoff Huffer, Peter Chapple-Hyam, Henry Cecil and John Gosden. Hardly a C-List, I'll grant you, but not what we've become accustomed to.

No Sir Michael Stoute among them, no Godolphin and, most surprisingly, no Aidan O'Brien. You have to go back to 1993 for the last time all those powerful stables drew a blank. Can we expect more of the same this year? I very much doubt it.

Sir Michael Stoute has signed up Ryan Moore as his stable jockey, so he's clearly not taking things lying down; Godolphin have any number of decent three-year-olds to represent them and Coolmore are Coolmore.

Godolphin, in particular, have much to look forward to. They were mere bit players in the 2007 Classics, but a look at the market for the 2,000 Guineas suggests 2008 will be very different.

At the time of writing, they have three of the first five in the betting: **Fast Company**, **Ibn Khaldun** and **Rio De La Plata**. Fast Company has come the "traditional" route, i.e. purchased for big bucks after doing very well for another trainer. Rio De La Plata was also bought in a breeze-up, but tellingly Ibn Khaldun is Godolphin born and bred – a Classic win from this one would be a huge boost for a breeding operation that has underperformed on a grand scale.

Which other trainers will do well this year?

Many fancy Henry Cecil to follow up last year's Oak's success with a Derby win with **Twice Over** the animal many are drooling over. He's a colt of immense potential, but he's not the only good prospect at Warren Place. **Kandahar Run** is a gorgeous grey son of Rock Of Gibraltar who got better and better last year and I fancy him to pick up a big prize or two.

Cecil's neighbour John Gosden is another who must feel very optimistic about his prospects.

Raven's Pass and **Sense Of Joy** have decent claims in the first two Classics, whilst **Dar Re Mi** (who is discussed at length in the following page) is a filly of whom I expect to hear plenty when upped to middle distances.

On the jockey front I claim no prizes for suggesting Ryan Moore will regain his title or that William Buick will continue to thrive. He had 67 winners in 2007 and I expect him to better that by some way this year.

KANDAHAR RUN

DAR RE MI
3yo brown filly
Singspiel – Darara (Top Ville)
John Gosden

This filly has really caught my imagination and I've a feeling we'll be hearing a fair bit about her this year.

Bred to need time and middle-distances and looking as though the run would bring her on, she nonetheless had the raw ability to finish runner-up in a big-field 7f Newmarket maiden.

Moreover, she'd have won but for showing her inexperience when first asked to pick up.

A lovely-looking filly, with loads of scope, a maiden looks a formality for her, once stepped up in trip.

In fact, it wouldn't surprise me in the least to see her develop into something pretty smart. It may be far-fetched but races like the Oaks and Ribblesdale could end up on her agenda.

SILVER SUITOR
4yo brown filly
Swain – Taatof (Lahib)
David Elsworth

Here's a horse we haven't seen the best of yet. Unraced at two and only seen five times last year, he has very few miles on the clock.

Despite those limited appearances he's already shown a decent level of ability, and it's encouraging that his form has got better each time he's run.

It's clear that he's improving with experience and it's also clear that he's a stayer.

He got off the mark at the fourth attempt, stepped up to 1m4f, and followed that with an even better effort on his final start over an extended 1m5f.

The way he kept on that day suggests even further will bring about more improvement. Elsworth excels with this type of animal and I can imagine he has races like the Ebor or the Northumberland Plate as possible targets.

SKY DIVE
3yo chestnut colt
Dr Fong – Free Flying (Groom Dancer)
Luca Cumani

The quality of horse contesting maiden races on the All-Weather has risen markedly in the last couple of years.

Most of the animals contesting these races are still moderate, but at places like Kempton and Lingfield you can come across a good one.

I certainly think I saw a horse worth following on a visit to Lingfield in September.

The beast in question is Sky Dive, who took a 14-runner maiden that was full of horses from powerful stables.

Luca Cumani's charge really took the eye beforehand (he's a big, rangy type) and, though this was his second start, he still

DAVID ELSWORTH: *trains Silver Suitor*

LUCA CUMANI: *his Sky Dive looks useful*

needed the run. He belied his burly appearance with a ready win despite not look entirely at ease with the sharp turns.

By Dr Fong from a good middle-distance family, he'll relish another furlong or two and, given his size, a more galloping track than Lingfield will also be a plus. Progressive and scopey, this is just the sort of animal that the patient Cumani excels with.

WEST WITH THE WIND
3yo brown colt
Fasliyev – Midnight Angel (Acatenango)
Tom Tate

Tom Tate is a trainer who gets the best out of his charges, and I reckon he'll be excited about plotting a campaign for this lad.

After showing promise on his debut at Doncaster (he stayed on nicely, having looked green in the early stages) he was unlucky not to score at Nottingham.

Forced wide on the first turn, he was always playing catch-up and, though putting in good late work, the damage was done.

His dam was a useful middle-distance performer and the way he kept on in that 1m maiden suggests that distances of 1m2f or further will suit him better.

A big, lengthy individual with loads of physical scope, he looks the type to thrive over the winter.

I'm hopeful he'll make up into a pretty good handicapper at least. However, one word of warning is that, given his size, I would think he'd always need a galloping track to be seen at his best.

WOOD CHORUS
3yo bay filly
Singspiel – Woodbeck (Terimon)
Michael Bell

On a visit to Yarmouth in October I was really taken with the performance of Wood Chorus in a 1m maiden.

I liked her in the paddock (though she very much looked as though the run would do her good) and I liked her performance in the race even more.

Held up towards the rear, she had a lot to do entering the final two furlongs but finished very strongly under hands-and-heels riding to finish a closing third.

The looked a good maiden beforehand and the form should work out.

Further encouragement is provided by her breeding, which has three-year old written all over it.

She's a Singspiel half-sister to the Mark Tompkins-trained Yorkshire Cup winner Franklins Gardens, so she ought to relish trips of 1m2f and more.

I'm more than hopeful she'll turn into a pretty decent performer.

FRANKLINS GARDENS: his half-sister Wood Chorus could be a useful sort this season

You have to specialise these days

THE 2008 Flat season scares me and having been on the track for the best part of 15 years, this is the first season that I really do feel that if I were starting out trying to make a living betting on the horses I would definitely check the situations vacant column before taking the plunge.

The reason is clear to me and that is that there is too much racing on the Flat. With the closure of jumping racecourses a couple of seasons ago the jumps form book has actually got smaller recently and it has been an enjoyable, if not massively profitable, winter so far.

The Flat form book is different and it virtually needs two men with strong backs to lift it by the end of the season.

That is too much for me. The key therefore is to rationalise your sphere of interest, specialise and stick to it.

As a punter who goes racing and bets through the card, I have had to bin the All-Weather and concentrate on the best meeting of the day.

That means there are now hundreds or even thousands of horses that I never see and don't need to know about.

This may not suit the stay-at-home punter but you must do something and I would recommend you either concentrate your efforts on age groups, the obvious one being two-year-olds, or divide things up by distance and cut things down that way.

All I will say, and I would bet just about anyone would back me up on this, is that if you try and keep tabs on everything then you will come a very very poor second and could end up doing the lot.

The other thing I am definitely going to do is use the advantage I have by attending the track to help me.

There are fewer and fewer reasons for going racing as opposed to sitting at home on the internet and betting away.

One of the advantages is that you may see the horses in the paddock (which as we know can be a double-edged sword on occasions) but perhaps more reliable is the ability to watch horses go to the start.

It is an absolute travesty that a lot of courses no longer insist that horses are paraded past the paying public before the race with clerks telling us that it preserves the ground.

I have never heard the clerks at tracks like Goodwood, where horses simply have to go down to post in front of the stands, moan about the situation.

IN THE JUNGLE: Dave in the ring

Sponsored by Stan James

JOHN BEST: overlooks his string, led by Ruff Diamond who has matured well

Equally I cannot remember ever seeing a horse go down to the start like a cripple and come back like a Classic winner.

If observing this stops me having just 20 bets this season then it will save me a fortune.

I will try to go to Doncaster as much as possible as I really believe we have a world-class track now after the recent renovations and if I cannot back winners at this venue then I will give up.

I have looked at my bets over the last year or so and there is a noticeable change in emphasis, and I believe it is caused by the now-mature betting-exchange markets becoming a major influence on prices.

In my early days pre-Betfair I used to specialise in outsiders and try desperately to find horses at prices to beat the favourites.

I was convinced this was where the value lay, and it was probably true, especially at the second and third cards of the day where I had more knowledge than other punters.

Nowadays I seem to get some fantastic prices about horses but very rarely get a winner, except on the odd occasion in a very big race at a big track, and if one does win it is usually because of some calamity in a race rather than my excellent form reading.

When I back a solid favourite the results are more positive and I really believe that backing outsiders is for mugs nowadays.

There is no point laying them because the spread between back and lay is too wide, but when a horse looks a huge price it is still probably the right price and finding the exceptions is not worth the effort you need to put in to find the odd gem.

Stick to rock-solid horses in rock-solid races.

With the sermon over, let's finish by finding some winners for the year. I reckon John Best will have a great season and my three to follow are all from his yard.

Ruff Diamond and **Meydan Dubai** have matured into seriously good three-year-olds and should be out and winning fairly early.

Meanwhile, I am managing some two-year-olds for a former City colleague and have high hopes already that **Square Eddie** will make up into a Royal Ascot runner.

Time Test *with Mark Nelson*

All to play for in the Classics

I BELIEVE it was W.C. Fields who said 'All I ever wanted out of life was an unfair advantage'. Perhaps he should have read the *RFO*.

Regular followers of speed figures will know the edge the numbers can give you over punters just reliant on form or whispers from the gallops.

In addition to highlighting the fast horses, they also give you a good idea of which horses to take on.

This is particularly relevant this year as some of last year's youngsters failed to impress on the clock, notably the fillies.

Compare the previous season's top filly Finsceal Beo, who achieved a *Time Test* figure of 75 during her juvenile campaign, with **Natagora**, who comes out best of last season's crop with a meagre 65.

In fairness, I think Jim Bolger's charge was an exceptional juvenile, but a 10lb gulf just goes to show that the youngsters really need to step up a gear.

As a result of this, I think the fillies who ended up near the top of my ratings after a handful of outings may be vulnerable to less exposed types in the season ahead.

Whilst Natagora is clearly a smart filly, she's already had five starts so wouldn't strike me as a winner of the Newmarket Guineas, especially with stamina unproven beyond 6f.

More interesting for the first fillies' Classic would be **Proviso** and **Zarkava**. There is currently only 1pt between the pair on my figures and both are lightly raced with the potential of better to come.

Proviso clocked a good time when successful on her second start and, although beaten at Ascot next time, she didn't benefit from the greatest ride by her usually astute jockey.

Zarkava is unbeaten in two starts and, in addition to being visually impressive in the Prix Marcel Boussac, she clocked a good time to boot.

While neither currently have figures to suggest they are Guineas winners in waiting , they at least have the potential to build on some solid times in the year ahead.

After outstanding colts in recent seasons such as George Washington, Teofilo and Holy Roman Emperor, I was worried that 2007's juveniles might come up short of what we have come to expect in this division.

That looked to be the case until the Dewhurst confirmed that **New Approach** had the speed to match the hype.

My numbers suggest that Jim Bolger's colt is not quite as good as last year's stablemate, but it's hard to knock a record of five unbeaten starts and his Newmarket success was a big step forward in terms of the times he had recorded.

However, it's possible the ground went against a few of his rivals that day and quotes as short as 7-4 look skinny enough for the 2,000 Guineas in May.

Solario Stakes winner **Raven's Pass** clocked a mighty figure at Sandown on fast ground and was far from disgraced behind New Approach in the Dewhurst.

His chance was almost certainly compromised by the softening of the ground and, at four times the odds of the Irish raider, he makes some appeal for the first colts' Classic.

Godolphin also have a couple of juveniles to consider in **Rio De La Plata** and **Ibn Khaldun**.

The latter ended the season on a high note by landing the Racing Post Trophy on his first venture into Group 1 company, but I have his stablemate as the fastest of the pair on what they have achieved to date.

I don't like making too many excuses for horses, but I have little doubt Rio De La Plata was unsuited by the muddling gallop when chasing home New Approach in the National Stakes.

Likewise, the rain-softened ground at Newmarket in the Dewhurst wouldn't have been ideal either and, while his form figures lack the profile of a typical Guineas winner, I wouldn't underestimate his chance if the ground is on the quick side in May.

Towards the end of the season **Endless Luck** made a good impression in what initially looked a nondescript Musselburgh maiden.

The Mark Johnston-trained juvenile clocked a time far above what one might normally expect for such a race and this son of Giant's Causeway may prove to be a decent type.

His *Time Test* figure is still some way below the very best juveniles, but there was a lot to like about the manner of the success and, if he improves significantly, like so many of the Mark Johnston horses do at three, he'll be one to take seriously in the season ahead.

Official ground descriptions are always a bone of contention and, as a punter, there is nothing worse than having a bet in the morning, only to find out during the course of the meeting that the ground is not as officially described.

The calculation of speed figures give a true insight into the ground and my numbers suggest that Hughie Morrison had a fair case when criticising ground staff at Haydock, after the Betfred Sprint Cup.

Morrison put the defeat of **Sakhee's Secret** down to the ground and the times from that Saturday support his accusations. Even on the preceding day, race times suggested the ground was good at best, despite the official description of good to firm.

A worse example came at Warwick racecourse earlier the same week when the meeting had to be abandoned after just two races as the track was deemed to be unsafe due to over-watering.

I'd like to see a less liberal approach to watering, but whether a common-sense approach will prevail in the season ahead remains to be seen.

The weight-for-age scale is designed to level the playing field for immature horses when they meet their elders, but a number of performances during the last couple of seasons have urged me to reconsider the adjustment I make to my speed figures.

The scale assumes that all horses of a particular age group are at the same level of development. Just as in human life, this is not the case.

Anyone with a child at school will know that despite a similarity in age, there will be a huge diversity in size, strength and speed among the pupils. The same is true with racehorses and I have found that making an allowance to suit all can skew the figures and have a detrimental effect.

Followers of my speed figures in the *Racing & Football Outlook* may wish to know that from the 2008 turf season onwards, my speed figures will be simply adjusted for the weight carried without any tinkering in terms of weight-for-age.

As speed figures tend to be more reliable the less they are manipulated, here's hoping our 'unfair advantage' may be even greater during 2008.

NEW APPROACH: has speed to match hype

	Horse	Speed rating	Distance in furlongs	Going	Track	Date achieved
1	**New Approach**	**78**	**7**	**Gs**	**Newmarket**	**Oct 20**
2	Fast Company	77	7	Gs	Newmarket	Oct 20
3	Kingsgate Native	71	5	Gd	York	Aug 23
4	Raven's Pass	70	7	Gf	Sandown	Sep 1
5	Rio De La Plata	65	7	Gd	Goodwood	Aug 1
6	Ibn Khaldun	64	8	Gd	Doncaster	Oct 27
6	Pomellato	64	6	Sf	Maisons-Laffittes	Nov 2
8	Myboycharlie	63	6	Sf	Deauville	Aug 19
8	Strike The Deal	63	6	Gf	Newbury	Sep 22
10	Captain Gerrard	61	5	Gs	Ascot	Oct 13

Top two-year-old fillies of 2007

	Horse	Speed rating	Distance in furlongs	Going	Track	Date achieved
1	**Natagora**	**65**	**6**	**Gd**	**Newmarket**	**Oct 5**
2	Fleeting Spirit	64	6	Gd	Newmarket	Oct 5
3	Proviso	62	7	Gd	Deauville	Aug 18
	Zarkava	61	8	Gs	Longchamp	Oct 7
5	Janina	60	5	Gd	York	May 18
	Laureldean Gale	60	7	Gd	Deauville	Aug 18
7	Eva's Request	59	7	Yd	Curragh	Sep 30
8	Elletelle	57	5	Gf	Ascot	Jun 20
	Listen	57	8	Sf	Ascot	Sep 29
	Nijoom Dubai	57	6	Gs	Ascot	Jun 22

Going key: F = firm, Gf = good to firm, G = good, Gs = good to soft, S = soft, H = heavy.

Time Test on call 0905 230 2269; ROI 1560 719 754 or subscribe to Nelson's sms tips by texting RFONELS to 84080; ROI 53307

Review of 2007

Outlook

News diary 2007

by Richard Williams

January

10 Henry Cecil reclaims the fillies' yard at Warren Place now that his string of horses has increased to 80 compared to 55 in 2006. The 17-box yard has been home to Bosra Sham and Ramruma. Cecil will continue to lease parts of Warren Place to Paul Howling, Ed Vaughan and Jonathan Jay. Cecil ended 2006 with 25 winners, up from 12 the previous year.

16 In the depths of winter, Flat enthusiasts emerge from hibernation to consider the World Thoroughbred Racehorse Rankings. It's the two-year-old class of 2006 that is the focus of attention. Jim Bolger's Teofilo comes out on top with 123 which is the median figure for a champion juvenile. Holy Roman Emperor is third on 122 and Dutch Art a point behind. Finsceal Beo and Mount Nelson are fourth equal on 119 giving Ireland four out of the top five. The ratings are a triumph for Bolger who also trains the top-rated filly Finsceal Beo. He had never before had a champion two-year-old. Teofilo beat Holy Roman Emperor by a head in the Dewhurst Stakes after a great duel and some observers argue that the two colts should have been treated equally. The best three-year-olds are the Americans, Bernardini and Discreet Cat, both on 128 ahead of George Washington and Rail Link, both on 127. The best older horse is Invasor (129) who won four from four in the US including the Breeders' Cup Classic. He is two points ahead of Japan's Deep Impact.

February

9 Coral expand by purchasing 44 betting shops in the northeast and Yorkshire from independent bookmaker Pagebet. Coral now have 1,550 shops but are still in third place behind Ladbrokes and William Hill, with Betfred in fourth place.

16 Robert Winston is banned from race riding for a year as a huge Horseracing Regulatory Authority investigation into corruption concludes with a series of verdicts against four jockeys. Winston will still be able to ride work giving him a life-line to continue his career. He is found guilty of passing on information for reward and for misleading investigators. However he is not in breach of not riding his mounts to their merits. On the other hand Robbie Fitzpatrick and Luke Fletcher are warned off for three years which means they can't ride work or step onto a racecourse. Fran Ferris is warned off for two years. The investigation centred on 37 races run between June 16, 2003 and February 29, 2004 together with the activities on betting exchanges of the Nottinghamshire bookmaker Ian Nicholl, who is warned off indefinitely.

March

10 The racing world is rocked when Coolmore announce that Holy Roman Emperor, officially 2006's second best two-year-old in the world and the second favourite for the 2,000 Guineas, is to be retired. He is to replace George Washington who has proved infertile at stud. Trainer Aidan O'Brien is "shell-shocked" when the the news is broken to him shortly after Holy Roman Emperor worked on the Ballydoyle gallops. "I don't know what to say," he says. "He worked brilliantly this morning but by lunchtime, the decision had been made to retire him. We were looking forward to taking on Teofilo again. Losing him is like having a football team and losing your best striker – maybe even two strikers. Like George Washington, Holy Roman Emperor is a Danehill and Coolmore wanted him to replace George with the best Danehill around." The decision to take a sound colt with Classic prospects out of training represents an unprecedented episode in bloodstock history. And one of the strangest ways for punters to lose their money.

11 Boylesports bookmakers are to refund ante-post stakes on Holy Roman Emperor due to the unique circumstances of his retirement. Coral say they won't do the same because it would set a dangerous precedent.

16/17/18 While most people are enjoying Gold Cup day at the Cheltenham Festival, champion Flat jockey Ryan Moore is being catapulted off his mount at Lingfield in the early stages of a 6f handicap. He breaks his arm and two days later has an operation at the John Radcliffe Hospital in Oxford.

19 Newmarket unveils a new sales race worth £1,000,000 for 2008 which will make it the second richest race in the UK. Only the Derby will be worth more. The Tattersalls Million will be open to two-year-old colts, fillies and geldings and there will also be an £800,000 race exclusively for fillies. They will take place at the same Cambridgeshire meeting as the Group 1 Middle Park Stakes and the Cheveley Park Stakes and will be restricted to graduates of the Tattersalls October Yearling Sale. There will also be a Tattersalls £400,000 three-year-old race run over 1m2f, staged at the Craven meeting in 2009. This will be open to horses for which the entry stake and first forfeit has been paid for either of the 2008 two-year-old races. Its prize-money is likely to easily exceed the prize-money for either the 1,000 or 2,000 Guineas. Newmarket's director of racing Michael Prosser says: "We are mindful of our black-type races and very protective of them. We've looked very closely at the potential impact and don't think it will make any difference." Leading breeder Philip Freedman opines: "I know these new two-year-old races are over 7f but they could attract horses that in the past might have run in the Middle Park or Cheveley Park or indeed take something away from the Dewhurst." Traditionalists may have their concerns but students of the form book less so. With huge prize-money all the way down to tenth place, all the horses involved will be off for their lives generating form than can be trusted.

21 It emerges that Finsceal Beo, 8-1 favourite for the Oaks, hasn't even been entered for the race. Jim Bolger says: "I've not put her in the Oaks because I don't think she will get a mile and a half. Nobody asked me. I've enough to do to mind my own business without organising things for the bookmakers."

27   Betting on the Flat jockeys championship begins with Totesport making Ryan Moore 5-4, Jamie Spencer 11-8, Frankie Dettori 7-1, Neil Callan 10-1 and Seb Sanders 12-1. Spencer says: "Winning the title isn't something you can be confident about but I'll be trying. I just want to stay in one piece and stay away from the stewards' room."

April

2/3   Brian Wright, 60, described as the UK's richest drugs dealer, faces the prospect of spending the rest of his life in prison after being found guilty of flooding Britain with cocaine. He is handed a 30-year sentence. He laundered his money by betting on horses. He headed the Jockey Club's most wanted list for more than a decade before being banned from racing for 20 years in 2002 when he was on the run in the Mediterranean. He was arrested in Spain in 2005.

15   Ryan Moore is facing another month on the sidelines because the lateral column fracture on his arm is proving more serious than first thought. He had a metal plate inserted in March and is having physiotherapy. The date for his comeback is pushed back to the middle of May.

16/17   Betting exchange layers come out in force for Teofilo in both the 2,000 Guineas and Derby while the bookmakers are inundated with requests for the colt's market rivals. The bookmakers suspend betting on the two colts' Classics. At 3pm he drifts out to 11 from 2.58 on Betfair and is then backed in again to around 4 at 10.30pm. Ladbrokes spokesman David Williams says: "It was a precautionary measure but we haven't found anything to substantiate the rumours. We are now back up and it's business as usual." The next day Bolger reveals: "When trotting yesterday Teofilo showed slight discomfort. His training will be restricted to walking and swimming for one week. Otherwise he is fit and well and on target for the 2,000 Guineas."

19   Shane Kelly has his licence suspended for a year after being found guilty of nine charges of passing information about rides and runners for reward to Bolton-based professional punter Ajaz Khan. The HRA also throws a nine-month ban at David Nolan and a four-month ban at Josh Byrne. Trainer Phil McEntee has his licence revoked for a year. The four can still work in racing.

20   Betting shops have to go without live pictures from Newbury. TurfTV and not SIS has the television rights to Newbury through its alignment with RacingUK. The big three bookmakers have a deal with SIS but not one with TurfTV. Squabbling among bookmakers and satellite broadcasters shows no sign of ending anytime soon.

25   Great Leighs, the new racecourse which has cancelled more times than a Virgin train, threatens to open its doors to the public on August 16. "And that's a promise," says Essex entrepreneur and track owner John Holmes speaking 24 hours after handing back three scheduled fixtures in June and July. "Only a catastophe with the weather will stop us now." Holmes has spent seven years planning and building his dream.

May

2   Ascot unveils the rebuild of the rebuild. The new grandstand, which had been deemed not fit for purpose, to borrow a phrase from former Labour Home Secretary John Reid, has had a £10 million facelift over the winter in order to improve viewing. According to an Ascot statement, the changes include the raising of the steppings (steps to me and you) at the base of the grandstand. Racegoers' reaction is mixed but their frustrations largely seem to have eased. The meeting features the Group 3 Sagaro Stakes which is won by Amanda Perrett's Tungsten Strike. Ascot's head of public

relations Nick Smith admits that a quiet mid-week Wednesday is not the right time to draw a conclusion on the modifications. The royal meeting will be the acid test. The £10 million spend comes on top of the original £220 million outlay.

3   Jim Bolger withdraws Teofilo from the 2,000 Guineas due to be run two days hence, citing an off-fore knee problem. The colt had been talked of as a Triple Crown contender but now Bolger has a battle to get him ready for the Derby. It is another bitter pill for punters following the defection of Holy Roman Emperor. They lose approximately £2 million.

6   On the day that the Jim Bolger-trained Finsceal Beo wins the 1,000 Guineas (in a record time for either the 1,000 or 2,000 Guineas) the trainer says that Teofilo will be on the easy list for at least six weeks which means that he will miss the Derby. "We won't race him beyond his three-year-old days," says Bolger looking further into the future. "Only one mare is booked so far and that is Finsceal Beo."

23   Having ridden a treble the day before, Jamie Spencer begins a 15-day ban which rules him out of the Derby meeting. He is now 4-6 to take the title from Ryan Moore, having been 1-3 ten days earlier. Totesport bring Moore in to 14-1 from 20-1 despite there being no sign of him returning.

24   Richard Quinn returns to the saddle 11 months after announcing his retirement. His three mounts at Goodwood draw a blank.

27   Frankie Dettori rides work on Derby favourite Authorized for trainer Peter Chapple-Hyam and afterwards gives a press conference at Newmarket. He dispels doubts about his fitness following his mid-race fall at Goodwood the previous week when he damaged his knee. He says: "I strapped the knee up with a strong bandage and a ski kneepad. I've won every other British Classic twice or more so nothing would give me more pleasure than to fulfil my childhood dreams with a Derby win." Looking further ahead, the 36-year-old says: "I don't think that there is any other job out there that can give me as much money or satisfaction. So as long as I'm still healthy and riding as good as ever, I've got to carry on as long as I can." He is of course talking about his job as a jockey and as not as (a) a restauranteur who heads the Frankie's Italian Bar and Grill chain (four outlets) (b) purveyor of Frankie Dettori's tinned tomatoes (average monthly sale 500,000 tins) (c) television presenter (Question Of Sport and Top Of The Pops on his cv so far).

June

1   The great Henry Cecil wins his eighth Oaks and 24th British Classic with Light Shift, who runs in the colours of the Niarchos family. After seven years in a relative racing wilderness, Cecil is back where he belongs. Light Shift, who returns at 13-2, is the stable's second string behind the favourite Passage Of Time. Cecil, 64, who has been undergoing treatment for stomach cancer, is warmly greeted by the crowd of 23,000 most of whom appear to respond to the man in the crowd near the winner's enclosure who shouts 'three cheers for Henry'.

2   Epsom is once again the scene of dream-fulfilment as Frankie Dettori wins his first Derby on Authorized. He does a flying dismount and says: "When I got to the furlong marker the world stopped, my heart stopped. I knew this was going to be my moment. Everything went so smoothly. I expected a dogfight but it was like an oil painting, beautiful and smooth." The colt, who is owned by two Kuwaiti businessmen Saleh Al Homaizi and Imad Al Sagar, goes off at 5-4 having been odds-on during the week. A spokesman for Coral says the race will be remembered by bookies as the worst result in Derby betting history. Neal Wilkins says that the result had cost VCbet £2m and that it was the worst single result for the firm in 61 years while Paddy Power claim that they face a payout of £2.5m.

3   Sheikh Mohammed buys up the stud rights to the first two in the Kentucky Derby, Street Sense and Hard Spun. They will stand in Lexington, Kentucky.

7   Kieren Fallon returns to the saddle at Tipperary where he rides the winner of the first race. His absence in Ireland has been due to a failed drugs test in France on July 9   He is still banned in Britain because he faces criminal charges. Ryan Moore returns from injury but is out of luck at Sandown.

20   On the first day of Royal Ascot, Godolphin win their first British Group 1 for nearly three years, Ramonti landing the Queen Anne Stakes. There are no complaints about the viewing but the crowds are down on the same day last year. The attendance was just over 40,191, a drop of 26 per cent.

21   There is another announcement from Great Leighs. It is much the same as previous ones. The track is postponing its opening date.

July

3   Southwell is facing many months of closure because of the floods in the centre of England. Simon Davis, the estate manager, tells the BBC: "The membrane is all salted up as well as the stone underneath, so the water can't get through. All the sand is contaminated with salt and debris from out of the ponds and surrounding dykes. The surface is basically ruined."

9   Tony Culhane is banned from riding for a year having been found guilty of corruption by the HRA. Dean Mernagh is banned for nine months at the end of a case that lifts to 12 the number of jockeys banned or warned off by the HRA in less than three years. Culhane's brother-in-law is warned off for two years and his father-in-law five years. The inquiry covered 37 races run between July 2003 and February 2004. On 32 out of the 37 occasions a horse was laid to lose or not be placed. Culhane's father-in-law made a profit of more than £56,000 from the races in question.

19   Owners in Britain will have to face up to a ten per cent cut in Levy Board prize-money contribution in 2008. The cuts, coming on top of a 14 per cent reduction in 2007, are made with a "heavy heart" according to Levy Board chairman Rob Hughes. Falling income from bookmakers forces the board to downgrade its working forecasts. Michael Harris, Racehorse Owners Association chief executive, says: "It's a stark warning to the industry that it must adapt to meet the demands of today's betting market. Racing's attractions are not being appreciated by young audiences."

22   Exercising horses in the dark in Newmarket is to be banned from October under a directive issued by the Health and Safety Executive. The HSE became involved after a road accident in December when a two-year-old was hit by a car crossing the Bury Road at 6.45am. Clive Brittain, usually the first on to the gallops, reacts thus: "Of all the hamfisted rules that have come in, this must be the worst. I would never put my horse or riders at risk if I didn't think it was safe to work in the dark. It's health and safety gone mad."

25   Sheikh Mohammed opens his chequebook again. This time he acquires Admire Moon for a reported £16m. The winner of the Duba Duty Free at Nad Al Sheba is the latest high-profile stallion prospect to be bought by the sheikh following the purchase of Authorized.

August

6   Sheikh Mohammed continues to add to his book of young stallions by bringing Teofilo to his Kildangan Stud in County Kildare. The recently retired colt never saw the racecourse as a three-year-old but won the Dewhurst as a two-year-old. Jim Bolger, his owner and trainer, retains ownership while the sheikh has unfettered breeding access. Despite a self-imposed boycott of Coolmore stallions, the sheikh has brought in sons of Coolmore sires, Teofilo being a son of Galileo and Authorized being a son of Montjeu.

9   The bloodstock empire pioneered and expanded by the late Robert Sangster over 40 year is to be broken up. His famous blue and green colours will continue to be seen on the racecourse though and Brian Meehan will continue training at Manton.

17   Doncaster is back in business, 20 months after its closure, and unveils its not-quite-ready new grandstand which cost £20 million. The racing is nothing special but the viewing is excellent. It is touch and go, however. The final British Horseracing Authority inspection takes place at 6.30am and it is not until late morning that the course receives the green light from Health and Safety.

20   The irresistible lure of Sheikh Mohammed's chequebook secures the breeding rights to Manduro, the five-year-old owned by Baron von Ullman and trained by Andre Fabre. The German-bred son of Monsun has been top-class throughout his career and has already won three Group 1s this season including the Prince Of Wales's Stakes at Royal Ascot when he memorably got the better of another multiple winner at the top level in Dylan Thomas.

26   A new era in Irish racing begins with an eight-race card on Dundalk's All-Weather (Polytrack) surface before a sellout crowd of 7,000. The new stadium incorporates a greyhound track and cost €35 million.

September

3   Jamie Spencer, the 2-9 favourite for the jockeys' title with William Hill, returns from an eight-day suspension with a winner at Goodwood, Lovelace in the Group 3 Supreme Stakes.

4   Gary Moore buys the yard near Horsham in Sussex about to be vacated by Charles Cyzer, who has recently announced his retirement from training because of the lack of return on his investment. The former jumps jockey intends keeping the family's base in Brighton, but Cisswold Racing Stables is to be his flagship yard once the building of additional boxes is complete. The father of champion jockey Ryan Moore, who is never one to waste words, says: "I am looking forward to moving in and getting on with the job."

8   The issue of watering triggered an angry reaction from trainer Hughie Morrison who accuses Haydock of drastically altering ground conditions and causing the defeat of Betfred Sprint Cup favourite Sakhee's Secret. Even Barry Hills, who trains the 9-1 winner Red Clubs, admits that the watering had changed the going significantly. During the week the ground was advertised as good to firm, prompting Peter Chapple-Hyam to scratch Dutch Art, a colt who likes a bit of give. "It's loose and it's overwatered," says Morrison. The Outlook's *Off The Bit* has pointed out, on more than one occasion, that overwatering has been with us for ages. It was only a few years ago that Ascot watered on a Sunday just before the royal meeting, only for heavy showers to arrive on Monday. Watering should only be used in exceptional circumstances. Let Mother Nature determine the going.

12   An outbreak of foot-and-mouth disease hits southern England and Kempton takes precautionary action for its evening meeting. Every horsebox and car arriving at the course goes through a disinfectant procedure. The Sunbury course, along with Ascot and Windsor, all fall within the ten-kilometre control zone surrounding the farm in Egham, Surrey at the centre of the outbreak. Meanwhile the BBC reports that its Ceefax section, dedicated to racing, is to be axed at the end of the year. The service offers viewers an up-to-the-minute guide to results, betting shows, declarations, going reports and racing news and has been operational for nearly 20 years. This follows the dropping after Royal Ascot of the two early-morning bulletins which Luke Harvey provided Radio Five Live with for six years.

16/17   Manduro is ruled out of the Prix de l'Arc de Triomphe because of an injury discovered after he had won the Prix Foy at Longchamp. The next day Andre Fabre hails the five-year-old as "the best I have trained and the best by a good margin." It's a bold statement by the Frenchman considering he handled Peintre Celebre, Zafonic, Arcangues and Hurricane Run. And it raises the eyebrow of Mark Nelson, who is responsible for the Outlook's speed figures. Manduro is only tenth equal in Nelson's 'best of the season three-year-olds and upwards' table, alongside Excellent Art, Notnowcato, Ramonti and Enticing.

20 Sheikh Mohammed comes to the rescue of racing on terrestrial TV with a two-year sponsorship package for Channel 4. With the Tote withdrawing its backing, things were looking bleak for the TV channel. The new backer is Dubai Holding, a company of which the sheikh is the founder and honorary chairman. Dubai Holding will sponsor for £2 million per year.

21/22 Seb Sanders is the new favourite for the jockeys' title after going four ahead of Jamie Spencer with 144 wins. He is 10-11 and Spencer is evens. The next day Sanders hardens to 8-11 because Spencer is hit with a two-day ban for his careless riding of Advanced on the way to Ayr Gold Cup victory. Just one more infringement would leave Spencer facing a lengthy totting-up suspension.

24 The trial of Kieren Fallon and five co-defendants for conspiracy to defraud opens at the Old Bailey under Mr Justice Forbes.

October

1/3 Sheikh Mohammed asks Trinity Mirror to give £10 million to four racing-related charities as part of the sale of the Racing Post. The sheikh owns the Racing Post trademark. Trinity Mirror hands £2.5 million each to the Injured Jockey's Fund, Racing Welfare, Re-training of Racehorses and the Barney Curley-founded Dafa (Direct Aid for Africa). Curley says: "What this will do for people is unbelievable."

7/8 The Aidan O'Brien-trained Dylan Thomas wins the Arc to complete a rare King George/Arc double. The four-year-old is ridden by Kieren Fallon who the following day appears in Court 12 at the Old Bailey. Fallon describes the victory as the best day of his life. He admits that earlier in the week he had considered riding Soldier Of Fortune but O'Brien had urged him to stick with Dylan Thomas. It is a first Arc for O'Brien but it is nearly a first Arc for Mick Channon too. His Youmzain finishes fast and late to be beaten a head. Dylan Thomas's Coolmore connections have to endure a 35-minute stewards' inquiry which prompts some frenzied betting on the exchanges. The first notion of the result of the inquiry comes when one punter shortens Dylan Thomas down to 1.05, reportedly after seeing Fallon leaving the stewards room with a grin on his face. BBC viewers are unable to participate in the excitement of the inquiry. The channel ends its Longchamp coverage in order to show highlights of a rugby league match that took place two days earlier.

22 Geoff Huffer, who prepared Cockney Rebel to win the 2,000 Guineas and Irish 2,000 Guineas, quits the training ranks for the second time. He says: "I have decided to to give up training for good this time." The former drummer with the Troggs initially trained in Newmarket between 1978 and 1991 enjoying succes with Persian Heights who won the St James's Palace Stakes.

27 A tragic night at Monmouth Park where the Breeders' Cup takes place. George Washington, the enigmatic colt who proved infertile at stud, is put down after sustaining an open fracture of the cannonbone in the right front fetlock joint. The injury appears to take place as he enters the rain-sodden straight and Mick Kinane jumps off when the horse stumbles. It is a poor night for Europe on the results side. For the first time since 1998 Europe suffers a whitewash.

29 Jamie Spencer shortens to 1-12 for the jockeys' title. He is five ahead and Sanders is sitting out a ban.

Nov 8   Great Leighs postpones again. It plans to have an open day on January 28 to prove that it really does exist.

Nov 10   On the morning of the last day of the Flat season Seb Sanders is one ahead of Jamie Spencer in the jockey's title race. They both go to Doncaster where Sanders takes his lead to two when gifted the 6f maiden in which the erratic newcomer Omnicat swerves and unseats Eddie Ahern. Spencer battles back with a double on Generous Thought and Inchnadamph to force a tie – 190 each. Spencer won the title in 2005 but this is a first for Sanders who admits: "I would have been devastated to lose. It was nerve-wracking to come here today. To share it is a great relief." Greg Fairley, who is attached to Mark Johnston's stable, secures the apprentice title with 65 winners. There will be no more winners for former champion Kevin Darley though. He draws a blank on the day of his retirement.

Dec 5   Ryan Moore accepts the job as stable jockey to Sir Michael Stoute. The post is likely to mean Moore regaining his position as champion rider. Kieren Fallon won three titles in a row when he had a retainer at Freemason Lodge.

Dec 7   Racing's corruption trial collapses at the Old Bailey leaving Kieren Fallon and his five co-defendants free to go. At the end of two months of prosecution evidence, Mr Justice Forbes says there is no case to answer after the prosecution's expert witness admitted he wasn't an expert. In a brief statement on leaving the court Fallon says: "I am relieved and delighted but also outraged. There was never any evidence against me." He later issues a stronger statement saying: "The BHA's actions have caused me enormous personal pain." The six-time champion jockey has been prevented from riding in Britain for the past 17 months. Jockeys Fergal Lynch and Darren Williams, the gambler Miles Rodgers, Philip Sherkle and Lynch's brother Shaun are the others to walk free. Lynch and Williams can now reapply for the riding licences although the BHA will review the evidence from the trial to determine whether there were any breaches of the rules of racing. The collapse of the trial hinges on the evidence of key prosecution witness Ray Murrihy, the chief steward of Racing New South Wales, who had admitted at the Old Bailey a few days earlier that he was no expert when it came to British racing. Yet he was recruited by the prosecution to persuade the court that jockeys in 13 of the 27 races in question had a prima facie case to answere for breaching the non-trier's rule. Justice Forbes says: "It is abundantly clear his evidence fell far short of establishing a prima faecie breach of UK racing rules. Remarkably it was only as a result of cross-examination that it first became apparent of the limitations of his [Murrihy's] expertise." The police, who produced 40,000 pages of evidence and who interviewed 500 people, have questions to answer as does the Crown Prosecution Service. The finger of blame for the fiasco also points at Paul Scotney, the BHA's director of integrity services and licensing. The taxpayer has a bill of £13 million to settle.

Dec 8   The trial and tribulations of Kieren Fallon continue with the news that the drug test he took in France after winning the Prix Morny on Myboycharlie shows traces of cocaine. Should the B sample prove positive too, Fallon faces a lengthy ban.

Dec 22   Eddie Ahern is handed a three-month ban for bringing racing into disrepute in relation to a riding offence. The BHA's disciplinary panel decide Ahern deliberately flouted the whip rules at Southwell in order to trigger a suspension under the totting-up process with the aim of serving the resulting ban during a relatively quiet period, while also ensuring he begins the Flat turf season with a clean record.

KIEREN FALLON: temporary relief after trial

Sponsored by Stan James

Group 1 review
by Dylan Hill

For two-year-old Group 1s, see 'Two-year-olds of 2007', page 96

1 **Stan James 2000 Guineas (Group 1), (1m) Newmarket May 5 (Good to Firm)**

1 **Cockney Rebel** 9-0   O Peslier
2 **Vital Equine** 9-0   C Catlin
3 **Dutch Art** 9-0   J Fortune
25-1, 33-1, 14-1. 1^1/2l, ^{3}/4l. 24 ran. 1m 35.3 (b8.64)
Mr Phil Cunningham (G Huffer, Newmarket).

An anti-climactic air hung over the season's first Classic with the two great juveniles of 2006 – Teofilo and Holy Roman Emperor – missing out, but it was lifted by a brilliant performance from **Cockney Rebel**. The field of 21 split into two groups and the stands' side held sway, with **Vital Equine** forcing the issue and enjoying a clear lead at one point before Cockney Rebel cut him down with an electrifying burst of speed and won comfortably. **Dutch Art** quickened up well to win the far-side race by almost 2l from French raider **US Ranger** and **Strategic Prince**, while Aidan O'Brien pair **Duke Of Marmalade** and **Eagle Mountain** finished best of the rest on the near side in fourth and fifth.

2 **Stan James 1000 Guineas Stakes (Fillies' Group 1), (1m) Newmarket May 6 (Good to Firm)**

1 **Finsceal Beo** 9-0   K J Manning
2 **Arch Swing** 9-0   M J Kinane
3 **Simply Perfect** 9-0   J Murtagh
5-4f, 10-1, 9-1. 2^1/2l, 1^1/4l. 21 ran. 1m 34.9 (b8.98)
M A Ryan (J Bolger, IRELAND).

A truly world-class display from **Finsceal Beo**, who slaughtered a strong field to lead Racing Post Ratings experts to label her the best filly in the world. While she failed to live up to such lofty billing subsequently, this remains a special performance as she led over 2f out and only needed to be pushed clear in the final furlong, seeing off Irish raider **Arch Swing** with a pair of future Group 1 winners in **Simply Perfect** and **Indian Ink** filling two of the next three places.

3 **Juddmonte Lockinge Stakes (Group 1), (1m) Newbury May 19 (Good to Soft)**

1 **Red Evie** 8-11   J P Spencer
2 **Ramonti** 9-0   L Dettori
3 **Passager** 9-0   R Hughes
8-1, 4-1, 20-1. hd, hd. 8 ran. 1m 40.4 (b2.37)
Mr Terry Neill (M Bell, Newmarket).

The fact that **Peeress**, without a win since the 2006 renewal, was sent off just 11-8 confirms that this race lacked quality, but it produced a great finish and went to **Red Evie**, who picked up well from the rear to get up close home in a driving finish. Godolphin were still learning with Italian recruit **Ramonti**, who was perhaps ridden with too much restraint and would soon find improvement, while **Passager**, underrated like several French milers, ran a blinder in third.

4 **Boylesports Irish 2,000 Guineas (Group 1), (1m) Curragh May 26 (Good to Firm)**

1 **Cockney Rebel** 9-0   O Peslier
2 **Creachadoir** 9-0   K J Manning
3 **He's A Decoy** 9-0   M J Kinane
6-4f, 7-1, 40-1. 1l, 1l. 12 ran. 1m 36.1 (b8.45)
Mr Phil Cunningham (G Huffer, Newmarket).

A race which brought together all the best three-year-old milers in Europe bar Dutch Art and Excellent Art, and confirmed **Cockney Rebel**'s superiority despite a workmanlike rather than spectacular performance. Ridden more prominently in a smaller field, Cockney Rebel was made to work hard by **Creachadoir** but ultimately won with a fair bit in hand again. Creachadoir, second in the French Guineas where Ireland was responsible for the first four home, ran another fine race, edging out **He's A Decoy** and **Duke Of Marmalade**, beaten exactly as far as he was at Newmarket. **Vital Equine** was sixth.

5 **Tattersalls Gold Cup (Group 1), (1m2f110yds) Curragh May 27 (Good to Firm)**

1 **Notnowcato** 9-0   J P Murtagh
2 **Dylan Thomas** 9-0   J A Heffernan
3 **Youmzain** 9-0   R Hughes
7-1, 1-2f, 7-1. hd, 4l. 9 ran. 2m 16.2 (b9.83)
Anthony & David De Rothschild (Sir M Stoute, Newmarket).

A major shock as 1-2 favourite **Dylan Thomas** suffered a rare off-day and was turned over by **Notnowcato**. Having returned with a classy comeback win in the Prix Ganay, Dylan Thomas seemed set for another impressive win when he eased up to Notnowcato at the 2f pole, but he was unable to produce his customary turn of foot and Notnowcato held on bravely, underlining his status as a high-class performer in his own right. The pair pulled 4l clear of **Youmzain**.

6 **Boylesports Irish 1,000 Guineas (Group 1), (1m) Curragh May 27 (Good to Firm)**

1 **Finsceal Beo** 9-0   K J Manning
2 **Dimenticata** 9-0   C D Hayes
3 **Peeping Fawn** 9-0   J A Heffernan
9-10f, 66-1, 12-1. nk, 2l. 11 ran. 1m 39.3 (b5.25)
M A Ryan (J Bolger, IRELAND).

Finsceal Beo's globe-trotting efforts had understandably taken their toll but she still showed enough guts to land a Classic double, gaining compensation for just being touched off by Darjina in France when attempting the second leg of what would have been an unprecedented treble. Ridden to lead over 1f out, she couldn't quicken clear as she had at Newmarket but stuck on gamely and just held the fast-finishing **Dimenticata**, whose performance makes sense only as a strange one-off. **Peeping Fawn**, 11 days after winning her maiden, began her rise to the top in third, but **Arch Swing** ran a shocker.

7 **Vodafone Coronation Cup (Group 1), (1m4f10yds) Epsom June 1 (Good to Soft)**

1 **Scorpion** 9-0   M J Kinane
2 **Septimus** 9-0   J Murtagh
3 **Maraahel** 9-0   R Hills
8-1, 3-1, 7-1. 1¼l, ½l. 7 ran. 2m 40.8 (b5.53)
Mrs John Magnier & Mr M Tabor (A P O'Brien, IRELAND).

A quality renewal on paper but one dominated tactically by Aidan O'Brien. **Septimus** set a stop-start gallop, tracked by stablemate **Scorpion**, and the pair dictated the pace so well that only **Maraahel** ever got close to them, Scorpion hitting the front 2f out and galloping on strongly. Maraahel ran a cracker in third as the trio were well clear of **Rising Cross** in fourth. Neither **Sir Percy** nor **Sixties Icon** ever threatened, both

unsuited by the pace but below-par as well.

8 **Vodafone Oaks (Fillies' Group 1), (1m4f10yds) Epsom June 1 (Good to Soft)**

1 **Light Shift** 9-0   T E Durcan
2 **Peeping Fawn** 9-0   Martin Dwyer
3 **All My Loving** 9-0   C Soumillon
13-2, 20-1, 5-1. ½l, 4l. 14 ran. 2m 40.4 (b5.97)
Niarchos Family (H Cecil, Newmarket).

A heartwarming return to Classic glory for Henry Cecil as his second-string **Light Shift** ran out a superb winner from **Peeping Fawn**. Racing in midfield, Light Shift put the race to bed 2f out with a stunning change of pace and was only idling as Peeping Fawn closed in, pulling out more when required. The runner-up came from an impossible position turning for home and ran a blinder, the pair pulling 4l clear of **All My Loving** with the rest massively strung out. However, **Passage Of Time** and **Simply Perfect** both flopped.

9 **Vodafone Derby Stakes (Group 1), (1m4f10yds) Epsom June 2 (Good)**

1 **Authorized** 9-0   L Dettori
2 **Eagle Mountain** 9-0   J Murtagh
3 **Aqaleem** 9-0   R Hills
5-4f, 6-1, 9-1. 5l, 2½l. 17 ran. 2m 34.8 (b11.58)
Saleh Al Homaizi & Imad Al Sagar (P Chapple-Hyam, Newmarket).

Only one horse in this race looked to have superstar potential and **Authorized** rose to the task magnificently, destroying the opposition to record a winning margin not bettered since Slip Anchor in 1985. Held up in rear, he was always going well as he cruised into contention 2f out and quickened clear in hugely impressive style. **Eagle Mountain** stayed on relentlessly in the straight to prove the best of Aidan O'Brien's eight-strong battalion, **Soldier Of Fortune** the only other to make the first seven in fifth. Trial winners **Aqaleem**, **Lucarno** and **Salford Mill** were the others to get in the mix.

10 **St James's Palace Stakes (Group 1), (1m) Ascot June 19 (Good)**

1 **Excellent Art** 9-0   J P Spencer
2 **Duke Of Marmalade** 9-0   M J Kinane
3 **Astronomer Royal** 9-0   C O'Donoghue
8-1, 11-1, 14-1. nk, 1¼l. 8 ran. 1m 39.3 (a0.52)
Mrs John Magnier, Michael Tabor, D Smith, M Green (A P O'Brien, IRELAND).

A sensational 1-2-3 for Aidan O'Brien but a race as much about the demise of **Cockney Rebel**, who looked a likely winner entering the final furlong but then drifted alarmingly to his left and lost all momentum to finish fifth – it subsequently transpired he had fractured his pelvis and he never raced again. It's impossible

RAMONTI (No. 6) just lands the Queen Anne from Jeremy (rails) and Turtle Bowl (hidden)

to say whether he would have won, though, which underlines the quality of **Excellent Art**, an unlucky fourth in the French Guineas, who had matched Cockney Rebel's acceleration through from the rear and cosily mastered **Duke Of Marmalade** by a neck. Duke Of Marmalade improved after bowling along in front, while French Guineas winner **Astronomer Royal** also ran a solid race. **Dutch Art** was disappointing in fourth, as were **Creachadoir** and **He's A Decoy**.

11 Queen Anne Stakes (Group 1) (Str), (1m) Ascot June 19 (Good to Firm)

1	**Ramonti** 9-0	
		L Dettori
2	**Jeremy** 9-0	R L Moore
3	**Turtle Bowl** 9-0	O Peslier

5-1, 14-1, 33-1. shd, shd. 8 ran. 1m 37.2 (b1.60)

Godolphin (S bin Suroor, Newmarket).

George Washington had dominated the build-up on his return from stud duties, but he was upstaged by a gritty display from **Ramonti**. Given his head in front, Ramonti was headed 2f out by **Jeremy** but battled on well and got back up in the dying strides, Jeremy having faded badly in the final furlong, while also holding the late swoop of French hope **Turtle Bowl**. George Washington pulled hard and never looked like winning but plugged on to lose by less than half a length. **Red Evie** found the going too fast.

12 Prince Of Wales's Stakes (Group 1), (1m2f) Ascot June 20 (Good)

1	**Manduro** 9-0	S Pasquier
2	**Dylan Thomas** 9-0	C Soumillon
3	**Notnowcato** 9-0	J Murtagh

15-8f, 2-1, 13-2. 1¼l, 4l. 6 ran. 2m 5.9 (a2.45)

Baron G von Ullmann (A Fabre, FRANCE).

Even in this exalted company the market rated **Manduro** and **Dylan Thomas** a class apart and so it proved, with the French superstar coming out on top. Much-improved since finishing third in the race in 2006, Manduro was ridden prominently and sent to the front 2f out, getting first run on Dylan Thomas and staying on well to maintain his advantage. Dylan Thomas produced a fine effort in second, while **Notnowcato** beat **Red Rocks** for third. A change in tactics failed to revitalise **Sir Percy**, who fell away tamely after making the running and was retired.

13 Gold Cup (Group 1), (2m4f) Ascot June 21 (Good to Firm)

1	**Yeats** 9-2	M J Kinane
2	**Geordieland** 9-2	J P Spencer
3	**Le Miracle** 9-2	D Boeuf

8-13f, 12-1, 50-1. 1½l, 3½l. 14 ran. 4m 20.8 (a7.25)

Mrs John Magnier & Mrs David Nagle (A P O'Brien, IRELAND).

A second successive win in the race for **Yeats** and remarkably straightforward as he reinforced his clear superiority. Perfectly poised just behind the leaders, he hit the front 2f out and soon had the race won, even though the frustrating but hugely talented **Geordieland** emerged from the pack to give chase in second. The rest were well strung out – it was more than 15l back to the sixth – with European challengers filling three of the next four places, underlining the lack of depth in Britain's staying ranks.

14 Coronation Stakes (Fillies' Group 1), (1m) Ascot June 22 (Good to Soft)

1	**Indian Ink** 9-0	R Hughes
2	**Mi Emma** 9-0	E Pedroza
3	**Darjina** 9-0	C Soumillon

8-1, 10-3j, 7-2. 6l, hd. 13 ran. 1m 42.3 (a3.45)

Mr Raymond Tooth (R Hannon, Marlborough).

A deluge transformed the ground and turned the form book on its head as **Indian Ink** stormed clear in astonishing fashion and left a trio of out-standing Guineas winners trailing. As the rain worked against big drifter **Finsceal Beo**, Indian Ink was backed from a morning 25-1 to 8-1 and the money was spot on as she quickened up 2f out and careered away down the outside, quickly pulling 6l clear. Three high-quality fillies chased her home, with **Mi Emma** – a 9l winner of the German 1000 – holding off French star **Darjina** and **Arch Swing**. Finsceal Beo cruised into contention 2f out before fading into eighth.

15 Golden Jubilee Stakes (Group 1), (6f) Ascot June 23 (Good)

1	**Soldier's Tale** 9-4	J Murtagh
2	**Takeover Target** 9-4	J Ford
3	**Asset** 9-4	R Hughes

9-1, 8-1, 14-1. hd, ½l. 21 ran. 1m 14.5 (a1.39)

Budget Stable (J Noseda, Newmarket).

Takeover Target upheld the honour of Australian sprinting but was denied by the superior stamina of **Soldier's Tale**, who relished the soft ground and needed every yard to get up in the dying strides. Takeover Target looked to have blitzed the opposition with a stunning display of speed, but he tired close home and allowed Soldier's Tale to pinch the prize. **Asset** and **Red Clubs** were next, that quartet nicely clear of the rest as several failed to perform.

16 Audi Pretty Polly Stakes (Group 1), (1m2f) Curragh June 30 (Soft)

1	**Peeping Fawn** 8-11	K Fallon
2	**Speciosa** 9-9	M Fenton
3	**West Wind** 8-11	J P Murtagh

7-4f, 8-1, 7-2. 2l, 2l. 9 ran. 2m 10.6 (b1.13)

Michael Tabor (A P O'Brien, IRELAND).

A pair of Classic winners and a pair of Classic runners-up made this a worthy Group 1 prize and it was won in great style by **Peeping Fawn**, who maintained her rapid progress. Held up off the pace set by **Speciosa**, she made headway 2f out and quickened inside the final furlong to win well. Speciosa held off the Prix de Diane heroine **West Wind** and well-fancied maiden winner **Timarwa** to take second, but **Echelon** and **Dimenticata** were major disappointments.

17 Budweiser Irish Derby (Group 1), (1m4f) Curragh July 1 (Soft)

1	**Soldier Of Fortune** 9-0	J A Heffernan
2	**Alexander Of Hales** 9-0	M J Kinane
3	**Eagle Mountain** 9-0	K Fallon

5-1, 33-1, 6-4f. 9l, shd. 11 ran. 2m 36.0 (b2.33)

Mrs John Magnier (A P O'Brien, IRELAND).

Aidan O'Brien finally found the star to crown his

PEEPING FAWN: claiming the second leg of her Group 1 four-timer in the Irish Oaks

legion of middle-distance three-year-olds as **Soldier Of Fortune** ran out a devastating winner. Having come into his own since Epsom according to connections, the apparent Ballydoyle second-string cruised into contention in the home straight and produced a decisive turn of foot 2f out to roar clear. **Alexander Of Hales** and **Eagle Mountain** were next to give the trainer another 1-2-3, the lightly-raced second bouncing back from a poor run in the French Derby, while soft ground seemed to blunt the favourite. Royal Ascot winner **Boscobel** ran a sound race in fourth ahead of **Mores Wells** with the field well strung out in the soft ground.

18 **Coral-Eclipse Stakes (Group 1), (1m2f7yds) Sandown July 7 (Good to Soft)**
1 **Notnowcato** 9-7   R L Moore
2 **Authorized** 8-10   L Dettori
3 **George Washington** 9-7   J A Heffernan
7-1, 4-7f, 4-1. 1¹/2l, hd. 8 ran. 2m 5.9 (b8.28)
Anthony & David De Rothschild (Sir M Stoute, Newmarket).

A race which will be remembered as the Eclipse stolen by Ryan Moore, whose solo tactics in racing up the stands' rail helped **Notnowcato** to a surprise win. As the eagerly-anticipated battle between **Authorized** and **George Washington** took place on the far side, Moore had chosen a different route on Notnowcato and the tough colt ploughed a lone furrow to come out on top. However, whether Moore really made the difference is open to conjecture as a subsequent solo win on the far side suggested the ground may not have been quicker and Authorized was certainly below-par with Frankie Dettori getting drawn into a speed battle over what looked a slightly inadequate trip. He just overcame George Washington, who again ran well without showing his old sparkle, with 50-1 shot **Yellowstone** just over 1l down in fourth.

19 **UAE Racing Federation Falmouth Stakes (Fillies' Group 1), (1m) Newmarket July 11 (Good)**
1 **Simply Perfect** 8-10   J Murtagh
2 **Irridescence** 9-5   W C Marwing
3 **Arch Swing** 8-10   M J Kinane
6-1, 11-2, 10-3. 1l, nk. 7 ran. 1m 37.1 (b6.22)
Mr D Smith, Mr M Tabor & Mrs J Magnier (J Noseda, Newmarket).

Simply Perfect was one of few fillies to give her running as she made all to beat South African hope **Irridescence**. Johnny Murtagh dictated a muddling pace on the Guineas third and, after she had kicked clear 2f out, the hold-up horses could never get back to her. Irridescence made the long trip pay by holding off **Arch Swing** for second, but **Nannina**, a wide-margin winner at Royal Ascot, looked unsuited by the gallop and **Red Evie** ran no sort of race.

20 **Darley July Cup (Group 1), (6f) Newmarket July 13 (Good to Firm)**
1 **Sakhee's Secret** 8-13   S Drowne
2 **Dutch Art** 8-13   J Fortune
3 **Red Clubs** 9-5   M Hills
9-2, 5-1, 16-1. ¹/2l, 1¹/4l. 18 ran. 1m 10.8 (b5.13)
Miss B Swire (H Morrison, East Ilsley).

An absolutely vintage renewal with two potential sprinting champions among the three-year-old entries, and **Sakhee's Secret** and **Dutch Art** both justified the hype in an enthralling contest. The pair came into the race very differently, Sakhee's Secret having burst on to the scene with three wins by a total of 12l while Dutch Art was brought back in trip, and that was arguably decisive as he couldn't live with the early pace, allowing Sakhee's Secret to quicken into a race-winning lead before he roared through the pack in the final furlong. The rest were put firmly in their place, although **Red Clubs** ran another cracker in third ahead of **Marchand d'Or**, **Dandy Man** and **Asset**.

21 **Darley Irish Oaks (Group 1), (1m4f) Curragh July 15 (Heavy)**
1 **Peeping Fawn** 9-0   J Murtagh
2 **Light Shift** 9-0   T E Durcan
3 **All My Loving** 9-0   J A Heffernan
3-1, 9-4f, 5-1. 3¹/2l, 2l. 12 ran. 2m 39.1 (a0.79)
Michael Tabor (A P O'Brien, IRELAND).

An eagerly-awaited rematch between **Light Shift** and **Peeping Fawn**, who confirmed her colossal rate of improvement by landing a quickfire Group 1 double. Peeping Fawn defied a major drift in the market as she was always travelling well and came with a sweeping run down the outside to head Light Shift approaching the final furlong and win comfortably. Light Shift, on ground seen as too testing, ran a solid race in second, confirming Epsom form with **All My Loving**.

22 **King George VI And Queen Elizabeth Stakes (Group 1), (1m4f) Ascot July 28 (Good to Soft)**
1 **Dylan Thomas** 9-7   J Murtagh
2 **Youmzain** 9-7   R Hughes
3 **Maraahel** 9-7   R Hills
5-4f, 12-1, 6-1. 4l, 3¹/2l. 7 ran. 2m 31.1 (a4.12)
Mrs John Magnier & Mr M Tabor (A P O'Brien, IRELAND).

A weak renewal rescued by a brilliant effort from **Dylan Thomas**. Already a red-hot favourite with no three-year-olds in the field, Dylan Thomas's task was made even easier when second-favourite **Scorpion** was sacrificed as a pacemaker when there was no early gallop. Dylan Thomas was always going well and easily drew clear when asked to assert 2f out, galloping on strongly. **Youmzain** was an excellent second, with plenty in hand over **Maraahel**, Group 1-placed for the sixth time, and Godolphin's dual French Group 1 winner **Laverock**.

23 BGC Sussex Stakes (Group 1), (1m) Goodwood August 1 (Good)

1 **Ramonti** 9-7 — L Dettori
2 **Excellent Art** 9-0 — J Spencer
3 **Jeremy** 9-7 — R Moore
9-2, 15-8f, 7-2. hd, 1³/4l. 8 ran. 1m 37.6 (b2.46)
Godolphin (S bin Suroor, Newmarket).

Not much strength in depth, but Royal Ascot winners **Ramonti** and **Excellent Art** were both there and produced a thriller as the Godolphin runner prevailed by a head. Ramonti travelled smoothly to the front 2f out, when Excellent Art was still trapped on the inside, and though the second was finishing best Ramonti managed to hang on. **Jeremy** should have been better suited by this faster track but was well beaten in third, confirming the progress Ramonti had made since Ascot, while UAE Derby winner **Asiatic Boy** was fourth on his British debut.

24 Blue Square Nassau Stakes (Fillies' Group 1), (1m2f) Goodwood August 4 (Good to Firm)

1 **Peeping Fawn** 8-10 — J Murtagh
2 **Mandesha** 9-5 — C Soumillon
3 **Light Shift** 8-10 — T E Durcan
2-1f, 7-2, 3-1. 1¹/2l, 3¹/2l. 8 ran. 2m 4.5 (b7.67)
Mr M Tabor & Mrs John Magnier (A P O'Brien, IRELAND).

A sensational Group 1 hat-trick for **Peeping Fawn** as she beat France's star older filly **Mandesha** and old rival **Light Shift** in a red-hot renewal. Dropping back to 1m2f, and on extremely fast ground, Peeping Fawn again demonstrated her astonishing versatility and class as she sat close to a frenetic early pace before being sent on 3f out, with only Mandesha emerging from the pack to throw down any sort of challenge. Light Shift was reportedly jarred up by the firm ground but was an honourable third.

25 Juddmonte International Stakes (Group 1), (1m2f88yds) York August 21 (Good)

1 **Authorized** 8-11 — L Dettori
2 **Dylan Thomas** 9-5 — J Murtagh
3 **Notnowcato** 9-5 — R L Moore
6-4f, 2-1, 7-2. 1l, 3l. 7 ran. 2m 11.8 (a9.33)
Saleh Al Homaizi & Imad Al Sagar (P Chapple-Hyam, Newmarket).

Authorized bounced back to his best and confirmed himself the best middle-distance horse in the country with a brilliant win over **Dylan Thomas**. Ridden more prominently than at Sandown, Authorized was always going a shade better than his Ballydoyle rival and quickened impressively 2f out. Though Dylan Thomas threw down a strong challenge, Authorized was always holding him and won comfortably in the end. The pair proved themselves head and shoulders above **Notnowcato** and another Group 1 performer in **Duke Of Marmalade**, pulling 3l clear of that pair, while **Asiatic Boy** was well beaten in fifth.

26 Darley Yorkshire Oaks (Fillies' Group 1), (1m4f) York August 22 (Good)

1 **Peeping Fawn** 8-11 — J Murtagh
2 **Allegretto** 9-7 — R L Moore
3 **Trick Or Treat** 9-7 — T P Queally
4-9f, 9-1, 66-1. 4l, 5l. 7 ran. 2m 32.7 (a6.19)
Mr M Tabor & Mrs John Magnier (A P O'Brien, IRELAND).

Yet another victory for **Peeping Fawn**, a fourth at the top level in eight weeks, though this looked a formality on the strength of her Nassau win and never remotely deviated from the script. She quickened to lead 2f out and put lengths into her rivals, only Goodwood Cup winner **Allegretto** staying in touch, while Ribblesdale heroine **Silkwood** was bitterly disappointing.

27 Coolmore Nunthorpe Stakes (Group 1), (5f) York August 23 (Good)

1 **Kingsgate Native** 8-1 — J Quinn
2 **Desert Lord** 9-11 — D Holland
3 **Dandy Man** 9-11 — P Shanahan
12-1, 20-1, 9-4f. 1³/4l, hd. 16 ran. 58.1 (a0.30)
Mr John Mayne (J R Best, Maidstone).

An astonishing victory for **Kingsgate Native**, a two-year-old maiden on only his third start, as he exposed the dearth of quality in the 5f ranks with a clearcut win. Given his chance after finishing second at Royal Ascot and Glorious Goodwood, he justified connections' bold decision by racing prominently and bursting clear in spectacular fashion in the final furlong. **Desert Lord** just edged the battle for second with **Dandy Man**, while **Red Clubs** ran a blinder in fourth over an inadequate trip.

28 Betfred Sprint Cup (Group 1), (6f) Haydock September 8 (Good to Firm)

1 **Red Clubs** 9-3 — M Hills
2 **Marchand D'or** 9-3 — D Bonilla
3 **Balthazaar's Gift** 9-3 — Jimmy Fortune
9-1, 13-2, 11-1. ³/4l, ¹/2l. 14 ran. 1m 13.1 (b1.89)
R Arculli (B Hills, Lambourn).

A hugely controversial race as over-watering led to going much softer than the official description, leading to a disappointing effort from **Sakhee's Secret** and a deserved Group 1 opportunity for the tough and consistent **Red Clubs** – though it was particularly galling for connections of Dutch Art, pulled out when the ground looked set to be genuinely fast. In his 12th attempt at the top level Red Clubs came from well off the pace to lead inside the final furlong, confirming July Cup superiority over **Marchand d'Or**, but Sakhee's Secret failed to pick up on the ground, running on at one pace in fifth. **Asset** was again a shade disappointing in sixth.

29 Coolmore Fusaichi Pegasus Matron Stakes (Fillies' Group 1), (1m) Leopardstown September 8 (Good to Firm)

1 **Echelon** 9-3   R L Moore
2 **Red Evie** 9-3   J P Spencer
3 **Arch Swing** 8-12   M J Kinane
9-4f, 7-2, 11-4. 1¹/₂l, nk. 9 ran. 1m 39.5 (b6.84)
Cheveley Park Stud (Sir M Stoute, Newmarket).

The fourth all-aged fillies' Group 1 of the campaign and a first win for the older generation, though it was fairly conclusive as **Echelon** saw off **Red Evie** with **Arch Swing** fourth past the post before being promoted into third. Better than ever at the age of five, Echelon was always prominent and quickly asserted entering the straight, getting first run on the fast-finishing runner-up. Arch Swing had no excuses, though she would have been third anyway but for late interference with the demoted **Eastern Anthem**.

30 Tattersalls Millions Irish Champion Stakes (Group 1), (1m2f) Leopardstown September 8 (Good to Firm)

1 **Dylan Thomas** 9-7   K Fallon
2 **Duke Of Marmalade** 9-0   J A Heffernan
3 **Red Rock Canyon** 9-0   C O'Donoghue
8-15f, 15-2, 100-1. 1¹/₂l, 2l. 6 ran. 2m 2.3 (b11.99)
Mrs John Magnier (A P O'Brien, IRELAND).

Not quite good enough for Authorized at York, **Dylan Thomas** reinforced his credentials as a superstar in his own right with a hugely impressive win as the Aidan O'Brien string was utterly dominant again. Pacemaker **Red Rock Canyon** gave way only in the straight when **Duke Of Marmalade** and finally Dylan Thomas, having slowly wound up his effort, stormed past down the outside. However, **Red Rocks**, **Maraahel** and **Finsceal Beo** all looked well below-par.

31 Irish Field St. Leger (Group 1), (1m6f) Curragh September 15 (Good to Firm)

1 **Yeats** 9-11   K Fallon
2 **Scorpion** 9-11   J A Heffernan
3 **Mores Wells** 9-0   D P McDonogh
4-7f, 7-2, 8-1. ¹/₂l, 4¹/₂l. 9 ran. 3m 3.4 (a0.22)
Mrs John Magnier (A P O'Brien, !RELAND).

Dropping back in trip had seen **Yeats** beaten as favourite in the previous two years, but he put the record straight with a fine victory over stable-companion **Scorpion**. Yeats briefly looked in trouble when Scorpion went for home

KINGSGATE NATIVE: the first two-year-old winner of the Nunthorpe since Lyric Fantasy

4f out, but he slowly wore him down and got on top in the final 100 yards for a gutsy win. Group 3 winner **Mores Wells**, the only other horse with even a slim form chance, was a decent third.

32 Ladbrokes St Leger Stakes (Group 1), (1m6f132yds) Doncaster September 15 (Good to Firm)

1	**Lucarno** 9-0	J Fortune
2	**Mahler** 9-0	M J Kinane
3	**Honolulu** 9-0	J Murtagh

7-2, 13-2, 13-8f. 1l, ³/4l. 10 ran. 3m 1.9 (b26.44)

Mr George Strawbridge (J Gosden, Newmarket).

Only one horse, **Lucarno**, carried previous Classic form into the contest and that proved good enough as he eased to a comfortable win. Only 4l separated the first eight, underlining the fact that this wasn't vintage form, but Lucarno was worth more than the winning margin as he travelled supremely well and even seemed to take a pull 2f out before storming to the front in the final furlong, defying stamina doubts which had allowed the Ebor second **Honolulu** to go off favourite. He ran well in third, behind front-running stable-mate **Mahler** who put his staying power to good use, while middle-distance types **Regal Flush** and **Macarthur** split another promising stayer, **Veracity**, just behind.

33 Queen Elizabeth II Stakes (Group 1), (1m) Ascot September 29 (Good to Soft)

1	**Ramonti** 9-3	L Dettori
2	**Excellent Art** 8-13	J P Spencer
3	**Duke Of Marmalade** 8-13	M J Kinane

5-1, 15-8f, 13-2. ¹/2l, ¹/2l. 7 ran. 1m 42.5 (a3.64)

Godolphin (S bin Suroor, Newmarket).

Ramonti cemented his status as champion miler by completing a Group 1 hat-trick with another narrow win over **Excellent Art** in a virtual carbon copy of their Goodwood battle. Once again Frankie Dettori always had Ramonti beautifully positioned and struck for home first in the straight, kicking past **Duke Of Marmalade** with Excellent Art still well back in rear. The Irish raider finished well, but Ramonti was always just about holding on. Duke Of Marmalade ran another terrific race in third, just beating the progressive **Cesare**, but French filly **Darjina**, who had beaten Ramonti and George Washington in the Prix du Moulin at Longchamp, again failed to act on rain-softened ground at Ascot.

34 Kingdom Of Bahrain Sun Chariot Stakes (Fillies' Group 1), (1m) Newmarket October 6 (Good to Firm)

1	**Majestic Roi** 8-13	D Holland
2	**Nannina** 9-2	J Fortune
3	**Echelon** 9-2	R L Moore

16-1, 5-1, 11-8f. ³/4l, 1l. 9 ran. 1m 37.8 (b6.09)

Mr Jaber Abdullah (M Channon, West Ilsley).

A surprise win for **Majestic Roi**, who left a trio of Group 1 winners in her wake when conjuring a late run to nail **Nannina** in the final furlong. Majestic Roi had looked like needing further after struggling to follow up an early-season win over Indian Ink at Newbury, but she benefited from an extremely fast-run race and enjoyed a smooth run as Nannina wandered off a true line and interfered with the favourite **Echelon**. **Simply Perfect** also compromised her chances by chasing **Speciosa**'s suicidal early gallop, leaving several questions over the form.

35 Prix de l'Arc de Triomphe Lucien Barriere (Group 1), (1m4f) Longchamp October 7 (Good to Soft)

1	**Dylan Thomas** 9-5	K Fallon
2	**Youmzain** 9-5	R Hughes
3	**Sagara** 8-11	T Gillet

11-2, 66-1, 33-1. hd, 1¹/2l. 12 ran. 2m 28.5

Mrs John Magnier (A P O'Brien, IRELAND).

Not the most satisfactory of renewals but still a stunning sixth Group 1 win for **Dylan Thomas**, confirmed after a half-hour stewards' enquiry. Always going well towards the rear, Dylan Thomas made smooth headway to hit the front just over 1f out but then veered right, interfering badly with those on his inside, and presumably kept the race only because runner-up **Youmzain** escaped the carnage. Nonetheless, in sealing a King George-Arc double, Dylan Thomas confirmed the impression that, despite numerous top efforts over 10f, he is best suited by the longer trip. Youmzain ran a stormer, though Dylan Thomas's swerve helped him to get significantly closer than when beaten 4l in the King George, while the French challenge was also poor, with Manduro missing out and **Soldier Of Fortune** beaten their best three-year-olds in the Prix Niel. He was only fifth this time, behind **Sagara** and **Getaway**, while **Authorized**'s career ended with an inexplicable flop down in tenth.

36 Emirates Airline Champion Stakes (Group 1), (1m2f) Newmarket October 20 (Good to Soft)

1	**Literato** 8-12	C P Lemaire
2	**Eagle Mountain** 8-12	J Murtagh
3	**Doctor Dino** 9-3	O Peslier

7-2, 5-1, 12-1. shd, 3l. 12 ran. 2m 4.2 (b7.46)

Mr H Morin (Jean Claude Rouget, FRANCE).

This looked wide-open with all the big guns over the trip missing, and **Literato** and **Eagle Mountain**, both Derby runners-up, duly stepped up in a thrilling finish. Eagle Mountain kicked for home 2f out to make use of his greater stamina, but French raider Literato emerged to cut him down and just prevailed, the pair pulling 3l clear of another French hope in **Doctor Dino** and a further 3l clear of non-staying **Creachadoir**. **Notnowcato** was a disappointing sixth.

Group 1 Index

All horses placed or commented on in our Group 1 review section, with race numbers

Alexander Of Hales 17

Allegretto 26

All My Loving 8, 21

Aqaleem 9

Arch Swing 2, 6, 14, 19, 29

Asiatic Boy 23, 25

Asset 15, 20, 28

Astronomer Royal 10

Authorized 9, 18, 25, 35

Balthazaar's Gift 28

Boscobel 17

Cesare..33

Cockney Rebel 1, 4, 10

Creachadoir 4, 10

Dandy Man 20, 27

Darjina 14, 33

Desert Lord 27

Dimenticata 6, 16

Doctor Dino..36

Duke Of Marmalade .1, 4, 10, 25, 30, 33

Dutch Art 1, 10, 20

Dylan Thomas 5, 12, 22, 25, 30, 35

Eagle Mountain 1, 9, 17, 36

Eastern Anthem 29

Echelon 16, 29, 34

Excellent Art 10, 23, 33

Finsceal Beo 2, 6, 14, 29

Geordieland 13

George Washington 11, 18

Getaway..35

He's A Decoy 4, 10

Honolulu 32

Indian Ink 2, 14

Irridescence 19

Jeremy 11, 23

Kingsgate Native 27

Laverock...22

Le Miracle 13

Light Shift 8, 21, 24

Literato 36

Lucarno 9, 32

Macarthur...32

Mahler 32

Majestic Roi 34

Mandesha 24

Manduro 12

Maraahel 7, 22, 29

Marchand D'or 20, 28

Mi Emma 14

Mores Wells 17, 31

Nannina 19, 34

Notnowcato 5, 12, 18, 25, 36

Passage Of Time...................................8

Passager 3

Peeping Fawn 6, 8, 16, 21, 24, 26

Peeress 3

Ramonti 3, 11, 23, 33

Red Clubs 15, 20, 27, 28

Red Evie 3, 11, 19, 29

Red Rock Canyon 30

Red Rocks...................................12, 29

Regal Flush 32

Rising Cross...7

Sagara...35

Sakhee's Secret 20, 28

Salford Mill 9

Scorpion 7, 22, 31

Septimus 7

Silkwood 26

Simply Perfect 2, 8, 19, 34

Sir Percy...7, 12

Sixties Icon...7

Soldier Of Fortune 9, 17, 35

Soldier's Tale 15

Speciosa 16, 34

Strategic Prince...................................1

Takeover Target 15

Timarwa..16

Trick Or Treat 26

Turtle Bowl 11

US Ranger..1

Veracity...82

Vital Equine.....................................1, 4

West Wind 16

Yeats 13, 31

Yellowstone 18

Youmzain 5, 22, 35

Two-year-olds of 2007
by Dylan Hill

1 **Langleys Solicitors E.B.F. Marygate Stakes (Fillies' Listed), (5f) York May 18 (Good)**

1	**Janina** 8-12	R Hills
2	**Tia Mia** 8-12	T P Queally
3	**Cristal Clear** 8-12	D Allan

5-2f, 8-1, 11-2. 1l, hd. 10 ran. 58.7
(a0.89)
Mr Hamdan Al Maktoum (B Hills, Lambourn).

With several of these taking a hand at a good level later in the campaign, and even the sixth, **Loch Jipp**, winning another Listed prize at Beverley next time out, this looked top-drawer for the time of year and suggests **Janina** could be more than useful if her trainer can bring her back from a lay-off – she wasn't seen out again after Royal Ascot. Janina was always travelling well and steadily wore down the front-running **Tia Mia** in the final furlong.

2 **Isabel Morris EBF Stakes (Listed), (5f) Curragh May 26 (Good to Firm)**

1	**Pencil Hill** 9-1	P Shanahan
2	**You'resothrilling** 8-12	C O'Donoghue
3	**Tuscan Evening** 8-12	D M Grant

12-1, 16-1, 50-1. 1³/4l, 1l. 7 ran. 58.8
(b3.88)
Mrs C Collins (Tracey Collins).

The first of several expensive failures for Aidan O'Brien colts as 2-5 shot **Achilles Of Troy** was only fourth, though punters couldn't have expected him to run into two such high-class recruits as the hugely impressive winner, **Pencil Hill**, and **You'resothrilling**, while even the 50-1 third, **Tuscan Evening**, went on to twice secure places at Group level.

3 **Betfair Mobile National Stakes (Listed), (5f6yds) Sandown May 31 (Good to Soft)**

1	**Sweepstake** 8-9	R Hughes
2	**Lady Avenger** 8-9	K McEvoy
3	**Al Muheer** 9-0	T E Durcan

11-4, 6-1, 33-1. ¹/2l, 1¹/2l. 7 ran. 1m 2.7
(b1.63)
Mr B Bull (R Hannon, Marlborough).

A decent renewal won in determined style by **Sweepstake**, who didn't have the easiest of runs but squeezed through in the final 100 yards to edge out another filly, **Lady Avenger**, the pair comfortably trumping the colts. Favourite **New Jersey** was only fourth.

4 **Vodafone Woodcote Stakes (Listed), (6f) Epsom June 2 (Good to Soft)**

1	**Declaration of War** 9-0	R Havlin
2	**Bespoke Boy** 9-0	L Dettori
3	**Mount Pleasure** 9-3	Martin Dwyer

9-2, 6-1, 8-1. 1l, nk. 13 ran. 1m 10.5
(b1.85)
Mrs Violet Mercer (P Chapple-Hyam, Newmarket).

Unusually solid form for a race losing its lustre, with **Declaration Of War** proving the best winner for some time. Having raced in midfield, he stayed on strongly for a commanding win, with **Mount Pleasure**, third under a 3lb penalty, the other to take out of the race, though **Berbice** in fourth also made further progress.

5 **Swordlestown Stud Sprint Stakes (Group 3), (6f) Naas June 4 (Good to Soft)**

1	**You'resothrilling** 8-12	J A Heffernan
2	**Saoirse Abu** 8-12	K J Manning
3	**May Day Queen** 8-12	J P Murtagh

13-8f, 7-2, 10-1. 1l, 1¹/4l. 9 ran. 1m 10.4
(b2.27)
Michael Tabor (A P O'Brien, IRELAND).

The first juvenile Group race of the season brought together two of the best fillies of the campaign, with **You'resothrilling** comfortably getting the better of **Saoirse Abu**, who was already crying out for a stiffer test, to point the way to Royal Ascot. However, the rest were a decidedly mixed bunch.

6 **Coventry Stakes (Group 2), (6f) Ascot June 19 (Good to Firm)**

1	**Henrythenavigator** 9-1	M J Kinane
2	**Swiss Franc** 9-1	T E Durcan
3	**Luck Money** 9-1	T Quinn

11-4f, 25-1, 13-2. ³/4l, shd. 20 ran. 1m 12.5
(b0.66)

Mrs John Magnier (A P O'Brien, IRELAND).

Now established as the opening race of the meeting, this drew a suitably top-class field – 18 previous winners, nine unbeaten – and was a belting contest. **Henrythenavigator** deserved huge respect as the Ballydoyle No. 1 and won impressively, racing prominently and getting the better of a protracted duel with **Pencil Hill** with enough in hand to hold the late bursts of **Swiss Franc** and **Luck Money**. **Mount Pleasure**, off the track subsequently, reversed Epsom form with **Declaration Of War** just behind.

7 Windsor Castle Stakes (Listed), (5f) Ascot June 19 (Good to Firm)

1	**Drawnfromthepast** 9-3	Martin Dwyer
2	**Kingsgate Native** 9-3	G Baker
3	**Hatta Fort** 9-3	J H Bowman

9-1, 66-1, 3-1f. hd, ½l. 20 ran. 59.8 (b0.74)
Elaine & Martyn Booth (J A Osborne, Upper Lambourn).

A fiercely competitive sprint which threw up a host of high-class future winners, two at Group 1 level in **Kingsgate Native** and **Dark Angel**. That makes **Drawnfromthepast** hugely disappointing given his subsequent failures, but he showed great speed and remains one to watch.

8 Queen Mary Stakes (Fillies' Group 2), (5f) Ascot June 20 (Good to Firm)

1	**Elletelle** 8-12	J Murtagh
2	**Starlit Sands** 8-12	S Sanders
3	**The Loan Express** 8-12	W M Lordan

20-1, 4-1f, 66-1. ½l, shd. 21 ran. 1m 0.6 (a0.13)
Jesse Club Syndicate (G Lyons, IRELAND).

Less than 3l covered the first ten past the post, making it little surprise that the race failed to throw up a star. However, several showed useful form, including **Elletelle**, who produced a smart turn of foot to nail the trail-blazing **Starlit Sands**. **Sweepstake** hated the ground and suffered pulled muscles back in 19th.

9 Norfolk Stakes (Group 2), (5f) Ascot June 21 (Good to Firm)

1	**Winker Watson** 9-1	J Fortune
2	**Art Advisor** 9-1	S Sanders
3	**Spirit of Sharjah** 9-1	K McEvoy

2-1f, 14-1, 9-2. 1¼l, shd. 11 ran. 1m 0.8 (a0.32)
The Comic Strip Heroes & Mrs JD Trotter (P Chapple-Hyam, Newmarket).

An eagerly-awaited clash between two of the best early-season Listed winners in **Warsaw** and **Spirit Of Sharjah**, but punters deserted both in favour of Newbury maiden winner **Winker Watson** and were vindicated as he quickened up impressively to win well. Spirit Of Sharjah and fifth-placed **Strike The Deal** gave the form a solid look, though Warsaw ran a shocker.

10 Albany Stakes (Fillies' Group 2), (6f) Ascot June 22 (Good to Firm)

1	**Nijoom Dubai** 8-12	J P Spencer
2	**You'resothrilling** 8-12	M J Kinane
3	**Baffled** 8-12	L Dettori

50-1, 7-4f, 6-1. 1¼l, 2l. 20 ran. 1m 15.6 (a2.43)
Mr Jaber Abdullah (M Channon, West Ilsley).

A 50-1 shock but no fluke as **Nijoom Dubai**, twice beaten when well fancied, rewarded Mick Channon's persistence with an impressive turn of foot in the final 2f to run out a decisive winner from **You'resothrilling**, the pair coming through from the rear to pull clear of the remainder. **Janina** seemed to race too keenly with a breakneck early pace and was a disappointing sixth.

11 Chesham Stakes (Listed), (7f) Ascot June 23 (Good)

1	**Maze** 9-3	R Ffrench
2	**Pegasus Again** 9-3	L Dettori
3	**Feared In Flight** 9-3	M J Kinane

11-2, 14-1, 15-8f. nk, nk. 12 ran. 1m 29.3 (a3.20)
Pinnacle Dr Fong Partnership (B Smart, Thirsk).

A race traditionally pinpointing those with long-term middle-distance prospects, and this looked just about up to scratch. **Maze** and **Feared In Flight**, both of whom went on to show patches of useful form, were the key players, Maze battling to a brave win while Feared In Flight was arguably denied victory by an extremely troubled passage.

12 Saoire Stakes (Fillies Listed), (6f) Curragh June 29 (Soft)

1	**Listen** 8-12	K Fallon
2	**Tuscan Evening** 8-12	D M Grant
3	**Charlotte Bronte** 8-12	W M Lordan

7-2, 7-1, 11-1. 1¼l, ½l. 7 ran. 1m 15.5 (b0.60)
Derrick Smith (A P O'Brien, IRELAND).

A stiff introduction for **Listen**, pitched into Listed company for her debut, but she proved well up to the task, leading over 1f out and staying on well to beat the rock-solid **Tuscan Evening** and another promising debutant, **Charlotte Bronte**. **Saoirse Abu** was a disappointing fifth.

13 Clipper Logistics Empress Stakes (Fillies' Listed), (6f) Newmarket June 30 (Soft)

1	**Polar Circle** 9-1	J Fortune
2	**Thought Is Free** 8-12	J F Egan
3	**Highland Daughter** 8-12	P Robinson

9-2, 66-1, 6-4f. nk, 1¼l. 9 ran. 1m 16.3 (a0.43)
Sangster Family (P Chapple-Hyam, Newmarket).

Polar Circle, who had beaten Nijoom Dubai on her debut before flopping in the Queen Mary, put that run behind her with a gutsy effort, though the race really took little winning – in

24 subsequent runs, the first six went on to win just one race between them.

14 **Anheuser-Busch Adventure Parks Railway Stakes (Group 2), (6f) Curragh July 1 (Soft)**

1 **Lizard Island** 9-1   J A Heffernan
2 **South Dakota** 9-1   K Fallon
3 **Irish Jig** 9-1   J P Murtagh
10-3, 7-4, 13-8f. ³/4l, nk. 4 ran. 1m 18.7 (a2.61)
Michael Tabor (A P O'Brien, IRELAND).

Aidan O'Brien maintained his stranglehold on this event as **Lizard Island** made all the running without looking like a superstar. None of the quartet was really fancied, with the result that **Irish Jig**'s modest Listed win at Cork saw him sent off favourite, but Lizard Island and **South Dakota** at least proved better than that, the winner exploiting the soft lead he was allowed for the first half-mile while Coventry ninth South Dakota stayed on well despite looking ill at ease on the soft ground.

15 **Golden Fleece Stakes (Listed), (7f) Leopardstown July 4 (Good to Soft)**

1 **Bruges** 9-1   N G McCullagh
2 **Going Public** 9-1   P J Smullen
3 **Minneapolis** 9-1   K Fallon
12-1, 4-1, 6-5f. 2l, hd. 5 ran. 1m 34.6 (a1.68)

Mrs P Myerscough (D Myerscough).

A new Listed race which attracted only five runners, but all were winners, four unbeaten, and **Bruges** triumphed in fine style, slowly winding up his effort to win going away. He wasn't seen out again, but **Going Public** franked the form and his return will be interesting.

16 **Aaim Dragon Stakes (Listed), (5f6yds) Sandown July 6 (Soft)**

1 **Western Art** 9-2   J Fortune
2 **New Jersey** 9-2   N Callan
3 **Miss Versatile** 8-11   J F Egan
11-2, 7-2f, 16-1. 1l, ¹/2l. 8 ran. 1m 4.1 (b0.28)
Matthew Green & Ben Sangster (P Chapple-Hyam, Newmarket).

Not an easy race to assess, with **New Jersey** going backwards while **Western Art** and **Miss Versatile** didn't race again, but the progress of the fourth, **Cute Ass**, lends hope that the winner could still be fairly smart, as does the way in which he swept through from last to first with a striking turn of foot.

17 **Irish Thoroughbred Cherry Hinton Stakes (Fillies' Group 2), (6f) Newmarket July 11 (Good)**

1 **You'resothrilling** 8-12   M J Kinane
2 **Festoso** 8-12   P Robinson
3 **Elletelle** 9-1   J Murtagh

YOU'RESOTHRILLING: comes from an impossible position to win the Cherry Hinton

        Sponsored by Stan James

6-4f, 40-1, 9-2. 1l, nk. 14 ran. 1m 11.7
(b4.24)
Mr M Tabor & Mrs John Magnier (A P O'Brien,
IRELAND).

A terrific win from **You'resothrilling**, who underlined her quality again by winning comfortably
from a seemingly impossible position, having
been 4l down at halfway after racing on the
unfavoured stands' side. **Festoso** settled far
better than she had when burning out in the
Albany and showed her true form in second,
while **Elletelle** stepped up on her Queen Mary
win, staying on strongly to snatch third from
Loch Jipp despite her 3lb penalty.

18 TNT July Stakes (Group 2), (6f) Newmarket July 12 (Good to Firm)
1 **Winker Watson** 9-1   J Fortune
2 **River Proud** 8-12   T Quinn
3 **Swiss Franc** 8-12   T E Durcan
11-4f, 3-1, 5-1. shd, 1¹/2l. 13 ran. 1m 11.6
(b4.34)
The Comic Strip Heroes & Mrs JD Trotter (P
Chapple-Hyam, Newmarket).

One of the more authoritative short-head wins
of the season as **Winker Watson** overhauled
River Proud in the final furlong for a brilliant
victory. Already giving 3lb all round to a red-
hot field, with a bad draw to contend with,
Winker Watson also missed the break and was
still at the back of the field 2f out, but he then
found his stride and roared to an ultimately cosy
victory. River Proud had almost been backed
into favouritism to emphasise the esteem in
which he was held by Paul Cole, and the pair
drew away from **Swiss Franc** and **Dark Angel**.

19 Weatherbys Superlative Stakes
(Group 2), (7f) Newmarket July 13
(Good to Firm)
1 **Hatta Fort** 9-0   J H Bowman
2 **Declaration of War** 9-0   R Havlin
3 **Ellmau** 9-0   C Catlin
4-1, 4-1, 25-1. nk, 1³/4l. 10 ran. 1m 25.9
(b4.53)
Sheikh Ahmed Al Maktoum (M Channon,
West Ilsley).

Not the strongest contest by Group 2 standards,
with **Hatta Fort** and **Declaration Of War** vastly
superior. The latter had looked the likely
winner 1f out, but Hatta Fort relished being
stepped right up in distance and won well.
Favourite **Feared In Flight** was a poor sixth.

20 Dubai Duty Free Anglesey Stakes
(Group 3), (6f63yds) Curragh July 15
(Heavy)
1 **Myboycharlie** 9-1   W M Lordan
2 **Tuscan Evening** 8-12   D M Grant
3 **Chun Tosaigh** 9-1   K J Manning
2-1, 11-2, 16-1. 7l, ¹/2l. 5 ran. 1m 21.7
(a1.52)
Hammersboy-I R S com Syndicate (T Stack,
IRELAND).

A stunning performance from **Myboycharlie**
as he romped to victory in the soft ground to
persuade Coolmore to add him to their empire.
He was cantering all over his rivals from an early
stage and quickened away in the final furlong
to beat **Tuscan Evening**, with **South Dakota**
a below-par fourth.

21 Irish Stallion Farms Silver Flash
Stakes (Fillies' Listed), (7f) Leopardstown July 18 (Good to Soft)
1 **Triskel** 8-12   W M Lordan
2 **Mad About You** 8-12   P J Smullen
3 **Saoirse Abu** 8-12   D J Moran
14-1, 11-4f, 8-1. 2l, ¹/2l. 9 ran. 1m 36.8
(a3.88)
Mrs W L O'Toole (T Stack, IRELAND).

Triskel left all other form behind to run out a
surprise winner, but the form and the manner
in which it was achieved brook little argument.
Mad About You was one of two highly-rated
unbeaten fillies behind, split by a back-to-form
Saoirse Abu, while the sixth, **Porto Marmay**,
won a weak Listed prize at Tipperary soon after.

22 Beat Charity Star Stakes (Listed),
(7f16yds) Sandown July 26 (Good)
1 **Muthabara** 8-12   R Hills
2 **Lady Deauville** 8-12   S Whitworth
3 **Hobby** 8-12   A Kirby
11-4f, 33-1, 20-1. ³/4l, 2l. 12 ran. 1m 30.4
(b2.73)
Mr Hamdan Al Maktoum (J Dunlop, Arundel).

An impressive win for **Muthabara**, who won with
more in hand than the winning margin suggests
from **Lady Deauville**, who would go on to prove
a consistent yardstick, as had the fourth, **Cute**,
earlier in the year. Though not seen out again,
this placed her not far behind the top fillies.

23 Kleenex Winkfield Stakes (Listed), (7f)
Ascot July 28 (Good to Soft)
1 **Raven's Pass** 9-2   J Fortune
2 **Unnefer** 9-2   T E Durcan
3 **Mister Hardy** 9-2   P Hanagan
9-2, 11-2, 14-1. 5l, 1¹/4l. 10 ran. 1m 30.5
(a4.46)
Stonerside Stable LLC (J Gosden, Newmarket).

This contained nine previous winners but only
one who went on to win again, suggesting it
wasn't the hot contest it had appeared, but that
needn't detract from the brilliant **Raven's Pass**.
He made virtually all the running and was different class when set alight 1f out, sprinting clear
of **Unnefer** to point the way to bigger things.

24 Tyros Stakes (Group 3), (7f) Leopardstown July 28 (Good to Soft)
1 **New Approach** 9-1   K J Manning
2 **Brazilian Star** 9-1   C D Hayes
3 **Norman Invader** 9-1   D P McDonogh
evensf, 6-1, 14-1. 2l, 1¹/2l. 4 ran. 1m 30.7
(b2.24)

VISIT (centre): beats Reel Gift in the Princess Margaret at Ascot in July

Mrs J S Bolger (J Bolger, IRELAND).

Jim Bolger had won this race with Teofilo 12 months previously and unleashed his next superstar in **New Approach**. He made all the running and found an extra gear when strongly pressed 2f out, soon taking total command with a trio of useful sorts, including a future Group 3 winner, behind.

25 **Princess Margaret Independent Newspaper Stakes (Fillies Gp3), (6f) Ascot July 29 (Good to Soft)**

1	**Visit** 8-12	R L Moore
2	**Reel Gift** 8-12	R Hughes
3	**Sweepstake** 8-12	P Dobbs

10-3j, 12-1, 11-1. 1¹/2l, 2¹/2l. 13 ran. 1m 17.0 (a3.85)
Mr K Abdulla (Sir M Stoute, Newmarket).

A wide-open renewal, with three Listed winners, but **Visit** and **Reel Gift** trumped them all. Reel Gift was the first to make her move but Visit's late burst was more decisive, with the pair beating the likes of **Loch Jipp** and **Kylayne** by around 3l more than You'resothrilling had at Newmarket, making the runner-up's subsequent poor efforts even more puzzling. **Sweepstake** bounced back to form in third.

26 **Betfair Molecomb Stakes (Group 3), (5f) Goodwood July 31 (Good)**

1	**Fleeting Spirit** 8-11	J Murtagh
2	**Kingsgate Native** 9-0	G Baker
3	**Captain Gerrard** 9-0	R Ffrench

8-1, 4-1, 11-2. nk, 2¹/2l. 16 ran. 58.0 (b1.79)
The Searchers (J Noseda, Newmarket).

One of the races of the season as **Fleeting Spirit** and **Kingsgate Native** fought out a thrilling finish and put several high-class horses firmly in their place, with an extremely good time to boot – between them the pair had a first and two seconds in Group 1 races by the end of the season. **Captain Gerrard** just couldn't live with the first two in the final furlong, while **Starlit Sands** was beaten around 4l in fourth. **Spirit Of Sharjah** ruined her chance with a slow start but stayed on eye-catchingly into sixth.

27 **Veuve Clicquot Vintage Stakes (Group 2), (7f) Goodwood August 1 (Good)**

1	**Rio de La Plata** 9-0	L Dettori
2	**Lizard Island** 9-3	J Murtagh
3	**Donegal** 9-0	L Keniry

8-13f, 7-1, 16-1. 2l, 4l. 7 ran. 1m 26.1 (b3.34)
Godolphin (S bin Suroor, Newmarket).

A small but select field were truly sorted out by a frenetic early pace, and Godolphin hotpot **Rio de la Plata** stayed on best of all for an outstanding win, easing to the front 2f out and winning comfortably. **Lizard Island** also ran a blinder under a 3lb penalty as there were serious gaps put into some useful opposition, with **Scintillo** beaten 7l and **Ellmau** 12l to underline the winner's quality.

28 **Richmond Stakes (Group 2), (6f) Goodwood August 3 (Good to Firm)**

1	**Strike The Deal** 9-0	E Ahern
2	**Fat Boy** 9-0	R Hughes
3	**Exhibition** 9-0	J P Spencer

3 **One Great Cat** 9-0   J Murtagh
7-1, 8-1, 7-1, 3-1f. 1¹/4l, 1¹/2l, dht. 9 ran. 1m
11.6
  (a0.37)
The Searchers (J Noseda, Newmarket).

Three late withdrawals deprived the race of much of its quality, but the two principles, both disappointing at Royal Ascot, were much-improved for a change of tactics as **Strike The Deal** finally learned to settle before quickening away from the newly front-running **Fat Boy**. **Drawnfromthepast** was a disappointing fifth.

29 Ad Valorem Stakes (Listed), (7f100yds) Tipperary August 9 (Soft)
1 **Lisvale** 9-1   W M Lordan
2 **Achill Island** 9-1   K Fallon
3 **Capt Chaos** 9-1   J P Murtagh
7-2, 2-1f, 7-1. 1¹/4l, nk. 6 ran. 1m 39.1
  (b4.91)
Mrs Moira McNamara (D Wachman, IRELAND).

Another new Listed event and a decent winner in **Lisvale**, who eased smoothly to the front at the furlong pole and comfortably beat a smart prospect in **Achill Island**, while a line through the fourth, **Norman Invader**, placed the form on a par with New Approach's Tyros win.

30 skybet.com Sweet Solera Stakes (Fillies' Group 3), (7f) Newmarket August 11 (Firm)
1 **Albabilia** 8-12   R L Moore
2 **Don't Forget Faith** 8-12   P Robinson
3 **Kay Es Jay** 8-12   M Hills
7-2, 5-2, 16-1. ¹/2l, ³/4l. 7 ran. 1m 25.7
  (b4.77)
Mr Saif Ali (C Brittain, Newmarket).

Four exciting maiden winners made this an interesting renewal, but the proximity of **Kay Es Jay**, who finished far closer than she did in five attempts at Listed or Group level, was a clue that **Albabilia** wouldn't live up to her trainer's typically overblown hopes. That said, this was still a good effort and she has a good future.

31 Independent Waterfood Wedgwood Phoenix Stakes (Group 1), (6f) Curragh August 12 (Good to Soft)
1 **Saoirse Abu** 8-12   K J Manning
2 **Henrythenavigator** 9-1   K Fallon
3 **Elletelle** 8-12   J P Murtagh
25-1, 1-2f, 9-2. 1l, 1³/4l. 6 ran. 1m 18.9
  (a2.80)
Ennistown Stud (J Bolger, IRELAND).

A massive upset as the filly **Saoirse Abu** claimed the scalp of 1-2 favourite **Henrythenavigator**, coping with the testing conditions far better than her rivals and stepping up hugely on her previous efforts. Always prominent, she took up the running 2f out and stayed on strongly, never looking threatened even as Henrythenavigator, who was under pressure early and looked ill at ease on the ground, battled on bravely in

second. **Elletelle** was another who looked a shade below-par in third, though **The Loan Express** and **Warsaw** were also well beaten and Saoirse Abu's subsequent efforts showed this form had been seriously underrated.

32 Ballygallon Stud Debutante Stakes (Fillies Group 2), (7f) Curragh August 12 (Good to Soft)
1 **Campfire Glow** 8-12   P J Smullen
2 **Listen** 8-12   K Fallon
3 **Tuscan Evening** 8-12   D M Grant
12-1, 9-10f, 25-1. nk, 1¹/4l. 9 ran. 1m 33.2
  (a4.19)
Dr R Lambe (D Weld, IRELAND).

Conditions were just as bad as in the earlier Phoenix Stakes, but the fillies went through it well and the only excuse heard afterwards was that **Listen** had been given too much to do to reel in **Campfire Glow**. The runner-up would certainly have won in another stride or two and emerged as clearly the best horse in the race.

33 Usk Valley Stud Stakes (Listed), (7f) Newbury August 18 (Good)
1 **Sharp Nephew** 9-0   L Dettori
2 **Latin Lad** 9-0   R L Moore
3 **Scintillo** 9-0   J P Spencer
7-2j, 5-1, 13-2. hd, ¹/2l. 10 ran. 1m 26.5
  (b4.40)
Saleh Al Homeizi & Imad Al Sagar (B Meehan, Manton).

Little over 1l covered the first six, even in testing conditions, to suggest the race wasn't up to much, but **Sharp Nephew** got the job done well enough, slowly wearing down his rivals and just holding off the fast-finishing **Latin Lad**.

34 Darley Prix Mornu (Group 1), (6f) Deauville August 19 (Soft)
1 **Myboycharlie** 9-0   K Fallon
2 **Natagora** 8-10   C P Lemaire
3 **Alexandros** 9-0   S Pasquier
2l, ¹/2l. 6 ran. 1m 13.1
  (a4.60)
Mme S Magnier (T Stack, IRELAND).

Myboycharlie had already shown his liking for a soft surface and produced another terrific performance to beat a pair of top-class French juveniles. Myboycharlie was always going well and pulled out of **Natagora**'s slipstream to win easily from the subsequent Cheveley Park heroine and the improving **Alexandros**, with the trio 6l clear of the rest.

35 Tattersalls Millions Acomb Stakes (Group 3), (7f) York August 21 (Good)
1 **Fast Company** 9-0   R L Moore
2 **Lucifer Sam** 9-0   J Murtagh
3 **Without A Prayer** 9-0   S Sanders
11-4, 2-1f, 14-1. 3¹/2l, hd. 7 ran. 1m 26.7
  (a3.95)
Mr Earle I Mack (B Meehan, Manton).

Fast Company burst into the Classic picture

with a stunning win as he produced a devastating burst of speed to rout a field of highly promising maiden winners, all of whom held Group 1 entries. Indeed, **Lucifer Sam** had been a 2l second to New Approach before winning his maiden, a rival with whom the winner would soon cross swords.

36 Ireland Gimcrack Stakes (Group 2), (6f) York August 22 (Good)

1 **Sir Gerry** 8-12 — J P Spencer
2 **Great Barrier Reef** 8-12 — J Murtagh
3 **Swiss Franc** 8-12 — R L Moore
4-1, 8-1, 5-4f. ³/4l, 3l. 8 ran. 1m 14.2 (a4.11)
Mrs Gerry Galligan (J Fanshawe, Newmarket).

An impressive win for **Sir Gerry**, who was forced to come wide to deliver his challenge but cut down the field and came clear along with the impressive debutant **Great Barrier Reef**. However, the first two were both beaten favourites next time out, suggesting the form should be treated with caution, with **Swiss Franc** well below his best in third.

37 Julia Graves Roses Stakes (Listed), (5f) York August 22 (Good)

1 **Captain Gerrard** 9-0 — R L Moore
2 **Cake** 8-12 — P Dobbs
3 **Fred's Lad** 9-0 — P Mulrennan
6-4f, 8-1, 11-1. 2l, 1¹/2l. 10 ran. 1m 0.3 (a2.46)
Mr R C Bond (B Smart, Thirsk).

Captain Gerrard's Molecomb third entitled him to win this comfortably, and he did exactly that with an authoritative all-the-way win. Set alight 2f out, he came clear of the speedy filly **Cake**, who had won a softer Listed event at Newbury the previous week and put several of the same opponents just as easily in their place.

38 300000 St Leger Yearling Stakes, (6f) York August 23 (Good)

1 **Dark Angel** 8-11 — M Hills
2 **Gypsy Baby** 8-7 — R Hughes
3 **Cosmic Art** 8-11 — K McEvoy
3-1f, 11-1, 14-1. 1l, ¹/2l. 20 ran. 1m 12.4 (a2.32)
The Hon Mrs J M Corbett & Mr C Wrig (B Hills, Lambourn).

Only a Class 2 affair, but the monster prize attracted a huge field and this would prove a great pointer. **Dark Angel** brought the best form to the table and won in fine style, paving the way to bigger things, while several of those behind also went from strength to strength. **Gypsy Baby** and **Cosmic Art**, neither of whom raced again, could well be two to watch.

39 Jaguar Cars Lowther Stakes (Fillies' Group 2), (6f) York August 23 (Good)

1 **Nahoodh** 8-12 — J P Spencer
2 **Visit** 8-12 — R L Moore
3 **Fleeting Spirit** 8-12 — J Murtagh
15-2, 6-4f, 11-4. ¹/2l, ³/4l. 10 ran. 1m 12.6 (a2.57)
Mr Jaber Abdullah (M Channon, West Ilsley).

An absolutely belting renewal on paper as **Visit** and **Fleeting Spirit** had no answer to the late challenge of the highly-rated **Nahoodh**, though in retrospect it's impossible to know what to make of the affair with Visit subsequently found to have been doped. Somehow she still had a pair of subsequent Listed winners behind her in fourth and sixth, split by the high-class **Festoso**, though Fleeting Spirit raced too keenly and failed to stay and **You'resothrilling** was short of room at a key stage.

40 Galileo EBF Futurity Stakes (Group 2), (7f) Curragh August 25 (Soft)

1 **New Approach** 9-1 — K J Manning
2 **Curtain Call** 9-1 — F M Berry
3 **Henrythenavigator** 9-4 — K Fallon
8-11f, 40-1, 11-10. 3l, nk. 5 ran. 1m 29.0 (a0.01)
Mrs J S Bolger (J Bolger, IRELAND).

New Approach took another smooth step to the top, proving himself a top-class colt with a hugely authoritative win. Having set a searching pace, one which saw fellow front-runner **Warsaw** drop out 2f from home, he maintained the gallop and never allowed **Henrythenavigator** a chance to get back at him, even with conditions slightly better for the Ballydoyle hope. Surprise package **Curtain Call** pounced to take second close home.

41 totescoop6 Prestige Stakes (Fillies' Group 3), (7f) Goodwood August 25 (Good)

1 **Sense of Joy** 9-0 — R Hughes
2 **Celtic Slipper** 9-0 — S Sanders
3 **Eva's Request** 9-0 — D Holland
4-7f, 17-2, 40-1. ¹/2l, 2l. 7 ran. 1m 29.6 (a0.18)
Mr K Abdulla (J Gosden, Newmarket).

Sense Of Joy appeared to have little to beat, but she did it well and with the form reading better and better as the season progressed this could prove to be an excellent performance. Ridden with huge confidence, she was given plenty to do but found her stride in the final furlong and swept past the improving **Celtic Slipper** with ease.

42 Ripon Champion Two-Year-Old Trophy (Listed), (6f) Ripon August 27 (Good to Firm)

1 **Fat Boy** 9-2 — R Hughes
2 **Anosti** 8-11 — T E Durcan
3 **Cristal Clear** 8-11 — D Allan
4-7f, 22-1, 7-2. 3l, 2¹/2l. 7 ran. 1m 12.6 (b3.94)
Mr M Sines (R Hannon, Marlborough).

A dire renewal, with only seven going to post and the placed horses officially rated 82 and

80, though **Fat Boy** confirmed the promise of his Goodwood second as he made all to rout the opposition.

43 Weatherbys Bank Stonehenge Stakes (Listed), (1m) Salisbury August 31 (Good to Firm)

1 **McCartney** 8-13   Greg Fairley
2 **Scintillo** 8-13   R Hughes
3 **Yahrab** 8-13   K McEvoy

13-8f, 4-1, 4-1. hd, 2l. 7 ran. 1m 44.2 (b4.92)
Sheikh Mohammed (M Johnston, Middleham).

The first 1m Listed race of the season for juveniles went to a smart middle-distance prospect in **McCartney**, who knuckled down well to hold off the challenge of **Scintillo**. The runner-up seemed to improve for the step up in trip and the pair pulled away from the useful **Yahrab**.

44 Iveco Solario Stakes (Group 3), (7f16yds) Sandown September 1 (Good to Firm)

1 **Raven's Pass** 9-0   J Fortune
2 **City Leader** 9-0   K Darley
3 **Gaspar Van Wittel** 9-0   Dane O'Neill

11-8f, 8-1, 12-1. 7l, shd. 9 ran. 1m 26.6 (b6.52)
Stonerside Stable LLC (J Gosden, Newmarket).

Another stunning victory for **Raven's Pass**, who barely had to come off the bridle to bolt clear of a decent field. This looked a far stiffer test than Ascot, with the Chesham first and second in opposition, but he was always travelling ominously well and stormed clear in the final furlong to destroy the two-year-old course record by 1.3sec, leaving the subsequent Royal Lodge winner **City Leader** trailing in his wake. **Maze** raced far too freely in front and faded into sixth, one place behind **Pegasus Again**.

45 Go And Go Round Tower Stakes (Group 3), (6f) Curragh September 2 (Good)

1 **Norman Invader** 9-1   C O'Donoghue
2 **Perfect Polly** 8-12   N G McCullagh
3 **Great Barrier Reef** 9-1   K Fallon

14-1, 25-1, 2-5f. hd, nk. 8 ran. 1m 12.1 (b3.97)
A Gannon (K Condon, IRELAND).

A major surprise as punters, not for the first time, were too keen to side with a Ballydoyle hotpot, allowing a couple of decent horses to go off at silly prices. **Norman Invader** had shown useful form on several occasions and battled on gamely to beat a high-class maiden winner in **Perfect Polly** and 2-5 favourite **Great Barrier Reef**, who may have found the race coming too soon after York.

46 Moyglare Stud Stakes (Fillies' Group 1), (7f) Curragh September 2 (Good)

1 **Saoirse Abu** 8-12   K J Manning
2 **Listen** 8-12   K Fallon
3 **Mad About You** 8-12   P J Smullen

13-2, 4-5f, 7-1. 1¹/2l, ¹/2l. 9 ran. 1m 25.0 (b3.99)
Ennistown Stud (J Bolger, IRELAND).

Saoirse Abu achieved a tremendous Group 1 double as she got the better of a strong field, punishing punters for refusing to give due credit for her Phoenix win. Repeating that gritty performance, she edged to the front just over 1f out and stayed on strongly to hold off **Listen**,

DARK ANGEL: earned a big payday for connections with this win at York

who was again given plenty to do, fairly comfortably. **Mad About You** enhanced her reputation in third, ahead of **Albabilia**.

47 E.B.F. Dick Poole Fillies' Stakes (Listed), (6f) Salisbury September 6 (Good to Firm)

1 **Fashion Rocks** 8-12 — J Fortune
2 **Vive Les Rouges** 8-12 — I Mongan
3 **Raymi Coya** 8-12 — T E Durcan
11-8f, 11-1, 16-1. nk, ¾l. 9 ran. 1m 15.0 (b3.78)
Mr Andrew Rosen (B Meehan, Manton).

Not a great race, with **Fashion Rocks** 11-8 on the strength of her Lowther sixth, and she prevailed in workmanlike style, while **Raymi Coya** also caught the eye with a fast-finishing third having had little luck in running.

48 totescoop6 Sirenia Stakes (Group 3), (6f) Kempton September 8 (Polytrack)

1 **Philario** 9-0 — D Sweeney
2 **Red Alert Day** 9-0 — B Doyle
3 **Lady Aquitaine** 8-11 — I Mongan
16-1, 13-2, 14-1. 1l, hd. 12 ran. 1m 12.3 (b1.21)
Mr Philip Richards (K R Burke, Leyburn).

Proof that the All-Weather can attract quality horses as the first three all went on to run with credit at a higher level, **Philario** leading the way with a convincing all-the-way win. **Reel Gift** drifted alarmingly and duly ran a shocker, setting the tone for the rest of her season.

49 Samsung 300000 St Leger 2-y-o Stakes, (6f110yds) Doncaster September 12 (Good to Firm)

1 **Dream Eater** 8-12 — F Norton
2 **Achilles Of Troy** 9-2 — J Murtagh
3 **Copywriter** 8-12 — J Fortune
15-2, 10-1, 16-1. 1¼l, hd. 22 ran. 1m 17.5 (b6.73)
Mr J C Smith (A Balding, Kingsclere).

Dream Eater had failed to win in six previous attempts, but it was worth the wait as he landed this rich payday. Battle-hardened, with a fourth in the Windsor Castle behind him, Dream Eater proved an ideal type for the 22-runner race as he burst clear entering the final furlong despite racing on the unfavoured side. **Achilles Of Troy** and **Copywriter** beat the rest well, and **Oasis Wind** emerged with credit on the wrong side.

50 Frenchgate For Fashion May Hill Stakes (Fills' Grp2) (Str), (1m) Doncaster September 13 (Good to Firm)

1 **Spacious** 8-12 — J P Spencer
2 **Kotsi** 8-12 — L Dettori
3 **Celtic Slipper** 8-12 — S Sanders
9-4f, 10-1, 16-1. ½l, hd. 12 ran. 1m 37.6 (b10.26)
Cheveley Park Stud (J Fanshawe, Newmarket).

Very little proven Pattern form for this Group 2 prize, but there were still several fillies of rich promise, headed by the winning 9-4 favourite **Spacious**, who travelled notably well before battling on gamely. **Celtic Slipper**'s third places the winner alongside Sense Of Joy, and both look equally exciting.

51 Parknasilla Hotel Goffs Fillies Million, (7f) Curragh September 14 (Good to Firm)

1 **Lush Lashes** 9-0 — K J Manning
2 **Rinterval** 9-0 — J Fortune
3 **Carribean Sunset** 9-0 — P Shanahan
10-1, 7-1, 25-1. 1½l, 1l. 22 ran. 1m 24.3 (b4.67)
Mrs J S Bolger (J Bolger, IRELAND).

Lush Lashes produced a remarkable debut performance as she raced to the front 2f out and strode away from Richard Hannon's maiden winner **Rinterval**, though with form picks **Campfire Glow** and **Albabilia** both flopping this looked an extremely soft prize.

52 Parknasilla Hotel Goffs (C & G) Million, (7f) Curragh September 14 (Good to Firm)

1 **Luck Money** 9-0 — T Quinn
2 **Hitchens** 9-0 — K Fallon
3 **Major Willy** 9-0 — J A Heffernan
9-2f, 9-1, 33-1. 2½l, 1¼l. 19 ran. 1m 23.3 (b5.67)
Mrs Stephanie Smith (P Cole, Whatcombe).

A clean sweep for the raiding party, led by the Coventry third **Luck Money**, who defied a three-month absence to blitz the opposition from the front, drawing clear in the final furlong with great authority. Again the opposition was modest, however, with **Lisvale** enduring a luckless run before staying on late into fourth.

53 Polypipe Flying Childers Stakes (Group 2), (5f) Doncaster September 14 (Good to Firm)

1 **Fleeting Spirit** 8-11 — L Dettori
2 **Spirit of Sharjah** 9-0 — R Hughes
3 **Cute Ass** 8-11 — T E Durcan
5-4f, 15-2, 28-1. 1¾l, ¾l. 8 ran. 58.5 (b6.99)
The Searchers (J Noseda, Newmarket).

A high-quality sprint championship missing only Kingsgate Native, and his Goodwood conqueror **Fleeting Spirit** confirmed her class with a terrific win, easing clear having chased the pace throughout. **Spirit Of Sharjah** bounced back to form by storming through the field into second, ahead of the highly progressive **Cute Ass** and **Captain Gerrard**. Irish raiders **The Loan Express** and **Warsaw** were well beaten, with **Dark Angel** disappointing.

54 Flame Of Tara EBF Stakes (Fillies Listed), (6f) Curragh September 15 (Good to Firm)

1 **Forthefirstime** 8-12 — F M Berry
2 **Longing To Dance** 8-12 — W M Lordan

FLEETING SPIRIT: ran away with the two-year-olds' 5f championship, the Flying Childers

3 **Bett's Spirit** 8-12   J A Heffernan
7-2j, 5-1, 14-1. nk, nk. 9 ran. 1m 11.6
(b4.49)
Byerley Racing (J Oxx, IRELAND).

Only two previous winners underlined the lack of depth, and with the third, **Bett's Spirit**, beaten a shade further in a modest Listed event at Newmarket later in the year, **Forthefirstime** probably achieved little in winning narrowly.

55 Urban-i Champagne Stakes (Group 2), (7f) Doncaster September 15 (Good to Firm)
1 **McCartney** 8-12   R L Moore
2 **Alexander Castle** 8-12   D O'Donohoe
3 **One Great Cat** 8-12   M J Kinane
8-1, 22-1, 25-1. 2$\frac{1}{2}$l, 1$\frac{1}{4}$l. 10 ran. 1m 25.0
(b7.78)
Sheikh Mohammed (M Johnston, Middleham).

This looked a red-hot field on paper, but with three of the most proven runners – **River Proud**, **Strike The Deal** and **Maze** – filling the last three places, **McCartney**'s runaway win may not quite rate as highly as it initially appeared. However, this was still a fine effort as he defied a drop back in trip to quicken clear in the closing stages, with several useful juveniles beaten fair and square behind him.

56 Rosaleen Kelly Blenheim Stakes (Listed), (6f) Curragh September 16 (Good to Firm)
1 **Rock Of Rochelle** 9-1   V R De Souza
2 **Domingues** 9-1   D P McDonogh

3 **Deal Breaker** 9-1   P J Smullen
15-2, 5-1, 12-1. shd, ³/4l. 8 ran. 1m 12.2
(b3.88)
Her Diamond Necklace Farms FZE (A Kinsella, IRELAND).

Little over 2l separated the first six and **Rock Of Rochelle**'s battling qualities just saw him home from **Domingues**, a well-beaten fifth behind Norman Invader on his previous run to confirm this was a modest contest.

57 Bank Of Scotland (Ire) National Stakes (Group 1), (7f) Curragh September 16 (Good to Firm)
1 **New Approach** 9-1   K J Manning
2 **Rio de La Plata** 9-1   L Dettori
3 **Myboycharlie** 9-1   K Fallon
9-4f, 5-2, 5-2. 1³/4l, 1³/4l. 9 ran. 1m 23.5
(b5.48)
Mrs J S Bolger (J Bolger, IRELAND).

An outstanding contest featuring three of the season's best juvenile colts and won in exceptional style by **New Approach**, who dictated affairs from the front and quickened again in the final furlong as **Rio de la Plata** threatened to reel him in. The runner-up also ran a stormer, comfortably beating **Myboycharlie**, who in turn ran a decent race on much quicker ground than previously encountered. The rest were well strung out behind, with **Lizard Island** and **Great Barrier Reef** next, from well-backed maiden winner **Famous Name**.

58 **James Barr Chartered Surveyors Harry Roseberry Stakes (Lstd), (5f) Ayr September 21 (Soft)**

1 **Captain Gerrard** 9-6   T Eaves
2 **Look Busy** 8-12   P Mathers
3 **Carleton** 9-3   P Hanagan
5-6f, 12-1, 12-1. 2l, ³/4l. 9 ran. 1m 0.7 (a0.71)
Mr R C Bond (B Smart, Thirsk).

For the second time **Captain Gerrard** bounced back from a good effort in Group company to run away with a Listed prize, proving different class as he broke sharply and was never in danger. However, he didn't even have to be at his best to prevail, with **New Jersey**, his main rival on the book, disappointing in sixth.

59 **Laundry Cottage Stud Firth Of Clyde Stakes (Fillies Group 3), (6f) Ayr September 22 (Good to Soft)**

1 **Unilateral** 8-12   L Dettori
2 **Broken Applause** 8-12   P Hanagan
3 **Highland Daughter** 8-12   P Robinson
5-1, 7-1, 14-1. ³/4l, 1¹/2l. 11 ran. 1m 14.3 (a0.33)
Prime Equestrian (B Smart, Thirsk).

Unilateral proved her 100-1 fourth in the Lowther was no fluke as she landed a highly competitive contest in style, leading 1f out and winning comfortably. Five of the next seven had been placed at Listed level before to give the form a reasonably solid look, although **Broken Applause** achieved little else.

60 **Dubai Duty Free Mill Reef Stakes (Group 2), (6f8yds) Newbury September 22 (Good to Firm)**

1 **Dark Angel** 9-1   M Hills
2 **Strike The Deal** 9-4   J Murtagh
3 **Berbice** 9-1   R L Moore
9-4f, 5-2, 4-1. nk, ³/4l. 6 ran. 1m 11.7 (b5.34)
The Hon Mrs J M Corbett & Mr C Wrig (B Hills, Lambourn).

Not a great renewal but still an excellent all-the-way win for **Dark Angel**, who had found the best 5f speedsters too fast at Doncaster but won cosily enough over the extra furlong. **Strike The Deal** ran well in second, just missing out under his penalty, while **Berbice**, fourth to Dark Angel at York, was another to advertise the form in third as he just edged out **Philario**, who ran his best race on turf.

61 **Juddmonte Royal Lodge Stakes (Group 2), (1m) Ascot September 29 (Good to Soft)**

1 **City Leader** 8-12   K Darley
2 **Achill Island** 8-12   J Murtagh
3 **Scintillo** 8-12   R L Moore
9-1, 13-2, 7-1. ³/4l, hd. 11 ran. 1m 43.6 (a4.83)
Sangster Family (B Meehan, Manton).

CITY LEADER: won the Royal Lodge

An enormous compliment to Raven's Pass as **City Leader**, beaten 7l at Sandown, fought his way to victory in a decent renewal. Barely 2l separated the first eight, but they included several highly-rated colts, with **Achill Island** going on to finish second at the Breeders' Cup and **Scintillo** maintaining the progress that saw him land an Italian Group 1 next time. **Ridge Dance** also caught the eye with a fast-finishing fourth.

62 **Meon Valley Stud Fillies' Mile (Group 1), (1m) Ascot September 29 (Good to Soft)**

1 **Listen** 8-12   J Murtagh
2 **Proviso** 8-12   S Pasquier
3 **Saoirse Abu** 8-12   K J Manning
10-3, 11-10f, 5-1. 1l, 2¹/2l. 7 ran. 1m 43.3 (a4.49)
Mr D Smith, Mrs J Magnier, Mr M Tab (A P O'Brien, IRELAND).

Listen came into the race as ante-post favourite for the Oaks and the step up in trip duly helped her to reverse placings with her Moyglare conqueror **Saoirse Abu**. In fact the French hotpot **Proviso** was expected to provide the main opposition, but Listen struck first turning for home and was always holding Proviso, who in turn quickened away from the front-running Saoirse Abu to underline this as seriously smart form. It was a further 5l back to **Kotsi**, who led a risible home defence in fourth.

63 **C.L.Weld Park Stakes (Fillies Group 3), (7f) Curragh September 30 (Good to Soft)**

1 **Eva's Request** 8-12   M J Kinane
2 **Kyniska** 8-12   W J Supple

Sponsored by Stan James

3 **Indiana Gal** 8-12   F M Berry
14-1, 12-1, 11-1. 1l, 2l. 12 ran. 1m 30.3
(a1.26)
Liam Mulryan (M Channon, West Ilsley).

This soft Group 3 prize allowed **Eva's Request**
to secure a first win on turf at the fifth attempt,
with the fact that the disappointing **Lady Jane
Digby**'s May Hill fifth was enough to make her
2-1 favourite speaking volumes for the form.

64 Juddmonte Beresford Stakes (Group 2), (1m) Curragh September 30 (Good to Soft)

1 **Curtain Call** 9-1   F M Berry
2 **Domestic Fund** 9-1   P J Smullen
3 **Going Public** 9-1   M J Kinane
9-2, 9-1, 20-1. 4l, 1½l. 9 ran. 1m 46.7
(a2.19)
Mrs P K Cooper (Mrs J Harrington, IRELAND).

A brilliant win from **Curtain Call**, who made
all to beat a good field in fine style, gradually
quickening the tempo from halfway and staying on well to slam highly-rated maiden winner
Domestic Fund. Each of the next six had won
or been placed at Group or Listed level, though
Lizard Island was below-par in sixth.

65 Somerville Tattersall Stakes (Group 3), (7f) Newmarket October 5 (Good)

1 **River Proud** 8-12   T Quinn
2 **Iguazu Falls** 8-12   L Dettori
3 **Yankadi** 8-12   R Hughes
11-4, 9-4f, 10-3. ¾l, nk. 8 ran. 1m 25.7
(b5.50)
Mrs Michael Spencer (P Cole, Whatcombe).

A slow early pace lessened some of the clues
this race tends to provide, but that couldn't stop
River Proud restoring his reputation with an
excellent win. Taking time to get on top of the
speedier **Iguazu Falls**, he ground out a battling win with another promising type, **Yankadi**,
staying on well in third.

66 skybet.com Cheveley Park Stakes (Fillies' Group 1), (6f) Newmarket October 5 (Good)

1 **Natagora** 8-12   C P Lemaire
2 **Fleeting Spirit** 8-12   L Dettori
3 **Festoso** 8-12   E Ahern
7-2, 7-2, 33-1. nk, 4l. 14 ran. 1m 11.6
(b3.51)
Mr Stefan Friborg (P Bary, FRANCE).

Another fillies' Group 1 to go abroad as
Natagora got the better of a thrilling battle with
Fleeting Spirit. Having made the running,
Natagora produced a devastating turn of foot
2f out and was always on top despite Fleeting
Spirit's valiant chase, the pair pulling well clear.
Festoso ran a stormer in third despite being
beaten around 3l further than she had been
by You'resothrilling and Nahoodh in previous
outings, leading home progressive pair **Pretty
Polly** and **Missit**, while **Elletelle** was far from

disgraced in sixth and **Visit** a poor eighth.

67 Shadwell Middle Park Stakes (Group 1), (6f) Newmarket October 5 (Good)

1 **Dark Angel** 8-12   M Hills
2 **Strike The Deal** 8-12   E Ahern
3 **Tajdeef** 8-12   R Hills
8-1, 9-1, 9-2. ½l, nk. 9 ran. 1m 12.1
(b2.98)
The Hon Mrs J M Corbett & Mr C Wrig (B Hills,
Lambourn).

The absence of Winker Watson and a lamen-
table performance from Sir Gerry left this looking
a weak renewal, with the Mill Reef one-two **Dark
Angel** and **Strike The Deal** holding sway again.
Dark Angel led 3f out and bravely held off the
challenges of Strike The Deal and **Tajdeef**, but
even assuming the trio behind all posted career-
best efforts as well it is still hard to see this as
true Group 1 form.

68 Finnforest Oh So Sharp Stakes (Fillies' Group 3), (7f) Newmarket October 6 (Good to Firm)

1 **Raymi Coya** 8-12   K McEvoy
2 **Step Softly** 8-12   J Fortune
3 **Annie Skates** 8-12   J F Egan
15-2, 9-1, 13-2. ½l, hd. 8 ran. 1m 27.5
(b3.70)
Mr C Pizarro (M Botti, Newmarket).

This didn't look strong by Group 3 standards,
though it was still an excellent win from **Raymi
Coya**, stepping up on her Salisbury third to
Fashion Rocks. She had to be switched to find
a run but picked up well to beat **Step Softly**.

69 totescoop6 Two-Year-Old Trophy (Listed), (6f) Redcar October 6 (Good)

1 **Dubai Dynamo** 9-2   Dean McKeown
2 **Vhujon** 9-0   T G McLaughlin
3 **Pelican Prince** 8-9   P Makin
40-1, 66-1, 50-1. ½l, ¾l. 23 ran. 1m 12.0
(b1.81)
Mrs Fitri Hay (J S Moore, Upper Lambourn).

A massive upset as **Dubai Dynamo** jumped
from winning a nursery off 75 to taking this competitive Listed prize, though with the first two
both beaten out of sight in three runs between
them subsequently the obvious conclusion is
that most of their rivals were well below-par.

70 Prix Marcel Boussac Royal Barriere de Deauville (Fills Grp1), (1m) Longchamp October 7 (Good to Soft)

1 **Zarkava** 8-11   C Soumillon
2 **Conference Call** 8-11   S Pasquier
3 **Mad About You** 8-11   P J Smullen
6-1, 9-2, 11-2. 2½l, 1½l. 10 ran. 1m 37.0
(a2.00)
S A Aga Khan (A De Royer Dupre, FRANCE).

Zarkava confirmed the superiority of France's
juvenile fillies with a spectacular victory, quickening brilliantly after she had been left with

plenty to do 2f out. **Mad About You** ran a fine race in third, while **Don't Forget Faith** was best of the British trio in fifth, with **Laureldean Gale**, bought by Godolphin after running Proviso to half a length at Deauville, a poor eighth.

71 Prix Jean-Luc Lagardere (Grand Criterium) (Group 1), (7f) Longchamp October 7 (Good to Soft)

1	**Rio de La Plata** 9-0	L Dettori
2	**Declaration of War** 9-0	R L Moore
3	**Shediak** 9-0	C Soumillon

8-13f, 16-1, 5-1. 2¹/2l, shd. 8 ran. 1m 21.5 (a2.50)
Godolphin (S bin Suroor, Newmarket).

An extremely British feel to this contest with only one French runner breaking the monopoly, and **Rio de la Plata** justified favouritism with a clearcut win. He was the only horse with serious Group 1 pretentions and was far too good for **Declaration Of War**, who reversed earlier form with **Hatta Fort**, the pair split by **Shediak**.

72 Irish Stallion Farms EBF Star Appeal Stakes (Listed), (7f) Dundalk October 12 (Standard)

1	**Great War Eagle** 9-1	J P Murtagh
2	**Going Public** 9-1	P J Smullen
3	**Billyford** 9-1	F M Berry

9-4f, 5-1, 6-1. hd, hd. 11 ran. 1m 26.1 (a4.24)
Michael Tabor (D Wachman, IRELAND).

A decent race which saw highly-tried trio **Minneapolis**, **Brazilian Star** and **Going Public** hoping to get off the mark at this level, but all again came up just short, the latter just pipped by the once-raced favourite Great War Eagle.

73 Willmott Dixon Cornwallis Stakes (Group 3), (5f) Ascot October 13 (Good to Soft)

1	**Captain Gerrard** 9-0	T Eaves
2	**Cute Ass** 8-11	T E Durcan
3	**Cake** 8-11	L Dettori

9-4f, 8-1, 14-1. 1¹/2l, shd. 12 ran. 1m 0.8 (a0.30)
Mr R C Bond (B Smart, Thirsk).

Captain Gerrard finally achieved a richly deserved first Group success as he set a blistering gallop and saw the race out well, reversing Doncaster form with **Cute Ass** with the benefit of an easier surface. **Cake** also ran a good race after being given too much to do, but **Spirit Of Sharjah** ran a shocker.

74 Deloitte Autumn Stakes (Group 3), (1m) Ascot October 13 (Good to Soft)

1	**Ibn Khaldun** 9-0	L Dettori
2	**Redolent** 9-0	R L Moore
3	**Yahrab** 9-0	K McEvoy

4-7f, 16-1, 5-1. 1l, 1¹/2l. 8 ran. 1m 44.2 (a5.43)
Godolphin (S bin Suroor, Newmarket).

A straightforward opportunity for **Ibn Khaldun** to bridge the gap from nursery to Pattern company in a modest contest. A stiffer test would follow, but the manner of victory caught the eye as he needed only to be shaken up to take command having been held up in rear.

KITTY MATCHAM (centre): comes good in the Rockfel Stakes at Newmarket

75 **Stowe Family Law Silver Jubilee Rockingham Stakes (Listed), (6f) York October 13 (Good to Soft)**

1 **Max One Two Three** 8-9   R Kingscote
2 **Maze** 9-3   R Ffrench
3 **Look Busy** 8-9   P Robinson
12-1, 14-1, 12-1. 2l, nk. 15 ran. 1m 13.1 (a3.03)
123 Racing Partnership (T Dascombe, Lambourn).

A big field and a cracking performance from **Max One Two Three**, who quickened up well but may have been slightly fortunate to beat the back-to-form **Maze**, who ducked sharply to his left in the final furlong when looking likely to concede weight all round.

76 **Darley Dewhurst Stakes (Group 1), (7f) Newmarket October 20 (Good to Soft)**

1 **New Approach** 9-1   K J Manning
2 **Fast Company** 9-1   T E Durcan
3 **Raven's Pass** 9-1   J Fortune
6-4f, 14-1, 3-1. 1/2l, 2 1/2l. 10 ran. 1m 25.3 (b5.92)
Mrs J S Bolger (J Bolger, IRELAND).

New Approach confirmed his status as champion juvenile with a gutsy win over **Fast Company** in a scintillating renewal which saw three unbeaten colts fill the places. Things didn't go according to plan for New Approach as he broke awkwardly and was pushed along behind the leaders before halfway, but he forced his way to the front 2f out and held on gamely to hold off Fast Company's late challenge. Fast Company ran a blinder in second and, for all the winner's troubles, the pair came clear of **Raven's Pass**, who hit the front early enough before being run out of things. There was a further gap to **Rio de la Plata**, who may have found the race coming too soon after Longchamp, though even then a line through the sixth, **Hatta Fort**, suggests he wasn't far behind that running despite being beaten by more than 5l. **Luck Money** was fifth, with **McCartney** disappointing in seventh, while **Dark Angel** looked a non-stayer in ninth.

77 **seriousquitters.co.uk Rockfel Stakes (Fillies' Group 2), (7f) Newmarket October 20 (Good to Soft)**

1 **Kitty Matcham** 8-12   J Murtagh
2 **Missit** 8-12   D Holland
3 **Royal Confidence** 8-12   M Hills
10-1, 4-1, 9-1. nk, 3/4l. 10 ran. 1m 27.0 (b4.20)
Mrs David Nagle & Mrs John Magnier (A P O'Brien, IRELAND).

Another kick in the teeth for the form of the British fillies as **Kitty Matcham**, the only Irish raider in a weak field, plundered the prize, winning a fine battle with the Middle Park fifth **Missit**. However, **Royal Confidence** and the fourth, **Rosa Grace**, had both been exposed behind Raymi Coya on their previous run.

78 **Lanwades & Staffordstown Studs Stakes (Fillies Listed), (1m) Curragh October 21 (Good to Soft)**

1 **Savethisdanceforme** 8-12 J A Heffernan
2 **Maryellen's Spirit** 8-12   P J Smullen
3 **Queen Jock** 8-12   P Shanahan
4-1, 3-1f, 20-1. 9l, nk. 11 ran. 1m 44.4 (b0.18)
Derrick Smith (A P O'Brien, IRELAND).

A breathtaking performance from **Savethisdanceforme**, who absolutely routed a useful field to put herself in Classic contention, storming clear in the final furlong to follow up her improved fourth in the Prix Marcel Boussac. Less than 2l separated the next five, so poor ground can't be held as exaggerating the distance, and they weren't mugs either, with **Maryellen's Spirit** looking a smart maiden winner and **Queen Jock** and **Indiana Gal** having shown form at Group level.

79 **totesport.com Silver Tankard Stakes, (1m4yds) Pontefract October 22 (Good)**

1 **Siberian Tiger** 9-2   T P O'Shea
2 **Latin Lad** 9-2   Dane O'Neill
3 **Alan Devonshire** 9-2   J Quinn
12-1, 9-4f, 9-1. 3/4l, 1 1/4l. 6 ran. 1m 46.8 (b2.28)
Ridgeway Downs Racing (Channon, West Ilsley).

A surprise result as **Siberian Tiger**, the outsider of six, swept through in the final furlong off a slow pace to turn over the favourite **Latin Lad**, who was finishing second at Listed level for a second time, though with other fancied runners disappointing the form doesn't look much.

80 **Coral Trophy Stakes (Listed), (6f) Doncaster October 27 (Good)**

1 **Floristry** 8-10   J P Spencer
2 **Fateh Field** 9-1   K McEvoy
3 **Nacho Libre** 9-1   M Hills
6-4f, 3-1, 25-1. 1 1/2l, 1 1/4l. 12 ran. 1m 12.4 (b6.31)
Gainsborough (Sir M Stoute, Newmarket).

A highly impressive victory for fast-improving filly **Floristry**, who was always cantering all over a decent field and blew her rivals away with a devastating burst of speed in the final furlong. Godolphin maiden winner **Fateh Field** was a good second, and with some reasonable yardsticks behind the winner looks very useful.

81 **Racing Post Trophy (Group 1) (Str), (1m) Doncaster October 27 (Good)**

1 **Ibn Khaldun** 9-0   K McEvoy
2 **City Leader** 9-0   K Darley
3 **Feared In Flight** 9-0   P Robinson
11-4f, 8-1, 66-1. 3l, shd. 12 ran. 1m 37.6 (b10.22)
Godolphin (S bin Suroor, Newmarket).

A bizarre race with 66-1 shots in third and fourth ahead of a string of well-fancied rivals, but whatever the merits of the form **Ibn Khaldun** ran out a stunning winner. Always going well, he eased to the front 1f out and powered clear with great authority, leaving behind the equally strong-travelling **City Leader**. **Feared In Flight** and **Art Master** belied their massive odds with fine efforts, beating a host of more proven runners and promising types. **Curtain Call** seemed to run a flat race in fifth, ahead of **Declaration Of War** and **River Proud**, while Aidan O'Brien's inexperienced pair **Frozen Fire** and **King Of Rome** both failed to justify single-figure odds.

82 Mountgrange Stud Stakes (Group 3), (7f) Newbury October 27 (Soft)

1	**Beacon Lodge** 8-12	A Kirby
2	**Stimulation** 8-12	S Drowne
3	**Iguazu Falls** 8-12	T E Durcan

14-1, 5-1, 4-1. hd, nk. 11 ran. 1m 29.3 (b1.66)
Mr & Mrs P Hargreaves (C G Cox, Hungerford).

Soft ground scuppered the chances of several runners, and **Beacon Lodge** and **Stimulation** handled it better than anyone to fight out the finish, with the runner-up looking the best horse in the race after a troubled passage. **Iguazu Falls** didn't look entirely comfortable in third, though, and favourite **Almajd** flopped in fifth.

83 Heatherwold Stud Stakes (Listed), (7f) Newbury October 27 (Soft)

1	**Lady Deauville** 8-12	E Ahern
2	**Missit** 8-12	D Holland
3	**Maramba** 8-12	R L Moore

7-1, 6-5f, 8-1. 1/2l, 1 1/2l. 10 ran. 1m 29.8 (b1.13)
P J Hughes Developments Ltd (P Blockley, Lambourn).

Lady Deauville had established herself as one of the best maidens in training with a string of good efforts at a high level and she finally broke her duck with a hard-fought win, **Missit** again just missing out with her Rockfel second possibly leaving its mark.

84 Killavullan Stakes (Group 3), (7f) Leopardstown October 29 (Good to Firm)

1	**Jupiter Pluvius** 9-1	J A Heffernan
2	**Famous Name** 9-1	P J Smullen
3	**Billyford** 9-1	F M Berry

6-4f, 4-1, 16-1. 3/4l, 1/2l. 14 ran. 1m 29.2 (b3.73)
Mrs John Magnier (A P O'Brien, IRELAND).

Jupiter Pluvius had looked a smart prospect when winning a hot maiden at the Curragh two weeks previously and he duly took a major step in the right direction when beating **Famous Name** in a highly competitive contest. **Billyford** and **Great War Eagle**, in fourth, had fought out the finish to another Listed prize at Dundalk in October, but the first two trumped that form, Jupiter Pluvius just doing enough to claim a narrow verdict. **Pencil Hill**, back from a four-month absence, was well below-par.

85 E.B.F. Bosra Sham Fillies' Stakes (Listed), (6f) Newmarket November 2 (Good)

1	**Spinning Lucy** 8-12	M Hills
2	**Dubai Princess** 8-12	J P Spencer
3	**Bett's Spirit** 8-12	R Hughes

10-1, 7-2, 9-1. 1l, 1/2l. 12 ran. 1m 12.6 (b2.50)
Mr Steve Jenkins (B Hills, Lambourn).

Confirmation of **Spinning Lucy**'s late-season improvement as she followed up a 5l maiden win – at the fifth time of asking – with another comfortable victory, taking command 1f out and running on strongly to beat decent yardsticks **Dubai Princess**, who had run with credit behind Natagora and Captain Gerrard on her previous two outings, and **Bett's Spirit**.

86 bet365.com E.B.F. Montrose Fillies' Stakes (Listed), (1m) Newmarket November 3 (Good)

1	**Classic Legend** 8-12	I Mongan
2	**Jazz Jam** 8-12	T Quinn
3	**Queen of Naples** 8-12	J Fortune

11-2, 12-1, 5-4f. shd, 1/2l. 10 ran. 1m 41.7 (b2.21)
Mrs Moira McNamara (B Meehan, Manton).

Less than 1l separated the first five, with several form lines confirming this as well below the best, but it was a courageous effort from **Classic Legend**, who made it two from two and marked herself out as a decent middle-distance prospect by keeping on bravely after she had hit the front 3f out.

87 Eyrefield Stakes (Listed), (1m1f) Leopardstown November 4 (Good to Firm)

1	**Alessandro Volta** 9-1	J A Heffernan
2	**The Fist Of God** 9-1	M J Kinane
3	**Dick Morris** 9-1	C D Hayes

6-4f, 5-2, 16-1. 2l, 1 1/4l. 7 ran. 1m 54.9 (b3.98)
Michael Tabor (A P O'Brien, IRELAND).

A very weak contest, with the third well exposed off just 85, but **Alessandro Volta** dominated his rivals to justify being backed into 6-4, reaping the benefits of a maiden third to show his true potential.

Two-year-olds index

All horses placed or commented on in our two-year-old review section, with race numbers

Achilles Of Troy 2, 49
Achill Island 29, 61
Alan Devonshire 79
Albabilia 30, 46, 51
Alessandro Volta 87
Alexander Castle 55
Alexandros 34
Almajd 82
Al Muheer 3
Annie Skates 68
Anosti 42
Art Advisor 9
Art Master 81
Baffled 10
Beacon Lodge 82
Berbice 4, 60
Bespoke Boy 4
Bett's Spirit 54, 85
Billyford 72, 84
Brazilian Star 24, 72
Broken Applause 59
Bruges 15
Cake 37, 73
Campfire Glow 32, 51
Captain Gerrard 26, 37, 53, 58, 73
Capt Chaos 29
Carleton 58
Carribean Sunset 51
Celtic Slipper 41, 50
Charlotte Bronte 12
Chun Tosaigh 20
City Leader 44, 61, 81
Classic Legend 86
Conference Call 70
Copywriter 49
Cosmic Art 38
Cristal Clear 1, 42
Curtain Call 40, 64, 81
Cute..22
Cute Ass 16, 53, 73
Dark Angel 7, 18, 38, 53, 60, 67, 76
Deal Breaker 56
Declaration of War 4, 6, 19, 71, 81
Dick Morris 87
Domestic Fund 64
Domingues 56

Donegal 27
Don't Forget Faith 30, 70
Drawnfromthepast 7, 28
Dream Eater 49
Dubai Dynamo 69
Dubai Princess 85
Elletelle 8, 17, 31, 66
Ellmau 19, 27
Eva's Request 41, 63
Exhibition 28
Famous Name 57, 84
Fashion Rocks 47
Fast Company 35, 76
Fat Boy 28, 42
Fateh Field 80
Feared In Flight 11, 19, 81
Festoso 17, 39, 66
Fleeting Spirit 26, 39, 53, 66
Floristry 80
Forthefirstime 54
Fred's Lad 37
Frozen Fire..81
Gaspar Van Wittel 44
Going Public 15, 64, 72
Great Barrier Reef 36, 45, 57
Great War Eagle 72, 84
Gypsy Baby 38
Hatta Fort 7, 19, 71, 76
Henrythenavigator 6, 31, 40
Highland Daughter 13, 59
Hitchens 52
Hobby 22
Ibn Khaldun 74, 81
Iguazu Falls 65, 82
Indiana Gal 63, 78
Irish Jig 14
Janina 1, 10
Jazz Jam 86
Jupiter Pluvius 84
Kay Es Jay 30
King Of Rome 81
Kingsgate Native 7, 26
Kitty Matcham 77
Kotsi 50, 62
Kylayne..25
Kyniska 63

Lady Aquitaine 48
Lady Avenger 3
Lady Deauville 22, 83
Lady Jane Digby.................................63
Latin Lad 33, 79
Laureldean Gale 70
Listen 12, 32, 46, 62
Lisvale 29, 52
Lizard Island 14, 27, 57, 64
Loch Jipp.............................1, 17, 25
Longing To Dance 54
Look Busy 58, 75
Lucifer Sam 35
Luck Money 6, 52, 76
Lush Lashes 51
Mad About You 21, 46, 70
Major Willy 52
Maramba 83
Maryellen's Spirit 78
Max One Two Three 75
May Day Queen 5
Maze 11, 44, 55, 75
McCartney 43, 55, 76
Minneapolis 15, 72
Missit 66, 77, 83
Miss Versatile 16
Mister Hardy 23
Mount Pleasure 4, 6
Muthabara 22
Myboycharlie 20, 34, 57
Nacho Libre 80
Nahoodh 39
Natagora 34, 66
New Approach 24, 40, 57, 76
New Jersey 3, 16, 58
Nijoom Dubai 10
Norman Invader 24, 29, 45
Oasis Wind..49
One Great Cat 28, 55
Pegasus Again 11, 44
Pelican Prince...................................69
Pencil Hill 2, 6, 84
Perfect Polly 45
Philario 48, 60
Polar Circle 13
Porto Marmay 21
Pretty Polly 66
Proviso 62
Queen Jock 78
Queen of Naples 86

Raven's Pass 23, 44, 76
Raymi Coya 47, 68
Red Alert Day 48
Redolent 74
Reel Gift 25, 48
Ridge Dance 61
Rinterval 51
Rio de la Plata 27, 57, 71, 76
River Proud 18, 55, 65, 81
Rock Of Rochelle 56
Rosa Grace 77
Royal Confidence 77
Saoirse Abu 5, 12, 21, 31, 46, 62
Savethisdanceforme 78
Scintillo 27, 33, 43, 61
Sense of Joy 41
Sharp Nephew 33
Shediak 71
Siberian Tiger 79
Sir Gerry 36
South Dakota 14, 20
Spacious 50
Spinning Lucy 85
Spirit of Sharjah 9, 26, 53, 73
Starlit Sands 8, 26
Step Softly 68
Stimulation 82
Strike The Deal 9, 28, 55, 60, 67
Sweepstake 3, 8, 25
Swiss Franc 6, 18, 36
Tajdeef 67
The Fist Of God 87
The Loan Express 8, 31, 53
Thought Is Free 13
Tia Mia 1
Triskel 21
Tuscan Evening 2, 12, 20, 32
Unilateral 59
Unnefer 23
Vhujon 69
Visit 25, 39, 66
Vive Les Rouges 47
Warsaw 9, 31, 40, 53
Western Art 16
Winker Watson 9, 18
Without A Prayer 35
Yahrab 43, 74
Yankadi 65
You'resothrilling 2, 5, 10, 17, 39
Zarkava 70

Trainer Statistics

McCARTNEY: storms up the stands' rail to land the Group 2 Champagne Stakes

Mark Johnston

Another terrific haul for the Middleham handler as he hit the target with 161 winners, but total prize money was significantly down as he suffered from a lack of top-class ammunition.

Only 29 Johnston inmates took their chance in a Group race, although from that total three winners wasn't a bad return.

A desperate July hurt Johnston last season – six out of 104 was his record in a dire month – and if he can keep his string firing all year round this time he could do even better.

By month

2007

	Overall			Two-year-olds			Three-year-olds			Older horses		
	W-R	%	£1	W-R	%	£1	W-R	%	£1	W-R	%	£1
January	8-24	33	-0.48	0-0		+0.00	7-18	39	+2.53	1-6	17	-3.00
February	7-28	25	-7.44	0-0		+0.00	7-23	30	-2.44	0-5		-5.00
March	12-35	34	+10.29	0-0		+0.00	10-28	36	-1.46	2-7	29	+11.75
April	19-76	25	+2.27	1-7	14	-3.75	14-54	26	-4.98	4-15	27	+11.00
May	18-113	16	-25.00	1-27	4	-22.00	15-63	24	+9.00	2-23	9	-12.00
June	16-120	13	-12.90	4-27	15	+7.23	8-65	12	-12.13	4-28	14	-8.00
July	6-104	6	-40.09	2-35	6	-26.09	4-60	7	-5.00	0-9		-9.00
August	28-143	20	+48.69	17-70	24	+51.26	11-63	17	+7.43	0-10		-10.00
September	21-145	14	-21.97	15-95	16	+1.15	5-41	12	-17.13	1-9	11	-6.00
October	14-132	11	-48.52	12-101	12	-30.02	2-25	8	-12.50	0-6		-6.00
November	7-46	15	-27.69	7-36	19	-17.69	0-7		-7.00	0-3		-3.00
December	5-32	16	+0.50	5-29	17	+3.50	0-1		-1.00	0-2		-2.00

2006

	Overall			Two-year-olds			Three-year-olds			Older horses		
	W-R	%	£1	W-R	%	£1	W-R	%	£1	W-R	%	£1
January	1-6	17	-3.13	0-0		+0.00	0-3		-3.00	1-3	33	-0.13
February	6-13	46	+11.31	0-0		+0.00	6-12	50	+12.31	0-1		-1.00
March	4-25	16	-9.25	0-0		+0.00	4-19	21	-3.25	0-6		-6.00
April	8-94	9	-57.58	1-12	8	-5.50	6-62	10	-35.83	1-20	5	-16.25
May	14-111	13	+10.82	3-24	13	-7.43	9-57	16	+37.00	2-30	7	-18.75
June	18-126	14	-27.46	6-29	21	-4.71	9-67	13	-19.00	3-30	10	-3.75
July	37-167	22	+4.25	20-54	37	+27.10	15-89	17	-6.35	2-24	8	-16.50
August	22-145	15	-32.52	10-59	17	-29.35	9-59	15	+0.50	3-27	11	-3.67
September	18-129	14	-13.31	10-67	15	+3.19	8-46	17	-0.50	0-16		-16.00
October	10-113	9	-30.00	7-75	9	-24.00	3-33	9	-1.00	0-5		-5.00
November	16-61	26	+58.16	13-41	32	+55.16	3-19	16	+4.00	0-1		-1.00
December	4-15	27	+0.86	3-9	33	+2.36	1-4	25	+0.50	0-2		-2.00

2005

	Overall			Two-year-olds			Three-year-olds			Older horses		
	W-R	%	£1	W-R	%	£1	W-R	%	£1	W-R	%	£1
January	1-7	14	-2.50	0-0		0.00	1-5	20	-0.50	0-2		-2.00
February	0-2		-2.00	0-0		0.00	0-2		-2.00	0-0		0.00
March	5-18	27	+7.50	0-0		0.00	3-13	23	-6.00	2-5	40	+13.50
April	13-98	13	-36.36	1-9	11	-5.25	11-72	15	-16.61	1-17	5	-14.50
May	14-123	11	-48.29	3-18	16	-3.50	10-83	12	-26.79	1-22	4	-18.00
June	20-162	12	-35.47	4-33	12	-24.39	13-100	13	-24.08	3-29	10	+13.00
July	26-138	18	-6.90	8-34	23	+10.06	16-79	20	-6.45	2-25	8	-10.50
August	21-115	18	+14.63	12-46	26	+17.50	8-57	14	-5.87	1-12	8	+3.00
September	23-117	19	+15.07	12-62	19	+3.77	7-46	15	-10.13	4-9	44	+21.42
October	13-72	18	+12.02	10-46	21	+24.67	3-21	14	-7.65	0-5		-5.00
November	4-24	16	+3.00	1-16	6	-13.00	2-6	33	+11.00	1-2	50	+5.00
December	1-7	14	+1.00	0-4		-4.00	0-0		0.00	1-3	33	+5.00

All runners

2007	Wins	Runs	%	2nd	3rd	4th	Win prize	Total prize	£1 Stake
2yo	64	427	15	60	51	37	£308,892.65	£431,521.58	-36.41
3yo	83	448	19	52	48	51	£779,755.16	£1,041,403.14	-44.67
4yo+	14	123	11	13	18	18	£100,143.65	£178,703.76	-41.25
TOTAL	161	998	16	125	117	106	£1,188,791.46	£1,651,628.48	-122.33

2006	Wins	Runs	%	2nd	3rd	4th	Win prize	Total prize	£1 Stake
2yo	73	370	20	51	48	44	384,213.80	601,809.09	+16.83
3yo	73	470	16	59	51	47	726,573.20	959,857.37	-14.62
4yo+	12	165	7	15	11	17	134,935.50	306,531.25	-90.04
TOTAL	158	1005	16	125	110	108	1,245,722.50	1,868,197.71	-87.83

2005	Wins	Runs	%	2nd	3rd	4th	Win prize	Total prize	£1 Stake
2yo	51	268	19	29	40	22	307,516.89	476,649.89	+5.86
3yo	74	484	15	56	59	51	593,887.26	995,476.08	-95.08
4yo+	16	131	12	14	15	12	216,969.00	392,548.07	+10.92
TOTAL	141	883	16	99	114	85	1,118,373.15	1,864,674.04	-78.30

By race type

2007

	Overall			Two-year-olds			Three-year-olds			Older horses		
	W-R		£1	W-R		£1	W-R		£1	W-R		£1
Handicap	74-510	15	-98.42	12-90	13	+0.41	51-315	16	-65.33	11-105	10	-33.50
Group 1,2,3	3-29	10	-6.00	1-7	14	+2.00	2-19	11	-5.00	0-3		-3.00
Maiden	65-389	17	-46.61	43-297	14	-44.03	22-92	24	-2.59	0-0		+0.00

2006

	Overall			Two-year-olds			Three-year-olds			Older horses		
	W-R		£1	W-R		£1	W-R		£1	W-R		£1
Handicap	68-518	13	-60.46	11-68	16	-13.79	47-315	15	+21.45	10-135	7	-68.13
Group 1,2,3	3-50	6	-36.50	1-18	6	-15.50	2-15	13	-4.00	0-17		-17.00
Maiden	68-349	19	+47.67	48-237	20	+47.87	20-110	18	+1.81	0-2		-2.00

2005

	Overall			Two-year-olds			Three-year-olds			Older horses		
	W-R	%	£1	W-R	%	£1	W-R	%	£1	W-R	%	£1
Handicap	63-464	13	-47.63	5-48	10	-8.75	46-312	14	-50.55	12-104	11	+11.67
Group 1,2,3	4-42	9	-19.09	1-9	11	-7.09	2-18	11	-8.00	1-15	6	-4.00
Maiden	56-314	17	-40.00	40-187	21	+25.07	16-125	12	-63.08	0-2		-2.00

By jockey

2007

	Overall			Two-year-olds			Three-year-olds			Older horses		
	W-R	%	£1	W-R	%	£1	W-R	%	£1	W-R	%	£1
G Fairley	59-304	19	+103.62	38-172	22	+90.15	18-107	17	+29.48	3-25	12	-16.00
J Fanning	44-212	21	-39.70	4-40	10	-26.11	37-141	26	-18.33	3-31	10	+4.75
K Darley	13-96	14	-50.61	2-22	9	-17.17	6-48	13	-27.19	5-26	19	-6.25
J-P G'bert	12-124	10	-53.40	5-61	8	-25.27	6-54	11	-28.13	1-9	11	+0.00
R Ffrench	11-76	14	+9.48	7-43	16	-3.52	3-24	13	+16.50	1-9	11	-3.50
R Hills	8-36	22	+3.64	2-12	17	-5.09	6-14	43	+18.73	0-10		-10.00
J Spencer	5-13	38	+5.36	2-9	22	-4.64	3-4	75	+10.00	0-0		+0.00
S Sanders	2-12	17	-8.93	0-6		-6.00	2-6	33	-2.93	0-0		+0.00
F Norton	1-1	100	+3.33	0-0		+0.00	1-1	100	+3.33	0-0		+0.00
D Fentiman	1-2	50	+0.75	0-0		+0.00	0-1		-1.00	1-1	100	+1.75

By jockey ctd

2006

	Overall			Two-year-olds			Three-year-olds			Older horses		
	W-R	%	£1	W-R	%	£1	W-R	%	£1	W-R	%	£1
J Fanning	56-379	15	-67.22	29-146	20	-6.40	23-174	13	-30.33	4-59	7	-30.50
K Darley	37-241	15	-54.15	17-107	16	-21.86	20-111	18	-9.29	0-23		-23.00
R Ffrench	21-115	18	+26.16	7-33	21	-4.55	11-54	20	+37.88	3-28	11	-7.17
G Fairley	17-91	19	+17.03	7-20	35	+23.28	7-48	15	+0.00	3-23	13	-6.25
J Guill'bert	12-56	21	-4.18	9-35	26	+9.45	3-15	20	-7.63	0-6		-6.00
D O'D'hoe	2-2	100	+16.00	1-1	100	+12.00	1-1	100	+4.00	0-0		+0.00
J Egan	2-5	40	+11.00	0-0		+0.00	2-4	50	+12.00	0-1		-1.00
R Winston	2-8	5	-0.63	0-1		-1.00	1-4	25	+0.50	1-3	33	-0.13
M Dwyer	2-15	13	-8.10	2-6	33	+0.90	0-7		-7.00	0-2		-2.00
R Hills	2-21	10	-13.25	0-3		-3.00	2-16	13	-8.25	0-2		-2.00

2005

	Overall			Two-year-olds			Three-year-olds			Older horses		
	W-R	%	£1	W-R	%	£1	W-R	%	£1	W-R	%	£1
K Darley	51-316	16	-72.94	17-114	14	-36.02	29-161	18	-27.42	5-41	12	-9.50
J Fanning	42-292	14	-44.61	18-89	20	+1.08	19-161	11	-53.36	5-42	11	+7.67
Greg Fairley	14-56	25	+39.13	0-6		-6.00	11-39	28	+25.38	3-11	27	+19.75
R Ffrench	11-74	14	-21.12	4-17	23	+0.06	7-50	14	-14.18	0-7		-7.00
R Hills	4-28	14	-18.71	2-6	33	-2.01	2-18	11	-12.70	0-4		-4.00
J Guillambert	3-9	33	+5.35	2-5	40	+7.25	1-3	33	-0.90	0-1		-1.00
W Supple	3-18	16	+5.22	1-5	20	+6.00	1-11	9	-9.78	1-2	50	+9.00
D McKeown	2-7	28	+26.00	2-4	50	+29.00	0-2		-2.00	0-1		-1.00
J F Egan	2-11	18	+4.62	1-3	33	+10.00	1-7	14	-4.38	0-1		-1.00
R Havlin	1-1	100	+10.00	0-0		0.00	0-0		0.00	1-1	100	+10.00

By horse

	Wins-Runs	%	£1 level stakes	Win prize	Total Prize
Zaham	5-10	50	+9.40	129,218.40	160,511.65
Boscobel	4-6	67	+7.86	141.327.50	145.059.50
Hearthstead Maison	2-9	22	+27.00	56,088.00	76,151.60
McCartney	3-5	60	+9.13	74.089.40	74.859.80
Annemasse	4-14	29	+4.50	35,519.23	62,996.78
Lovelace	4-8	50	+11.50	60.540.70	61.888.90
Hinton Admiral	1-4	25	+0.50	42,585.00	51,459.00
Dubai's Touch	2-4	50	+17.50	31.796.80	31.796.80
Peppertree Lane	2-4	50	+3.75	23,889.20	31,658.20
Laa Rayb	3-8	38	+16.50	21.843.40	31.173.40
Colorado Rapid	2-5	40	-1.23	9,715.50	29,145.90
Players Please	3-12	25	-0.43	14.924.16	27.614.56
Eradicate	2-11	18	-5.17	16,871.88	26,939.58
Luberon	1-7	14	+10.00	24.928.00	24.928.00
Fongs Gazelle	4-9	44	+11.63	22,669.00	24,210.10
Regal Parade	3-11	27	+0.50	20.883.00	22.704.80
Record Breaker	3-7	43	+1.88	19,387.35	20,030.85
Campanologist	2-4	50	+8.25	17.487.90	19.727.90
Serengeti	2-4	50	+0.82	14,573.25	19,240.50
Atlantic Coast	4-10	40	+17.71	15.522.80	18.703.25
Feisty Royale	2-8	25	+11.00	10,363.20	15,426.15
Ramatni	2-10	20	-1.50	8.096.25	14.069.55
Doctor Scott	2-13	15	-4.50	11,010.90	13,767.85
White Deer	1-9	11	-5.50	5.181.60	13.157.40
Zar Solitario	3-4	75	+3.08	12,307.81	13,146.05
Soapy Danger	0-2		-2.00	0.00	13.022.30
Voodoo Moon	1-10	10	+5.00	7,124.70	12,493.70
Black Charmer	1-6	17	+3.00	12.464.00	12.464.00
Gigs Magic	3-8	38	+3.25	9,113.70	11,152.50
Plane Painter	1-12	8	-7.50	2,914.65	11,020.03

By course

2007

HEARTHSTEAD MAISON: winning at Newmarket in July

	Overall			Two-year-olds			Three-year-olds			Older horses		
	W-R	%	£1	W-R	%	£1	W-R	%	£1	W-R	%	£1
Ascot	2-45	4	-32.50	0-11		-11.00	2-23	9	-10.50	0-11		-11.00
Ayr	2-24	8	-17.59	2-14	14	-7.59	0-5		-5.00	0-5		-5.00
Bath	6-15	40	+7.71	1-7	14	-2.00	4-6	67	+7.71	1-2	50	+2.00
Beverley	6-33	18	+8.38	3-12	25	+9.00	3-16	19	+4.38	0-5		-5.00
Brighton	1-7	14	+0.50	1-6	17	+1.50	0-1		-1.00	0-0		+0.00
Carlisle	0-8		-8.00	0-2		-2.00	0-5		-5.00	0-1		-1.00
Catterick	10-35	29	+11.55	4-17	24	+5.75	4-14	29	-1.20	2-4	50	+7.00
Chepstow	0-5		-5.00	0-4		-4.00	0-1		-1.00	0-0		+0.00
Chester	3-21	14	-7.63	0-5		-5.00	3-13	23	+0.38	0-3		-3.00
Doncaster	3-17	18	+15.00	3-13	23	+19.00	0-2		-2.00	0-2		-2.00
Epsom	1-5	20	-0.50	0-0		+0.00	1-3	33	+1.50	0-2		-2.00
Folkestone	0-6		-6.00	0-3		-3.00	0-3		-3.00	0-0		+0.00
Goodwood	6-31	19	+20.20	0-10		-10.00	6-19	32	+32.20	0-2		-2.00
Hamilton	13-48	27	+30.80	6-15	40	+22.30	5-26	19	+9.50	2-7	29	-1.00
Haydock	6-37	16	-9.25	3-19	16	-6.25	3-15	20	+0.00	0-3		-3.00
Kempton	11-48	23	+22.32	3-23	13	+8.50	7-18	39	+3.82	1-7	14	+10.00
Leicester	6-23	26	+9.95	3-15	20	+10.00	2-7	29	-1.55	1-1	100	+1.50
Lingfield	0-3		-3.00	0-1		-1.00	0-2		-2.00	0-0		+0.00
Lingfield (AW)	12-80	15	-33.07	3-34	9	-14.50	9-36	25	-8.57	0-10		-10.00
Musselburgh	6-30	20	-8.07	4-11	36	+2.68	2-16	13	-7.75	0-3		-3.00
Newbury	7-24	29	+9.24	3-12	25	+2.91	3-9	33	+3.83	1-3	33	+2.50
Newcastle	4-31	13	-18.75	4-17	24	-4.75	0-10		-10.00	0-4		-4.00
Newmarket	2-33	6	-18.00	0-8		-8.00	2-21	10	-6.00	0-4		-4.00
Newmarket (J)	1-25	4	+1.00	0-7		-7.00	1-17	6	+9.00	0-1		-1.00
Nottingham	1-27	4	-23.75	1-19	5	-15.75	0-5		-5.00	0-3		-3.00
Pontefract	5-31	16	-18.70	2-12	17	-7.52	3-16	19	-8.17	0-3		-3.00
Redcar	5-27	19	+23.00	3-16	19	+2.00	2-10	20	+22.00	0-1		-1.00
Ripon	4-29	14	-17.48	1-8	13	-2.50	2-15	13	-11.23	1-6	17	-3.75
Salisbury	1-1	100	+1.63	1-1	100	+1.63	0-0		+0.00	0-0		+0.00
Sandown	4-30	13	+9.00	2-11	18	+10.50	1-15	7	-6.50	1-4	25	+5.00
Southwell	1-2	50	+0.75	0-0		+0.00	1-1	100	+1.75	0-1		-1.00
Southwell (AW)	8-28	29	+1.03	1-8	13	-2.00	6-17	35	+2.28	1-3	33	+0.75
Thirsk	3-25	12	+0.00	1-13	8	+4.00	2-10	20	-2.00	0-2		-2.00
Warwick	0-16		-16.00	0-9		-9.00	0-7		-7.00	0-0		+0.00
Windsor	1-10	10	-1.00	1-2	50	+7.00	0-6		-6.00	0-2		-2.00
Wolves	17-92	18	-13.46	7-39	18	-0.30	7-41	17	-21.91	3-12	25	+8.75
Yarmouth	2-13	15	-6.63	0-9		-9.00	2-3	67	+3.38	0-1		-1.00
York	1-33	3	-30.00	1-14	7	-11.00	0-14		-14.00	0-5		-5.00

Sponsored by Stan James

Richard Hannon

A better season for Hannon, who managed 145 winners after a relatively slow 2006 by his extremely high standards, and also topped the £2 million mark in total prize money again.

Despite Indian Ink's Group 1 win in the Coronation Stakes, it was a poor year for Hannon at the top level – only three per cent of his runners in Group races were successful.

However, he excelled in handicaps and maidens, with his older horses returning a profit to level stakes.

By month

2007

	Overall			Two-year-olds			Three-year-olds			Older horses		
	W-R	%	£1	W-R	%	£1	W-R	%	£1	W-R	%	£1
January	3-24	13	+6.25	0-0		+0.00	0-14		-14.00	3-10	30	+20.25
February	0-13		-13.00	0-0		+0.00	0-3		-3.00	0-10		-10.00
March	3-38	8	-1.00	0-0		+0.00	1-25	4	-15.00	2-13	15	+14.00
April	9-59	15	-20.79	3-12	25	-2.88	5-33	15	-7.67	1-14	7	-10.25
May	17-124	14	-36.38	7-43	16	-2.05	9-58	16	-19.33	1-23	4	-15.00
June	28-152	18	+24.33	10-60	17	-14.17	13-61	21	+40.50	5-31	16	-2.00
July	26-135	19	+19.23	11-67	16	+1.85	12-44	27	+17.38	3-24	13	+0.00
August	19-178	11	-80.51	10-108	9	-35.65	4-49	8	-38.08	5-21	24	-6.79
September	21-144	15	+3.00	13-85	15	-26.00	5-35	14	+6.50	3-24	13	+22.50
October	9-153	6	-94.92	5-94	5	-61.17	3-42	7	-24.75	1-17	6	-9.00
November	8-42	19	+10.58	3-23	13	-3.75	3-10	30	+2.33	2-9	22	+12.00
December	5-13	38	+4.97	4-8	50	+8.17	1-2	50	-0.20	0-3		-3.00

2006

	Overall			Two-year-olds			Three-year-olds			Older horses		
	W-R	%	£1	W-R	%	£1	W-R	%	£1	W-R	%	£1
January	3-23	13	+8.50	0-0		+0.00	1-9	11	-4.50	2-14	14	+13.00
February	1-10	10	-6.75	0-0		+0.00	1-5	20	-1.75	0-5		-5.00
March	5-29	17	+1.50	0-1		-1.00	3-15	20	+0.00	2-13	15	+2.50
April	13-85	15	-11.65	3-15	20	-2.90	6-44	14	8.00	4-26	15	-0.75
May	21-154	14	-43.82	9-39	23	-6.34	11-87	13	-15.48	1-28	4	-22.00
June	25-162	15	+9.89	11-59	19	-13.61	12-75	16	+42.25	2-28	7	-18.75
July	17-138	12	-24.60	10-68	15	+16.08	6-53	11	-30.68	1-17	6	-10.00
August	9-148	6	-66.83	5-87	6	-42.83	4-47	9	-10.00	0-14		-14.00
September	15-159	9	-67.78	13-99	13	-23.78	2-39	5	-23.00	0-21		-21.00
October	8-82	10	-28.04	8-52	15	+1.96	0-23		-23.00	0-7		-7.00
November	3-46	7	-31.50	2-27	7	-17.00	1-15	7	-10.50	0-4		-4.00
December	7-31	23	-0.33	5-18	28	+5.67	2-7	29	+0.00	0-6		-6.00

2005

	Overall			Two-year-olds			Three-year-olds			Older horses		
	W-R	%	£1	W-R	%	£1	W-R	%	£1	W-R	%	£1
January	1-10	10	-7.80	0-0		+0.00	1-7	14	-4.80	0-3		-3.00
February	0-2		-2.00	0-0		+0.00	0-1		-1.00	0-1		-1.00
March	3-33	9	-7.00	0-3		-3.00	2-17	11	+4.00	1-13	7	-8.00
April	13-98	13	-8.20	4-19	21	-0.20	5-49	10	-3.50	4-30	13	-4.50
May	19-163	11	-63.37	8-47	17	-17.20	6-70	8	-32.67	5-46	10	-13.50
June	32-193	16	+11.22	18-68	26	+8.89	9-81	11	-12.17	5-44	11	+14.50
July	18-222	8	-9.56	8-91	8	+35.53	6-77	7	-16.09	4-54	7	-29.00
August	23-186	12	-64.07	10-85	11	-45.22	7-61	11	-11.86	6-40	15	-7.00
September	19-164	11	-49.44	11-88	12	-17.97	5-49	10	-24.05	3-27	11	-7.43
October	6-119	5	-77.25	5-65	7	-31.25	1-38	2	-30.00	0-16		-16.00
November	7-40	17	+4.75	3-21	14	+1.00	0-7		-7.00	4-12	33	+10.75
December	4-29	13	-8.63	2-13	15	-2.37	0-8		-8.00	2-8	25	+1.75

All runners

2007	Wins	Runs	%	2nd	3rd	4th	Win prize	Total prize	£1 Stake
2yo	66	500	13	67	41	55	£336,308.52	£720,535.24	-135.64
3yo	56	376	15	49	42	46	£528,072.63	£795,252.86	-55.32
4yo+	26	199	13	24	20	23	£327,965.52	£568,187.05	+12.71
TOTAL	148	1075	14	140	103	124	£1,192,346.67	£2,083,975.15	-178.25

2006	Wins	Runs	%	2nd	3rd	4th	Win prize	Total prize	£1 Stake
2yo	66	465	14	72	64	50	638,077.35	913,497.85	-83.76
3yo	49	419	12	35	50	37	335,307.41	605,235.74	-84.66
4yo+	12	183	7	21	19	22	69,639.50	234,094.95	-93.00
TOTAL	127	1067	12	128	133	109	1,043,024.26	1,752,828.54	-261.41

2005	Wins	Runs	%	2nd	3rd	4th	Win prize	Total prize	£1 Stake
2yo	69	500	14	69	55	44	554,815.12	858,248.46	-71.79
3yo	42	465	9	39	52	45	242,991.62	482,115.56	-147.13
4yo+	34	294	12	34	32	25	412,199.30	688,832.99	-62.43
TOTAL	145	1259	12	142	139	114	1,210,006.04	2,029,197.01	-281.35

By race type

2007

	Overall			Two-year-olds			Three-year-olds			Older horses		
	W-R	%	£1	W-R	%	£1	W-R	%	£1	W-R	%	£1
Handicap	71-500	14	-31.31	10-105	10	-36.00	43-265	16	-27.02	18-130	14	+31.71
Group 1,2,3	2-63	3	-49.67	0-20		-20.00	2-20	10	-6.67	0-23		-23.00
Maiden	49-349	14	-83.66	44-295	15	-50.07	5-54	9	-33.58	0-0		+0.00

2006

	Overall			Two-year-olds			Three-year-olds			Older horses		
	W-R	%	£1	W-R	%	£1	W-R	%	£1	W-R	%	£1
Handicap	50-510	10	-129.25	8-88	9	-28.00	31-280	11	-42.75	11-142	8	-58.50
Group 1,2,3	3-45	7	-32.00	2-21	10	-10.50	1-15	7	-12.50	0-9		-9.00
Maiden	43-342	13	-79.09	37-274	14	-43.74	6-66	9	-33.35	0-2		-2.00

2005

	Overall			Two-year-olds			Three-year-olds			Older horses		
	W-R	%	£1	W-R	%	£1	W-R	%	£1	W-R	%	£1
Handicap	48-577	8	-148.46	9-88	10	-18.05	17-271	6	-87.17	22-218	10	-43.25
Group 1,2,3	7-64	10	-19.50	4-26	15	-1.00	0-22		-22.00	3-16	18	+3.50
Maiden	52-372	13	-139.21	39-283	13	-97.36	13-88	14	-40.85	0-1		-1.00

By jockey

2007

	Overall			Two-year-olds			Three-year-olds			Older horses		
	W-R	%	£1	W-R	%	£1	W-R	%	£1	W-R	%	£1
R Hughes	53-319	17	-59.75	27-136	20	-30.60	16-109	15	-10.02	10-74	14	-19.13
R Moore	33-170	19	+11.63	14-97	14	-44.90	12-44	27	+40.70	7-29	24	+15.83
P Dobbs	22-177	12	-51.43	10-93	11	-26.30	12-64	19	-5.13	0-20		-20.00
H Frost	12-57	21	+27.79	3-12	25	+7.67	5-23	22	+1.63	4-22	18	+18.50
E Ahern	5-16	31	+22.00	3-9	33	+19.00	2-7	29	+3.00	0-0		+0.00
J Fortune	4-40	10	-10.83	0-16		-16.00	3-15	20	-0.33	1-9	11	+5.50
F Norton	3-21	14	+21.50	2-11	18	+28.00	1-7	14	-3.50	0-3		-3.00
D O'Neill	3-72	4	-44.00	0-27		-27.00	1-23	4	-18.50	2-22	9	+1.50
D Kinsella	2-9	22	+7.00	1-7	14	+1.50	0-1		-1.00	1-1	100	+6.50
M Dwyer	2-11	18	-2.50	1-6	17	-1.00	1-5	20	-1.50	0-0		+0.00

By jockey ctd

2006

	Overall			Two-year-olds			Three-year-olds			Older horses		
	W-R	%	£1	W-R	%	£1	W-R	%	£1	W-R	%	£1
R Hughes	48-342	14	-62.64	26-137	19	-4.01	16-129	12	-22.88	6-76	8	-35.75
R Moore	40-304	13	-122.15	19-145	13	-76.87	18-128	14	-31.03	3-31	10	-14.25
D O'Neill	9-77	12	-15.93	3-28	11	-21.43	5-34	15	+14.50	1-15	7	-9.00
P Dobbs	8-103	8	-46.67	6-47	13	-2.67	2-43	5	-31.00	0-13		-13.00
R Smith	6-41	15	+47.23	4-30	13	+38.23	2-8	25	+12.00	0-3		-3.00
J Fortune	6-42	14	+1.25	4-19	21	+17.00	2-17	12	-9.75	0-6		-6.00
S Breux	5-68	7	-15.50	1-13	8	-7.00	2-29	7	-9.50	2-26	8	+1.00
G Baker	1-1	100	+2.00	1-1	100	+2.00	0-0		+0.00	0-0		+0.00
M Henry	1-1	100	+20.00	0-0		+0.00	1-1	100	+20.00	0-0		+0.00
T Queally	1-1	100	+2.00	1-1	100	+2.00	0-0		+0.00	0-0		+0.00

2005

	Overall			Two-year-olds			Three-year-olds			Older horses		
	W-R	%	£1	W-R	%	£1	W-R	%	£1	W-R	%	£1
R Hughes	59-351	16	-5.40	28-149	18	+1.55	16-123	13	-13.78	15-79	18	+6.83
R L Moore	35-345	10	-163.92	20-133	15	-52.42	7-115	6	-65.76	8-97	8	-45.75
Dane O'Neill	21-169	12	-47.63	9-66	13	-33.51	8-67	11	-7.62	4-36	11	-6.50
P Dobbs	10-123	8	-41.18	6-47	12	-5.51	1-45	2	-40.67	3-31	9	+5.00
S Sanders	2-5	40	+11.00	0-1		-1.00	1-2	50	+1.00	1-2	50	+11.00
J F Egan	2-11	18	-7.30	0-4		-4.00	2-6	33	-2.30	0-1		-1.00
J Quinn	2-14	14	+4.00	0-5		-5.00	2-5	40	+13.00	0-4		-4.00
J Fortune	2-27	7	-10.75	1-12	8	-8.75	1-9	11	+4.00	0-6		-6.00
N Callan	1-2	50	+1.75	0-1		-1.00	0-0		0.00	1-1	100	+2.75
R Winston	1-2	50	+0.63	1-1	100	+1.63	0-0		0.00	0-1		-1.00

By horse

	Wins-Runs	%	£1 level stakes	Win prize	Total Prize
Indian Ink	1-3	33%	+6.00	141,950.00	161,694.60
Ordnance Row	2-11	18%	+3.75	73,537.60	104,751.00
Asset	1-7	14%	-3.25	15,898.40	103,391.57
Gypsy Baby	1-6	17%	-3.90	2,914.65	87,012.20
Malt Or Mash	4-7	57%	+11.13	68,255.10	73,631.31
Galeota	3-8	38%	+9.00	47,721.00	61,818.10
Orchard Supreme	2-15	13%	+21.00	46,740.00	59,740.80
Fat Boy	3-7	43%	+6.82	29,988.00	45,794.50
Medley	2-7	29%	+12.50	33,973.50	45,582.30
Vitznau	2-9	22%	-1.50	28,159.50	45,321.16
Major Cadeaux	1-3	33%	+1.33	27,254.40	42,393.91
Song Of Passion	2-7	29%	+11.50	38,176.90	40,159.30
Reel Gift	1-6	17%	+0.50	3,886.20	38,338.96
Assertive	1-10	10%	-6.25	14,762.80	37,851.10
Cake	3-10	30%	+4.58	21,599.35	36,971.15
Berbice	1-6	17%	-4.60	5,019.67	36,173.44
Selinka	1-5	20%	+0.50	14,762.80	33,692.62
Mr Aviator	1-9	11%	+0.00	7,478.40	32,786.40
Talk Of Saafend	1-9	11%	-0.50	18,696.00	31,221.00
Scintillo	1-7	14%	-4.50	6,477.00	30,856.05
Danehillsundance	3-9	33%	+10.00	26,046.55	28,385.00
Ronaldsay	1-9	11%	-5.50	11,658.60	27,009.85
Eastern Gift	1-9	11%	-6.13	6,800.85	25,483.49
Solent	1-7	14%	+7.50	10,179.00	24,826.20
Latin Lad	1-3	33%	+31.00	10,363.20	22,522.00
Edge Closer	3-5	60%	+3.35	19,809.20	21,736.20
Sweepstake	2-4	50%	+14.75	16,417.75	20,725.75
Dazed And Amazed	1-12	8%	+1.00	14,762.80	19,893.60
Red Spell	1-5	20%	+1.50	9,971.20	19,764.40
Cracking	2-8	25%	+0.00	17,124.96	19,375.96

By course

2007

	Overall			Two-year-olds			Three-year-olds			Older horses		
	W-R	%	£1	W-R	%	£1	W-R	%	£1	W-R	%	£1
Ascot	5-75	7	-19.25	0-30		-30.00	3-26	12	-10.75	2-19	11	+21.50
Ayr	0-2		-2.00	0-2		-2.00	0-0		+0.00	0-0		+0.00
Bath	2-22	9	-13.00	1-14	7	-7.00	0-5		-5.00	1-3	33	-1.00
Brighton	4-16	25	+3.50	3-12	25	-2.50	1-3	33	+7.00	0-1		-1.00
Catterick	0-2		-2.00	0-2		-2.00	0-0		+0.00	0-0		+0.00
Chepstow	2-17	12	-8.92	0-9		-9.00	1-5	20	-1.25	1-3	33	+1.33
Chester	5-12	42	+11.88	3-5	60	+7.38	1-2	50	+2.00	1-5	20	+2.50
Doncaster	5-22	23	+23.00	0-14		-14.00	3-5	60	+25.00	2-3	67	+12.00
Epsom	2-12	17	+2.50	0-2		-2.00	1-4	25	-0.50	1-6	17	+5.00
Folkestone	4-15	27	+3.60	3-8	38	+7.10	1-7	14	-3.50	0-0		+0.00
Goodwood	6-96	6	-32.73	4-48	8	-0.73	2-30	7	-14.00	0-18		-18.00
Haydock	5-12	42	+8.38	2-4	50	+4.00	3-6	50	+6.38	0-2		-2.00
Kempton	18-118	15	-19.15	10-54	19	-0.67	8-44	18	+1.52	0-20		-20.00
Leicester	2-8	25	+7.00	1-3	33	+2.00	1-5	20	+5.00	0-0		+0.00
Lingfield	4-17	24	-2.00	2-10	20	-4.00	2-7	29	+2.00	0-0		+0.00
Lingfield (AW)	18-130	14	-5.24	6-40	15	-6.13	7-52	13	-12.87	5-38	13	+13.75
Newbury	7-79	9	-30.42	4-50	8	-28.25	2-20	10	+1.33	1-9	11	-3.50
Newmarket	6-54	11	-15.25	2-22	9	-10.25	1-20	5	-16.75	3-12	25	+11.75
Newmarket (J)	8-58	14	-11.97	5-35	14	-3.67	3-16	19	-1.30	0-7		-7.00
Nottingham	5-14	36	+6.58	2-6	33	+4.83	2-6	33	+1.75	1-2	50	+0.00
Pontefract	0-9		-9.00	0-3		-3.00	0-4		-4.00	0-2		-2.00
Ripon	1-1	100	+0.57	1-1	100	+0.57	0-0		+0.00	0-0		+0.00
Salisbury	8-67	12	-21.30	2-32	6	-14.80	4-26	15	-8.25	2-9	22	+1.75
Sandown	12-66	18	+3.33	8-26	31	+19.45	3-28	11	-16.13	1-12	8	+0.00
Warwick	2-12	17	-3.00	2-7	29	+2.00	0-1		-1.00	0-4		-4.00
Windsor	10-90	11	-46.27	2-42	5	-37.65	4-34	12	-10.25	4-14	29	+1.63
Wolves	7-31	23	+10.92	3-8	38	+5.67	3-17	18	+1.25	1-6	17	+4.00
Yarmouth	0-4		-4.00	0-4		-4.00	0-0		+0.00	0-0		+0.00
York	0-14		-14.00	0-7		-7.00	0-3		-3.00	0-4		-4.00

MALT OR MASH: sweeps through the field to land the November Handicap at Doncaster

Sir Michael Stoute

Stoute made the decision to employ Ryan Moore as his stable jockey on a permanent basis for 2008, and looking at the trainer's stats tells you why.

Moore won with 25 per cent of his rides for Stoute, returning a profit of £34 to £1 level stakes into the bargain.

That is excellent even given the fact that Stoute's overall strike-rate is massively higher than any other trainer near the top of our list – he sits third in the standings despite sending out far fewer runners than anyone in the top seven.

By month

2007

	Overall			Two-year-olds			Three-year-olds			Older horses		
	W-R	%	£1	W-R	%	£1	W-R	%	£1	W-R	%	£1
January	1-1	100	+0.36	0-0		+0.00	0-0		+0.00	1-1	100	+0.36
February	0-1		-1.00	0-0		+0.00	0-0		+0.00	0-1		-1.00
March	0-0		+0.00	0-0		+0.00	0-0		+0.00	0-0		+0.00
April	10-38	26	-1.46	0-0		+0.00	7-27	26	+0.54	3-11	27	-2.00
May	18-77	23	-17.08	0-1		-1.00	11-52	21	-17.74	7-24	29	+1.66
June	12-71	17	-21.32	0-6		-6.00	8-46	17	-8.65	4-19	21	-6.67
July	15-64	23	+23.93	3-13	23	-3.57	8-39	21	+11.63	4-12	33	+15.88
August	24-88	27	+33.61	6-29	21	+2.25	11-40	28	+2.61	7-19	37	+28.75
September	17-72	24	-16.27	7-23	30	-1.96	6-33	18	-8.38	4-16	25	-5.94
October	15-68	22	-9.37	12-32	38	+11.26	2-23	9	-10.00	1-13	8	-10.63
November	1-18	6	-16.33	0-16		-16.00	1-2	50	-0.33	0-0		+0.00
December	0-0		+0.00	0-0		+0.00	0-0		+0.00	0-0		+0.00

2006

	Overall			Two-year-olds			Three-year-olds			Older horses		
	W-R	%	£1	W-R	%	£1	W-R	%	£1	W-R	%	£1
January	0-0		0.00	0-0		0.00	0-0		0.00	0-0		0.00
February	0-0		0.00	0-0		0.00	0-0		0.00	0-0		0.00
March	0-1		-1.00	0-0		+0.00	0-0		+0.00	0-1		-1.00
April	12-46	26	-2.51	0-0		+0.00	9-38	24	-8.51	3-8	38	+6.00
May	29-81	36	-4.35	0-1		-1.00	21-62	34	-8.27	8-18	44	+4.91
June	11-74	15	-28.85	0-0		+0.00	9-58	16	-21.23	2-16	13	-7.63
July	15-54	28	+8.22	0-2		-2.00	15-43	35	+19.22	0-9		-9.00
August	12-91	13	-36.72	3-22	14	-15.47	8-55	15	-16.25	1-14	7	-5.00
September	12-69	17	+12.42	6-27	22	+3.92	5-37	14	+7.50	1-5	20	+1.00
October	14-65	22	-8.45	7-35	20	-5.85	6-24	25	-1.10	1-6	17	-1.50
November	1-5	20	-3.60	1-2	50	-0.60	0-3		-3.00	0-0		+0.00
December	1-1	100	+0.33	1-1	100	+0.33	0-0		+0.00	0-0		+0.00

2005

	Overall			Two-year-olds			Three-year-olds			Older horses		
	W-R	%	£1	W-R	%	£1	W-R	%	£1	W-R	%	£1
January	0-0		0.00	0-0		0.00	0-0		0.00	0-0		0.00
February	0-0		0.00	0-0		0.00	0-0		0.00	0-0		0.00
March	0-0		0.00	0-0		0.00	0-0		0.00	0-0		0.00
April	10-47	21	-5.25	0-0		0.00	8-36	22	-3.13	2-11	18	-2.12
May	16-54	29	+12.19	0-1		-1.00	12-41	29	+9.36	4-12	33	+3.83
June	19-62	30	+42.62	0-3		-3.00	14-44	31	+10.29	5-15	33	+35.33
July	11-64	17	-16.08	4-13	30	+16.00	4-35	11	-24.33	3-16	18	-7.75
August	9-58	15	-3.74	2-23	8	-4.56	4-25	1	-7.93	3-10	30	+8.75
September	12-76	15	-16.07	4-34	11	-23.78	5-31	16	+8.50	3-11	27	-0.79
October	17-71	23	+36.44	11-44	25	+20.69	4-18	22	-4.25	2-9	22	+20.00
November	1-9	11	+6.00	1-8	12	+7.00	0-1		-1.00	0-0		0.00
December	0-2		-2.00	0-2		-2.00	0-0		0.00	0-0		0.00

All runners

2007	Wins	Runs	%	2nd	3rd	4th	Win prize	Total prize	£1 Stake
2yo	28	120	23	21	8	10	£140,762.43	£200,684.90	-15.02
3yo	54	262	21	45	35	27	£483,372.52	£746,014.14	-30.32
4yo+	31	116	27	13	16	16	£1,067,255.17	£1,627,637.08	+20.42
TOTAL	113	498	23	79	59	53	£1,691,390.12	£2,574,336.12	-24.92

2006	Wins	Runs	%	2nd	3rd	4th	Win prize	Total prize	£1 Stake
2yo	18	90	20	11	10	9	74,666.55	110,861.25	-20.67
3yo	73	320	23	51	42	28	978,575.51	1,541,774.68	-31.63
4yo+	16	77	21	13	5	8	789,340.30	1,374,659.20	-12.21
TOTAL	107	487	22	75	57	45	1,842,582.36	3,027,295.13	-64.52

2005	Wins	Runs	%	2nd	3rd	4th	Win prize	Total prize	£1 Stake
2yo	22	128	17	25	14	12	114,164.30	215,827.76	+9.36
3yo	51	231	22	34	22	21	521,107.00	799,622.17	-12.48
4yo+	22	84	26	8	12	11	822,332.24	1,238,065.48	+57.25
TOTAL	95	443	21	67	48	44	1,457,603.54	2,253,515.41	+54.13

By race type

2007

	Overall			Two-year-olds			Three-year-olds			Older horses		
	W-R	%	£1	W-R	%	£1	W-R	%	£1	W-R	%	£1
Handicap	35-168	21	+11.75	4-13	31	+10.00	22-112	20	+10.13	9-43	21	-8.38
Group 1,2,3	19-79	24	+22.56	1-6	17	-1.67	3-21	14	-9.25	15-52	29	+33.48
Maiden	51-204	25	-27.03	21-93	23	-20.85	28-107	26	-4.94	2-4	50	-1.24

2006

	Overall			Two-year-olds			Three-year-olds			Older horses		
	W-R	%	£1	W-R	%	£1	W-R	%	£1	W-R	%	£1
Handicap	24-147	16	-12.44	1-5	20	+2.00	21-117	18	-3.44	2-25	8	-11.00
Group 1,2,3	19-86	22	-9.08	0-5		-5.00	9-41	22	-2.60	10-40	25	-1.48
Maiden	52-207	25	-31.54	17-76	22	-13.67	35-131	27	-17.87	0-0		+0.00

2005

	Overall			Two-year-olds			Three-year-olds			Older horses		
	W-R	%	£1	W-R	%	£1	W-R	%	£1	W-R	%	£1
Handicap	24-121	19	+26.29	2-9	22	+2.50	17-93	18	-3.59	5-19	26	+27.38
Group 1,2,3	13-85	15	+11.46	0-4		-4.00	2-29	6	-12.50	11-52	21	+27.96
Maiden	44-178	24	+15.71	18-102	17	+12.61	26-76	34	+3.11	0-0		0.00

By jockey

2007

	Overall			Two-year-olds			Three-year-olds			Older horses		
	W-R	%	£1	W-R	%	£1	W-R	%	£1	W-R	%	£1
R Moore	47-186	25	+33.93	12-64	19	-20.31	21-80	26	+20.05	14-42	33	+34.19
K McEvoy	17-78	22	-20.91	1-6	17	-1.00	7-48	15	-23.90	9-24	38	+3.99
R Hills	13-42	31	+5.50	4-8	50	+7.75	6-22	27	+0.50	3-12	25	-2.75
L Dettori	6-16	38	+3.79	0-2		-2.00	3-8	38	+3.17	3-6	50	+2.63
J Spencer	6-18	33	-4.02	3-6	50	+2.16	2-9	22	-4.54	1-3	33	-1.64
S Sanders	6-19	32	+16.45	1-2	50	-0.78	4-13	31	+8.23	1-4	25	+9.00
J-P G'bert	2-5	40	+2.38	0-0		+0.00	2-4	50	+3.38	0-1		-1.00
N Callan	2-9	22	-4.33	1-4	25	-1.00	1-4	25	-2.33	0-1		-1.00
K Darley	2-13	15	-5.09	2-8	25	-0.09	0-5		-5.00	0-0		+0.00
J Hamblett	2-14	14	-6.25	0-2		-2.00	2-11	18	-3.25	0-1		-1.00

By jockey ctd

2006

	Overall			Two-year-olds			Three-year-olds			Older horses		
	W-R	%	£1	W-R	%	£1	W-R	%	£1	W-R	%	£1
R Moore	24-107	22	-9.66	3-22	14	-15.24	20-76	26	+5.58	1-9	11	+0.00
R Winston	21-97	22	-19.73	2-17	12	-10.63	18-73	25	-4.21	1-7	14	-4.90
K Fallon	11-34	32	+4.56	0-0		+0.00	7-24	29	+0.15	4-10	40	+4.41
R Hills	10-47	21	-11.56	3-8	38	-3.34	4-23	17	-5.08	3-16	19	-3.14
K McEvoy	9-33	27	+18.73	6-12	50	+26.50	3-20	15	-6.77	0-1		-1.00
M J Kinane	7-35	20	-8.25	0-0		+0.00	3-22	14	-7.50	4-13	31	-0.75
M Dwyer	4-19	21	-7.43	0-3		-3.00	3-13	23	-5.93	1-3	33	+1.50
R Ffrench	3-6	50	+17.00	0-1		-1.00	3-5	60	+18.00	0-0		+0.00
J Hamblett	3-11	27	+4.50	0-1		-1.00	3-10	30	+5.50	0-0		+0.00
R Hughes	3-26	12	-9.33	1-4	25	+3.00	0-12		-12.00	2-10	20	-0.33

2005

	Overall			Two-year-olds			Three-year-olds			Older horses		
	W-R	%	£1	W-R	%	£1	W-R	%	£1	W-R	%	£1
K Fallon	13-39	33	+21.21	5-13	38	-0.07	2-9	22	-3.81	6-17	35	+25.08
R Winston	13-43	30	+20.21	1-3	33	+3.00	10-37	27	+11.71	2-3	66	+5.50
R L Moore	13-75	17	-6.43	3-24	12	+0.50	9-40	22	-4.93	1-11	9	-2.00
R Hills	10-36	27	+18.27	0-6		-6.00	5-18	27	+0.23	5-12	41	+24.04
J P Spencer	10-59	16	-3.34	4-28	14	+3.50	6-26	23	-1.84	0-5		-5.00
M J Kinane	9-54	16	+0.75	1-6	16	-0.50	3-29	10	-9.00	5-19	26	+10.26
R Hughes	7-33	21	-7.77	2-10	20	-3.06	4-21	19	-8.72	1-2	50	+4.00
J P Murtagh	5-26	19	-1.42	1-4	25	+8.00	3-13	23	-2.80	1-9	11	-6.63
J Fortune	3-10	30	+7.41	1-4	25	-2.09	2-4	50	+11.50	0-2		-2.00
L Dettori	2-5	40	+0.20	0-1		-1.00	2-4	50	+1.20	0-0		0.00

By horse

	Wins-Runs	%	£1 level stakes	Win prize	Total Prize
Notnowcato	1-5	20	+3.00	259,314.26	363,890.07
Maraahel	3-6	50	+3.25	143,653.40	251,353.40
Allegretto	2-6	33	+16.00	105,043.00	181,987.00
Jeremy	1-4	25	-1.00	48,263.00	143,626.60
Echelon	3-5	60	+7.48	118,897.32	142,318.82
Regal Flush	2-6	33	+14.00	101,549.50	133,715.63
Hi Calypso	4-5	80	+22.00	98,703.55	98,703.55
Papal Bull	2-5	40	+9.50	77,788.60	89,028.50
Ask	2-2	100	+5.25	70,975.00	70,975.00
Queen's Best	2-6	33	+6.25	43,152.80	63,649.30
Heaven Sent	1-6	17	-3.25	25,908.00	61,610.70
Galactic Star	3-6	50	+5.63	52,249.50	57,844.00
Greek Well	3-9	33	+5.25	32,385.00	51,426.60
Visit	1-4	25	+0.33	22,712.00	43,687.50
Adagio	1-3	33	-0.75	28,390.00	36,445.00
Promising Lead	2-4	50	+3.83	28,053.40	36,120.40
Al Shemali	0-4		-4.00	0.00	29,494.60
Red Gala	2-4	50	+1.50	25,260.30	28,272.10
Floristry	3-5	60	+7.72	27,282.65	28,149.35
Gulf Express	3-7	43	+0.75	21,159.79	26,806.59
Ea	1-5	20	-3.00	3,238.50	26,508.00
Al Tharib	2-6	33	-0.75	13,979.90	25,439.30
Distinction	1-5	20	-3.69	10,179.00	24,946.50
Mountain High	1-2	50	-0.39	22,712.00	24,057.00
Arabian Gulf	1-2	50	+6.00	5,181.60	19,169.60
Gyroscope	2-8	25	-1.17	11,334.75	17,495.75
Ogee	1-8	13	-5.13	12,954.00	17,470.70
Cabinet	1-5	20	+0.00	7,772.40	17,345.45
Lacework	2-4	50	+2.75	14,573.25	16,905.75
Ladies Best	0-7		-7.00	0.00	16,751.40

By course

2007

	Overall			Two-year-olds			Three-year-olds			Older horses		
	W-R	%	£1	W-R	%	£1	W-R	%	£1	W-R	%	£1
Ascot	8-41	20	-14.91	2-3	67	+4.33	0-18		-18.00	6-20	30	-1.24
Ayr	0-2		-2.00	0-0		+0.00	0-1		-1.00	0-1		-1.00
Bath	3-9	33	+5.10	2-3	67	+1.10	1-6	17	+4.00	0-0		+0.00
Beverley	1-8	13	-3.50	0-1		-1.00	1-5	20	-0.50	0-2		-2.00
Brighton	1-4	25	-1.13	0-1		-1.00	1-3	33	-0.13	0-0		+0.00
Catterick	1-1	100	+4.50	1-1	100	+4.50	0-0		+0.00	0-0		+0.00
Chepstow	1-2	50	+1.25	1-1	100	+2.25	0-1		-1.00	0-0		+0.00
Chester	3-11	27	-2.83	0-0		+0.00	1-8	13	-5.00	2-3	67	+2.17
Doncaster	5-19	26	-2.25	2-9	22	-2.75	1-5	20	+0.50	2-5	40	+0.00
Epsom	1-5	20	-2.25	0-0		+0.00	0-2		-2.00	1-3	33	-0.25
Folkestone	1-3	33	+0.75	0-0		+0.00	1-3	33	+0.75	0-0		+0.00
Goodwood	8-30	27	+17.12	0-4		-4.00	5-15	33	+12.24	3-11	27	+8.88
Hamilton	0-1		-1.00	0-0		+0.00	0-1		-1.00	0-0		+0.00
Haydock	1-7	14	-2.00	0-1		-1.00	1-5	20	+0.00	0-1		-1.00
Kempton	6-21	29	-2.17	3-8	38	+0.08	3-11	27	-0.25	0-2		-2.00
Leicester	1-14	7	-9.00	1-8	13	-3.00	0-5		-5.00	0-1		-1.00
Lingfield	0-9		-9.00	0-1		-1.00	0-6		-6.00	0-2		-2.00
Lingfield (AW)	5-18	28	+4.53	1-8	13	-1.50	3-7	43	+7.67	1-3	33	-1.64
Newbury	7-33	21	-5.54	0-6		-6.00	3-15	20	+0.71	4-12	33	-0.25
Newcastle	1-2	50	-0.60	0-0		+0.00	0-1		-1.00	1-1	100	+0.40
Newmarket	5-45	11	-26.90	1-9	11	-5.25	2-21	10	-10.75	2-15	13	-10.90
Newmarket (J)	6-31	19	-0.63	2-15	13	-7.00	3-11	27	-0.63	1-5	20	+7.00
Nottingham	6-14	43	+3.22	4-6	67	+6.72	2-8	25	-3.50	0-0		+0.00
Pontefract	2-8	25	-3.25	0-1		-1.00	2-7	29	-2.25	0-0		+0.00
Redcar	2-3	67	+5.25	1-1	100	+5.00	1-1	100	+1.25	0-1		-1.00
Ripon	1-4	25	+2.50	0-0		+0.00	1-4	25	+2.50	0-0		+0.00
Salisbury	5-14	36	+6.67	1-4	25	-1.90	4-10	40	+8.57	0-0		+0.00
Sandown	9-38	24	+14.00	1-7	14	-1.50	3-19	16	-1.75	5-12	42	+17.25
Southwell (AW)	1-2	50	+0.88	0-0		+0.00	1-2	50	+0.88	0-0		+0.00
Thirsk	3-7	43	-1.46	1-1	100	+0.91	2-5	40	-1.36	0-1		-1.00
Warwick	1-8	13	-4.25	1-2	50	+1.75	0-5		-5.00	0-1		-1.00
Windsor	10-32	31	+3.94	1-3	33	+1.33	8-26	31	-3.39	1-3	33	+6.00
Wolves	4-18	22	+4.03	1-8	13	-6.09	3-10	30	+10.13	0-0		+0.00
Yarmouth	1-11	9	-6.00	0-5		-5.00	1-6	17	-1.00	0-0		+0.00
York	3-23	13	+2.00	1-3	33	+6.00	0-9		-9.00	2-11	18	+5.00

Mick Channon

A season of contrasts for Channon, who was unable to follow up a stellar 2006 in terms of winners but enjoyed a tremendous year at Group level, not least in the final weeks of the turf season when Majestic Roi won the Sun Chariot Stakes at Newmarket and Youmzain so nearly added the Prix de l'Arc de Triomphe.

A rich pool of juvenile fillies suggest Channon has the ammunition to secure more top prizes, but he will hope to improve his overall strike-rate of ten per cent.

By month

2007

	Overall			Two-year-olds			Three-year-olds			Older horses		
	W-R	%	£1	W-R	%	£1	W-R	%	£1	W-R	%	£1
January	0-10		-10.00	0-0		+0.00	0-7		-7.00	0-3		-3.00
February	1-19	5	-14.00	0-0		+0.00	0-13		-13.00	1-6	17	-1.00
March	4-37	11	-13.50	0-0		+0.00	2-27	7	-18.00	2-10	20	+4.50
April	11-93	12	-22.15	3-22	14	-13.02	7-49	14	+6.88	1-22	5	-16.00
May	17-128	13	-25.21	8-40	20	-0.08	7-60	12	-8.63	2-28	7	-16.50
June	10-116	9	+13.72	5-47	11	+22.60	1-39	3	-37.39	4-30	13	+28.50
July	15-134	11	+6.75	7-55	13	-8.25	5-51	10	+18.50	3-28	11	-3.50
August	17-192	9	-51.52	13-101	13	+8.15	3-58	5	-32.67	1-33	3	-27.00
September	20-194	10	-55.51	9-107	8	-43.51	4-45	9	-14.00	7-42	17	+2.00
October	12-130	9	+3.25	6-68	9	-9.75	3-32	9	+16.00	3-30	10	-3.00
November	2-29	7	-7.00	2-15	13	+7.00	0-5		-5.00	0-9		-9.00
December	0-4		-4.00	0-2		-2.00	0-1		-1.00	0-1		-1.00

2006

	Overall			Two-year-olds			Three-year-olds			Older horses		
	W-R	%	£1	W-R	%	£1	W-R	%	£1	W-R	%	£1
January	0-11	-1	1.00	0-0		+0.00	0-10		-10.00	0-1		-1.00
February	1-1	100	+25.00	0-0		+0.00	0-0		+0.00	1-1	100	+25.00
March	4-30	13	-9.13	1-5	20	+2.50	3-12	25	+1.38	0-13		-13.00
April	12-84	14	-17.13	2-16	13	-7.75	8-46	17	-13.38	2-22	9	+4.00
May	10-120	8	-38.45	2-25	8	-7.00	5-68	7	-31.45	3-27	1	+0.00
June	22-144	15	+57.97	11-61	8	8.22	7-63	11	+15.25	4-20	20	+34.50
July	25-199	13	-34.36	12-84	14	-7.70	9-73	12	-7.42	4-42	10	19.25
August	22-177	12	-41.55	17-93	18	-12.55	5-52	10	+3.00	0-32		-32.00
September	16-158	10	-44.43	10-84	12	13.93	6-44	14	-0.50	0-30		-30.00
October	11-78	14	-3.26	7-44	16	-15.26	3-22	14	+13.00	1-12	8	-1.00
November	3-18	17	+11.50	2-9	22	+7.50	0-6		-6.00	1-3	33	+10.00
December	1-7	14	-2.50	1-4	25	+0.50	0-1		-1.00	0-2		-2.00

2005

	Overall			Two-year-olds			Three-year-olds			Older horses		
	W-R	%	£1	W-R	%	£1	W-R	%	£1	W-R	%	£1
January	1-9	11	-1.50	0-0		0.00	0-4		-4.00	1-5	20	+2.50
February	1-18	5	-15.38	0-0		0.00	1-9	11	-6.38	0-9		-9.00
March	6-37	16	+25.12	2-5	40	+3.13	3-24	12	+9.00	1-8	12	+13.00
April	14-107	13	-0.67	4-18	22	+8.38	9-63	14	-0.05	1-26	3	-9.00
May	18-139	12	-28.48	7-31	22	+4.90	10-72	13	-2.88	1-36	2	-30.50
June	15-156	9	-15.37	10-56	17	+28.63	3-69	4	-30.50	2-31	6	-13.50
July	18-162	11	-51.76	12-79	15	-19.59	2-47	4	-24.00	4-36	11	-8.17
August	12-148	8	-72.26	5-68	7	-38.84	5-46	10	-11.75	2-34	5	-21.67
September	9-136	6	-81.96	8-78	10	-40.96	1-34	2	-17.00	0-24		-24.00
October	7-106	6	-39.76	6-59	10	-4.76	0-26		-26.00	1-21	4	-9.00
November	3-18	16	+12.73	2-12	16	+17.00	1-4	25	-2.27	0-2		-2.00
December	0-6		-6.00	0-5		-5.00	0-0		0.00	0-1		-1.00

All runners

2007	Wins	Runs	%	2nd	3rd	4th	Win prize	Total prize	£1 Stake
2yo	53	457	12	44	57	49	£403,474.78	£588,706.39	-38.87
3yo	32	387	8	51	40	42	£348,078.77	£560,297.93	-95.30
4yo+	24	242	10	21	22	25	£235,244.92	£554,195.93	-45.00
TOTAL	109	1086	10	116	119	116	£986,798.47	£1,703,200.25	-179.17

2006	Wins	Runs	%	2nd	3rd	4th	Win prize	Total prize	£1 Stake
2yo	65	425	15	52	49	56	348,524.00	609,277.16	-45.47
3yo	46	397	12	48	39	40	383,125.35	661,820.47	-37.12
4yo+	16	205	8	21	19	22	146,999.25	277,528.09	-24.75
TOTAL	127	1027	12	121	107	118	878,648.60	1,548,625.72	-107.34

2005	Wins	Runs	%	2nd	3rd	4th	Win prize	Total prize	£1 Stake
2yo	56	411	14	63	45	50	374,971.99	695,963.48	-47.12
3yo	35	398	9	40	46	37	217,616.20	435,642.02	-115.83
4yo+	13	233	6	21	26	27	96,316.80	218,520.11	-112.33
TOTAL	104	1042	10	124	117	114	688,904.99	1,350,125.61	-275.28

By race type

2007

	Overall			Two-year-olds			Three-year-olds			Older horses		
	W-R	%	£1	W-R	%	£1	W-R	%	£1	W-R	%	£1
Handicap	52-607	9	-131.17	13-131	10	+26.00	17-275	6	-135.67	22-201	11	-21.50
Group 1,2,3	8-63	13	+75.50	3-23	13	+41.50	4-20	20	+43.00	1-20	5	-9.00
Maiden	26-280	9	-150.98	22-225	10	-129.09	4-55	7	-21.89	0-0		+0.00

2006

	Overall			Two-year-olds			Three-year-olds			Older horses		
	W-R	%	£1	W-R	%	£1	W-R	%	£1	W-R	%	£1
Handicap	58-562	10	-15.18	13-107	12	-24.01	30-273	11	+17.08	15-182	8	-8.25
Group 1,2,3	3-46	7	+6.00	2-14	14	+25.00	1-24	4	-11.00	0-8		-8.00
Maiden	40-275	15	-62.95	35-217	16	-23.95	5-58	9	-39.00	0-0		+0.00

2005

	Overall			Two-year-olds			Three-year-olds			Older horses		
	W-R	%	£1	W-R	%	£1	W-R	%	£1	W-R	%	£1
Handicap	33-547	6	-207.92	9-91	9	-7.75	15-262	5	-98.00	9-194	4	-102.17
Group 1,2,3	3-45	6	-31.09	2-24	8	-17.09	0-16		-16.00	1-5	20	+2.00
Maiden	42-281	14	-15.80	34-216	15	+1.12	8-62	12	-13.92	0-3		-3.00

By jockey

2007

	Overall			Two-year-olds			Three-year-olds			Older horses		
	W-R	%	£1	W-R	%	£1	W-R	%	£1	W-R	%	£1
T O'Shea	25-216	12	-13.58	13-101	13	+9.81	8-78	10	-22.39	4-37	11	-1.00
D Holland	22-192	11	-3.15	10-101	10	-32.15	7-55	13	+7.50	5-36	14	+21.50
J Bowman	16-152	11	-58.75	10-70	14	-21.50	4-51	8	-19.25	2-31	6	-18.00
C Catlin	11-94	12	-2.42	5-33	15	+24.83	2-28	7	-22.75	4-33	12	-4.50
S Hitchcott	7-68	10	-40.27	4-32	13	-16.02	2-25	8	-18.75	1-11	9	-5.50
M Davies	6-66	9	-18.67	0-11		-11.00	3-28	11	+1.33	3-27	11	-9.00
R Mullen	3-11	27	+5.62	3-7	43	+9.62	0-3		-3.00	0-1		-1.00
J Spencer	3-16	19	+69.50	2-6	33	+53.50	1-9	11	+17.00	0-1		-1.00
T O'Brien	3-26	12	-1.50	2-13	15	+7.50	0-3		-3.00	1-10	10	-6.00
F Norton	2-9	22	+4.75	1-5	20	-1.25	1-4	25	+6.00	0-0		+0.00

By jockey ctd

2006

	Overall			Two-year-olds			Three-year-olds			Older horses		
	W-R	%	£1	W-R	%	£1	W-R	%	£1	W-R	%	£1
T E Durcan	26-204	13	-42.89	14-94	15	-17.65	10-77	13	-1.49	2-33	6	-23.75
T Culhane	21-199	11	-33.01	7-65	11	-5.39	12-96	13	-6.13	2-38	5	-21.50
C Catlin	19-156	12	-44.98	12-70	17	-4.98	4-46	9	-24.00	3-40	8	-16.00
E Creighton	13-122	11	-30.00	11-63	17	+7.00	0-37		-37.00	2-22	9	+0.00
T O'Shea	8-33	24	+8.38	6-18	33	+9.13	2-11	18	+3.25	0-4		-4.00
S Hitchcott	6-47	13	+26.00	2-17	12	+4.00	1-16	6	+5.00	3-14	21	+17.00
R Winston	5-26	19	+7.30	3-18	17	-2.20	1-6	17	+0.50	1-2	50	+9.00
T Quinn	4-42	10	-1.75	1-10	10	-2.50	2-28	7	-21.25	1-4	25	+22.00
R Hughes	3-10	30	+29.50	1-7	14	-1.50	2-3	67	+31.00	0-0		+0.00
J Fanning	3-17	18	+16.75	0-4		-4.00	3-9	33	+24.75	0-4		-4.00

2005

	Overall			Two-year-olds			Three-year-olds			Older horses		
	W-R	%	£1	W-R	%	£1	W-R	%	£1	W-R	%	£1
T E Durcan	41-330	12	-67.52	25-156	16	-22.20	14-137	10	-20.82	2-37	5	-24.50
C Catlin	19-145	13	+7.25	9-56	16	+1.87	8-63	12	+11.88	2-26	7	-6.50
A Culhane	18-187	9	-104.49	10-81	12	-31.44	6-52	11	-30.88	2-54	3	-42.17
S Hitchcott	11-157	7	-39.84	5-45	11	-3.18	3-66	4	-27.00	3-46	6	-9.67
E Creighton	5-74	6	+4.00	3-28	10	+38.50	0-23		-23.00	2-23	8	-11.50
G Gibbons	1-1	100	+1.66	1-1	100	+1.66	0-0		0.00	0-0		0.00
K McEvoy	1-2	50	-0.09	1-1	100	+0.91	0-1		-1.00	0-0		0.00
L Dettori	1-4	25	-1.25	0-2		-2.00	1-2	50	+0.75	0-0		0.00
F Lynch	1-4	25	+2.00	1-2	50	+4.00	0-1		-1.00	0-1		-1.00
T Quinn	1-5	20	-1.25	1-3	33	+0.75	0-1		-1.00	0-1		-1.00

By horse

	Wins-Runs	%	£1 level stakes	Win prize	Total Prize
Youmzain	0-1		-1.00	0.00	161,400.00
Majestic Roi	2-5	40	+38.00	132,297.40	135,322.40
Halicarnassus	3-9	33	+15.50	78,356.40	96,883.00
Championship Point	2-7	29	+28.00	62,389.00	65,116.60
Dan Tucket	3-12	25	+15.83	48,253.65	54,303.20
Hatta Fort	2-5	40	+5.00	44,279.90	53,759.30
Nahoodh	1-3	33	+5.50	50,379.50	51,342.50
Sweet Lilly	1-6	17	+1.00	14,762.80	46,702.70
Man Of Vision	2-7	29	+3.00	14,205.75	37,072.90
Nijoom Dubai	1-3	33	+48.00	34,068.00	36,698.40
Johar Jamal	2-6	33	+7.00	17,164.05	36,689.80
South Cape	3-14	21	+14.00	30,000.90	35,747.30
Siberian Tiger	3-7	43	+21.00	29,588.50	30,406.80
Silver Touch	1-3	33	+8.00	26,686.60	28,973.10
Missit	1-5	20	-2.63	2,914.65	28,815.18
Ajigolo	3-18	17	-2.50	21,697.95	28,295.95
Wovoka	1-12	8	-2.00	6,477.00	24,259.00
Mango Mischief	1-6	17	+0.50	17,034.00	23,311.90
Treat	0-4		-4.00	0.00	22,991.40
Baddam	0-8		-8.00	0.00	22,842.00
Meeriss	3-7	43	+14.00	19,292.45	21,717.95
Thunder Bay	3-13	23	-0.77	12,751.95	20,015.30
Malapropism	4-24	17	-1.00	13,925.55	19,665.11
Compton's Eleven	1-14	7	-8.00	12,464.00	19,624.00
Mutawaajid	0-4		-4.00	0.00	19,455.51
Capable Guest	1-13	8	-7.00	12,464.00	17,316.40
Tuanku	2-6	33	+25.00	16,038.60	16,416.20
Massive	1-4	25	+9.00	14,762.80	15,140.80
Majuro	1-11	9	-5.50	7,570.80	14,688.00
Carleton	2-13	15	+0.50	9,067.80	14,421.00

HALICARNASSUS (left): wins the Superlative Stakes at Newmarket

By course
2007

	Overall			Two-year-olds			Three-year-olds			Older horses		
	W-R	%	£1	W-R	%	£1	W-R	%	£1	W-R	%	£1
Ascot	5-63	8	+34.00	3-21	14	+40.00	0-17		-17.00	2-25	8	+11.00
Ayr	1-16	6	-10.00	0-7		-7.00	1-3	33	+3.00	0-6		-6.00
Bath	7-42	17	+9.33	3-27	11	-0.50	1-10	10	-5.67	3-5	60	+15.50
Beverley	2-16	13	-3.50	1-7	14	+1.00	0-5		-5.00	1-4	25	+0.50
Brighton	1-32	3	-29.63	0-13		-13.00	1-16	6	-13.63	0-3		-3.00
Carlisle	0-1		-1.00	0-1		-1.00	0-0		+0.00	0-0		+0.00
Catterick	3-17	18	+1.63	1-8	13	+5.00	2-9	22	-3.38	0-0		+0.00
Chepstow	0-19		-19.00	0-7		-7.00	0-5		-5.00	0-7		-7.00
Chester	4-21	19	+1.12	2-10	20	+2.62	1-6	17	-1.50	1-5	20	+0.00
Doncaster	0-22		-22.00	0-13		-13.00	0-4		-4.00	0-5		-5.00
Epsom	1-8	13	+3.00	0-1		-1.00	1-4	25	+7.00	0-3		-3.00
Folkestone	6-39	15	+46.83	2-15	13	-4.17	3-15	20	+45.00	1-9	11	+6.00
Goodwood	8-83	10	-5.00	3-35	9	-2.50	1-24	4	-19.50	4-24	17	+17.00
Hamilton	1-4	25	+2.50	1-2	50	+4.50	0-1		-1.00	0-1		-1.00
Haydock	1-30	3	-20.00	0-11		-11.00	1-10	10	+0.00	0-9		-9.00
Kempton	4-67	6	-39.00	2-26	8	-12.00	2-35	6	-21.00	0-6		-6.00
Leicester	3-19	16	-7.25	2-15	13	-7.75	1-3	33	+1.50	0-1		-1.00
Lingfield	2-26	8	-21.79	2-15	13	-10.79	0-8		-8.00	0-3		-3.00
Lingfield (AW)	6-65	9	-32.00	2-8	25	+2.50	2-43	5	-32.00	2-14	14	-2.50
Musselburgh	1-18	6	-14.25	1-8	13	-4.25	0-6		-6.00	0-4		-4.00
Newbury	4-58	7	+5.00	0-29		-29.00	4-20	20	+43.00	0-9		-9.00
Newcastle	2-23	9	+9.50	1-10	10	+16.00	0-6		-6.00	1-7	14	-0.50
Newmarket	2-55	4	-32.00	0-14		-14.00	1-21	5	-4.00	1-20	5	-14.00
Newmarket (J)	9-46	20	+25.75	7-22	32	+32.75	0-15		-15.00	2-9	22	+8.00
Nottingham	2-25	8	-3.50	2-14	14	+7.50	0-10		-10.00	0-1		-1.00
Pontefract	3-25	12	+14.50	1-11	9	+2.00	2-7	29	+19.50	0-7		-7.00
Redcar	4-13	31	+12.22	2-7	29	+12.10	1-4	25	-2.39	1-2	50	+2.50
Ripon	2-25	8	-17.50	2-9	22	-1.50	0-7		-7.00	0-9		-9.00
Salisbury	2-29	7	-20.50	1-12	8	-8.00	1-12	8	-7.50	0-5		-5.00
Sandown	6-33	18	+7.75	2-12	17	-3.25	3-14	21	+12.00	1-7	14	-1.00
Southwell (AW)	2-6	33	+6.50	0-0		+0.00	1-3	33	+0.50	1-3	33	+6.00
Thirsk	3-15	20	-8.72	3-8	38	-1.72	0-5		-5.00	0-2		-2.00
Warwick	1-18	6	-14.50	1-10	10	-6.50	0-7		-7.00	0-1		-1.00
Windsor	5-29	17	-1.90	4-15	27	+6.60	0-4		-4.00	1-10	10	-4.50
Wolves	4-42	10	-16.25	1-15	7	-2.00	1-20	5	-16.25	2-7	29	+2.00
Yarmouth	0-19		-19.00	0-11		-11.00	0-4		-4.00	0-4		-4.00
York	2-17	12	-0.50	1-8	13	+0.50	1-4	25	+4.00	0-5		-5.00

Kevin Ryan

Another season of tremendous progress for Ryan, who is getting more and more horses and more than justifying his rise by maintaining a strike-rate of around 11 per cent, resulting in his first century of winners last year.

Handicaps are the races in which to follow Ryan – he won with 54 out of 496 runners in them last year, and level-stakes losses of £42 are respectable given the size of the sample.

They certainly contrast favourably with overall losses of £218 to £1 level stakes.

By month

2007

	Overall			Two-year-olds			Three-year-olds			Older horses		
	W-R	%	£1	W-R	%	£1	W-R	%	£1	W-R	%	£1
January	9-53	17	+11.50	0-0		+0.00	2-14	14	-3.50	7-39	18	+15.00
February	8-47	17	-8.88	0-0		+0.00	2-21	10	-12.47	6-26	23	+3.58
March	7-36	19	+1.47	0-0		+0.00	3-7	43	+6.22	4-29	14	-4.75
April	8-65	12	-26.14	2-14	14	-0.50	3-22	14	-11.64	3-29	10	-14.00
May	5-92	5	-64.13	2-31	6	-22.13	0-28		-28.00	3-33	9	-14.00
June	9-82	11	-33.24	3-25	12	-3.59	2-22	9	-13.25	4-35	11	-16.40
July	13-109	12	-11.67	3-35	9	-22.13	2-34	6	-15.00	8-40	20	+25.46
August	16-138	12	-34.28	8-62	13	-0.39	2-27	7	-11.50	6-49	12	-22.40
September	11-117	9	-16.93	7-54	13	-10.43	2-18	11	+12.50	2-45	4	-19.00
October	11-88	13	+6.88	6-44	14	-15.63	1-17	6	+9.00	4-27	15	+13.50
November	3-54	6	-34.50	0-21		-21.00	1-9	11	-3.50	2-24	8	-10.00
December	7-51	14	-8.29	4-19	21	+4.88	2-11	18	+3.50	1-21	5	-16.67

2006

	Overall			Two-year-olds			Three-year-olds			Older horses		
	W-R	%	£1	W-R	%	£1	W-R	%	£1	W-R	%	£1
January	8-51	16	+10.43	0-0		+0.00	2-15	13	-1.38	6-36	17	+11.80
February	6-34	18	+8.19	0-0		+0.00	1-9	11	-7.56	5-25	20	+15.75
March	3-51	6	-33.00	0-2		-2.00	3-12	25	+6.00	0-37		-37.00
April	12-62	19	+16.75	3-18	17	-7.00	4-18	22	+0.50	5-26	19	+23.25
May	19-91	21	+23.78	13-31	42	+37.65	1-22	5	-19.38	5-38	13	+5.50
June	10-76	13	+6.58	4-25	16	-8.42	1-14	7	-9.00	5-37	14	+24.00
July	7-80	9	-32.00	3-24	13	-7.00	2-22	9	-1.00	2-34	6	-24.00
August	9-116	8	-55.88	5-48	10	-8.83	0-23		-23.00	4-45	9	-24.04
September	7-93	8	-44.25	4-43	9	-10.75	1-19	5	-13.50	2-31	6	-20.00
October	4-57	7	-22.50	1-28	4	-24.50	1-12	8	+9.00	2-17	12	-7.00
November	2-49	4	-37.00	1-15	7	-7.00	1-13	8	-9.00	0-21		-21.00
December	8-67	12	-36.64	2-20	10	-10.50	2-17	12	-12.14	4-30	13	-14.00

2005

	Overall			Two-year-olds			Three-year-olds			Older horses		
	W-R	%	£1	W-R	%	£1	W-R	%	£1	W-R	%	£1
January	6-38	16	+26.25	0-0		+0.00	1-12	8	-6.00	5-26	19	+32.25
February	2-30	7	-21.75	0-0		+0.00	0-3		-3.00	2-27	7	-18.75
March	1-20	5	-15.00	0-2		-2.00	0-1		-1.00	1-17	6	-12.00
April	15-63	24	+44.79	3-9	33	+7.17	4-16	25	+19.50	8-38	21	+18.13
May	10-82	12	-10.50	3-27	11	+4.25	3-18	17	+3.50	4-37	11	-18.25
June	11-73	15	+11.69	3-20	15	-1.25	2-16	13	-5.50	6-37	16	+18.44
July	9-71	13	-28.63	5-27	19	-6.13	0-17		-17.00	4-27	15	-5.50
August	7-75	9	-6.25	3-29	10	+1.00	0-20		-20.00	4-26	15	+12.75
September	8-75	11	-11.50	4-32	13	-4.00	0-12		-12.00	4-31	13	+4.50
October	7-56	13	+6.50	4-23	17	+19.50	1-13	8	-4.00	2-20	10	-9.00
November	3-29	10	-12.00	1-16	6	-12.00	0-3		-3.00	2-10	20	+3.00
December	3-31	10	-19.50	0-12		-12.00	0-4		-4.00	3-15	20	-3.50

All runners

2007	Wins	Runs	%	2nd	3rd	4th	Win prize	Total prize	£1 Stake
2yo	35	305	11	50	34	36	£136,745.54	£371,203.20	-90.90
3yo	22	230	10	22	19	20	£90,071.29	£172,873.31	-67.63
4yo+	50	397	13	36	36	35	£401,933.64	£567,785.17	-59.67
TOTAL	107	932	11	108	89	91	£628,750.47	£1,111,861.68	-218.21

2006	Wins	Runs	%	2nd	3rd	4th	Win prize	Total prize	£1 Stake
2yo	36	254	14	24	28	32	217,765.00	437,540.85	-48.35
3yo	19	196	10	25	25	14	89,304.90	366,977.60	-80.44
4yo+	40	377	11	36	40	27	314,842.92	510,108.37	-66.74
TOTAL	95	827	11	85	93	73	621,912.82	1,314,626.82	-195.53

2005	Wins	Runs	%	2nd	3rd	4th	Win prize	Total prize	£1 Stake
2yo	26	197	13	26	25	19	424,675.85	567,483.77	-5.46
3yo	11	135	8	14	12	10	52,318.52	107,221.02	-52.50
4yo+	45	311	14	31	31	23	245,273.75	356,276.31	+22.07
TOTAL	82	643	13	71	68	52	722,268.12	1,030,981.10	-35.89

By race type

2007

	Overall		Two-year-olds		Three-year-olds		Older horses	
	W-R	£1	W-R	£1	W-R	£1	W-R	£1
Handicap	54-496 11	-42.83	6-46 13	+8.88	12-147 8	-26.50	36-303 12	-25.21
Group 1,2,3	1-29 3	-25.00	0-5	-5.00	0-10	-10.00	1-14 7	-10.00
Maiden	24-211 11	-77.43	21-173 12	-52.65	3-36 8	-22.78	0-2	-2.00

2006

	Overall		Two-year-olds		Three-year-olds		Older horses	
	W-R	£1	W-R	£1	W-R	£1	W-R	£1
Handicap	42-509 8	-163.00	4-49 8	-15.00	11-144 8	-70.25	27-316 9	-77.75
Group 1,2,3	1-28 4	-24.25	1-20 5	-16.25	0-7	-7.00	0-1	-1.00
Maiden	29-162 18	+10.43	22-129 17	-0.02	5-22 23	+4.12	2-11 18	+6.33

2005

	Overall		Two-year-olds		Three-year-olds		Older horses	
	W-R	£1	W-R	£1	W-R	£1	W-R	£1
Handicap	44-394 11	-17.75	4-43 9	-10.13	9-96 9	-24.50	31-255 12	+16.88
Group 1,2,3	3-11 27	+23.00	3-10 30	+24.00	0-1	-1.00	0-0	+0.00
Maiden	15-113 13	-32.83	12-87 14	-18.33	1-20 5	-15.00	2-6 33	+0.50

By jockey

2007

	Overall			Two-year-olds			Three-year-olds			Older horses		
	W-R	%	£1	W-R	%	£1	W-R	%	£1	W-R	%	£1
N Callan	57-389	15	-61.35	17-124	14	-30.23	11-91	12	-20.35	29-174	17	-10.77
P Mulrennan	7-53	13	-14.43	6-27	22	+2.58	1-12	8	-3.00	0-14		-14.00
J Spencer	6-27	22	+15.38	2-8	25	-2.00	1-7	14	-1.50	3-12	25	+18.88
D O'Donohoe	6-132	5	-90.50	1-52	2	-48.00	2-43	5	-24.00	3-37	8	-18.50
P Cosgrave	5-39	13	+26.00	2-11	18	+13.00	0-8		-8.00	3-20	15	+21.00
A Mullen	5-85	6	-35.13	3-22	14	-1.63	1-23	4	-14.50	1-40	3	-19.00
D Holland	3-11	27	+9.72	1-3	33	+12.00	2-3	67	+2.72	0-5		-5.00
J Egan	3-16	19	+17.10	0-6		-6.00	1-4	25	+22.00	2-6	33	+1.10
K Darley	2-5	40	+7.00	0-1		-1.00	2-3	67	+9.00	0-1		-1.00
Miss A Ryan	2-10	20	-1.50	0-0		+0.00	0-0		+0.00	2-10	20	-1.50

By jockey ctd

2006

	Overall			Two-year-olds			Three-year-olds			Older horses		
	W-R	%	£1	W-R	%	£1	W-R	%	£1	W-R	%	£1
N Callan	51-342	15	+4.18	19-99	19	+22.98	10-79	13	-13.81	22-164	13	-4.99
D O'Donohoe	11-113	10	-35.20	7-51	14	-18.70	2-25	8	-13.50	2-37	5	-3.00
A Mullen	6-107	6	-59.50	1-13	8	-7.50	1-32	3	-27.00	4-62	6	-25.00
J Spencer	4-9	44	+6.25	1-3	33	-1.50	0-1		-1.00	3-5	60	+8.75
C Gannon	4-83	5	-56.89	0-35		-35.00	3-21	14	-4.39	1-27	4	-17.50
J Jones	2-7	29	-1.75	0-2		-2.00	1-1	100	+2.25	1-4	25	-2.00
P Hanagan	2-13	15	+1.50	2-5	40	+9.50	0-4		-4.00	0-4		-4.00
R Winston	2-14	14	-3.50	1-4	25	+1.00	0-4		-4.00	1-6	17	-0.50
P Mulrennan	2-16	13	-2.00	1-8	13	+1.00	0-4		-4.00	1-4	25	+1.00
T Hamilton	1-1	100	+2.75	1-1	100	+2.75	0-0		+0.00	0-0		+0.00

2005

	Overall			Two-year-olds			Three-year-olds			Older horses		
	W-R	%	£1	W-R	%	£1	W-R	%	£1	W-R	%	£1
N Callan	52-344	15	+17.61	19-107	18	+19.17	9-77	12	-10.00	24-160	15	+8.44
A Mullen	8-62	13	+6.50	0-10		-10.00	0-9		-9.00	8-43	19	+25.50
N Carberry	4-14	29	+0.63	0-0		+0.00	0-2		-2.00	4-12	33	+2.63
J Fanning	3-17	18	+4.00	0-4		-4.00	0-3		-3.00	3-10	30	+11.00
R Winston	3-23	13	+0.88	2-11	18	-4.13	0-0		+0.00	1-12	8	+5.00
F Lynch	2-5	40	+4.00	1-3	33	+3.00	0-1		-1.00	1-1	100	+2.00
J Carroll	2-6	33	+21.50	1-2	50	+19.00	1-2	50	+4.50	0-2		-2.00
A Nicholls	2-40	5	-25.50	2-24	8	-9.50	0-3		-3.00	0-13		-13.00
K Fallon	1-2	50	+15.00	1-2	50	+15.00	0-0		+0.00	0-0		+0.00
C Timmons	1-3	33	+6.00	0-0		+0.00	1-2	50	+7.00	0-1		-1.00

By horse

	Wins-Runs	%	£1 level stakes	Win prize	Total Prize
Anosti	1-6	17	+0.00	2,388.75	92,564.52
Advanced	1-8	13	+13.00	75,407.20	86,190.80
Desert Lord	0-5		-5.00	0.00	58,552.52
Amadeus Wolf	1-5	20	-1.00	56,780.00	56,780.00
Tamagin	4-7	57	+40.00	34,993.40	42,316.00
King Orchisios	3-11	27	+10.50	42,160.00	42,160.00
Green Manalishi	2-9	22	+3.00	24,734.00	29,765.30
Alexander Castle	1-2	50	+4.00	4,100.85	25,620.85
Imperial Mint	2-5	40	+1.38	13,989.00	22,202.00
Wi Dud	0-6		-6.00	0.00	22,182.12
Cobo Bay	3-7	43	+32.00	20,884.10	21,759.81
Melalchrist	3-17	18	-3.92	15,220.95	19,820.00
Captain Jacksparra	3-10	30	+1.72	13,655.92	19,437.98
My Paris	1-11	9	-3.50	11,658.60	18,169.40
New Jersey	1-8	13	-2.00	8,420.10	16,460.70
Eastern Romance	1-8	13	-6.09	3,238.50	16,117.12
Golan Knight	2-7	29	+17.00	13,601.70	15,816.60
Danetime Lord	3-11	27	+6.50	10,843.65	15,041.84
Philanthropy	1-5	20	+21.00	11,658.60	14,305.70
High Curragh	1-12	8	-7.00	9,715.50	13,928.95
Harry Up	1-16	6	-10.00	4,857.75	13,771.29
Wigwam Willie	2-7	29	+2.00	12,709.00	13,286.20
Mazzanti	1-7	14	-5.09	2,590.80	12,995.06
Distinctly Game	2-14	14	+6.00	9,132.57	12,852.12
Milla's Rocket	2-8	25	+12.00	7,929.00	12,596.04
Mutamared	0-7		-7.00	0.00	11,109.50
Evens And Odds	0-8		-8.00	0.00	10,512.30
Fast Feet	1-12	8	-9.50	2,968.87	10,494.11
Louisiade	4-9	44	+13.25	9,610.30	10,335.05
Fontana Amorosa	1-3	33	+3.00	4,728.21	10,323.41

By course

2007

	Overall			Two-year-olds			Three-year-olds			Older horses		
	W-R	%	£1	W-R	%	£1	W-R	%	£1	W-R	%	£1
Ascot	1-23	4	-2.00	0-6		-6.00	0-4		-4.00	1-13	8	+8.00
Ayr	5-44	11	+5.62	2-14	14	+2.62	0-10		-10.00	3-20	15	+13.00
Bath	0-1		-1.00	0-1		-1.00	0-0		+0.00	0-0		+0.00
Beverley	4-33	12	-18.68	2-13	15	-6.76	0-8		-8.00	2-12	17	-3.92
Carlisle	1-10	10	-7.50	1-5	20	-2.50	0-3		-3.00	0-2		-2.00
Catterick	3-30	10	-18.67	2-12	17	-6.17	0-9		-9.00	1-9	11	-3.50
Chepstow	0-1		-1.00	0-1		-1.00	0-0		+0.00	0-0		+0.00
Chester	4-25	16	+0.00	2-12	17	+0.50	1-5	20	+1.00	1-8	13	-1.50
Doncaster	1-30	3	-22.00	0-11		-11.00	0-4		-4.00	1-15	7	-7.00
Epsom	0-7		-7.00	0-1		-1.00	0-2		-2.00	0-4		-4.00
Goodwood	0-13		-13.00	0-1		-1.00	0-3		-3.00	0-9		-9.00
Hamilton	7-25	28	+12.13	2-7	29	+8.00	1-8	13	-5.25	4-10	40	+9.38
Haydock	2-37	5	-24.00	1-18	6	-10.00	0-5		-5.00	1-14	7	-9.00
Kempton	3-21	14	+9.00	0-1		-1.00	1-5	20	+1.00	2-15	13	+9.00
Leicester	6-30	20	+38.75	3-16	19	+14.50	3-10	30	+28.25	0-4		-4.00
Lingfield	1-1	100	+3.50	0-0		+0.00	1-1	100	+3.50	0-0		+0.00
Lingfield (AW)	14-63	22	+21.60	3-11	27	+6.50	2-14	14	-2.50	9-38	24	+17.60
Musselburgh	2-36	6	-28.59	1-10	10	-8.09	1-7	14	-1.50	0-19		-19.00
Newbury	1-9	11	-3.50	0-1		-1.00	0-5		-5.00	1-3	33	+2.50
Newcastle	3-18	17	-2.00	1-7	14	-1.00	1-5	20	+1.00	1-6	17	-2.00
Newmarket	0-25		-25.00	0-7		-7.00	0-8		-8.00	0-10		-10.00
Newmarket (J)	2-22	9	-3.00	1-5	20	+7.00	0-7		-7.00	1-10	10	-3.00
Nottingham	0-12		-12.00	0-7		-7.00	0-3		-3.00	0-2		-2.00
Pontefract	1-22	5	-17.00	0-11		-11.00	1-5	20	+0.00	0-6		-6.00
Redcar	3-35	9	+5.50	2-20	10	-8.50	0-6		-6.00	1-9	11	+20.00
Ripon	5-30	17	+10.00	2-15	13	+4.50	1-6	17	+1.00	2-9	22	+4.50
Salisbury	0-3		-3.00	0-1		-1.00	0-1		-1.00	0-1		-1.00
Sandown	0-6		-6.00	0-2		-2.00	0-4		-4.00	0-0		+0.00
Southwell	0-3		-3.00	0-0		+0.00	0-1		-1.00	0-2		-2.00
Southwell (AW)	9-67	13	-27.45	1-10	10	-7.50	3-20	15	-8.28	5-37	14	-11.67
Thirsk	2-45	4	-24.50	0-16		-16.00	1-14	7	-1.00	1-15	7	-7.50
Warwick	0-4		-4.00	0-2		-2.00	0-1		-1.00	0-1		-1.00
Windsor	2-5	40	-0.40	1-2	50	+0.88	0-0		+0.00	1-3	33	-1.27
Wolves	22-156	14	-46.02	7-42	17	-4.88	4-39	10	-19.85	11-75	15	-21.29
York	3-40	8	-4.00	1-17	6	-11.00	1-7	14	+19.00	1-16	6	-12.00

AMADEUS WOLF: pleased connections when winning the Duke of York Stakes in May

Barry Hills

A rare year in which Hills failed to reach 100 winners, but contrary to the rumour mill that hasn't persuaded him to call it a day and he will be looking to set the record straight this time.

A midsummer wobble was the reason for Hills' lower total, but he finished the season strongly and has several interesting contenders for the top prizes in the months ahead.

Note the contrasting records of sons Michael and Richard in the saddle, with Richard's significantly better strike-rate.

By month

2007

	Overall			Two-year-olds			Three-year-olds			Older horses		
	W-R	%	£1	W-R	%	£1	W-R	%	£1	W-R	%	£1
January	0-5		-5.00	0-0		+0.00	0-5		-5.00	0-0		+0.00
February	0-6		-6.00	0-0		+0.00	0-5		-5.00	0-1		-1.00
March	1-6	17	-4.56	0-0		+0.00	1-6	17	-4.56	0-0		+0.00
April	13-58	22	-2.59	2-8	25	+5.00	10-41	24	-3.59	1-9	11	-4.00
May	13-86	15	-5.61	5-12	42	+4.27	6-56	11	+0.63	2-18	11	-10.50
June	6-76	8	-36.75	2-21	10	-7.00	3-41	7	-19.00	1-14	7	-10.75
July	10-86	12	+14.25	1-27	4	-24.75	7-40	18	+35.00	2-19	11	+4.00
August	20-115	17	-20.53	7-42	17	-17.48	10-56	18	-5.05	3-17	18	+2.00
September	17-106	16	-6.57	9-51	18	-0.48	5-42	12	-14.59	3-13	23	+8.50
October	6-96	6	-51.45	5-55	9	-31.45	1-27	4	-6.00	0-14		-14.00
November	4-18	22	+2.63	3-11	27	+6.38	0-1		-1.00	1-6	17	-2.75
December	1-1	100	+8.00	0-0		+0.00	0-0		+0.00	1-1	100	+8.00

2006

	Overall			Two-year-olds			Three-year-olds			Older horses		
	W-R	%	£1	W-R	%	£1	W-R	%	£1	W-R	%	£1
January	0-2		-2.00	0-0		+0.00	0-0		+0.00	0-2		-2.00
February	0-4		-4.00	0-0		+0.00	0-2		-2.00	0-2		-2.00
March	1-11	9	-7.00	0-0		+0.00	1-10	10	-6.00	0-1		-1.00
April	12-77	16	+17.53	1-9	11	-1.00	6-54	11	+7.33	5-14	36	+11.20
May	10-66	15	-32.55	1-10	10	-7.63	8-46	17	-17.42	1-10	10	-7.50
June	17-116	15	-36.24	4-25	16	-8.85	11-72	15	-21.39	2-19	11	-6.00
July	12-88	14	-23.46	4-33	12	-10.03	4-42	10	-31.43	4-13	31	+18.00
August	18-119	15	+0.64	5-46	11	-25.50	11-60	18	+24.64	2-13	15	+1.50
September	20-136	15	+2.25	11-68	16	+6.50	9-57	16	+6.75	0-11		-11.00
October	8-79	10	-34.93	4-41	10	-23.68	4-33	12	-6.25	0-5		-5.00
November	5-32	16	-11.45	2-13	15	-7.95	2-16	13	-6.50	1-3	33	+3.00
December	0-4		-4.00	0-0		+0.00	0-3		-3.00	0-1		-1.00

2005

	Overall			Two-year-olds			Three-year-olds			Older horses		
	W-R	%	£1	W-R	%	£1	W-R	%	£1	W-R	%	£1
January	0-4		-4.00	0-0			0-1		-1.00	0-3		-3.00
February	0-3		-3.00	0-0			0-0		0.00	0-3		-3.00
March	0-13		-13.00	0-1		-1.00	0-9		-9.00	0-3		-3.00
April	11-57	19	+18.58	2-3	66	+11.00	7-45	15	-6.42	2-9	22%	+14.00
May	14-84	16	+4.54	2-11	18	-5.05	10-58	17	-12.41	2-15	13	+22.00
June	8-59	13	-19.25	3-12	25	+6.00	5-42	11	-20.25	0-5		-5.00
July	19-122	15	+2.66	4-38	10	+6.38	13-70	18	-12.22	2-14	14	+8.50
August	19-95	20	-22.62	8-28	28	-9.24	10-57	17	-11.38	1-10	10	-2.00
September	20-125	16	-25.65	8-58	13	-20.96	9-55	16	-4.32	3-12	25	-0.37
October	9-84	10	-15.65	3-40	7	-26.65	6-40	15	+15.00	0-4		-4.00
November	1-22	4	-5.00	1-10	10	+7.00	0-11		-11.00	0-1		-1.00
December	0-0		0.00	0-0		0.00	0-0		0.00	0-0		0.00

All runners

2007	Wins	Runs	%	2nd	3rd	4th	Win prize	Total prize	£1 Stake
2yo	34	227	15	25	33	25	£502,245.03	£670,676.44	-65.52
3yo	43	320	13	39	35	26	£366,931.63	£563,944.31	-28.17
4yo+	14	112	13	14	13	18	£343,847.57	£562,149.29	-20.50
TOTAL	91	659	14	78	81	69	£1,213,024.23	£1,796,770.04	-114.19

2006	Wins	Runs	%	2nd	3rd	4th	Win prize	Total prize	£1 Stake
2yo	32	245	13	42	28	19	274,013.17	507,776.10	-78.13
3yo	56	395	14	45	62	41	555,636.62	1,000,652.07	-55.27
4yo+	15	94	16	9	13	8	271,440.80	315,316.20	-1.80
TOTAL	103	734	14	96	103	68	1,101,090.59	1,823,744.37	-135.20

2005	Wins	Runs	%	2nd	3rd	4th	Win prize	Total prize	£1 Stake
2yo	31	201	15	29	20	26	200,968.48	480,643.66	-32.52
3yo	60	388	15	50	35	38	496,540.80	747,100.18	-73.00
4yo+	10	79	13	10	10	7	254,459.24	419,351.28	+23.13
TOTAL	101	668	15	89	65	71	951,968.52	1,647,095.12	-82.39

By race type

2007

	Overall			Two-year-olds			Three-year-olds			Older horses		
	W-R	%	£1	W-R	%	£1	W-R	%	£1	W-R	%	£1
Handicap	32-302	11	-59.01	1-28	4	-22.00	19-194	10	-35.26	12-80	15	-1.75
Group 1,2,3	4-64	6	-20.75	2-23	9	-10.75	1-22	5	-1.00	1-19	5	-9.00
Maiden	49-242	20	-12.06	28-152	18	-27.27	21-89	24	+16.22	0-1		-1.00

2006

	Overall			Two-year-olds			Three-year-olds			Older horses		
	W-R	%	£1	W-R	%	£1	W-R	%	£1	W-R	%	£1
Handicap	39-310	13	-11.21	6-32	19	+19.13	22-199	11	-29.08	11-79	14	-1.25
Group 1,2,3	8-62	13	-12.50	3-19	16	-2.00	4-35	11	-7.00	1-8	13	-3.50
Maiden	46-306	15	-92.03	20-167	12	-77.43	26-139	19	-14.60	0-0		+0.00

2005

	Overall			Two-year-olds			Three-year-olds			Older horses		
	W-R	%	£1	W-R	%	£1	W-R	%	£1	W-R	%	£1
Handicap	28-266	10	-45.13	0-16		-16.00	21-197	10	-50.75	7-53	13	+21.63
Group 1,2,3	3-49	6	-29.00	1-17	5	-10.50	1-16	6	-10.50	1-16	6	-8.00
Maiden	59-294	20	-12.80	25-141	17	+6.92	34-153	22	-19.72	0-0		0.00

By jockey

2007

	Overall			Two-year-olds			Three-year-olds			Older horses		
	W-R		£1	W-R		£1	W-R		£1	W-R		£1
M Hills	39-305	13	-75.13	16-118	14	-35.67	17-129	13	-17.47	6-58	10	-22.00
R Hills	15-75	20	+10.36	7-36	19	-11.01	6-30	20	+19.61	2-9	22	+1.75
R Hughes	6-43	14	-3.50	2-14	14	+0.50	4-27	15	-2.00	0-2		-2.00
J Spencer	5-12	42	+4.00	2-4	50	+1.00	2-5	40	+2.00	1-3	33	+1.00
W Buick	4-17	24	+11.91	1-5	20	+1.00	3-9	33	+13.91	0-3		-3.00
M Dwyer	4-26	15	+0.75	2-7	29	-0.25	2-16	13	+4.00	0-3		-3.00
D O'Neill	3-13	23	+18.50	1-6	17	+5.00	2-7	29	+13.50	0-0		+0.00
P Robinson	2-10	20	+10.25	0-3		-3.00	0-3		-3.00	2-4	50	+16.25
T E Durcan	2-10	20	-3.90	1-3	33	-0.90	1-6	17	-2.00	0-1		-1.00
C Catlin	2-17	12	-6.00	0-3		-3.00	2-11	18	+0.00	0-3		-3.00

By jockey ctd

2006

	Overall			Two-year-olds			Three-year-olds			Older horses		
	W-R		£1	W-R		£1	W-R		£1	W-R		£1
M Hills	55-341	16	-38.57	21-115	18	-16.38	27-175	15	-25.19	7-51	14	+3.00
R Hills	15-78	19	-14.99	2-26	8	-20.63	10-43	23	+4.69	3-9	33	+0.95
R Hughes	10-50	20	+44.50	5-21	24	+13.38	5-29	17	+31.13	0-0		+0.00
R Moore	5-18	28	+4.92	0-4		-4.00	5-14	36	+8.92	0-0		+0.00
O Urbina	3-23	13	-5.00	0-4		-4.00	0-7		-7.00	3-12	25	+6.00
A Medeiros	2-9	22	+12.00	1-6	17	+0.00	1-2	50	+13.00	0-1		-1.00
R Ffrench	2-10	20	+8.50	1-3	33	+9.00	0-6		-6.00	1-1	100	+5.50
J Spencer	2-16	13	-7.50	1-7	14	-1.50	1-9	11	-6.00	0-0		+0.00
T Culhane	2-30	7	-21.25	1-10	10	-5.00	0-18		-18.00	1-2	50	+1.75
M Dwyer	2-36	6	-21.00	0-5		-5.00	2-27	7	-12.00	0-4		-4.00

2005

	Overall			Two-year-olds			Three-year-olds			Older horses		
	W-R	%	£1	W-R	%	£1	W-R	%	£1	W-R	%	£1
M Hills	42-314	13	-99.68	13-104	12	-41.92	22-158	13	-64.76	7-52	13	+7.00
R Hills	10-51	19	+5.66	2-15	13	-11.08	7-34	20	+15.61	1-2	50	+1.13
Martin Dwyer	8-35	22	+35.00	2-7	28	+14.00	6-23	26	+26.00	0-5		-5.00
R Hughes	8-36	22	+6.85	4-14	28	+3.38	4-22	18	+3.48	0-0		0.00
W Supple	6-24	25	+12.38	1-8	12	-1.00	5-16	31	+13.38	0-0		0.00
P Hanagan	4-15	26	+0.75	0-3		-3.00	4-12	33	+3.75	0-0		0.00
E Ahern	4-21	19	-4.52	2-6	33	+0.73	2-13	15	-3.25	0-2		-2.00
O Urbina	2-5	40	+5.75	2-3	66	+7.75	0-2		-2.00	0-0		0.00
T Quinn	2-8	25	+20.50	1-2	50	+24.00	1-6	16	-3.50	0-0		0.00
S Sanders	2-15	13	-5.00	1-4	25	+1.00	1-11	9	-6.00	0-0		0.00

By horse

	Wins-Runs	%	£1 level stakes	Win prize	Total Prize
Dark Angel	4-9	44	+8.65	335,620.31	341,306.31
Red Clubs	1-6	17	+4.00	179,027.34	272,607.10
Giganticus	3-8	38	+18.50	90,987.20	100,305.00
Miss Lucifer	2-8	25	+17.50	71,997.04	91,337.54
The Illies	3-8	38	+14.91	85,847.00	90,509.00
Under The Rainbow	0-10		-10.00	0.00	49,660.50
Prime Defender	2-8	25	-2.13	31,796.80	45,193.00
Royal Confidence	2-7	29	+0.44	29,794.20	43,913.30
Mashaahed	1-6	17	-2.75	14,762.80	41,022.20
Feared In Flight	1-4	25	+3.00	7,837.17	36,245.67
Desert Dew	1-3	33	+5.00	12,464.00	32,375.50
Tajdeef	1-3	33	-0.63	5,829.30	30,660.69
Zaahid	3-7	43	+17.50	21,654.30	25,665.70
Spinning Lucy	2-5	40	+7.80	18,511.89	21,305.19
Janina	2-3	67	+4.50	18,056.00	18,866.00
Dubai Twilight	1-9	11	-7.82	2,817.49	18,635.59
Dabbers Ridge	1-8	13	-3.00	12,954.00	18,085.50
Kay Es Jay	1-7	14	-4.75	3,886.20	16,805.42
Celestial Halo	1-7	14	-5.33	3,562.35	16,055.35
Parisian Dream	2-6	33	+5.00	13,558.05	15,966.35
Thousand Words	0-5		-5.00	0.00	15,887.90
Persian Express	2-9	22	+4.50	14,249.40	14,600.40
Yandina	1-7	14	-3.75	7,772.40	14,364.15
Urban Spirit	1-6	17	+3.00	9,715.50	13,803.50
Soul Mountain	2-10	20	-4.00	9,126.49	13,506.09
Nacho Libre	1-7	14	-3.00	2,914.65	13,072.35
Zifaaf	1-7	14	-4.00	6,477.00	11,848.02
Rule Of Life	2-7	29	-1.56	8,743.95	11,585.40
Huzzah	1-9	11	-4.50	4,533.90	11,261.41
Yankadi	1-2	50	+7.00	4,533.90	10,995.90

By course

2007

	Overall			Two-year-olds			Three-year-olds			Older horses		
	W-R	%	£1	W-R	%	£1	W-R	%	£1	W-R	%	£1
Ascot	2-40	5	-20.50	0-11		-11.00	2-18	11	+1.50	0-11		-11.00
Bath	4-18	22	-4.88	1-8	13	-5.38	3-9	33	+1.50	0-1		-1.00
Beverley	0-4		-4.00	0-0		+0.00	0-4		-4.00	0-0		+0.00
Brighton	0-3		-3.00	0-1		-1.00	0-2		-2.00	0-0		+0.00
Catterick	0-3		-3.00	0-0		+0.00	0-3		-3.00	0-0		+0.00
Chepstow	0-6		-6.00	0-0		+0.00	0-5		-5.00	0-1		-1.00
Chester	4-29	14	-18.90	1-6	17	-4.60	3-17	18	-8.30	0-6		-6.00
Doncaster	3-32	9	-18.59	2-20	10	-8.50	1-9	11	-7.09	0-3		-3.00
Epsom	0-2		-2.00	0-0		+0.00	0-2		-2.00	0-0		+0.00
Folkestone	2-14	14	-9.39	0-3		-3.00	1-7	14	-5.64	1-4	25	-0.75
Goodwood	2-35	6	-17.50	2-12	17	+5.50	0-20		-20.00	0-3		-3.00
Haydock	12-30	40	+33.73	6-12	50	+15.85	4-16	25	+4.88	2-2	100	+13.00
Kempton	4-36	11	+5.42	2-11	18	-7.08	1-13	8	+21.00	1-12	8	-8.50
Leicester	4-19	21	-2.44	3-8	38	-1.44	1-10	10	+0.00	0-1		-1.00
Lingfield	1-8	13	-0.50	0-3		-3.00	1-5	20	+2.50	0-0		+0.00
Lingfield (AW)	5-39	13	-15.87	0-5		-5.00	3-22	14	-13.87	2-12	17	+3.00
Newbury	4-54	7	-14.88	2-28	7	-22.38	2-22	9	+11.50	0-4		-4.00
Newcastle	2-3	67	+3.67	0-0		+0.00	1-2	50	-0.33	1-1	100	+4.00
Newmarket	10-69	14	+3.38	5-35	14	+0.38	3-24	13	+3.25	2-10	20	-0.25
Newmarket (J)	5-50	10	-2.00	1-18	6	-9.00	2-18	11	-0.50	2-14	14	+7.50
Nottingham	0-14		-14.00	0-4		-4.00	0-7		-7.00	0-3		-3.00
Pontefract	5-14	36	+9.88	2-6	33	+7.88	3-8	38	+2.00	0-0		+0.00
Redcar	1-4	25	-2.20	1-4	25	-2.20	0-0		+0.00	0-0		+0.00
Ripon	1-6	17	-2.00	0-1		-1.00	1-5	20	-1.00	0-0		+0.00
Salisbury	2-16	13	-4.50	1-5	20	-0.50	1-10	10	-3.00	0-1		-1.00
Sandown	5-29	17	+2.94	1-7	14	-5.56	3-15	20	+8.00	1-7	14	+0.50
Southwell (AW)	3-7	43	+18.50	0-1		-1.00	3-6	50	+19.50	0-0		+0.00
Thirsk	0-1		-1.00	0-1		-1.00	0-0		+0.00	0-0		+0.00
Warwick	1-7	14	-2.50	0-1		-1.00	1-5	20	-0.50	0-1		-1.00
Windsor	2-16	13	-5.00	1-6	17	-2.00	0-6		-6.00	1-4	25	+3.00
Wolves	3-26	12	-12.56	0-2		-2.00	2-20	10	-10.56	1-4	25	+0.00
York	4-25	16	-4.50	3-8	38	+6.50	1-10	10	-4.00	0-7		-7.00

Richard Fahey

A fairly disappointing year for Fahey, whose growing stock meant he was able to send out nearly 200 more runners than in 2006.

That should have seen him pushing for a first century of winners, but instead his total was two lower at 85 with his strike-rate dropping to an extremely modest nine per cent.

Fahey's strength lies with his older handicappers, and while one or two led the way last year, he will hope for more consistency in 2008.

By month

2007

	Overall			Two-year-olds			Three-year-olds			Older horses		
	W-R	%	£1	W-R	%	£1	W-R	%	£1	W-R	%	£1
January	3-37	8	-26.13	0-0		+0.00	0-11		-11.00	3-26	12	-15.13
February	4-32	13	+9.50	0-0		+0.00	1-13	8	+0.00	3-19	16	+9.50
March	2-31	6	-20.50	1-1	100	+5.50	0-5		-5.00	1-25	4	-21.00
April	7-68	10	-32.65	1-1	100	+0.73	0-29		-29.00	6-38	16	-4.38
May	9-109	8	-49.00	1-9	11	-5.50	2-36	6	-21.00	6-64	9	-22.50
June	11-104	11	-11.25	1-14	7	-2.00	1-37	3	-32.50	9-53	17	+23.25
July	12-117	10	-20.75	2-25	8	-15.25	8-39	21	+30.50	2-53	4	-36.00
August	14-142	10	-60.35	2-32	6	-21.25	6-46	13	-14.10	6-64	9	-25.00
September	11-129	9	-77.75	2-36	6	-25.25	3-29	10	-17.00	6-64	9	-35.50
October	7-88	8	-47.80	3-33	9	-18.80	0-18		-18.00	4-37	11	-11.00
November	1-37	3	-28.50	0-7		-7.00	1-13	8	-4.50	0-17		-17.00
December	4-32	13	+37.40	0-9		-9.00	1-10	10	-1.00	3-13	23	+47.40

2006

	Overall			Two-year-olds			Three-year-olds			Older horses		
	W-R	%	£1	W-R	%	£1	W-R	%	£1	W-R	%	£1
January	5-29	17	-1.29	0-0		+0.00	1-1	100	+3.33	4-28	14	-4.63
February	1-22	5	-18.25	0-0		+0.00	0-1		-1.00	1-21	5	-17.25
March	3-11	27	+8.83	0-0		+0.00	0-1		-1.00	3-10	30	+9.83
April	3-33	9	-15.70	0-0		+0.00	0-3		-3.00	3-30	10	-12.70
May	11-78	14	+3.02	1-6	17	-0.50	4-25	16	+18.50	6-47	13	-14.98
June	14-107	13	-24.83	0-7		-7.00	3-33	9	-11.00	11-67	16	-6.83
July	17-119	14	-22.60	3-13	23	+29.25	5-35	14	-16.75	9-71	13	-35.10
August	14-132	11	-2.25	4-33	12	-11.13	4-34	12	-0.50	6-65	9	+9.38
September	10-102	10	+26.25	4-24	17	+53.75	0-20		-20.00	6-58	10	-7.50
October	3-55	5	-24.63	0-7		-7.00	3-18	17	+12.38	0-30		-30.00
November	1-22	5	-19.25	0-3		-3.00	0-11		-11.00	1-8	13	-5.25
December	5-24	21	-7.35	0-1		-1.00	2-8	25	+0.67	3-15	20	-7.02

2005

	Overall			Two-year-olds			Three-year-olds			Older horses		
	W-R	%	£1	W-R	%	£1	W-R	%	£1	W-R	%	£1
January	2-15	13	-3.00	0-0		0.00	0-4		-4.00	2-11	18	+1.00
February	3-16	18	0.00	0-0		0.00	0-4		-4.00	3-12	25	+4.00
March	1-19	5	-10.50	0-0		0.00	0-5		-5.00	1-14	7	-5.50
April	7-63	11	+14.50	0-4		-4.00	2-27	7	+3.00	5-32	15	+15.50
May	12-102	11	+4.62	1-14	7	+7.00	4-33	12	-10.75	7-55	12	+8.37
June	7-125	5	-56.88	1-20	5	-13.50	1-38	2	-31.50	5-67	7	-11.88
July	21-113	18	+38.46	4-15	26	+11.75	8-26	30	+32.38	9-72	12	-5.67
August	13-110	11	-22.40	2-26	7	-10.50	3-34	8	-16.50	8-50	16	+4.60
September	7-92	7	-40.50	2-22	9	+3.00	2-29	6	-18.50	3-41	7	-25.00
October	3-52	5	-34.50	0-9		-9.00	1-16	6	-9.50	2-27	7	-16.00
November	2-35	5	-5.00	1-6	16	+3.00	0-12		-12.00	1-17	5	+4.00
December	1-24	4	-16.50	1-3	33	+4.50	0-11		-11.00	0-10		-10.00

All runners

2007	Wins	Runs	%	2nd	3rd	4th	Win prize	Total prize	£1 Stake
2yo	13	167	8	19	14	21	£63,190.25	£146,623.78	-97.82
3yo	23	286	8	26	35	35	£104,428.90	£197,738.49	-122.60
4yo+	49	473	10	56	58	50	£476,374.93	£788,114.70	-107.35
TOTAL	85	926	9	101	107	106	£643,994.08	£1,132,476.97	-327.77

2006	Wins	Runs	%	2nd	3rd	4th	Win prize	Total prize	£1 Stake
2yo	12	94	13	12	13	11	54,575.85	88,258.29	+53.38
3yo	22	190	12	23	19	18	186,619.32	279,548.68	-29.38
4yo+	53	450	12	61	39	46	436,684.91	730,600.38	-122.05
TOTAL	87	734	12	96	71	75	677,880.08	1,098,407.35	-98.05

2005	Wins	Runs	%	2nd	3rd	4th	Win prize	Total prize	£1 Stake
2yo	12	119	10	6	12	13	73,624.42	98,940.81	-7.75
3yo	21	239	9	25	19	24	112,485.41	172,727.53	-87.38
4yo+	46	408	11	41	44	32	301,452.78	530,221.89	-36.57
TOTAL	79	766	10	72	75	69	487,562.61	801,890.23	-131.70

By race type

2007

	Overall			Two-year-olds			Three-year-olds			Older horses		
	W-R	%	£1	W-R	%	£1	W-R	%	£1	W-R	%	£1
Handicap	61-676	9	-193.50	3-44	7	-29.25	19-220	9	-73.50	39-412	9	-90.75
Group 1,2,3	0-16		-16.00	0-1		-1.00	0-1		-1.00	0-14		-14.00
Maiden	11-141	8	-77.15	7-91	8	-48.55	4-49	8	-27.60	0-1		-1.00

2006

	Overall			Two-year-olds			Three-year-olds			Older horses		
	W-R	%	£1	W-R	%	£1	W-R	%	£1	W-R	%	£1
Handicap	61-545	11	-116.23	1-18	6	-15.25	17-146	12	-10.75	43-381	11	-90.23
Group 1,2,3	0-13		-13.00	0-1		-1.00	0-1		-1.00	0-11		-11.00
Maiden	11-91	12	+48.38	8-57	14	+62.63	2-29	7	-14.25	1-5	20	+0.00

2005

	Overall			Two-year-olds			Three-year-olds			Older horses		
	W-R	%	£1	W-R	%	£1	W-R	%	£1	W-R	%	£1
Handicap	60-543	11	-33.57	5-26	19	+27.00	15-160	9	-47.63	40-357	11	-12.94
Group 1,2,3	0-6		-6.00	0-2		-2.00	0-2		-2.00	0-2		-2.00
Maiden	6-116	5	-62.25	4-75	5	-35.25	1-34	2	-25.00	1-7	14	-2.00

By jockey

2007

	Overall			Two-year-olds			Three-year-olds			Older horses		
	W-R	%	£1	W-R	%	£1	W-R	%	£1	W-R	%	£1
P Hanagan	43-422	10	-146.93	7-80	9	-42.55	10-127	8	-67.00	26-215	12	-37.38
T Hamilton	18-140	13	-35.10	5-33	15	-3.00	7-48	15	-13.10	6-59	10	-19.00
J Moriarty	12-147	8	-30.00	1-26	4	-24.27	1-40	3	-27.00	10-81	12	+21.28
S De Sousa	2-5	40	+24.50	0-3		-3.00	2-2	100	+27.50	0-0		+0.00
D Gibson	2-76	3	-58.00	0-14		-14.00	1-29	3	-20.00	1-33	3	-24.00
J H Bowman	1-1	100	+5.00	0-0		+0.00	0-0		+0.00	1-1	100	+5.00
T P Queally	1-1	100	+6.50	0-0		+0.00	0-0		+0.00	1-1	100	+6.50
Miss A Ryan	1-2	50	+6.50	0-0		+0.00	1-1	100	+7.50	0-1		-1.00
S Drowne	1-2	50	+3.00	0-0		+0.00	0-0		+0.00	1-2	50	+3.00
P Cosgrave	1-4	25	+9.00	0-1		-1.00	0-0		+0.00	1-3	33	+10.00

By jockey ctd

2006

	Overall			Two-year-olds			Three-year-olds			Older horses		
	W-R	%	£1	W-R	%	£1	W-R	%	£1	W-R	%	£1
P Hanagan	57-384	15	-58.33	7-55	13	-21.13	16-90	18	+13.88	34-239	14	-51.08
T Hamilton	12-152	8	-6.61	3-26	12	+27.50	3-46	7	-19.50	6-80	8	-14.61
J Moriarty	5-53	9	-11.52	0-2		-2.00	2-22	9	+5.50	3-29	10	-15.02
D Gibson	4-21	19	+2.25	1-4	25	+5.00	0-7		-7.00	3-10	30	+4.25
Mr B McHugh	3-14	21	+7.50	0-0		+0.00	0-0		+0.00	3-14	21	+7.50
J-P Guillambert	1-1	100	+6.00	0-0		+0.00	0-0		+0.00	1-1	100	+6.00
S Sanders	1-2	50	+0.75	0-0		+0.00	1-1	100	+1.75	0-1		-1.00
G Fairley	1-3	33	+6.00	0-0		+0.00	0-1		-1.00	1-2	50	+7.00
R Ffrench	1-10	10	-3.00	0-1		-1.00	0-2		-2.00	1-7	14	+0.00
J Reveley	1-13	8	-11.09	0-0		+0.00	0-1		-1.00	1-12	8	-10.09

2005

	Overall			Two-year-olds			Three-year-olds			Older horses		
	W-R	%	£1	W-R	%	£1	W-R	%	£1	W-R	%	£1
P Hanagan	39-309	12	-23.05	8-44	18	+34.75	7-96	7	-61.63	24-169	14	+3.83
T Hamilton	22-247	8	-95.90	2-44	4	-30.50	8-83	9	-29.00	12-120	10	-36.40
R Ffrench	6-29	20	+27.50	1-7	14	+1.00	1-8	12	+13.00	4-14	28	+13.50
F Norton	2-3	66	+24.50	0-1		-1.00	1-1	100	+5.50	1-1	100	+20.00
N Lawes	2-31	6	-2.00	0-2		-2.00	0-9		-9.00	2-20	10	+9.00
S O'Hara	1-1	100	+4.00	0-0		0.00	0-0		0.00	1-1	100	+4.00
J Fanning	1-2	50	+1.75	0-0		0.00	1-1	100	+2.75	0-1		-1.00
Mr D Cottle	1-2	50	+4.50	0-0		0.00	0-0		0.00	1-2	50	+4.50
S Sanders	1-2	50	+9.00	1-1	100	+10.00	0-1		-1.00	0-0		0.00
W Supple	1-3	33	+3.50	0-0		0.00	1-2	50	+4.50	0-1		-1.00

By horse

	Wins-Runs	%	£1 level stakes	Win prize	Total Prize
Charlie Tokyo	2-8	25	+11.50	104,697.60	114,852.30
Greenwich Meantime	1-8	13	+7.00	74,784.00	80,641.50
Anna Pavlova	1-3	33	+2.00	28,390.00	52,612.50
Flying Clarets	2-11	18	+3.50	12,630.15	50,322.00
Mister Hardy	2-8	25	+0.23	12,012.30	39,259.19
Knot In Wood	1-9	11	-4.00	21,812.00	36,955.90
Fonthill Road	1-10	10	-2.50	22,669.50	36,471.35
Utmost Respect	1-4	25	-0.25	21,812.00	30,209.00
Benandonner	1-10	10	-4.00	17,234.00	26,654.00
Green Park	1-11	9	-4.50	18,696.00	26,250.00
St Savarin	2-6	33	+0.40	9,172.20	23,693.70
Sadler's Kingdom	3-11	27	+4.25	17,532.67	21,476.97
Bo McGinty	1-20	5	-12.00	6,477.00	21,469.70
Broken Applause	1-6	17	+6.00	2,817.49	20,703.74
Bolodenka	1-6	17	+1.50	12,464.00	19,093.40
Wyatt Earp	1-11	9	-3.50	12,954.00	18,645.90
Mutawaffer	0-3		-3.00	0.00	18,610.00
Peruvian Prince	1-10	10	+16.00	5,505.45	18,166.35
Fortunate Isle	2-9	22	+0.00	14,205.75	17,584.35
Music Review	2-12	17	-2.00	9,391.65	17,491.25
Torrens	2-17	12	-10.50	9,391.65	16,166.05
Rainbow Fox	2-16	13	+3.50	9,067.80	14,864.79
Rose Siog	2-5	40	+2.25	6,477.00	14,386.90
Flying Bantam	3-12	25	+7.00	10,843.65	13,808.65
Beldon Hill	3-8	38	+5.88	11,010.90	12,341.03
Trojan Flight	1-7	14	-0.50	3,886.20	11,657.50
Valley Of The Moon	0-12		-12.00	0.00	11,178.27
Dark Charm	1-13	8	-5.00	7,772.40	10,490.83
Cat Whistle	1-5	20	+2.00	9,715.50	10,394.48
Graceful Descent	1-6	17	-2.25	5,829.30	10,376.77

By course

	Overall			Two-year-olds			Three-year-olds			Older horses		
	W-R	%	£1	W-R	%	£1	W-R	%	£1	W-R	%	£1
Ascot	1-20	5	-14.00	0-2		-2.00	0-3		-3.00	1-15	7	-9.00
Ayr	7-51	14	-10.80	2-15	13	-9.05	2-15	13	+1.75	3-21	14	-3.50
Beverley	9-56	16	-6.75	0-8		-8.00	4-22	18	+2.00	5-26	19	-0.75
Carlisle	4-22	18	+17.50	0-5		-5.00	3-9	33	+26.50	1-8	13	-4.00
Catterick	1-23	4	-20.13	0-6		-6.00	0-7		-7.00	1-10	10	-7.13
Chester	3-20	15	+4.25	0-3		-3.00	0-5		-5.00	3-12	25	+12.25
Doncaster	0-18		-18.00	0-6		-6.00	0-0		+0.00	0-12		-12.00
Epsom	0-8		-8.00	0-1		-1.00	0-3		-3.00	0-4		-4.00
Folkestone	0-2		-2.00	0-0		+0.00	0-1		-1.00	0-1		-1.00
Goodwood	0-17		-17.00	0-2		-2.00	0-4		-4.00	0-11		-11.00
Hamilton	5-40	13	-15.25	0-3		-3.00	3-17	18	-5.25	2-20	10	-7.00
Haydock	3-38	8	+8.00	1-9	11	+3.00	0-11		-11.00	2-18	11	+16.00
Kempton	0-17		-17.00	0-3		-3.00	0-4		-4.00	0-10		-10.00
Leicester	1-11	9	-6.00	0-1		-1.00	0-6		-6.00	1-4	25	+1.00
Lingfield (AW)	1-18	6	-14.00	1-2	50	+2.00	0-3		-3.00	0-13		-13.00
Musselburgh	4-47	9	-30.50	2-5	40	+2.25	0-14		-14.00	2-28	7	-18.75
Newbury	0-11		-11.00	0-0		+0.00	0-1		-1.00	0-10		-10.00
Newcastle	6-43	14	+1.23	3-8	38	+8.23	1-13	8	-4.50	2-22	9	-2.50
Newmarket	0-13		-13.00	0-2		-2.00	0-3		-3.00	0-8		-8.00
Newmarket (J)	0-11		-11.00	0-2		-2.00	0-3		-3.00	0-6		-6.00
Nottingham	1-8	13	-5.50	0-2		-2.00	1-5	20	-2.50	0-1		-1.00
Pontefract	3-46	7	-28.75	0-10		-10.00	1-14	7	-7.00	2-22	9	-11.75
Redcar	4-35	11	-14.60	2-9	22	+4.00	2-17	12	-9.60	0-9		-9.00
Ripon	3-28	11	-7.50	0-7		-7.00	1-9	11	-0.50	2-12	17	+0.00
Salisbury	0-2		-2.00	0-0		+0.00	0-0		+0.00	0-2		-2.00
Sandown	0-5		-5.00	0-1		-1.00	0-1		-1.00	0-3		-3.00
Southwell	0-5		-5.00	0-0		+0.00	0-3		-3.00	0-2		-2.00
Southwell (AW)	12-63	19	+20.78	0-3		-3.00	2-18	11	+4.00	10-42	24	+19.78
Thirsk	4-32	13	-7.50	0-9		-9.00	2-14	14	-3.00	2-9	22	+4.50
Warwick	1-6	17	-0.50	0-0		+0.00	0-2		-2.00	1-4	25	+1.50
Wolves	5-130	4	-59.00	0-24		-24.00	1-49	2	-40.50	4-57	7	+5.50
Yarmouth	0-5		-5.00	0-1		-1.00	0-1		-1.00	0-3		-3.00
York	7-75	9	-24.75	2-18	11	-7.25	0-9		-9.00	5-48	10	-8.50

GREENWICH MEANTIME (left): nicely clear in the Chester Cup

Saeed bin Suroor

Godolphin emerged from the doldrums in no uncertain terms last year, moving Bin Suroor back up our list, and their hopes for 2008 will be pinned on Ibn Khaldun, the Racing Post Trophy winner born and bred by Sheikh Mohammed's operation.

The Godolphin trademark has become buying and improving older horses like Group 1 hat-trick hero Ramonti, and the stats show they are still underestimated in this sphere – their older Group runners returned a £25 profit last year to just £44 staked.

By month

2007

	Overall			Two-year-olds			Three-year-olds			Older horses		
	W-R	%	£1	W-R	%	£1	W-R	%	£1	W-R	%	£1
January	0-0		+0.00	0-0		+0.00	0-0		+0.00	0-0		+0.00
February	0-0		+0.00	0-0		+0.00	0-0		+0.00	0-0		+0.00
March	0-0		+0.00	0-0		+0.00	0-0		+0.00	0-0		+0.00
April	0-0		+0.00	0-0		+0.00	0-0		+0.00	0-0		+0.00
May	6-25	24	-7.41	0-1		-1.00	2-16	13	-11.14	4-8	50	+4.73
June	7-32	22	-12.08	0-2		-2.00	4-13	31	-5.08	3-17	18	-5.00
July	10-35	29	+0.21	1-2	50	+1.75	5-15	33	-4.34	4-18	22	+2.80
August	9-42	21	-12.35	1-7	14	-5.39	7-21	33	+1.53	1-14	7	-8.50
September	19-62	31	+4.44	6-11	55	+8.24	8-21	38	+7.74	5-30	17	-11.55
October	21-78	27	+19.46	7-32	22	-3.69	8-26	31	+4.17	6-20	30	+18.98
November	1-11	9	-8.38	1-3	33	-0.38	0-1		-1.00	0-7		-7.00
December	0-0		+0.00	0-0		+0.00	0-0		+0.00	0-0		+0.00

2006

	Overall			Two-year-olds			Three-year-olds			Older horses		
	W-R	%	£1	W-R	%	£1	W-R	%	£1	W-R	%	£1
January	0-0		+0.00	0-0		+0.00	0-0		+0.00	0-0		+0.00
February	0-0		+0.00	0-0		+0.00	0-0		+0.00	0-0		+0.00
March	0-0		+0.00	0-0		+0.00	0-0		+0.00	0-0		+0.00
April	0-0		+0.00	0-0		+0.00	0-0		+0.00	0-0		+0.00
May	1-12	8	-9.13	0-0		+0.00	1-8	13	-5.13	0-4		-4.00
June	6-19	32	+3.98	0-0		+0.00	3-11	27	+1.24	3-8	38	+2.74
July	8-25	32	-2.59	0-2		-2.00	4-11	36	-1.28	4-12	33	+0.69
August	16-40	40	+9.06	0-0		+0.00	9-22	41	+6.80	7-18	39	+2.26
September	17-51	33	+24.02	1-1	100	+1.20	7-24	29	+5.41	9-26	35	+17.41
October	18-73	25	-0.06	4-14	29	-2.02	9-33	27	+3.97	5-26	19	-2.00
November	4-27	15	-12.14	0-8		-8.00	3-13	23	-4.14	1-6	17	+0.00
December	0-0		+0.00	0-0		+0.00	0-0		+0.00	0-0		+0.00

2005

	Overall			Two-year-olds			Three-year-olds			Older horses		
	W-R	%	£1	W-R	%	£1	W-R	%	£1	W-R	%	£1
January	0-0			0-0			0-0			0-0		
February	0-0			0-0			0-0			0-0		
March	0-0			0-0			0-0			0-0		
April	1-3	33	+2.50	0-0		0.00	0-2		-2.00	1-1	100	+4.50
May	6-29	20	+17.16	1-3	33	+0.25	3-12	25	+5.41	2-14	14	+11.50
June	8-65	12	-35.71	1-12	8	-3.00	4-36	11	-24.08	3-17	17	-8.63
July	9-51	17	-8.18	5-14	35	+9.20	1-25	4	-16.50	3-12	25	-0.87
August	19-82	23	-7.34	7-33	21	-5.27	9-31	29	-0.40	3-18	16	-1.67
September	18-91	19	-16.90	10-52	19	-17.40	6-20	30	+7.00	2-19	10	-6.50
October	14-78	17	-7.67	10-42	23	+5.33	4-26	15	-2.99	0-10		-10.00
November	3-7	42	+3.65	3-6	50	+4.65	0-1		-1.00	0-0		0.00
December	0-0			0-0			0-0			0-0		

All runners

2007	Wins	Runs	%	2nd	3rd	4th	Win prize	Total prize	£1 Stake
2yo	16	58	28	14	6	4	£239,927.60	£297,442.97	-2.45
3yo	34	113	30	21	11	10	£200,326.60	£285,363.43	-8.11
4yo+	23	114	20	16	15	14	£794,286.48	£1,105,308.23	-5.55
TOTAL	73	285	26	51	32	28	£1,234,540.68	£1,688,114.63	-16.11

2006	Wins	Runs	%	2nd	3rd	4th	Win prize	Total prize	£1 Stake
2yo	5	25	20	4	3	3	18,459.45	24,238.50	-10.82
3yo	36	122	30	20	9	11	236,725.95	365,369.32	+6.88
4yo+	29	100	29	16	9	8	680,220.25	1,220,596.20	+17.10
TOTAL	70	247	28	40	21	22	935,405.65	1,610,204.02	+13.15

2005	Wins	Runs	%	2nd	3rd	4th	Win prize	Total prize	£1 Stake
2yo	37	162	23	31	22	12	194,094.70	274,683.90	-6.24
3yo	27	153	18	27	17	14	343,609.50	655,849.69	-34.58
4yo+	14	91	15	10	10	11	363,964.50	591,835.66	-11.67
TOTAL	78	406	19	68	49	37	901,668.70	1,522,369.25	-52.49

By race type

2007

	Overall			Two-year-olds			Three-year-olds			Older horses		
	W-R	%	£1	W-R	%	£1	W-R	%	£1	W-R	%	£1
Handicap	14-59	24	-11.82	1-3	33	+0.25	8-28	29	-6.05	5-28	18	-6.02
Group 1,2,3	12-44	27	+25.44	3-7	43	-0.06	1-5	20	-1.25	8-32	25	+26.75
Maiden	32-108	30	+5.71	10-44	23	-3.64	22-64	34	+9.35	0-0		+0.00

2006

	Overall			Two-year-olds			Three-year-olds			Older horses		
	W-R	%	£1	W-R	%	£1	W-R	%	£1	W-R	%	£1
Handicap	16-82	20	-0.09	0-0		+0.00	10-52	19	-11.84	6-30	20	+11.75
Group 1,2,3	9-42	21	-6.40	0-0		+0.00	0-7		-7.00	9-35	26	+0.60
Maiden	22-57	39	+1.94	5-24	21	-9.82	17-33	52	+11.76	0-0		+0.00

2005

	Overall			Two-year-olds			Three-year-olds			Older horses		
	W-R	%	£1	W-R	%	£1	W-R	%	£1	W-R	%	£1
Handicap	10-96	10	-30.37	3-12	25	+7.50	6-60	10	-22.88	1-24	4	-15.00
Group 1,2,3	5-54	9	-15.25	0-6		-6.00	2-16	12	-7.75	3-32	9	-1.50
Maiden	41-174	23	-14.14	29-126	23	-1.32	12-48	25	-12.82	0-0		0.00

By jockey

2007

	Overall			Two-year-olds			Three-year-olds			Older horses		
	W-R	%	£1	W-R	%	£1	W-R	%	£1	W-R	%	£1
L Dettori	37-120	31	-12.32	12-31	39	-0.83	15-39	38	-2.32	10-50	20	-9.18
K McEvoy	18-79	23	-16.18	3-12	25	+10.75	9-34	26	-13.96	6-33	18	-12.97
T E Durcan	10-35	29	+18.23	1-10	10	-7.38	3-15	20	-3.00	6-10	60	+28.60
K Darley	2-5	40	+9.50	0-0		+0.00	2-4	50	+10.50	0-1		-1.00
J Fortune	1-1	100	+1.50	0-0		+0.00	1-1	100	+1.50	0-0		+0.00
S Drowne	1-2	50	+5.00	0-0		+0.00	1-1	100	+6.00	0-1		-1.00
R Hills	1-4	25	+2.50	0-0		+0.00	1-2	50	+4.50	0-2		-2.00
D Holland	1-6	17	-2.00	0-0		+0.00	1-2	50	+2.00	0-4		-4.00
J Spencer	1-6	17	+3.00	0-2		-2.00	0-2		-2.00	1-2	50	+7.00
M Dwyer	1-8	13	-6.33	0-1		-1.00	1-6	17	-4.33	0-1		-1.00

By jockey ctd

2006

	Overall			Two-year-olds			Three-year-olds			Older horses		
	W-R	%	£1	W-R	%	£1	W-R	%	£1	W-R	%	£1
L Dettori	42-126	33	-3.44	4-14	29	-2.07	17-56	30	-10.02	21-56	38	+8.65
K McEvoy	16-52	31	+28.75	0-1		-1.00	9-27	33	+7.31	7-24	29	+22.44
T Durcan	4-25	16	+0.50	0-1		-1.00	4-14	29	+11.50	0-10		-10.00
T Queally	3-5	60	+4.45	0-0		+0.00	3-5	60	+4.45	0-0		+0.00
M Dwyer	2-4	50	+0.05	1-1	100	+1.25	1-2	50	-0.20	0-1		-1.00
S Sanders	1-2	50	+5.50	0-0		+0.00	1-2	50	+5.50	0-0		+0.00
D O'Donohoe	1-3	33	+1.33	0-0		+0.00	1-3	33	+1.33	0-0		+0.00
R Hills	1-6	17	+0.00	0-2		-2.00	0-1		-1.00	1-3	33	+3.00
D O'Neill	0-1		-1.00	0-0		+0.00	0-1		-1.00	0-0		+0.00
J Fortune	0-1		-1.00	0-1		-1.00	0-0		+0.00	0-0		+0.00

2005

	Overall			Two-year-olds			Three-year-olds			Older horses		
	W-R	%	£1	W-R	%	£1	W-R	%	£1	W-R	%	£1
K McEvoy	36-146	25	+47.66	14-52	27	+18.83	13-58	22	+2.88	9-36	25	+25.96
L Dettori	30-150	20	-30.69	17-58	29	+7.74	9-56	16	-16.92	4-36	11	-21.50
J Spencer	3-14	21	-6.75	1-6	17	-2.25	2-4	50	-0.50	0-4		-4.00
T P Queally	2-15	13	-9.13	1-6	17	-3.00	0-7		-7.00	1-2	50	+0.88
C Catlin	1-1	100	+9.00	0-0		+0.00	1-1	100	+9.00	0-0		+0.00
D O'Neill	1-1	100	+4.50	1-1	100	+4.50	0-0		+0.00	0-0		+0.00
S Kelly	1-3	33	+0.25	0-2		-2.00	1-1	100	+2.25	0-0		+0.00
S Sanders	1-5	20	-3.43	1-5	20	-3.43	0-0		+0.00	0-0		+0.00
W J Supple	1-7	14	-3.25	1-3	33	+0.75	0-4		-4.00	0-0		+0.00
E Ahern	1-9	11	-7.27	0-1		-1.00	1-7	14	-5.27	0-1		-1.00

By horse

	Wins-Runs	%	£1 level stakes	Win prize	Total Prize
Ramonti	3-4	75	+13.50	446,293.63	489,333.63
Ibn Khaldun	4-5	80	+5.02	146,904.75	147,169.30
Blue Ksar	2-7	29	-2.50	29,498.00	66,100.35
Rio De La Plata	2-4	50	+1.37	49,461.50	64,569.08
Stage Gift	1-1	100	+8.00	56,780.00	56,780.00
Laverock	0-3		-3.00	0.00	56,150.50
Scriptwriter	2-4	50	+5.73	32,614.00	51,917.50
Creachadoir	1-2	50	+1.75	28,390.00	49,418.92
Greek Renaissance	2-3	67	+12.20	34,476.60	34,476.60
Echo Of Light	1-2	50	+0.25	29,635.00	34,199.50
Winged Cupid	1-4	25	-1.25	14,762.80	30,892.80
Amarna	4-6	67	+5.41	27,136.09	30,223.69
Windsor Knot	1-2	50	+6.00	26,686.60	29,702.20
Kirklees	2-2	100	+2.48	28,362.40	28,362.40
Crime Scene	1-2	50	+7.00	26,686.60	28,136.50
Iguazu Falls	1-4	25	-2.70	2,914.65	24,629.05
Army Of Angels	1-2	50	+0.00	15,410.20	21,866.20
Fairmile	1-3	33	+1.50	9,348.00	20,724.20
Emirates Skyline	1-3	33	+3.50	16,516.35	18,580.85
Gongidas	3-6	50	+0.08	16,516.35	18,144.00
Bygone Days	0-4		-4.00	0.00	17,101.40
Short Skirt	1-1	100	+1.38	15,330.60	15,330.60
Measured Tempo	1-3	33	-1.64	14,762.80	14,762.80
Formal Decree	0-3		-3.00	0.00	14,741.20
New Guinea	1-4	25	-1.90	5,678.10	14,024.70
Opera Cape	1-4	25	+1.50	12,464.00	13,727.10
Fateh Field	1-2	50	+2.33	5,829.30	12,104.10
Dustoori	2-4	50	+4.17	8,355.33	11,714.13
Familiar Territory	1-3	33	+0.25	6,855.20	11,520.20
Tam Lin	0-4		-4.00	0.00	10,200.60

By course

2007

	Overall			Two-year-olds			Three-year-olds			Older horses		
	W-R	%	£1	W-R	%	£1	W-R	%	£1	W-R	%	£1
Ascot	4-23	17	-6.18	2-3	67	+1.82	0-3		-3.00	2-17	12	-5.00
Ayr	0-3		-3.00	0-0		+0.00	0-1		-1.00	0-2		-2.00
Bath	1-9	11	-2.50	0-2		-2.00	1-5	20	+1.50	0-2		-2.00
Beverley	1-2	50	+2.00	0-0		+0.00	1-2	50	+2.00	0-0		+0.00
Chester	0-3		-3.00	0-0		+0.00	0-1		-1.00	0-2		-2.00
Doncaster	2-17	12	-10.50	1-4	25	-0.25	1-5	20	-2.25	0-8		-8.00
Epsom	0-3		-3.00	0-0		+0.00	0-2		-2.00	0-1		-1.00
Folkestone	1-3	33	-0.63	1-2	50	+0.38	0-1		-1.00	0-0		+0.00
Goodwood	7-25	28	-2.28	2-4	50	+0.49	3-8	38	-3.27	2-13	15	+0.50
Hamilton	2-4	50	+3.23	0-0		+0.00	0-2		-2.00	2-2	100	+5.23
Haydock	0-4		-4.00	0-1		-1.00	0-0		+0.00	0-3		-3.00
Kempton	6-13	46	+1.21	2-3	67	+0.93	3-7	43	+0.03	1-3	33	+0.25
Leicester	2-7	29	-3.46	1-4	25	-2.56	0-2		-2.00	1-1	100	+1.10
Lingfield	2-4	50	+2.00	0-0		+0.00	1-3	33	+0.50	1-1	100	+1.50
Lingfield (AW)	3-11	27	+5.41	2-4	50	+8.91	1-7	14	-3.50	0-0		+0.00
Newbury	3-9	33	+5.70	1-2	50	+2.33	1-2	50	-0.64	1-5	20	+4.00
Newcastle	0-3		-3.00	0-1		-1.00	0-2		-2.00	0-0		+0.00
Newmarket	4-26	15	+1.13	0-5		-5.00	1-8	13	-4.25	3-13	23	+10.38
Newmarket (J)	1-12	8	-8.25	1-3	33	+0.75	0-4		-4.00	0-5		-5.00
Nottingham	6-9	67	+13.68	0-2		-2.00	5-5	100	+15.88	1-2	50	-0.20
Pontefract	3-8	38	+5.50	0-1		-1.00	2-4	50	+7.50	1-3	33	-1.00
Redcar	2-6	33	-2.99	0-1		-1.00	2-3	67	+0.02	0-2		-2.00
Ripon	2-3	67	+1.72	0-0		+0.00	2-2	100	+2.72	0-1		-1.00
Salisbury	0-2		-2.00	0-0		+0.00	0-1		-1.00	0-1		-1.00
Sandown	3-16	19	-7.00	0-2		-2.00	2-8	25	-1.50	1-6	17	-3.50
Thirsk	2-4	50	+4.00	0-0		+0.00	2-4	50	+4.00	0-0		+0.00
Warwick	0-6		-6.00	0-2		-2.00	0-3		-3.00	0-1		-1.00
Windsor	6-18	33	-6.10	0-2		-2.00	4-10	40	-2.85	2-6	33	-1.25
Wolves	2-7	29	+3.50	1-3	33	+5.00	1-4	25	-1.50	0-0		+0.00
Yarmouth	2-9	22	-3.05	1-5	20	-1.25	0-1		-1.00	1-3	33	-0.80
York	6-16	38	+11.75	1-2	50	+0.00	1-3	33	+0.50	4-11	36	+11.25

David Nicholls

A return to form for Nicholls, back in the top ten after a fairly rotten 2006 as he sent out 68 winners at a strike-rate of 12 per cent with almost as many seconds and thirds.

Known as the king of the sprint handicaps, Nicholls' big-race roll of honours bears out such a distinction, but it is more significant for punters to pay attention when Nicholls runs one in a maiden.

His runners in those races have returned healthy profits in two of the last three years, and in nearly every age category.

By month

2007

	Overall			Two-year-olds			Three-year-olds			Older horses		
	W-R	%	£1	W-R	%	£1	W-R	%	£1	W-R	%	£1
January	2-19	11	-10.25	0-0		+0.00	0-0		+0.00	2-19	11	-10.25
February	2-14	14	+5.00	0-0		+0.00	0-0		+0.00	2-14	14	+5.00
March	6-51	12	+3.50	0-2		-2.00	0-7		-7.00	6-42	14	+12.50
April	9-57	16	+37.00	0-0		+0.00	5-14	36	+41.50	4-43	9	-4.50
May	6-97	6	-73.75	0-4		-4.00	1-16	6	-11.50	5-77	6	-58.25
June	6-77	8	-18.63	1-10	10	-2.50	1-9	11	-6.13	4-58	7	-10.00
July	12-63	19	+16.38	1-7	14	-3.50	5-17	29	+7.13	6-39	15	+12.75
August	11-85	13	+49.41	4-13	31	+44.50	2-16	13	+25.00	5-56	9	-20.09
September	10-76	13	+32.33	4-9	44	+53.50	1-8	13	+13.00	5-59	8	-34.17
October	4-32	13	-9.88	0-0		+0.00	1-5	20	+4.00	3-27	11	-13.88
November	0-6		-6.00	0-0		+0.00	0-0		+0.00	0-6		-6.00
December	0-0		+0.00	0-0		+0.00	0-0		+0.00	0-0		+0.00

2006

	Overall			Two-year-olds			Three-year-olds			Older horses		
	W-R	%	£1	W-R	%	£1	W-R	%	£1	W-R	%	£1
January	2-40	5	-28.00	0-0		+0.00	0-1		-1.00	2-39	5	-27.00
February	1-11	9	-6.67	0-0		+0.00	0-0		+0.00	1-11	9	-6.67
March	3-48	6	-21.00	0-0		+0.00	0-4		-4.00	3-44	7	-17.00
April	6-75	8	-12.97	0-3		-3.00	1-6	17	-4.47	5-66	8	-5.50
May	7-100	7	-16.50	0-12		-12.00	0-6		-6.00	7-82	9	+1.50
June	8-89	9	+8.50	1-7	14	-2.00	0-6		-6.00	7-76	9	+16.50
July	8-92	9	-31.50	0-10		-10.00	2-11	18	-3.25	6-71	8	-18.25
August	15-115	13	-10.63	2-15	13	-2.00	3-12	25	-1.13	10-88	11	-7.50
September	6-75	8	-33.52	1-6	17	+11.00	0-7		-7.00	5-62	8	-37.52
October	3-20	15	-4.00	1-3	33	+1.50	0-3		-3.00	2-14	14	-2.50
November	0-6		-6.00	0-0		+0.00	0-1		-1.00	0-5		-5.00
December	0-3		-3.00	0-0		+0.00	0-0		+0.00	0-3		-3.00

2005

	Overall			Two-year-olds			Three-year-olds			Older horses		
	W-R	%	£1	W-R	%	£1	W-R	%	£1	W-R	%	£1
January	4-25	16	+47.00	0-0		0.00	2-3	66	+22.00	2-22	9	+25.00
February	0-11		-11.00	0-0		0.00	0-2		-2.00	0-9		-9.00
March	2-12	16	+39.00	0-0		0.00	0-1		-1.00	2-11	18	+40.00
April	4-84	4	-33.50	1-2	50	+2.00	2-8	25	+33.50	1-74	1	-69.00
May	12-112	10	+25.70	3-7	42	+20.88	0-15		-15.00	9-90	10	+19.83
June	17-93	18	+17.18	0-5		-5.00	1-10	10	-3.50	16-78	20	+25.68
July	14-100	14	-6.04	1-5	20	+2.00	3-10	30	+11.00	10-85	11	-19.04
August	9-65	13	-7.00	1-7	14	+3.00	2-8	25	+2.25	6-50	12	-12.25
September	5-66	7	-22.78	0-1		-1.00	0-7		-7.00	5-58	8	-14.78
October	0-15		-15.00	0-0		0.00	0-3		-3.00	0-12		-12.00
November	0-5		-5.00	0-0		0.00	0-0		0.00	0-5		-5.00
December	0-3		-3.00	0-0		0.00	0-0		0.00	0-3		-3.00

All runners

2007	Wins	Runs	%	2nd	3rd	4th	Win prize	Total prize	£1 Stake
2yo	10	45	22	8	5	3	£49,346.09	£61,574.26	+86.00
3yo	16	92	17	9	14	8	£72,800.94	£104,475.84	+66.00
4yo+	42	440	10	49	38	36	£266,534.95	£460,970.58	-126.88
TOTAL	68	577	12	66	57	47	£388,681.98	£627,020.68	+25.12

2006	Wins	Runs	%	2nd	3rd	4th	Win prize	Total prize	£1 Stake
2yo	5	56	9	3	8	8	£28,996.65	£41,928.51	-16.50
3yo	6	57	11	3	6	7	£36,260.55	£61,663.65	-36.84
4yo+	48	561	9	50	52	50	£355,895.74	£631,098.16	-111.94
TOTAL	59	674	9	56	66	65	£421,152.94	£734,690.32	-165.28

2005	Wins	Runs	%	2nd	3rd	rest	Win prize	Total prize	£1 Stake
2yo	6	27	22	7	1	3	71,040.45	108,752.90	+21.88
3yo	10	67	15	2	6	6	125,336.25	134,064.05	+37.25
4yo+	51	497	10	44	42	38	449,656.95	671,712.65	-33.57
TOTAL	67	591	11	53	49	47	646,033.65	914,529.60	+25.56

By race type

2007

	Overall			Two-year-olds			Three-year-olds			Older horses		
	W-R	%	£1	W-R	%	£1	W-R	%	£1	W-R	%	£1
Handicap	42-412	10	-25.29	2-6	33	+21.50	11-65	17	+40.75	29-341	9	-87.54
Group 1,2,3	1-8	13	-5.63	0-0		+0.00	0-0		+0.00	1-8	13	-5.63
Maiden	11-60	18	+89.88	7-30	23	+70.50	4-23	17	+26.38	0-7		-7.00

2006

	Overall			Two-year-olds			Three-year-olds			Older horses		
	W-R	%	£1	W-R	%	£1	W-R	%	£1	W-R	%	£1
Handicap	35-478	7	-113.38	1-9	11	-1.00	4-36	11	-20.13	30-433	7	-92.25
Group 1,2,3	0-14		-14.00	0-0		+0.00	0-1		-1.00	0-13		-13.00
Maiden	5-57	9	-35.97	3-37	8	-22.50	1-12	8	-10.47	1-8	13	-3.00

2005

	Overall			Two-year-olds			Three-year-olds			Older horses		
	W-R	%	£1	W-R	%	£1	W-R	%	£1	W-R	%	£1
Handicap	34-386	8	-103.82	0-2		-2.00	5-42	11	-11.25	29-342	8	-90.57
Group 1,2,3	2-13	15	+5.00	1-2	50	+5.00	0-0		0.00	1-11	9	0.00
Maiden	7-41	17	+73.00	4-10	40	+29.00	2-20	10	+21.00	1-11	9	+23.00

By jockey

2007

	Overall			Two-year-olds			Three-year-olds			Older horses		
	W-R	%	£1	W-R	%	£1	W-R	%	£1	W-R	%	£1
A Nicholls	40-297	13	+85.49	8-34	24	+89.50	7-53	13	+23.00	25-210	12	-27.01
S De Sousa	12-93	13	-15.25	1-7	14	-2.50	5-11	45	+18.25	6-75	8	-31.00
A Rothery	4-41	10	+14.88	0-0		+0.00	1-4	25	+17.00	3-37	8	-2.13
A Mullen	3-14	21	-2.13	1-1	100	+2.00	1-2	50	+0.88	1-11	9	-5.00
L Dettori	2-4	50	+4.50	0-0		+0.00	0-0		+0.00	2-4	50	+4.50
G Gibbons	2-5	40	+26.50	0-0		+0.00	1-1	100	+25.00	1-4	25	+1.50
Miss A Ryan	1-2	50	+4.00	0-0		+0.00	0-0		+0.00	1-2	50	+4.00
P J McDonald	1-3	33	-0.25	0-0		+0.00	0-0		+0.00	1-3	33	-0.25
P Hanagan	1-7	14	+12.00	0-0		+0.00	0-0		+0.00	1-7	14	+12.00
J Spencer	1-8	13	-4.50	0-0		+0.00	0-0		+0.00	1-8	13	-4.50

By jockey ctd

2006

	Overall			Two-year-olds			Three-year-olds			Older horses		
	W-R	%	£1	W-R	%	£1	W-R	%	£1	W-R	%	£1
A Nicholls	23-298	8	-165.53	5-39	13	+0.50	3-33	9	-23.84	15-226	7	-142.19
S De Sousa	10-81	12	+31.00	0-7		-7.00	1-5	20	-0.50	9-69	13	+38.50
V Behan	8-50	16	+37.75	0-0		+0.00	1-2	50	+1.75	7-48	15	+36.00
R Winston	4-24	17	+22.00	0-0		+0.00	0-0		+0.00	4-24	17	+22.00
J Fanning	4-38	11	-13.25	0-3		-3.00	1-1	100	+1.75	3-34	9	-12.00
S Carson	2-3	67	+17.50	0-0		+0.00	0-0		+0.00	2-3	67	+17.50
P Fessey	2-5	40	+31.00	0-0		+0.00	0-0		+0.00	2-5	40	+31.00
Mr S Dobson	1-2	50	+5.00	0-0		+0.00	0-0		+0.00	1-2	50	+5.00
T Culhane	1-5	20	-1.25	0-0		+0.00	0-0		+0.00	1-5	20	-1.25
M Stainton	1-6	17	+4.00	0-0		+0.00	0-0		+0.00	1-6	17	+4.00

2005

	Overall			Two-year-olds			Three-year-olds			Older horses		
	W-R	%	£1	W-R	%	£1	W-R	%	£1	W-R	%	£1
A Nicholls	40-273	14	+164.69	6-23	26	+25.88	7-39	17	+44.75	27-211	12	+94.06
D R McCabe	6-65	9	-15.38	0-3		-3.00	0-12		-12.00	6-50	12	-0.38
Victoria Behan	5-37	13	-8.88	0-0		0.00	1-4	25	+1.00	4-33	12	-9.88
P J Benson	3-40	7	-27.75	0-0		0.00	0-0		0.00	3-40	7	-27.75
K Fallon	2-3	66	+5.13	0-0		0.00	0-0		0.00	2-3	66	+5.13
J P Spencer	2-4	50	+3.75	0-0		0.00	0-0		0.00	2-4	50	+3.75
R Winston	2-11	18	+0.50	0-0		0.00	0-0		0.00	2-11	18	+0.50
F Norton	2-29	6	-16.00	0-0		0.00	1-5	20	+3.00	1-24	4	-19.00
M Halford	1-1	100	+6.50	0-0		0.00	1-1	100	+6.50	0-0		0.00
I Mongan	1-1	100	+3.00	0-0		0.00	0-0		0.00	1-1	100	+3.00

By horse

	Wins-Runs	%	£1 level stakes	Win prize	Total Prize
Tax Free	2-5	40	+1.13	35,868.40	44,161.30
Indian Trail	2-13	15	-4.50	29,913.60	38,822.10
Fremen	3-10	30	+26.00	33,067.90	37,375.20
Northern Fling	2-8	25	+37.00	25,540.50	29,436.90
Fol Hollow	3-9	33	+18.50	20,481.40	25,134.63
Northern Dare	3-10	30	+20.25	12,208.30	24,042.95
Turnkey	1-14	7	-3.00	9,348.00	22,910.00
Peace Offering	0-4		-4.00	0.00	22,239.20
Bahamian Pirate	1-12	8	+1.00	11,334.75	21,734.20
Moss Vale	0-3		-3.00	0.00	18,292.00
Continent	2-13	15	+18.00	15,544.80	17,901.90
Royal Dignitary	1-10	10	+11.00	9,348.00	14,795.35
Kabis Amigos	4-14	29	+19.00	11,784.80	14,329.25
Ice Planet	1-8	13	-2.00	9,715.50	13,591.60
Mandurah	3-11	27	+5.25	8,023.73	12,341.28
Machinist	1-7	14	+2.00	10,363.20	12,275.40
Merlin's Dancer	1-3	33	+10.00	11,217.60	11,870.80
Buachaill Dona	1-7	14	-2.67	7,772.40	11,141.90
Cape Vale	2-2	100	+33.50	11,010.90	11,010.90
Crocodile Bay	1-8	13	-1.00	3,562.35	9,470.27
Lucayan Dancer	1-14	7	-10.50	5,829.30	9,172.20
Shot To Fame	0-13		-13.00	0.00	9,161.05
Funfair Wane	2-17	12	-7.00	5,505.45	8,719.15
Sawwaah	3-6	50	+12.25	7,692.15	7,920.63
Tencendur	1-8	13	+7.00	4,728.21	7,692.76
Blackheath	1-17	6	-11.50	2,388.75	7,508.66
Fire Up The Band	1-9	11	+1.00	6,477.00	7,411.00
Pieter Brueghel	0-11		-11.00	0.00	7,262.35
Just James	3-8	38	+0.63	6,634.95	7,239.45
Maia	2-5	40	+8.00	5,968.50	6,546.30

By course

	Overall			Two-year-olds			Three-year-olds			Older horses		
	W-R	%	£1	W-R	%	£1	W-R	%	£1	W-R	%	£1
Ascot	0-14		-14.00	0-0		+0.00	0-0		+0.00	0-14		-14.00
Ayr	5-33	15	+7.25	3-4	75	+24.50	1-6	17	-2.25	1-23	4	-15.00
Bath	0-1		-1.00	0-0		+0.00	0-1		-1.00	0-0		+0.00
Beverley	0-13		-13.00	0-1		-1.00	0-2		-2.00	0-10		-10.00
Brighton	0-2		-2.00	0-0		+0.00	0-0		+0.00	0-2		-2.00
Carlisle	3-17	18	+7.50	0-3		-3.00	2-3	67	+15.50	1-11	9	-5.00
Catterick	6-39	15	-12.25	1-4	25	+0.50	3-12	25	+3.88	2-23	9	-16.63
Chester	2-20	10	-12.50	0-0		+0.00	0-3		-3.00	2-17	12	-9.50
Doncaster	0-12		-12.00	0-0		+0.00	0-1		-1.00	0-11		-11.00
Epsom	0-14		-14.00	0-0		+0.00	0-0		+0.00	0-14		-14.00
Goodwood	3-21	14	+32.00	1-1	100	+20.00	0-2		-2.00	2-18	11	+14.00
Hamilton	4-29	14	-7.25	0-4		-4.00	0-5		-5.00	4-20	20	+1.75
Haydock	4-18	22	+36.50	2-4	50	+37.50	1-5	20	+4.00	1-9	11	-5.00
Kempton	1-5	20	-1.50	0-1		-1.00	0-1		-1.00	1-3	33	+0.50
Leicester	1-7	14	+14.00	0-1		-1.00	0-2		-2.00	1-4	25	+17.00
Lingfield (AW)	2-14	14	+5.50	0-1		-1.00	0-1		-1.00	2-12	17	+7.50
Musselburgh	7-43	16	+8.37	1-3	33	+0.50	3-7	43	+19.63	3-33	9	-11.76
Newbury	0-1		-1.00	0-0		+0.00	0-0		+0.00	0-1		-1.00
Newcastle	3-32	9	-13.13	0-6		-6.00	1-6	17	+3.00	2-20	10	-10.13
Newmarket	1-9	11	-6.63	0-0		+0.00	0-2		-2.00	1-7	14	-4.63
Newmarket (J)	0-6		-6.00	0-0		+0.00	0-2		-2.00	0-4		-4.00
Nottingham	1-6	17	+4.00	0-0		+0.00	0-0		+0.00	1-6	17	+4.00
Pontefract	1-13	8	-2.00	0-0		+0.00	0-1		-1.00	1-12	8	-1.00
Redcar	1-18	6	-12.00	0-1		-1.00	0-3		-3.00	1-14	7	-8.00
Ripon	3-25	12	+18.00	1-7	14	-4.00	1-7	14	+12.00	1-11	9	+10.00
Sandown	1-6	17	-1.50	0-0		+0.00	0-0		+0.00	1-6	17	-1.50
Southwell	1-3	33	+0.75	0-0		+0.00	1-1	100	+2.75	0-2		-2.00
Southwell (AW)	5-44	11	-13.25	0-1		-1.00	0-4		-4.00	5-39	13	-8.25
Thirsk	5-41	12	+29.75	1-2	50	+27.00	1-10	10	+11.00	3-29	10	-8.25
Windsor	0-2		-2.00	0-0		+0.00	0-0		+0.00	0-2		-2.00
Wolves	6-38	16	+8.00	0-0		+0.00	0-2		-2.00	6-36	17	+10.00
Yarmouth	0-1		-1.00	0-0		+0.00	0-0		+0.00	0-1		-1.00
York	2-30	7	+1.50	0-1		-1.00	2-3	67	+28.50	0-26		-26.00

TAX FREE (centre): gets up on the line in the Palace House Stakes

Michael Jarvis

A mixed year for Jarvis, whose return of 68 winners was decent yet offset by a sharp fall in prize money.

Having topped £1 million in each of the previous two years, Jarvis managed just £685,000 in 2007 and will hope to reverse that trend this time.

Like Stoute and Bin Suroor, he is another of those trainers who place a small but select string of horses to good effect and therefore his runners are always worth a second look, winning with 18 per cent in both 2006 and 2007.

By month

2007

	Overall			Two-year-olds			Three-year-olds			Older horses		
	W-R	%	£1	W-R	%	£1	W-R	%	£1	W-R	%	£1
January	2-9	22	-1.42	0-0		+0.00	2-4	50	+3.58	0-5		-5.00
February	3-5	60	+5.74	0-0		+0.00	2-3	67	+0.24	1-2	50	+5.50
March	2-6	33	-1.34	0-0		+0.00	1-4	25	-2.09	1-2	50	+0.75
April	11-30	37	+21.95	0-0		+0.00	10-27	37	+21.70	1-3	33	+0.25
May	8-56	14	-30.44	0-2		-2.00	8-45	18	-19.44	0-9		-9.00
June	8-51	16	+5.00	2-10	20	+19.50	5-32	16	-13.00	1-9	11	-1.50
July	8-47	17	-17.44	0-5		-5.00	8-38	21	-8.44	0-4		-4.00
August	10-59	17	-8.72	1-13	8	-7.50	8-40	20	-8.22	1-6	17	+7.00
September	8-45	18	-14.75	3-18	17	-9.75	5-22	23	+0.00	0-5		-5.00
October	8-55	15	-8.88	7-34	21	+1.13	1-15	7	-4.00	0-6		-6.00
November	0-14		-14.00	0-7		-7.00	0-4		-4.00	0-3		-3.00
December	0-5		-5.00	0-1		-1.00	0-1		-1.00	0-3		-3.00

2006

	Overall			Two-year-olds			Three-year-olds			Older horses		
	W-R	%	£1	W-R	%	£1	W-R	%	£1	W-R	%	£1
January	3-11	27	+7.50	0-0		+0.00	1-4	25	+7.00	2-7	29	+0.50
February	0-6		-6.00	0-0		+0.00	0-1		-1.00	0-5		-5.00
March	0-6		-6.00	0-0		+0.00	0-4		-4.00	0-2		-2.00
April	8-35	23	+4.18	0-0		+0.00	8-28	29	+11.18	0-7		-7.00
May	9-46	20	-8.33	0-5		-5.00	7-28	25	-1.13	2-13	15	-2.20
June	7-60	12	-23.00	3-10	30	+7.25	2-37	5	-29.75	2-13	15	-0.50
July	9-45	20	+5.46	0-13		-13.00	7-24	29	+4.96	2-8	25	+13.50
August	11-59	19	-13.04	3-24	13	-14.25	8-26	31	+10.21	0-9		-9.00
September	10-52	19	-30.87	8-30	27	-14.59	2-13	15	-7.27	0-9		-9.00
October	11-50	22	+27.54	8-35	23	+21.04	1-9	11	-4.50	2-6	33	+11.00
November	1-13	8	-7.00	0-8		-8.00	1-3	33	+3.00	0-2		-2.00
December	4-13	31	+1.05	3-9	33	-2.95	1-1	100	+7.00	0-3		-3.00

2005

	Overall			Two-year-olds			Three-year-olds			Older horses		
	W-R	%	£1	W-R	%	£1	W-R	%	£1	W-R	%	£1
January	0-0		+0.00	0-0		+0.00	0-0		+0.00	0-0		+0.00
February	2-3	67	+13.00	0-0		+0.00	2-3	67	+13.00	0-0		+0.00
March	2-10	20	-1.50	0-0		+0.00	1-5	20	-0.50	1-5	20	-1.00
April	6-38	16	+27.50	0-0		+0.00	6-26	23	+39.50	0-12		-12.00
May	11-59	19	+5.10	2-4	50	+6.00	5-39	13	-21.40	4-16	25	+20.50
June	6-56	11	-31.50	0-11		-11.00	5-35	14	-13.75	1-10	10	-6.75
July	5-58	9	-21.95	0-17		-17.00	2-25	8	-20.45	3-16	19	+15.50
August	7-60	12	-14.25	2-21	10	-9.00	4-28	14	+3.00	1-11	9	-8.25
September	10-53	19	+0.03	5-22	23	+7.20	3-18	17	-6.50	2-13	15	-0.67
October	8-61	13	+11.25	2-32	6	-2.00	4-24	17	+10.00	2-5	40	+3.25
November	1-15	7	-3.00	0-5		-5.00	1-8	13	+4.00	0-2		-2.00
December	1-7	14	+4.00	0-2		-2.00	0-3		-3.00	1-2	50	+9.00

All runners

2007	Wins	Runs	%	2nd	3rd	4th	Win prize	Total prize	£1 Stake
2yo	13	90	14	16	8	11	£62,293.97	£94,056.01	-11.63
3yo	50	235	21	35	28	21	£361,474.35	£521,794.72	-34.67
4yo+	5	57	9	6	7	3	£27,683.10	£69,437.43	-23.00
TOTAL	68	382	18	57	43	35	£451,451.42	£685,288.16	-69.29

2006	Wins	Runs	%	2nd	3rd	4th	Win prize	Total prize	£1 Stake
2yo	25	134	19	24	19	13	£171,938.14	£261,548.52	-29.50
3yo	38	178	21	35	20	19	£260,353.90	£463,179.35	-4.31
4yo+	10	84	12	8	11	12	£203,698.30	£307,670.75	-14.70
TOTAL	73	396	18	67	50	44	£635,990.34	£1,032,398.62	-48.51

2005	Wins	Runs	%	2nd	3rd	rest	Win prize	Total prize	£1 Stake
2yo	11	114	10	5	10	15	£48,184.50	£77,033.60	-32.80
3yo	33	214	15	21	31	22	£425,527.24	£620,273.90	+3.90
4yo+	15	92	16	15	8	5	£474,620.98	£662,528.97	+17.58
TOTAL	59	420	14	41	49	42	£948,332.72	£1,359,836.47	-11.32

By race type

2007

	Overall			Two-year-olds			Three-year-olds			Older horses		
	W-R	%	£1	W-R	%	£1	W-R	%	£1	W-R	%	£1
Handicap	27-174	16	-42.48	1-6	17	-3.25	21-120	18	-25.23	5-48	10	-14.00
Group 1,2,3	1-13	8	-8.00	0-2		-2.00	1-10	10	-5.00	0-1		-1.00
Maiden	37-169	22	-3.15	11-73	15	+0.38	26-96	27	-3.52	0-0		+0.00

2006

	Overall			Two-year-olds			Three-year-olds			Older horses		
	W-R	%	£1	W-R	%	£1	W-R	%	£1	W-R	%	£1
Handicap	29-150	19	+18.50	2-11	18	+1.50	21-83	25	+16.00	6-56	11	+1.00
Group 1,2,3	1-22	5	-16.50	1-6	17	-0.50	0-6		-6.00	0-10		-10.00
Maiden	36-186	19	-57.11	19-104	18	-40.80	16-79	20	-15.31	1-3	33	-1.00

2005

	Overall			Two-year-olds			Three-year-olds			Older horses		
	W-R	%	£1	W-R	%	£1	W-R	%	£1	W-R	%	£1
Handicap	21-184	11	-11.50	2-18	11	-5.50	10-102	10	-14.25	9-64	14	+8.25
Group 1,2,3	4-24	17	+3.50	0-2		-2.00	1-9	11	-5.25	3-13	23	+10.75
Maiden	28-179	16	+2.10	9-89	10	-20.30	19-87	22	+25.40	0-3		-3.00

By jockey

2007

	Overall			Two-year-olds			Three-year-olds			Older horses		
	W-R	%	£1	W-R	%	£1	W-R	%	£1	W-R	%	£1
P Robinson	39-204	19	-37.94	11-60	18	+12.38	27-122	22	-31.56	1-22	5	-18.75
N Callan	11-48	23	-5.15	0-3		-3.00	10-33	30	+7.10	1-12	8	-9.25
R Hills	6-33	18	-8.29	1-11	9	-7.75	5-19	26	+2.46	0-3		-3.00
K Darley	3-7	43	+10.00	0-0		+0.00	3-7	43	+10.00	0-0		+0.00
M Henry	2-32	6	-20.17	0-7		-7.00	2-19	11	-7.17	0-6		-6.00
C Catlin	1-1	100	+6.50	0-0		+0.00	0-0		+0.00	1-1	100	+6.50
E Ahern	1-1	100	+9.00	0-0		+0.00	1-1	100	+9.00	0-0		+0.00
G Baker	1-1	100	+6.00	0-0		+0.00	1-1	100	+6.00	0-0		+0.00
J Fortune	1-2	50	+11.00	0-0		+0.00	0-0		+0.00	1-2	50	+11.00
R Moore	1-2	50	+0.50	0-1		-1.00	1-1	100	+1.50	0-0		+0.00

By horse

	Wins-Runs	%	£1 level stakes	Win prize	Total Prize
Silkwood	3-5	60	+4.80	90,337.49	91,744.20
Veracity	2-6	33	+1.12	15,922.87	65,909.30
Fragrancy	2-8	25	+8.00	25,005.00	31,722.96
Black Rock	3-6	50	+5.00	23,334.80	24,971.90
Yaqeen	2-5	40	-0.92	19,765.00	24,490.00
Blue Echo	1-5	20	-1.00	14,762.80	20,695.80
Kal Barg	2-4	50	+1.00	19,186.00	20,642.30
Harland	2-3	67	+3.24	18,649.00	18,649.00
We'll Come	1-5	20	-3.33	2,914.65	16,117.05
Irish Quest	2-9	22	-3.75	9,715.50	15,817.48
Mutanaseb	2-6	33	+0.38	11,010.90	14,088.10
Dichoh	2-11	18	-0.75	9,715.50	13,959.80
Ebn Reem	1-4	25	-1.00	9,971.20	13,443.60
Marozi	2-4	50	+2.00	12,940.07	13,421.07
Sunlight	1-5	20	+3.00	11,334.75	12,201.54
Rasaman	2-8	25	+2.25	9,391.65	11,982.63
Malyana	2-6	33	+2.75	11,789.25	11,789.25
Pressing	0-1		-1.00	0.00	10,006.13

By course

2007

	Overall			Two-year-olds			Three-year-olds			Older horses		
	W-R	%	£1	W-R	%	£1	W-R	%	£1	W-R	%	£1
Ascot	2-21	10	-11.00	0-4		-4.00	2-9	22	+1.00	0-8		-8.00
Ayr	1-2	50	+3.50	0-0		+0.00	1-2	50	+3.50	0-0		+0.00
Bath	0-4		-4.00	0-0		+0.00	0-3		-3.00	0-1		-1.00
Beverley	1-4	25	+7.00	0-1		-1.00	1-3	33	+8.00	0-0		+0.00
Brighton	1-2	50	+1.00	1-1	100	+2.00	0-1		-1.00	0-0		+0.00
Chepstow	0-1		-1.00	0-0		+0.00	0-1		-1.00	0-0		+0.00
Chester	2-8	25	+2.00	0-0		+0.00	2-5	40	+5.00	0-3		-3.00
Doncaster	2-8	25	+4.75	2-4	50	+8.75	0-4		-4.00	0-0		+0.00
Epsom	1-3	33	+0.25	0-0		+0.00	1-2	50	+1.25	0-1		-1.00
Folkestone	1-7	14	-3.25	0-1		-1.00	1-5	20	-1.25	0-1		-1.00
Goodwood	3-23	13	-10.50	1-5	20	+0.50	2-16	13	-9.00	0-2		-2.00
Hamilton	0-1		-1.00	0-0		+0.00	0-1		-1.00	0-0		+0.00
Haydock	4-15	27	+6.00	0-5		-5.00	3-8	38	+9.75	1-2	50	+1.25
Kempton	5-29	17	+4.63	2-6	33	+17.25	3-16	19	-5.63	0-7		-7.00
Leicester	1-14	7	-12.09	0-3		-3.00	1-9	11	-7.09	0-2		-2.00
Lingfield	3-7	43	+0.63	0-1		-1.00	3-6	50	+1.63	0-0		+0.00
Lingfield (AW)	8-34	24	-4.20	2-7	29	+3.63	6-17	35	+2.17	0-10		-10.00
Musselburgh	0-3		-3.00	0-2		-2.00	0-1		-1.00	0-0		+0.00
Newbury	1-9	11	-3.50	0-2		-2.00	1-7	14	-1.50	0-0		+0.00
Newcastle	1-4	25	-2.09	0-1		-1.00	1-1	100	+0.91	0-2		-2.00
Newmarket	3-25	12	-14.92	1-9	11	-6.25	2-14	14	-6.67	0-2		-2.00
Newmarket (J)	0-25		-25.00	0-2		-2.00	0-21		-21.00	0-2		-2.00
Nottingham	2-11	18	-6.00	0-3		-3.00	2-6	33	-1.00	0-2		-2.00
Pontefract	0-8		-8.00	0-2		-2.00	0-5		-5.00	0-1		-1.00
Redcar	1-6	17	+5.00	0-1		-1.00	1-5	20	+6.00	0-0		+0.00
Ripon	2-6	33	+2.50	0-1		-1.00	2-4	50	+4.50	0-1		-1.00
Salisbury	0-3		-3.00	0-0		+0.00	0-3		-3.00	0-0		+0.00
Sandown	4-22	18	-8.17	0-4		-4.00	4-18	22	-4.17	0-0		+0.00
Southwell (AW)	3-9	33	+11.25	0-2		-2.00	1-3	33	+7.00	2-4	50	+6.25
Thirsk	0-3		-3.00	0-1		-1.00	0-2		-2.00	0-0		+0.00
Warwick	2-5	40	+0.90	0-3		-3.00	2-2	100	+3.90	0-0		+0.00
Windsor	4-15	27	+19.00	1-4	25	+4.50	1-9	11	-4.00	2-2	100	+18.50
Wolves	4-16	25	-7.90	0-3		-3.00	4-12	33	-3.90	0-1		-1.00
Yarmouth	6-18	33	+4.92	3-10	30	+2.00	3-8	38	+2.92	0-0		+0.00
York	0-11		-11.00	0-2		-2.00	0-6		-6.00	0-3		-3.00

Top trainers by winners (Turf)

All runs			Trainer	First time out			Horses		
Won	Ran	%		Won	Ran	%	Won	Ran	%
113	750	15	M Johnston	22	170	13	70	170	41
105	796	13	R Hannon	7	134	5	69	134	51
97	438	22	Sir M Stoute	26	130	20	69	130	53
93	906	10	M Channon	7	125	6	62	125	50
76	551	14	B Hills	16	120	13	54	120	45
67	698	10	R Fahey	9	99	9	53	99	54
62	254	24	S bin Suroor	26	104	25	46	104	44
59	623	9	K Ryan	10	104	10	42	104	40
57	649	9	T Easterby	3	102	3	39	102	38
54	410	13	J Dunlop	11	97	11	39	97	40
54	476	11	D Nicholls	5	49	10	35	49	71
52	309	17	J Gosden	11	100	11	35	100	35
51	280	18	W Haggas	10	66	15	32	66	48
48	294	16	M Jarvis	11	83	13	32	83	39
45	202	22	H Cecil	9	56	16	27	56	48
45	403	11	B Meehan	11	118	9	36	118	31
41	238	17	L Cumani	9	64	14	25	64	39
39	274	14	G A Swinbank	10	60	17	24	60	40
39	397	10	T Barron	9	58	16	28	58	48
38	355	11	M Dods	2	47	4	24	47	51
37	284	13	M Bell	7	64	11	28	64	44
35	164	21	Sir M Prescott	5	35	14	15	35	43
35	277	13	B Smart	8	56	14	21	56	38
35	289	12	E Dunlop	8	72	11	28	72	39
35	354	10	J Goldie	7	41	17	22	41	54
35	409	9	K R Burke	5	74	7	26	74	35
34	179	19	J Noseda	5	53	9	20	53	38
32	213	15	R Charlton	5	58	9	21	58	36
32	214	15	J Fanshawe	6	61	10	25	61	41
32	329	10	W Brisbourne	2	40	5	15	40	38
31	296	10	B Millman	0	37	0	18	37	49
31	302	10	Mrs A Perrett	10	69	14	23	69	33
31	332	9	M Tompkins	2	58	3	22	58	38
30	193	16	P Chapple-Hyam	8	63	13	19	63	30
30	237	13	R M Beckett	10	58	17	26	58	45
30	296	10	I Semple	3	40	8	19	40	48
29	192	15	J A Osborne	1	37	3	12	37	32
29	243	12	H Morrison	5	41	12	16	41	39
29	244	12	R Harris	1	21	5	12	21	57
26	229	11	C G Cox	5	48	10	16	48	33
26	271	10	D Barker	1	22	5	12	22	55
26	297	9	C Brittain	0	48	0	19	48	40
25	185	14	B Ellison	4	26	15	13	26	50
25	261	10	D Elsworth	3	43	7	17	43	40
24	202	12	Mrs A Duffield	2	44	5	15	44	34
24	383	6	M W Easterby	3	64	5	14	64	22
22	258	9	A Balding	4	60	7	16	60	27
22	332	7	P Evans	4	44	9	12	44	27
21	144	15	C Wall	2	36	6	9	36	25
21	256	8	E Alston	3	37	8	16	37	43
20	185	11	P Cole	6	46	13	15	46	33

Top trainers by prize money (Turf)

Total prizemoney	Trainer	Win prizemoney	Wins
3,475,904	A P O'Brien	1,669,482	18
2,457,155	Sir M Stoute	1,636,310	97
1,884,031	P Chapple-Hyam	1,485,577	30
1,765,635	R Hannon	984,922	105
1,686,607	B Hills	1,132,743	76
1,646,577	S bin Suroor	1,215,777	62
1,581,574	M Channon	920,028	93
1,528,570	J Gosden	973,158	52
1,356,721	M Johnston	959,312	113
1,053,131	R Fahey	605,025	67
947,624	J Noseda	644,562	34
849,173	K Ryan	446,561	59
811,176	B Meehan	534,254	45
785,351	L Cumani	523,457	41
722,520	H Cecil	564,131	45
683,473	M Bell	528,288	37
669,652	W Haggas	490,888	51
668,075	J Dunlop	406,814	54
605,589	A Balding	452,795	22
578,083	M Jarvis	373,972	48
563,668	H Morrison	420,576	29
559,341	D Nicholls	338,141	54
542,650	T Easterby	319,915	57
527,433	J Fanshawe	394,888	32
488,337	R Charlton	383,858	32
481,688	B Smart	348,469	35
475,617	J A Osborne	233,871	29
465,341	E Dunlop	209,020	35
452,990	D Elsworth	209,890	25
421,986	C Brittain	201,677	26
416,624	C G Cox	272,033	26
395,112	K R Burke	197,848	35
373,338	J Bolger	348,289	2
372,989	M Tregoning	131,328	18
336,050	Mrs A Perrett	208,701	31
327,088	T Barron	192,800	39
327,086	J S Moore	221,666	18
319,085	A Fabre	267,987	3
298,862	B Millman	209,583	31
297,255	M Tompkins	174,285	31
283,370	G A Swinbank	191,519	39
282,251	R M Beckett	167,529	30
276,765	J Given	136,518	20
262,938	P Cole	173,460	20
260,972	J J Quinn	189,289	16
256,183	Mrs A Duffield	219,269	24
255,485	C Wall	171,937	21
252,741	B Ellison	147,388	25
248,291	J Goldie	150,261	35
245,407	G Huffer	219,229	4
245,116	M Dods	157,261	38

Top trainers by winners (AW)

Won	Ran	%	Trainer	Won	Ran	%	Won	Ran	%
	All runs			First time out			Horses*		
48	248	19	M Johnston	19	77	25	37	77	48
48	306	16	K Ryan	7	63	11	34	63	54
45	418	11	D Shaw	0	52	0	23	52	44
43	279	15	R Hannon	9	56	16	33	56	59
34	252	13	G L Moore	7	65	11	25	65	38
32	188	17	J A Osborne	3	41	7	21	41	51
31	147	21	Sir M Prescott	9	39	23	24	39	62
31	255	12	P Evans	5	40	13	17	40	43
27	174	16	K R Burke	5	39	13	15	39	38
24	177	14	J Boyle	3	35	9	15	35	43
24	204	12	R Hollinshead	3	35	9	12	35	34
23	205	11	D Ivory	2	41	5	11	41	27
23	230	10	J R Best	2	36	6	13	36	36
23	298	8	R Harris	2	51	4	15	51	29
22	79	28	J Noseda	4	22	18	19	22	86
22	123	18	H Morrison	9	31	29	14	31	45
22	269	8	P Howling	1	34	3	11	34	32
21	213	10	A J McCabe	0	32	0	8	32	25
20	88	23	M Jarvis	10	28	36	17	28	61
19	124	15	D Carroll	5	29	17	13	29	45
18	107	17	M Wallace	3	29	10	11	29	38
18	172	10	P Blockley	4	46	9	13	46	28
18	228	8	R Fahey	2	46	4	11	46	24
18	332	5	P Grayson	2	52	4	10	52	19
17	84	20	Jane Chapple-Hyam	3	22	14	13	22	59
17	101	17	I McInnes	2	23	9	8	23	35
17	126	13	P Cole	5	32	16	15	32	47
17	152	11	A Balding	5	37	14	14	37	38
17	255	7	W Brisbourne	2	37	5	12	37	32
16	59	27	Sir M Stoute	2	14	14	11	14	79
16	73	22	M Tregoning	8	32	25	13	32	41
16	91	18	G A Butler	2	18	11	7	18	39
16	94	17	M W Easterby	2	20	10	8	20	40
16	102	16	E Dunlop	4	32	13	11	32	34
16	129	12	S Kirk	2	17	12	13	17	76
16	141	11	B Meehan	5	37	14	12	37	32
16	172	9	N Littmoden	3	32	9	11	32	34
15	63	24	L Cumani	3	13	23	9	13	69
15	85	18	M G Quinlan	3	24	13	8	24	33
15	92	16	J Gosden	3	25	12	12	25	48
15	96	16	W Haggas	4	26	15	11	26	42
15	108	14	B Hills	4	30	13	14	30	47
15	125	12	S C Williams	4	23	17	11	23	48
15	158	9	P Hiatt	3	21	14	9	21	43
15	179	8	M Channon	3	37	8	10	37	27
14	67	21	T Dascombe	3	16	19	7	16	44
14	80	18	T Barron	2	19	11	11	19	58
14	83	17	I Semple	1	16	6	6	16	38
14	99	14	P Makin	3	18	17	10	18	56
14	101	14	D Nicholls	3	40	8	9	40	23
13	69	19	D M Simcock	4	17	24	9	17	53

Top trainers by prize money (AW)

Total prizemoney	Trainer	Win prizemoney	Wins
305,934	R Hannon	213,269	43
303,189	M Johnston	234,438	48
256,550	K Ryan	181,774	48
187,004	D Shaw	122,066	45
180,153	G L Moore	120,280	34
158,948	M W Easterby	144,445	16
149,324	K R Burke	107,695	27
149,102	G A Butler	112,421	16
144,040	J A Osborne	98,395	32
136,010	N Littmoden	79,377	16
124,568	P Evans	89,356	31
119,075	M Channon	73,001	15
118,477	Sir M Prescott	90,495	31
114,426	C Brittain	67,587	11
112,672	P Cole	78,617	17
110,159	J R Best	59,667	23
108,949	M Jarvis	79,122	20
108,805	J Boyle	69,562	24
108,025	J Noseda	79,678	22
105,908	R Hollinshead	75,239	24
105,691	A Balding	72,250	17
98,749	P Howling	59,795	22
98,253	E Dunlop	67,904	16
97,795	R Harris	62,690	23
97,164	A J McCabe	79,601	21
96,841	Jane Chapple-Hyam	74,540	17
96,733	W Haggas	57,241	15
94,289	Sir M Stoute	65,092	16
93,921	H Morrison	69,154	22
93,420	J Gosden	60,508	15
90,334	R Fahey	49,479	18
90,235	J S Moore	44,129	13
89,297	D Ivory	61,445	23
87,794	J Pearce	62,806	7
87,318	B Meehan	53,543	16
85,671	M Wallace	69,041	18
83,030	B Hills	53,694	15
82,710	P Grayson	47,142	18
82,187	I Semple	68,772	14
80,199	J Hills	39,299	13
75,935	D Nicholls	53,082	14
75,500	A Jarvis	43,613	13
75,011	L Cumani	57,117	15
73,913	P Makin	53,509	14
72,271	G Wragg	23,412	4

Profiles for punters looks at Clive Cox and Ann Duffield, see page 6

W-R	%	Jockey & Weight	Best Trainer	W-R
136-704	19	**J P Spencer** 8-7	M Bell	18-70
127-737	17	**S Sanders** 8-7	Sir M Prescott	21-93
115-574	20	**R L Moore** 8-6	Sir M Stoute	44-168
96-634	15	**R Hughes** 8-7	R Hannon	36-233
86-695	12	**T E Durcan** 8-5	H Cecil	27-121
84-488	17	**K McEvoy** 8-3	Sir M Stoute	17-77
83-568	15	**J Fortune** 8-6	J Gosden	29-158
79-645	12	**N Callan** 8-5	K Ryan	29-267
71-669	11	**P Hanagan** 8-0	R Fahey	36-309
69-351	20	**L Dettori** 8-7	S bin Suroor	32-112
65-596	11	**S Drowne** 8-5	R Charlton	17-105
60-376	16	**R Hills** 8-4	B Hills	12-68
59-700	8	**T Eaves** 8-5	I Semple	19-191
57-493	12	**K Darley** 8-4	M Johnston	12-89
57-637	9	**R Ffrench** 8-0	Mrs A Duffield	15-130
56-410	14	**Greg Fairley** 8-3	M Johnston	46-228
55-513	11	**D Holland** 8-0	M Channon	18-171
54-530	10	**D Allan** 8-2	T Easterby	42-337
52-486	11	**Martin Dwyer** 8-0	J A Osborne	6-32
51-346	15	**P Robinson** 8-3	M Jarvis	29-169
47-504	9	**Jim Crowley** 9-0	Mrs A Perrett	16-156
47-565	8	**E Ahern** 8-3	J Dunlop	8-72
46-517	9	**C Catlin** 8-0	M Channon	10-64
45-579	8	**P Mulrennan** 8-4	W Haggas	7-34
44-380	12	**M Hills** 8-6	B Hills	34-258
42-460	9	**P Makin** 8-4	M Dods	16-159
41-331	12	**T P Queally** 8-5	J Given	11-91
41-376	11	**F Norton** 8-0	A Balding	10-72
40-308	13	**William Buick** 8-5	A Balding	7-63
38-307	12	**Liam Jones** 7-8	W Haggas	12-53
38-512	7	**J Quinn** 7-12	M Tompkins	16-127
36-473	8	**J F Egan** 8-2	J S Moore	8-99
36-477	8	**T Hamilton** 8-2	R Fahey	16-122
35-388	9	**R Mullen** 8-2	E S McMahon	9-43
34-262	13	**J Fanning** 8-2	M Johnston	18-131
34-359	9	**T P O'Shea** 8-2	M Channon	22-196
34-452	8	**M Fenton** 8-5	T Tate	11-73
33-469	7	**Dane O'Neill** 8-5	H Candy	6-74
32-421	8	**P Cosgrave** 8-4	K R Burke	12-112
31-262	12	**G Baker** 8-9	C Wall	9-44
31-281	11	**J H Bowman** 8-5	M Channon	14-140
30-354	8	**A Nicholls** 7-12	D Nicholls	29-238
27-338	8	**T Quinn** 8-4	P Cole	8-62
27-367	7	**P Fessey** 7-12	T Barron	14-134
26-221	12	**N Mackay** 7-12	L Cumani	16-87
25-241	10	**Luke Morris** 7-8	R Harris	8-64
25-310	8	**G Gibbons** 8-2	J J Quinn	10-133
25-367	7	**D Sweeney** 8-6	W S Kittow	4-24
24-310	8	**A Elliott** 7-6	I McInnes	4-21
24-351	7	**A Kirby** 9-7	W R Swinburn	14-151
23-304	8	**Jamie Moriarty** 8-5	B Ellison	6-27

Sponsored by Stan James

W-R	%	Jockey & Weight	Best Trainer	W-R
91-490	19	**N Callan** 8-5	K Ryan	20-89
86-504	17	**S Sanders** 8-7	Sir M Prescott	17-72
71-327	22	**J P Spencer** 8-7	L Cumani	6-13
65-761	9	**C Catlin** 8-0	E J O'Neill	8-37
59-467	13	**Dane O'Neill** 8-5	D Shaw	4-43
47-370	13	**T P Queally** 8-5	J Given	9-41
44-331	13	**G Baker** 8-9	G L Moore	13-55
44-425	10	**Jim Crowley** 9-0	J A Osborne	4-16
42-230	18	**R Hughes** 8-7	R Hannon	16-81
42-392	11	**E Ahern** 8-3	M Wallace	6-18
41-295	14	**J F Egan** 8-2	Jane Chapple-Hyam	7-22
41-368	11	**S Drowne** 8-5	H Morrison	8-40
39-198	20	**J Fanning** 8-2	M Johnston	19-62
37-344	11	**D Sweeney** 8-6	K R Burke	10-33
34-362	9	**R Havlin** 8-4	R Ingram	6-40
33-408	8	**Hayley Turner** 7-9	M Usher	5-49
32-370	9	**A Kirby** 9-7	C G Cox	6-24
31-292	11	**S Donohoe** 8-5	P Evans	8-49
30-336	9	**M Fenton** 8-5	Stef Liddiard	8-48
29-455	6	**L Keniry** 8-3	S Kirk	7-41
28-197	14	**P Cosgrave** 8-4	J Boyle	8-33
28-254	11	**P Mulrennan** 8-4	M W Easterby	5-28
27-177	15	**D Tudhope** 8-4	I McInnes	7-38
27-299	9	**Dean McKeown** 8-3	D Shaw	16-122
26-226	12	**William Buick** 8-5	B Johnson	2-4
26-314	8	**Liam Jones** 7-8	W Haggas	8-38
25-146	17	**J Fortune** 8-6	J Gosden	12-49
25-198	13	**I Mongan** 8-6	P Howling	6-40
24-327	7	**J Quinn** 7-12	P Howling	3-29
24-356	7	**J Doyle** 7-12	N Littmoden	4-49
23-153	15	**R Kingscote** 8-2	T Dascombe	6-26
20-141	14	**N Mackay** 7-12	M Wigham	7-16
20-169	12	**Greg Fairley** 8-3	M Johnston	10-68
20-267	7	**J-P Guillambert** 8-6	R Brotherton	3-14
19-146	13	**S W Kelly** 8-6	J A Osborne	3-18
19-265	7	**P Hanagan** 8-0	R Fahey	5-81
18-129	14	**P Makin** 8-4	I Semple	6-16
18-159	11	**Martin Dwyer** 8-0	J A Osborne	6-14
17-186	9	**P Doe** 8-3	W J Knight	5-33
17-209	8	**J M O'Dwyer** 8-8	M G Quinlan	4-16
16-142	11	**A Elliott** 7-6	A Hales	2-4
16-164	10	**P Dobbs** 8-4	R Hannon	7-50
16-177	9	**R Kennemore** 7-11	R Hollinshead	10-72
16-216	7	**F Norton** 8-0	A Balding	4-30
15-112	13	**Kirsty Milczarek** 7-12	D M Simcock	7-16
15-125	12	**A Culhane** 8-2	D Cantillon	1-2
15-126	12	**P Hills** 7-10	D Shaw	5-25
15-151	10	**S Hitchcott** 8-7	N J Vaughan	4-12
15-191	8	**D Fentiman** 7-8	M Johnston	1-1
14-134	10	**Hadden Frost** 8-5	R Hannon	5-24
13-45	29	**R Hills** 8-4	Sir M Stoute	4-5

Top apprentices

W-R	%	Jockey & Weight	Best Trainer	W-R
76-579	13	**Greg Fairley** 8-2	M Johnston	56-296
64-621	10	**Liam Jones** 7-8	W Haggas	20-91
52-656	8	**S Donohoe** 8-4	P Evans	19-186
44-369	12	**R Kingscote** 8-4	T Dascombe	13-52
40-452	9	**A Elliott** 7-13	I McInnes	6-30
40-616	6	**J Doyle** 8-4	R M Beckett	7-48
38-368	10	**Luke Morris** 7-8	R Harris	13-98
30-542	6	**D Fentiman** 7-7	T Easterby	7-133
26-392	7	**T Dean** 7-8	P Cole	7-35
26-397	7	**A Mullen** 8-0	W J H Ratcliffe	5-39
25-331	8	**R Kennemore** 7-12	R Hollinshead	14-126
25-382	7	**J M O'Dwyer** 8-8	M G Quinlan	7-62
24-251	10	**M Stainton** 8-2	R Whitaker	8-109

Figures include all riders who were apprentices at the start of the year

GREG FAIRLEY: driving out another winner as Suzi Spends triumphs at Windsor

Sponsored by Stan James

Group One records

Year	Winner	Age (if appropriate)	Trainer	Jockey	SP	draw/ran

2,000 Guineas (1m) Newmarket

Year	Winner	Trainer	Jockey	SP	draw/ran
1998	**King Of Kings**	A O'Brien	M Kinane	7-2	17/18
1999	**Island Sands**	S bin Suroor	L Dettori	10-1	3/16
2000	**King's Best**	Sir M Stoute	K Fallon	13-2	12/27
2001	**Golan**	Sir M Stoute	K Fallon	11-1	19/18
2002	**Rock Of Gibraltar**	A O'Brien	J Murtagh	9-1	22/22
2003	**Refuse To Bend**	D Weld	P Smullen	9-2	18/20
2004	**Haafhd**	B Hills	R Hills	11-2	4/14
2005	**Footstepsinthesand**	A O'Brien	K Fallon	13-2	17/19
2006	**George Washington**	A O'Brien	K Fallon	6-4f	6/14
2007	**Cockney Rebel**	G Huffer	O Peslier	25-1	15/24

THE FIRST colts' Classic was first run in 1809 and is usually held on the first Saturday in May. It's increasingly become a specialist miler's race rather than a stepping stone to the Derby, with only Golan going on to meet any success over middle distances among recent winners. As with the 1,000 Guineas, you don't get many winners who haven't earned themselves a high place in the International Classifications, although Island Sands and, to a lesser extent, Cockney Rebel bucked that trend. King Of Kings, Rock of Gibraltar and George Washington were all Group One winners at two, Rock of Gibraltar taking the Dewhurst, which has proved the best trial (the Racing Post Trophy, in contrast, has produced only one winner, High Top). It therefore follows that winners have nearly all been well fancied, though favourites had a desperate record until George Washington's win, with Xaar and One Cool Cat the most high-profile failures. Newmarket's Craven Stakes has traditionally proved a far better guide than Newbury's Greenham, with Haafhd winning in 2004, but most winners are now making their seasonal debuts, including Cockney Rebel, George Washington, Footstepsinthesand, Rock Of Gibraltar, Golan, Island Sands, King Of Kings, Entrepreneur, Mark Of Esteem and Mister Baileys since the mid-Nineties.

1,000 Guineas (1m) Newmarket

Year	Winner	Trainer	Jockey	SP	draw/ran
1998	**Cape Verdi**	S bin Suroor	L Dettori	10-3jf	7/16
1999	**Wince**	H Cecil	K Fallon	4-1f	19/22
2000	**Lahan**	J Gosden	R Hills	14-1	10/18
2001	**Ameerat**	M Jarvis	P Robinson	11-1	10/18
2002	**Kazzia**	S bin Suroor	L Dettori	14-1	12/17
2003	**Russian Rhythm**	Sir M Stoute	K Fallon	12-1	2/19
2004	**Attraction**	M Johnston	K Darley	11-2	8/16
2005	**Virginia Waters**	A O'Brien	K Fallon	12-1	1/20

| 2006 | **Speciosa** | | Mrs P Sly | M Fenton | 10-1 | 3/13 |
| 2007 | **Finsceal Beo** | | J Bolger | K Manning | 5-4f | 8/21 |

FIRST RUN in 1814, since 1995 the first fillies' Classic has been run on a Sunday. A more worrying change for punters has been the parade of fancied horses beaten, with Finsceal Beo the first winning favourite since Wince in 1999 and only the second returned at single-figures. The early-season form of Newbury's Fred Darling and Newmarket's Nell Gwyn has often worked out well, but six winners were making their seasonal reappearance – traditionally the Prix Marcel Boussac and the Cheveley Park are the races to study from the previous year. Proven course form is key – Attraction had won the Cheveley Park, Russian Rhythm had come second, and Finsceal Beo, Lahan and Speciosa won the Rockfel, Speciosa following up in the Nell Gwyn.

Lockinge (1m) Newbury

1998	**Cape Cross**	4	S bin Suroor	D O'Donohoe	20-1	8/10
1999	**Fly To The Stars**	5	S bin Suroor	W Supple	9-1	6/6
2000	**Aljabr**	4	S bin Suroor	L Dettori	8-13f	1/7
2001	**Medicean**	4	Sir M Stoute	K Fallon	3-1	5/7
2002	**Keltos**	4	C Laffon-Parias	O Peslier	9-1	7/10
2003	**Hawk Wing**	4	A O'Brien	M Kinane	2-1f	4/6
2004	**Russian Rhythm**	4	Sir M Stoute	K Fallon	3-1f	3/15
2005	**Rakti**	6	M Jarvis	P Robinson	7-4f	5/8
2006	**Soviet Song**	6	J Fanshawe	J Spencer	7-2f	10/10
2007	**Red Evie**	4	M Bell	J Spencer	8-1	7/8

OFTEN QUITE weak for a Group 1, the Lockinge was a Godolphin benefit in the late 1990s. Now, though, it is more for the benefit of punters, with four of the last five favourites doing the business. Four-year-olds had long held sway until Rakti and Soviet Song bucked the trend. Russian Rhythm bucked another strong trend when becoming the first winning filly for 20 years in 2004, since when Soviet Song and Red Evie have also triumphed.

Coronation Cup (1m4f) Epsom

1998	**Silver Patriarch**	4	J Dunlop	Pat Eddery	7-2	2/7
1999	**Daylami**	5	S bin Suroor	L Dettori	9-2	3/7
2000	**Daliapour**	4	Sir M Stoute	K Fallon	11-8f	2/4
2001	**Mutafaweq**	5	S bin Suroor	L Dettori	11-2	1/6
2002	**Boreal**	4	P Schiergen	K Fallon	4-1	3/6
2003	**Warrsan**	5	C Brittain	P Robinson	9-2	4/9
2004	**Warrsan**	5	C Brittain	D Holl5and	7-1	5/11
2005	**Yeats**	4	A O'Brien	K Fallon	5-1	9/7
2006	**Shirocco**	5	A Fabre	C Soumillon	8-11f	5/6
2007	**Scorpion**	5	A O'Brien	M Kinane	8-1	2/7

IT'S HARD to escape the conclusion that this race is suffering a fall from grace, with the quality of winner dropping markedly, even within the last ten years, though Shirocco was at least out of the top drawer. That might sound harsh on a grand campaigner like Warrsan, but even that tough old favourite was hardly outstanding and Yeats and Scorpion were able to win over trips probably short of their best. The race almost always features a small field, and bearing that in mind the record of favourites is fairly poor with only two successful in the last ten years. The combination of a false pace and the tricky course could be responsible for some funny results, such as Silver Patriarch beating Swain in 1998.

The Oaks (1m4f) Epsom

Year	Horse	Trainer	Jockey	Odds	
1998	**Shahtoush**	A O'Brien	M Kinane	12-1	5/8
1999	**Ramruma**	H Cecil	K Fallon	3-1	5/10
2000	**Love Divine**	H Cecil	T Quinn	9-4f	3/16
2001	**Imagine**	A O'Brien	M Kinane	3-1f	10/14
2002	**Kazzia**	S bin Suroor	L Dettori	100-30f	13/14
2003	**Casual Look**	A Balding	Martin Dwyer	10-1	7/15
2004	**Ouija Board**	E Dunlop	K Fallon	7-2	3/7
2005	**Eswarah**	M Jarvis	R Hills	11-4jf	2/12
2006	**Alexandrova**	A O'Brien	K Fallon	9-4f	1/10
2007	**Light Shift**	H Cecil	T Durcan	13-2	11/14

FIRST RUN in 1779, the Oaks is one year older then the Derby. Breeding is critical since so few three-year-old fillies stay so far at this time of the year. However, there seems few clues from the racecourse performances of the winners – Shahtoush, Imagine, Kazzia and Casual Look had never run beyond a mile previously, whereas Ramruma, Love Divine, Ouija Board, Eswarah and Light Shift had all won over at least 10 furlongs (and Alexandrova was second in the Musidora). It rarely pays to look beyond the market principles – Light Shift was one of only two winners since 1999 priced bigger than 7-2.

The Derby (1m4f) Epsom

Year	Horse	Trainer	Jockey	Odds	
1998	**High-Rise**	L Cumani	O Peslier	20-1	14/15
1999	**Oath**	H Cecil	K Fallon	13-2	1/16
2000	**Sinndar**	J Oxx	J Murtagh	7-1	15/15
2001	**Galileo**	A O'Brien	M Kinane	11-4j	10/12
2002	**High Chaparral**	A O'Brien	J Murtagh	7-2	9/12
2003	**Kris Kin**	Sir M Stoute	K Fallon	6-1	4/20
2004	**North Light**	Sir M Stoute	K Fallon	7-2jf	6/14
2005	**Motivator**	M Bell	J Murtagh	3-1f	5/13
2006	**Sir Percy**	M Tregoning	M Dwyer	6-1	10/18
2007	**Authorized**	P Chapple-Hyam	L Dettori	5-4f	14/17

MANY HIGH-CLASS colts are beaten here due to lack of stamina. It's important to have a top-class sire plus a staying pedigree on the dam's side. Since the golden years of Nijinsky and Mill Reef (1970 and 1971) only one horse, Nashwan, has won both the 2,000 Guineas and Derby, although Dancing Brave was unlucky at Epsom having landed the Newmarket race and Sir Percy built on his Guineas second. The previous nine winners had all won recognised trials with four Dante winners (Benny The Dip, North Light, Motivator and Authorized), three Leopardstown winners (Sinndar, Galileo and High Chaparral), two Chester winners (Oath and Kris Kin) and one Lingfield winner (High-Rise). Generally this is a race for fancied runners from the first four in the betting – 20-1 winner High-Rise was the biggest priced winner for 25 years.

Queen Anne Stakes (1m) Royal Ascot

Year	Horse	Age	Trainer	Jockey	Odds	
1998	**Intikhab**	4	S bin Suroor	L Dettori	9-4	6/9
1999	**Cape Cross**	5	S bin Suroor	G Stevens	7-1	2/8
2000	**Kalanisi**	4	Sir M Stoute	K Fallon	11-2	11/11
2001	**Medicean**	4	Sir M Stoute	K Fallon	11-2	8/10
2002	**No Excuse Needed**	4	Sir M Stoute	J Murtagh	13-2	11/12
2003	**Dubai Destination**	4	S bin Suroor	L Dettori	9-2	10/10
2004	**Refuse To Bend**	4	S bin Suroor	L Dettori	12-1	1/16
2005	**Valixir**	4	A Fabre	C Soumillon	4-1	1/10*

| 2006 | **Ad Valorem** | 4 | A O'Brien | K Fallon | 13-2 | 2/7 |
| 2007 | **Ramonti** | 5 | S bin Suroor | L Dettori | 5-1 | 2/8 |

Formerly Group 3. Group 2 from 1985, Group 1 from 2003.
**Note – all Royal Ascot races were run at York in 2005*

USUALLY won by Saeed bin Suroor or Sir Michael Stoute. Unbelievably, from Nicolotte's win in 1995 to Valixir's defeat of Rakti ten years later, Godolphin or Stoute won every single renewal, and the pair had the one-two last year. Four-year-olds who were once considered Classic contenders fit the bill and this age group has taken 12 of the last 14 runnings. The Lockinge Stakes was a key race but is becoming slightly unreliable as a guide. Medicean won both races in 2001 and Ramonti had been second at Newbury, but No Excuse Needed ran a feeble race there before landing this and two of the most impressive Group 1 winners of recent times, Hawk Wing and Rakti, were beaten when well fancied to follow up here while Soviet Song could only fill second to Ad Valorem last year.

Prince Of Wales's Stakes (1m2f) Royal Ascot

1998	**Faithful Son**	4	S bin Suroor	J Reid	11-2	7/8
1999	**Lear Spear**	4	D Elsworth	M Kinane	20-1	5/8
2000	**Dubai Millennium**	4	S bin Suroor	J Bailey	5-4	7/6
2001	**Fantastic Light**	5	S bin Suroor	L Dettori	100-30	8/9
2002	**Grandera**	4	S bin Suroor	L Dettori	4-1	3/12
2003	**Nayef**	5	M Tregoning	R Hills	5-1	6/10
2004	**Rakti**	5	M Jarvis	P Robinson	3-1	10/10
2005	**Azamour**	4	J Oxx	M Kinane	11-8f	3/8*
2006	**Ouija Board**	5	E Dunlop	O Peslier	8-1	5/7
2007	**Manduro**	5	A Fabre	S Pasquier	15-8f	4/6

Formerly Group 2, Group 1 from 2000.

FIRST RUN in 1968 and now one of the best races of the week since becoming a Group 1 in 2000. Godolphin were largely responsible for its rise in profile with three top-class winners between 2000 and 2002 (with Dubai Millennium's victory one of the outstanding moments in the history of the meeting), but since then Moon Ballad and Sulamani were beaten favourites and Electrocutionist was second to Ouija Board when well fancied. Traditional trials like the Brigadier Gerard Stakes, the Gordon Richards Stakes and the Tattersalls Gold Cup are largely being eschewed in favour of international preparations, a route taken by Grandera, Nayef, Rakti, Ouija Board and, of course, French star Manduro.

St James's Palace Stakes (1m) Royal Ascot

1998	**Dr Fong**	H Cecil	K Fallon	4-1	4/8
1999	**Sendawar**	A de Royer-Dupre	G Mosse	2-1f	11/11
2000	**Giant's Causeway**	A O'Brien	M Kinane	7-2f	3/11
2001	**Black Minnaloushe**	A O'Brien	J Murtagh	8-1	1/11
2002	**Rock Of Gibraltar**	A O'Brien	M Kinane	4-5f	4/9
2003	**Zafeen**	M Channon	D Holland	8-1	5/11
2004	**Azamour**	J Oxx	M Kinane	9-2	1/11
2005	**Shamardal**	S bin Suroor	K McEvoy	7-4f	2/8
2006	**Araafa**	J Noseda	A Munro	2-1f	2/11
2007	**Excellent Art**	A O'Brien	J Spencer	8-1	1/8

GUINEAS form holds the key to this prize with winners and also-rans from the Irish, French and English versions forming the vast majority of the line-up. Seven of the last ten winners had made the frame at Newmarket, while six of the last seven also ran in the Irish Guineas – Black Minnaloushe and Rock Of Gibraltar won at the Curragh, Giant's Causeway, Azamour and Araafa took second, while Zafeen was a dismal 14th. Shamardal had taken the French Classic double and Excellent Art was probably the moral winner at Longchamp. Essentially, the profile adds up to an out-and-out miler proven at the top level.

Coronation Stakes (1m) Royal Ascot

1998	**Exclusive**	Sir M Stoute	W Swinburn	5-1	10/9
1999	**Balisada**	G Wragg	M Roberts	16-1	8/9
2000	**Crimplene**	C Brittain	P Robinson	4-1j	6/9
2001	**Banks Hill**	A Fabre	O Peslier	4-1j	4/13
2002	**Sophisticat**	A O'Brien	M Kinane	11-2	3/11
2003	**Russian Rhythm**	Sir M Stoute	K Fallon	4-7f	11/9
2004	**Attraction**	M Johnston	K Darley	6-4f	10/11
2005	**Maids Causeway**	B Hills	M Hills	9-2	9/10
2006	**Nannina**	J Gosden	J Fortune	6-1jf	13/15
2007	**Indian Ink**	R Hannon	R Hughes	8-1	2/13

A CHAMPIONSHIP race for three-year-old fillies, first run in 1870. The English 1,000 Guineas has generally been a dreadful guide – Russian Rhythm and Attraction are the only winners to follow up since 1979, while Harayir, Las Meninas, Shadayid, Sleepytime, Ameerat, Speciosa and Finsceal Beo were among several expensive flops since the mid-Nineties and the last three Ascot winners had been beaten at Newmarket. The Irish Guineas has often proved a better trial, with Crimplene and Attraction the last to do the double, and Banks Hill and Sophisticat followed up fine efforts in the French Guineas.

Golden Jubilee Stakes (6f) Royal Ascot

1998	**Tomba**	4	B Meehan	M Tebbutt	4-1	13/12
1999	**Bold Edge**	4	R Hannon	D O'Neill	16-1	16/19
2000	**Superior Premium**	6	R Fahey	J Murtagh	20-1	17/16
2001	**Harmonic Way**	6	R Charlton	S Drowne	10-1	1/21
2002	**Malhub**	4	J Gosden	K Darley	16-1	12/12
2003	**Choisir**	4	P Perry	J Murtagh	13-2	20/17
2004	**Fayr Jag**	4	T Easterby	W Supple	12-1	9/14
2005	**Cape of Good Hope**	7	D Oughton	M Kinane	6-1	2/15
2006	**Les Arcs**	6	T Pitt	J Egan	33-1	4/18
2007	**Soldier's Tale**	6	J Noseda	J Murtagh	9-1	11/21

AKA 'The Cork And Orrery'. Formerly Group 3. Group 2 from 1999, Group 1 from 2002.
A RACE whose profile has been steadily on the rise and has now reached fever pitch with its inauguration into the Global Sprint Challenge, attracting the best sprinters from around the world. Its essense hasn't changed, though, as this is a fiercely competitive sprint which throws up more than its share of shocks, not least when former failed hurdler Les Arcs was a 33-1 springer in 2006. Three-year-olds have often run well at big prices, but five of the last eight winners have been six or older.

Gold Cup (2m4f) Royal Ascot

1998	**Kayf Tara**	4	S bin Suroor	L Dettori	11-1	17/16
1999	**Enzeli**	4	J Oxx	J Murtagh	20-1	16/17
2000	**Kayf Tara**	6	S bin Suroor	M Kinane	11-8f	6/11
2001	**Royal Rebel**	5	M Johnston	J Murtagh	8-1	10/12
2002	**Royal Rebel**	6	M Johnston	J Murtagh	16-1	8/15
2003	**Mr Dinos**	4	P Cole	K Fallon	3-1	6/12
2004	**Papineau**	4	S bin Suroor	L Dettori	5-1	4/13
2005	**Westerner**	6	E Lellouche	O Peslier	7-4f	4/17

| 2006 | **Yeats** | 5 | A O'Brien | K Fallon | 7-1 | 8/12 |
| 2007 | **Yeats** | 6 | A O'Brien | M Kinane | 8-13f | 2/14 |

ROYAL ASCOT'S most famous race and the only British Group One race run over 2m4f. Many winners, including Yeats and Royal Rebel, have followed up from the year before – this is due to the fact that winners have to possess a blend of speed and stamina which is very rare in modern racing stock. Indeed, but for not quite matching Papineau's turn of foot in 2004, Westerner would have added his name to this list of greats by now, having made amends by battling past Distinction the following year. The key trial is Sandown's Henry II Stakes, won by Mr Dinos and Papineau en route to Ascot.

Eclipse (1m2f) Sandown

1998	**Daylami**	4	S bin Suroor	L Dettori	6-4f	5/7
1999	**Compton Admiral**	3	G Butler	D Holland	20-1	7/8
2000	**Giant's Causeway**	3	A O'Brien	G Duffield	8-1	4/8
2001	**Medicean**	4	Sir M Stoute	K Fallon	7-2	7/8
2002	**Hawk Wing**	3	A O'Brien	M Kinane	8-15f	6/5
2003	**Falbrav**	5	L Cumani	D Holland	8-1	14/15
2004	**Refuse To Bend**	4	S bin Suroor	L Dettori	15-2	9/12
2005	**Oratorio**	3	A O'Brien	K Fallon	12-1	1/7
2006	**David Junior**	4	B Meehan	J Spencer	9-4	2/9
2007	**Notnowcato**	5	Sir M Stoute	R Moore	7-1	1/8

CHANGES IN the weight-for-age scale meant that, from 1990 onwards, three-year-olds became 2lb worse off with their elders, and after a spell of four winners in seven years from 1999 to 2005 the Classic generation is enduring its usual drought with just one in the last six now. Derby winners have a poor record, with Authorized and Motivator the latest hotpots to get turned over. Similarly, fillies are to be avoided – Pebbles, in the mid-Eighties, was the first filly to succeed since the 19th century, and Bosra Sham and Ouija Board were beaten favourites. Royal Ascot form is the key. Daylami, Falbrav and David Junior, all beaten in the Prince of Wales's Stakes, kept up the good record of runners from that race, Giant's Causeway had won the St James's Palace, and Medicean and Refuse To Bend won the Queen Anne.

July Cup (6f) Newmarket

1998	**Elnadim**	4	J Dunlop	R Hills	3-1f	18/17
1999	**Stravinsky**	3	A O'Brien	M Kinane	8-1	6/17
2000	**Agnes World**	5	H Mori	Y Take	4-1f	6/10
2001	**Mozart**	3	A O'Brien	M Kinane	4-1f	19/18
2002	**Continent**	5	D Nicholls	D Holland	12-1	2/14
2003	**Oasis Dream**	3	J Gosden	R Hughes	9-2	11/16
2004	**Frizzante**	5	J Fanshawe	J Murtagh	14-1	18/20
2005	**Pastoral Pursuits**	4	H Morrison	J Egan	22-1	10/19
2006	**Les Arcs**	6	T Pitt	J Egan	10-1	15/15
2007	**Sakhee's Secret**	3	H Morrison	S Drowne	9-2	16/18

THE BLUE RIBAND event of Newmarket's July meeting, this was first staged in 1876. This is a race for specialist sprinters with the Golden Jubilee (Les Arcs doubled up in 2006), the King's Stand and the Duke of York (York, May) giving the most helpful clues. However, horses dropping down in trip shouldn't be ruled out – everyone remembers greats like Ajdal and Soviet Song achieving the seemingly impossible in the late Eighties, while Mozart had won the 7f Jersey Stakes and finished second in the Irish Guineas in 2001 and Pastoral Pursuits was a Guineas horses until his stamina limitations were exposed in 2004. A high draw looks increasingly vital – the first four came from the highest six stalls in 2006.

King George VI and Queen Elizabeth Diamond Stakes (1m4f) Ascot

1998	**Swain**	6	S bin Suroor	L Dettori	11-2	5/8
1999	**Daylami**	5	S bin Suroor	L Dettori	3-1	8/8
2000	**Montjeu**	4	J Hammond	M Kinane	1-3f	5/7
2001	**Galileo**	3	A O'Brien	M Kinane	1-2f	7/12
2002	**Golan**	4	Sir M Stoute	K Fallon	11-2	8/9
2003	**Alamshar**	3	J Oxx	J Murtagh	13-2	5/12
2004	**Doyen**	4	S bin Suroor	L Dettori	11-10f	5/11
2005	**Azamour**	4	J Oxx	M Kinane	5-2f	12/12*
2006	**Hurricane Run**	4	A Fabre	C Soumillon	5-6f	4/6
2007	**Dylan Thomas**	4	A O'Brien	J Murtagh	5-4f	5/7

Run at Newbury

ALTHOUGH IT has less prestige than the Arc, the King George is always won by a top-class horse. A seriously good three-year-old has long been seen as getting a head-start by the weight-for-age scale, but no three-year-old has won this in recent times without having made the frame in the Derby – Lammtarra and Galileo came into this race as Derby winners, King's Theatre had been second at Epsom and Alamshar third. Given the stiffness of the task fewer horses are taking their chances from the Classic generation (there were no representatives last year) and a top-class older horse, trained by an established handler, best fits the bill as Doyen, Azamour, Hurricane Run and Dylan Thomas proved. Golan was the first horse ever to win this on his seasonal debut, while Godolphin have had the winner five times in the last 13 years and love to unleash their superstars in this.

Sussex Stakes (1m) Goodwood

1998	**Among Men**	4	Sir M Stoute	M Kinane	4-1	10/10
1999	**Aljabr**	3	S Bin Suroor	L Dettori	11-10f	6/8
2000	**Giant's Causeway**	3	A O'Brien	M Kinane	3-1j	6/10
2001	**Noverre**	3	S Bin Suroor	L Dettori	9-2	11/10
2002	**Rock Of Gibraltar**	3	A O'Brien	M Kinane	8-13f	3/5
2003	**Reel Buddy**	5	R Hannon	Pat Eddery	20-1	7/9
2004	**Soviet Song**	5	J Fanshawe	J Murtagh	3-1	5/11
2005	**Proclamation**	3	J Noseda	M Kinane	3-1	7/12
2006	**Court Masterpiece**	6	E Dunlop	E Dunlop	15-2	5/7
2007	**Ramonti**	5	Sir M Stoute	L Dettori	9-2	8/8

THIS TRADITIONALLY featured a glamorous three-year-old sent off a well-backed favourite and landing the odds, but the outlook has changed in recent years. After four winning three-year-olds in a row, Proclamation is their only victor in the last five years, during which time Excellent Art, Araafa and Trade Fair were all losing jollies while Reel Buddy, Soviet Song (also second in the following two years), Court Masterpiece and Ramonti have notched victories for the older brigade.

Nassau Stakes (1m1f192yds) Goodwood

1998	**Alborada**	3	Sir M Prescott	G Duffield	4-1	5/9
1999	**Zahrat Dubai**	3	S bin Suroor	G Stevens	5-1	3/8
2000	**Crimplene**	3	C Brittain	P Robinson	7-4f	3/7
2001	**Lailani**	3	E Dunlop	L Dettori	5-4f	5/7
2002	**Islington**	3	Sir M Stoute	K Fallon	100-30	6/10
2003	**Russian Rhythm**	3	Sir M Stoute	K Fallon	4-5f	7/8
2004	**Favourable Terms**	4	Sir M Stoute	K Fallon	11-2	2/6
2005	**Alexander Goldrun**	4	J Bolger	K Manning	13-8f	9/11

| 2006 | **Ouija Board** | 5 | E Dunlop | L Dettori | Evensf | 7/7 |
| 2007 | **Peeping Fawn** | 3 | A O'Brien | J Murtagh | 2-1f | 4/18 |

AN AMAZINGLY good race for favourites, pointing up a real lack of strength in depth among fillies at this distance and at this level, with six of the last eight winners being the market leader. Three-year-olds dominated to the exclusion of their elders until 2004, though Russian Rhythm was the first Guineas winner to triumph for many a year. Favourable Terms then completed a hat-trick for Sir Michael Stoute, and Alexander Goldrun and Ouija Board were other older winners before the brilliant Peeping Fawn last year.

Juddmonte International Stakes (1m2f85yds) York

1998	**One So Wonderful**	4	L Cumani	Pat Eddery	6-1	5/8
1999	**Royal Anthem**	4	H Cecil	G Stevens	3-1f	9/12
2000	**Giant's Causeway**	3	A O'Brien	M Kinane	10-11f	5/6
2001	**Sakhee**	4	S bin Suroor	L Dettori	7-4f	5/8
2002	**Nayef**	4	M Tregoning	R Hills	6-4f	5/7
2003	**Falbrav**	5	L Cumani	D Holland	5-2	2/8
2004	**Sulamani**	5	S bin Suroor	L Dettori	3-1	9/9
2005	**Electrocutionist**	4	V Valiani	M Kinane	9-2	5/7
2006	**Notnowcato**	4	Sir M Stoute	R Moore	8-1	5/7
2007	**Authorized**	3	P Chapple-Hyam	L Dettori	6-4f	1/7

FAMOUS FOR its many upsets since Brigadier Gerard suffered his only defeat to Roberto in 1972, the race has turned in punters' favour in recent times. Halling twice won as favourite in the mid-Nineties and no winner has returned bigger than 8-1 since then. Favourites won four in a row before 2003 and Authorized was another successful jolly last year, while Falbrav, Sulamani and Electrocutionist were all well fancied in between. Older horses, especially lightly-raced ones such as the subsequent Arc winner Sakhee, have mostly kept on top of the three-year-olds, though two great ones – Authorized and Giant's Causeway – bucked the trend. Note the previous year's running and the Eclipse for other clues.

Yorkshire Oaks (1m3f195yds) York

1998	**Catchascatchcan**	3	H Cecil	K Fallon	2-1f	7/6
1999	**Ramruma**	3	H Cecil	Pat Eddery	5-6f	9/11
2000	**Petrushka**	3	Sir M Stoute	J Murtagh	5-4f	1/6
2001	**Super Tassa**	5	V Valiani	K Darley	25-1	7/9
2002	**Islington**	3	Sir M Stoute	K Fallon	2-1	9/11
2003	**Islington**	4	Sir M Stoute	K Fallon	8-11f	5/8
2004	**Quiff**	3	Sir M Stoute	K Fallon	7-2	3/8
2005	**Punctilious**	4	S bin Suroor	K McEvoy	13-2	5/11
2006	**Alexandrova**	3	A O'Brien	M Kinane	4-9f	4/6
2007	**Peeping Fawn**	3	A O'Brien	J Murtagh	4-9f	8/8

SIR MICHAEL STOUTE has a good grip on what it takes to land this, with four victories in the last seven years, including two for the brilliant Islington, though even he finds it hard to match the Ballydoyle might now with Alexandrova and Peeping Fawn winning at a canter. All fit the general mould of well-fancied runners (six winning favourites in ten years) trained by an established handler. Super Tassa was remarkable in this respect, being the first Italian winner in Britain for 41 years and consequently sent off at 25-1. The Classic generation have the edge, with six wins in the last decade.

Nunthorpe Stakes (5f) York

| 1998 | **Lochangel** | 4 | I Balding | L Dettori | 6-1 | 2/17 |
| 1999 | **Stravinsky** | 3 | A O'Brien | M Kinane | Evensf | 13/16 |

2000	**Nuclear Debate**	5	J Hammond	G Mosse	5-2f	1/13
2001	**Mozart**	3	A O'Brien	M Kinane	4-9f	4/10
2002	**Kyllachy**	4	H Candy	J Spencer	3-1f	15/17
2003	**Oasis Dream**	3	J Gosden	R Hughes	4-9f	2/8
2004	**Bahamian Pirate**	9	D Nicholls	S Sanders	16-1	5/12
2005	**La Cucaracha**	4	B Hills	M Hills	7-1	8/16
2006	**Reverence**	5	E Ahern	K Darley	5-1	6/14
2007	**Kingsgate Native**	2	J Best	J Quinn	12-1	13/16

AN EXCELLENT race for punters with five winning favourites between 1999 and 2003 and two more fancied horses, La Cucaracha and Reverence, triumphing after the shock of nine-year-old Bahamian Pirate. Both matched the profile of relatively young horses still on the upgrade, and that was certainly the case with Kingsgate Native last year, the first winning juvenile since Lyric Fantasy in 1992. Six of the last eight winners were drawn low.

Stanley Leisure Sprint Cup (6f) Haydock

1998	**Tamarisk**	3	R Charlton	T Sprake	13-2	5/13
1999	**Diktat**	4	S bin Suroor	L Dettori	13-8f	16/16
2000	**Pipalong**	4	T Easterby	K Darley	3-1	7/13
2001	**Nuclear Debate**	6	J Hammond	G Mosse	11-2	9/12
2002	**Invincible Spirit**	5	J Dunlop	J Carroll	25-1	10/14
2003	**Somnus**	3	T Easterby	T Durcan	12-1	7/10
2004	**Tante Rose**	4	R Charlton	R Hughes	10-1	14/19
2005	**Goodricke**	3	D Loder	J Spencer	14-1	4/17
2006	**Reverence**	5	E Alston	K Darley	5-1	6/14
2007	**Red Clubs**	4	B Hills	M Hills	33-1	4/18

THIS CAN often be run on ground with plenty of give, so there have been a string of minor upsets as midsummer form proves misleading. Sakhee's Secret was the latest favourite to get turned over last year and there hasn't been a winning jolly since Diktat in 1999. High draws were traditionally favoured, but the last three winners were drawn low.

St Leger (1m6f127yds) Doncaster

1998	**Nedawi**	S bin Suroor	J Reid	5-2	1/9
1999	**Mutafaweq**	S bin Suroor	R Hills	11-2	6/9
2000	**Millenary**	J Dunlop	T Quinn	11-4	5/11
2001	**Milan**	A O'Brien	M Kinane	13-8f	7/10
2002	**Bollin Eric**	T Easterby	K Darley	7-1	3/8
2003	**Brian Boru**	A O'Brien	J Spencer	5-4f	9/12
2004	**Rule Of Law**	S bin Suroor	K McEvoy	3-1f	9/9
2005	**Scorpion**	A O'Brien	L Dettori	10-11f	2/6
2006	**Sixties Icon**	J Noseda	L Dettori	11-8f	11/11*
2007	**Lucarno**	J Gosden	J Fortune	11-8f	11/11

*Run at Newbury

THE OLDEST of the five Classics, first run in 1776, but it has rather suffered in recent years from an obsession with keeping class horses to shorter trips and only three of the last 11 winners came via the traditional route of stepping up on strong Derby form – Silver Patriarch and Rule Of Law were second at Epsom, and Lucarno was third. The key race has been the Great Voltigeur at York – Bollin Eric led a repeat of the York 1-2-3 in 2002, while Lucarno, Rule Of Law and Milan won that race and Brian Boru was second.

Queen Elizabeth II Stakes (1m) Ascot

| 1998 | **Desert Prince** | 3 | D Loder | O Peslier | 100-30f | 1/7 |

1999	**Dubai Millennium**	3	S bin Suroor	L Dettori	4-9f	3/4
2000	**Observatory**	3	J Gosden	K Darley	14-1	6/12
2001	**Summoner**	4	S bin Suroor	R Hills	33-1	7/8
2002	**Where Or When**	3	T Mills	K Darley	7-1	3/5
2003	**Falbrav**	5	L Cumani	D Holland	6-4f	4/8
2004	**Rakti**	5	M Jarvis	P Robinson	9-2	13/11
2005	**Starcraft**	3	L Cumani	C Lemaire	7-2	2/6
2006	**George Washington**	3	A O'Brien	K Fallon	13-8f	7/8
2007	**Ramonti**	5	S bin Suroor	L Dettori	5-1	8/7

KNOWN AS the mile championship of Europe, and one in which the Classic generation have firmly held sway. Summoner, Falbrav and Rakti did briefly interrupt their hegemony, but Starcraft and George Washington redressed the balance prior to Ramonti just beating Excellent Art. There have been four winning favourites in the last ten years, but some short-priced hotpots have been turned over such as Hawk Wing (1-2 when second to Where Or When in 2002) and Giant's Causeway (11-10 when beaten by Observatory in 2000).

Prix De l'Arc De Triomphe (1m4f) Longchamp

1998	**Sagamix**	3	A Fabre	O Peslier	5-2j	7/14
1999	**Montjeu**	3	J Hammond	M Kinane	6-4c	4/14
2000	**Sinndar**	3	J Oxx	J Murtagh	6-4	7/10
2001	**Sakhee**	4	S bin Suroor	L Dettori	22-10f	15/17
2002	**Marienbard**	5	S bin Suroor	L Dettori	158-10	3/16
2003	**Dalakhani**	3	A de Royer-Dupre	C Soumillon	9-4	14/13
2004	**Bago**	3	J Pease	T Gillet	10-1	5/20
2005	**Hurricane Run**	3	A Fabre	K Fallon	11-4	6/15
2006	**Rail Link**	3	A Fabre	S Pasquier	8-1	4/8
2007	**Dylan Thomas**	4	A O'Brien	K Fallon	11-2	6/12

THIS RACE has restored its reputation as the premier middle-distance championship of Europe, with top-class 12f horses now trained specifically for the race from the summer. Dylan Thomas, though, had been on the go for a while and bucked every trend going. Winners had followed a very clear pattern – lightly-raced, progressive three-year-olds trained on home territory – with only Godolphin breaking the mould. Andre Fabre has a stunning record with five of the last 15 winners. Trials day at Longchamp three weeks prior to the race has to be watched – the last four three-year-old winners warmed up in the Prix Niel.

Dubai Champion Stakes (1m2f) Newmarket

1998	**Alborada**	3	Sir M Prescott	G Duffield	6-1	5/10
1999	**Alborada**	4	Sir M Prescott	G Duffield	5-1	10/13
2000	**Kalanisi**	4	Sir M Stoute	J Murtagh	5-1	3/15
2001	**Nayef**	3	M Tregoning	R Hills	3-1	1/12
2002	**Storming Home**	4	B Hills	M Hills	8-1	4/11
2003	**Rakti**	4	M Jarvis	P Robinson	11-1	3/12
2004	**Haafhd**	3	B Hills	R Hills	12-1	9/11
2005	**David Junior**	3	B Meehan	J Spencer	25-1	13/15
2006	**Pride**	6	A de Royer-Dupre	C Lemaire	7-2	2/8
2007	**Literato**	3	J-C Rouget	C Lemaire	7-2	5/12

THE FINAL major contest of the year but a clash with the Breeders' Cup means the quality is dipping, particularly among the home defence, and the last two renewals have gone to France. Guineas winners of the same year or the year before have traditionally had a great record, a trend reaffirmed by Haafhd's runaway win in 2004, while there has been a mixture of fancied winners and outsiders, the most notable being David Junior in 2005.

Big handicap records

Lincoln Handicap (1m) Doncaster

Year	Winner	Age	Weight	Trainer	Jockey	SP	Draw/ran
1998	**Hunters Of Brora**	8	9-0	J Bethell	J Weaver	16-1	23/23
1999	**Right Wing**	5	9-5	J Dunlop	T Quinn	9-2f	8/24
2000	**John Ferneley**	5	8-10	P Cole	J Fortune	7-1j	1/24
2001	**Nimello**	5	8-9	P Cole	J Fortune	9-2f	1/23
2002	**Zucchero**	6	8-13	D Arbuthnot	S Whitworth	33-1	7/23
2003	**Pablo**	4	8-11	B Hills	M Hills	5-1	6/24
2004	**Babodana**	4	9-10	M Tompkins	P Robinson	20-1	23/24
2005	**Stream of Gold**	4	9-0	Sir M Stoute	R Winston	5-1f	13/22
2006	**Blythe Knight**	6	8-10	J Quinn	G Gibbons	22-1	9/30*
2007	**Very Wise**	5	8-11	W Haggas	J Fanning	9-1	16/20

*Run at Redcar

BET ANTE-POST or, better still, take a morning price but, whatever you do, don't bet at SP. The perennial question is what effect the draw will have – low numbers won five renewals in a row from 1999 to 2003, but two of the last three run at Doncaster went to a high berth. The best advice for punters is to watch the Spring Mile, run a day earlier. Weight was traditionally a major barrier to success but has become less so since Hunters of Brora's victory in 1998. At the time he was the first winner to carry 9st or more since 1985, but since then Right Wing, Babodana and Stream of Gold have followed suit. Not surprisingly the vast majority of winners and runners have been enjoying their first outing of the season, but Very Wise was having his seventh run since December and maybe the increasing quality of the All-Weather will take effect. Northern-based trainers no longer dominate and Paul Cole has done particularly well in the last ten years.

Royal Hunt Cup Handicap (1m) Royal Ascot

Year	Winner	Age	Weight	Trainer	Jockey	SP	Draw/ran
1998	**Refuse To Lose**	4	7-11	J Eustace	J Tate	20-1	6/32
1999	**Showboat**	5	8-6	B Hills	N Pollard	14-1	30/32
2000	**Caribbean Monarch**	5	8-10	Sir M -oute	K Fallon	11-2	28/32
2001	**Surprise Encounter**	5	8-9	E Dunlop	L Dettori	8-1	29/30
2002	**Norton**	5	8-9	T Mills	J Fortune	25-1	10/30
2003	**Macadamia**	4	8-13	J Fanshawe	D O'Neill	8-1	6/32
2004	**Mine**	6	9-5	J Bethell	T Quinn	16-1	8/31
2005	**New Seeker**	5	9-0	C Cox	P Robinson	11-1	6/22*
2006	**Cesare**	5	8-8	J Fanshawe	J Spencer	14-1	3/30
2007	**Royal Oath**	4	9-0	J Gosden	J Fortune	9-1	14/26

*Royal Hunt Cup and the Wokingham run at York in 2005

A GREAT betting race in which there are few pointers and plots are thick on the ground, so most winners go off at a decent price – Yeast (at 8-1) was the last winning favourite in 1996. That said, there haven't been any real shocks and punters should look to horses just trading below the market leaders. Draw trends have changed markedly in recent years. Even ignoring 2005 (run at York), the run of winners from high stalls (all 28 or higher between 1999 and 2001) saw a sea change towards low numbers, with the first seven in 2006 all drawn 11 or lower, before Royal Oath's win from the middle of the track last year saw an even sweep of runners across the course. Mine and New Seeker were also rare in managing to carry 9st or more to victory.

Wokingham Handicap (6f) Royal Ascot

1998	Selhurstpark Flyer	7	9-7	J Berry	C Lowther	16-1	20/29
1999	Deep Space	4	8-7	E Dunlop	G Carter	14-1	3/30
2000	Harmonic Way	5	9-6	R Charlton	R Hughes	12-1	28/29
2001	Nice One Clare	5	9-3	J Payne	J Murtagh	7-1f	4/30
2002	Capricho	5	8-11	J Akehurst	T Quinn	20-1	21/28
2003	Fayr Jag	4	9-6	T Easterby	W Supple	10-1	13/29
	Ratio	5	9-3	J Hammond	L Dettori	14-1	22/29
2004	Lafi	5	8-13	D Nicholls	E Ahern	6-1f	30/29
2005	Iffraaj	4	9-6	M Jarvis	P Robinson	9-4f	6/17
2006	Baltic King	6	9-10	H Morrison	J Fortune	10-1	6/28
2007	Dark Missile	4	8-6	A Balding	W Buick	22-1	27/26

FIRST run in 1896 and generally a tough race in which to find a winner, although Lafi and Iffraaj have put the poor record of favourites right in recent years. Class horses have been increasingly successful since the turn of the century, with seven of the last 11 winners carrying at least 9-3 to victory. A key trial is the Victoria Cup at the same track in May. Winners tend to be aged four to six, with only two having been older in the history of the race, including dual winner Selhurstpark Flyer for Jack Berry in 1998.

Northumberland Plate (2m) Newcastle

1998	Cyrian	4	7-13	P Cole	T Sprake	12-1	2/20
1999	Far Cry	4	8-10	M Pipe	K Darley	9-2j	6/20
2000	Bay Of Islands	8	8-4	D Morris	K Darley	7-1	4/18
2001	Archduke Ferdinand	3	8-4	P Cole	F Norton	12-1	17/18
2002	Bangalore	6	9-5	A Perrett	S Sanders	8-1	9/16
2003	Unleash	4	8-11	P Hobbs	J Spencer	10-1	1/20
2004	Mirjan	8	8-3	L Lungo	P Hanagan	25-1	5/19
2005	Sergeant Cecil	6	8-8	D Millman	A Munro	14-1	7/20
2006	Toldo	4	8-2	G Moore	N de Souza	33-1	16/20
2007	Juniper Girl	4	8-11	M Bell	L Morris	5-1f	13/20

A RACE traditionally identified with providing an opportunity for older, experienced stayers to grind out victory, though whether this still applies is open to debate. Younger, less exposed types took over around the turn of the century, since when four of the last eight winners have been six or older (including a couple of eight-year-olds) but the other four have been three or four. For the time being age doesn't seem to have a bearing. Paul Cole, though, does particularly well with his youngsters. The first bend comes shortly after the start, so those drawn high can be disadvantaged, though the first three in 2006 were all 16 or higher and Juniper Girl defied stall 13 last year.

Bunbury Cup (7f) Newmarket

1998	Ho Leng	3	9-7	L Perratt	M Kinane	14-1	20/20
1999	Grangeville	4	9-3	I Balding	K Fallon	13-2j	20/19
2000	Tayseer	6	8-9	D Nicholls	G Mosse	9-1	8/19
2001	Atavus	4	8-9	G Margarson	J Mackay (3)	10-1	14/19

2002	**Mine**	4	8-12	J Bethell	K Fallon	5-1f	3/17
2003	**Patavellian**	5	9-1	R Charlton	S Drowne	4-1f	2/20
2004	**Material Witness**	7	9-3	W Muir	M Dwyer	25-1	6/19
2005	**Mine**	7	9-9	J Bethell	T Quinn	16-1	6/18
2006	**Mine**	8	9-10	J Bethell	M Kinane	10-1	14/19
2007	**Giganticus**	4	8-8	B Hills	P Robinson	16-1	3/18

THE AWESOME figure of Mine stands tall over the other winners of this race as he picked up the prize on three occasions between 2002 and 2006. Mine's last two wins were further evidence that weight is no barrier to success (seven out of the last 11 winners have carried 9-1 or more) and smaller yards tend to do well. Course management have struggled with the fairness of the draw in recent years. A huge bias towards high numbers in the late Nineties was followed by a string of low-drawn winners. The last two runnings featured strong biases both ways – the first four all came from the top six stalls in 2006, before six of the first nine came from the bottom seven last year.

John Smith's Cup (1m2f85yds) York

1998	**Porto Foricos**	3	8-3	H Cecil	J Quinn	6-1	7/20
1999	**Achilles**	4	8-11	K Burke	J Weaver	25-1	6/15
2000	**Sobriety**	3	8-8	R F J'-Houghton	J Reid	20-1	8/22
2001	**Foreign Affairs**	3	8-6	Sir M Prescott	G Duffield	5-2f	8/19
2002	**Vintage Premium**	5	9-9	R Fahey	P Hanagan	20-1	9/20
2003	**Far Lane**	4	9-4	B Hills	M Hills	7-1	4/20
2004	**Arcalis**	4	9-2	H Johnson	R Win-on	20-1	18/21
2005	**Mullins Bay**	4	9-7	A O'Brien	K Fallon	4-1f	19/20
2006	**Fairmile**	4	8-12	W Swinburn	A Kirby	6-1j	9/20
2007	**Charlie Tokyo**	4	8-9	R Fahey	J Moriarty	11-1	4/17

ANOTHER handicap at the mercy of draw analysts for a number of years, and even though Arcalis and Mullins Bay have defied the bias towards low numbers in the last four years it's still worth bearing in mind the overwhelming amount of evidence. Given the field are turning left for almost the first half of the race, it clearly takes a class horse to get into the race from a high draw, and both of that pair fit such a description. Sir Mark Prescott has proved his liking for the race, while runners older than four increasingly struggle. It has always been worth overlooking the favourite until recent years.

Stewards' Cup Handicap (6f) Goodwood

1998	**Superior Premium**	4	8-12	R Fahey	R Winston	14-1	28/29
1999	**Harmonic Way**	4	8-6	R Charlton	R Hughes	12-1	8/30
2000	**Tayseer**	6	8-11	D Nicholls	R Hughes	13-2	28/30
2001	**Guinea Hunter**	5	9-0	T Ea-erby	J Spencer	33-1	19/30
2002	**Bond Boy**	5	8-2	B Smart	C Catlin	14-1	29/28
2003	**Patavellian**	5	8-11	R Charlton	S Drowne	4-1	27/29
2004	**Pivotal Point**	4	8-11	P Makin	S Sanders	7-1c	1/28
2005	**Gift Horse**	5	9-7	D Nicholls	K Fallon	9-2	19/27
2006	**Borderlescott**	4	9-5	R Bastiman	R Ffrench	10-1	19/27
2007	**Zidane**	5	9-1	J Fanshawe	J Spencer	6-1f	11/27

INAUGURATED IN 1840, this is a major betting heat with a strong ante-post market. However, in the last decade or so the race has been altered by the opening up of a fresh strip of ground on the far rail which has given high numbers a huge advantage, to the detriment of ante-post punters. A high draw has been thought essential and even a casual glance at the results above will tell you why, with Patavellian's win in 2003 (leading home a 1-2-3 for the widest four stalls) fairly typical. Pivotal Point managed a scorching win from stall one in 2004 before Gift Horse and Borderlescott succeeded from the same stall 19 in the following two years. It must be hoped that last year's thrilling win for Zidane marks a shift back towards fairness as there was no bias whatsoever evident that day. The Wokingham Handicap at Royal Ascot has the most bearing.

Ebor Handicap (1m6f) York

1998	Tuning	3	8-7	H Cecil	K Fallon	9-2	1/21
1999	Vicious Circle	5	8-4	L Cumani	K Darley	11-1	7/21
2000	Give The Slip	3	8-8	Mrs A Perrett	Pat Eddery	8-1	16/22
2001	Mediterranean	3	8-4	A O'Brien	M Kinane	16-1	20/22
2002	Hugs Dancer	5	8-5	J Given	D McKeown	25-1	20/22
2003	Saint Alebe	4	8-8	D Elsworth	T Quinn	20-1	17/22
2004	Mephisto	4	9-4	L Cumani	D Holland	6-1	3/19
2005	Sergeant Cecil	6	8-12	B Millman	A Munro	11-1	18/20
2006	Mudawin	5	8-4	J Chapple-Hyam	J Egan	100-1	13/22
2007	Purple Moon	4	9-4	L Cumani	J Spencer	7-2f	14/19

ONE OF the oldest and most famous handicaps, first run in 1847, again with an extremely strong ante-post market. Sea Pigeon brought the house down when lumping top-weight home in 1979. In general, though, low weights are massively favoured with only three winners carrying more than 8-8 in the last ten years – one the remarkable Sergeant Cecil and another who went on to come second in the Melbourne Cup (Purple Moon). Perceived no-hopers can triumph off light burdens, such as 100-1 Mudawin in 2006. Watch the Northumberland Plate (Newcastle, June) and the Duke Of Edinburgh Handicap (Royal Ascot, June).

Ayr Gold Cup Handicap (6f) Ayr

1998	Always Alight	4	8-7	K Burke	J Egan	16-1	8/29
1999	Grangeville	4	9-0	I Balding	K Fallon	11-1	17/28
2000	Bahamian Pirate	5	8-0	D Nicholls	A Nicholls	33-1	7/28
2001	Continent	4	8-10	D Nicholls	D Holland	10-1	22/28
2002	Funfair Wane	3	9-3	D Nicholls	A Nicholls	16-1	16/28
2003	Quito	6	8-6	D Chapman	A Culhane	20-1	10/26
2004	Funfair Wane	5	8-6	D Nicholls	P Doe	33-1	8/24
2005	Presto Shinko	4	9-2	R Hannon	S Sanders	12-1	2/27
2006	Fonthill Road	6	9-2	R Fahey	P Hanagan	16-1	6/28
2007	Advanced	4	9-9	K Ryan	J Spencer	20-1	22/28

A HISTORIC race first run in 1804, and yet another boasting a lively ante-post book. That still hasn't done the punters any favours, though, when it comes to getting things right on the day – Continent was the most-fancied winner of the last ten years at 10-1. The effect of the draw can be gleaned from the Ayr Silver Cup, run the day before, as there seems little obvious pattern from recent runnings. A horse with good recent form who can settle in large fields and come from off the pace is required. Key races are the Wokingham Handicap (Royal Ascot, June), the Tote Portland Handicap (Doncaster, September) and the Stewards' Cup (Goodwood, August). Take a second look at Dandy Nicholls' runners – there are a few but his record is brilliant, particularly with less fancied runners.

Cambridgeshire Handicap (1m1f) Newmarket

1998	Lear Spear	3	7-13	D Elsworth	N Pollard	20-1	33/35
1999	She's Our Mare	6	7-12	A Martin	F Norton	11-1	14/33
2000	Katy Nowaitee	4	8-8	P Harris	J Reid	6-1	34/35
2001	I Cried For You	6	8-6	J Given	M Fenton	33-1	11/35
2002	Beauchamp Pilot	4	9-5	G Butler	E Ahern	9-1	26/30

2003	**Chivalry**	4	8-1	Sir M Prescott	G Duffield	14-1	17/34
2004	**Spanish Don**	6	8-7	D Elsworth	L Keniry	100-1	3/32
2005	**Blue Monday**	4	9-3	R Charlton	S Drowne	5-1f	28/30
2006	**Formal Decree**	3	8-9	G Swinbank	J Spencer	9-1	17/33
2007	**Pipedreamer**	3	8-12	J Gosden	J Fortune	5-1f	11/34

THE FIRST leg of the Autumn Double, dating back to 1839. Because of its unusual distance and its straight course, the Cambridgeshire has thrown up a number of specialists down the years so consider horses who have run well in the race before. Apart from that, the traditional winner was a late-maturing three-year-old bred to find improvement over longer trips which are not attempted until after the weights are set – in the last two years Formal Decree and Pipedreamer have won for this age group after a seven-year gap. Two races at Doncaster on St Leger day, a 0-105 handicap over the straight mile and a 0-95 over an extended 1m2f, should provide clues.

Cesarewitch Handicap (2m2f) Newmarket

1998	**Spirit Of Love**	3	8-8	M Johnston	O Peslier	11-1	19/29
1999	**Top Cees**	9	8-10	I Balding	K Fallon	7-1	17/32
2000	**Heros Fatal**	6	8-1	M Pipe	G Carter	11-1	18/33
2001	**Distant Prospect**	4	8-8	I Balding	M Dwyer	14-1	32/31
2002	**Miss Fara**	7	8-0	M Pipe	R Moore	12-1	36/36
2003	**Landing Light**	8	9-4	N Henderson	Pat Eddery	12-1	36/36
2004	**Contact Dancer**	5	8-2	M Johnston	R Ffrench	16-1	18/34
2005	**Sergeant Cecil**	6	9-8	B Millman	A Munro	10-1	28/34
2006	**Detroit City**	4	9-1	P Hobbs	J Spencer	9-2f	29/32
2007	**Leg Spinner**	6	8-11	A Martin	J Murtagh	14-1	23/33

THE SECOND leg of the Autumn Double. Few trends leap off the page, though this is another race in which a long sweeping bend makes the draw far more important than you would think from the trip with Leg Spinner the first winner drawn lower than 17 since Turnpole in 1997. It generally takes a fair amount of experience to win this race, and three-year-old winners are a very rare breed. Horses from traditional jumping yards also tend to go well with Martin Pipe (twice), Mary Reveley, Nicky Henderson, Philip Hobbs and Tony Martin sending out winners in the last 11 years.

November Handicap (1m4f) Doncaster

1998	**Yavana's Pace**	6	9-10	M John-on	D Holland	8-1	12/23
1999	**Flossy**	3	7-7	C Thornton	A Beech	5-1	10/16
2000	**Batswing**	5	8-8	B Ellison	R Win-on	14-1	14/20
2001	**Royal Cavalier**	4	7-10	R Hollinshead	P Quinn	50-1	5/14
2002	**Red Wine**	3	8-1	J Osborne	M Dwyer	16-1	20/23
2003	**Turbo**	4	9-2	G Balding	A Clark	25-1	14/24
2004	**Carte Diamond**	4	9-6	B Ellison	K Fallon	12-1	3/24
2005	**Come On Jonny**	3	8-0	K Beckett	N de Souza	14-1	18/21
2006	**Group Captain**	4	9-5	R Charlton	R Hughes	10-1	20/20
2007	**Malt Or Mash**	3	8-10	R Hannon	R Moore	5-1	13/21

THE LAST big betting heat of the season traces back to 1876. Lightly-raced, progressive three-year-olds are most likely to succeed. The Ladbroke Handicap run over course and distance at the previous meeting is worth studying. As far as detailed trends are concerned, there is quite little that stands out. Prices and weights of the winners vary, but favourites have a desperate record which makes the colossal gamble on Scriptwriter in 2006 (down to 2-1 in a 20-runner race) all the more amazing. Only Royal Cavalier and Carte Diamond have won from single-figure draws in the last ten years.

Big Race Dates, Fixtures and Track Facts

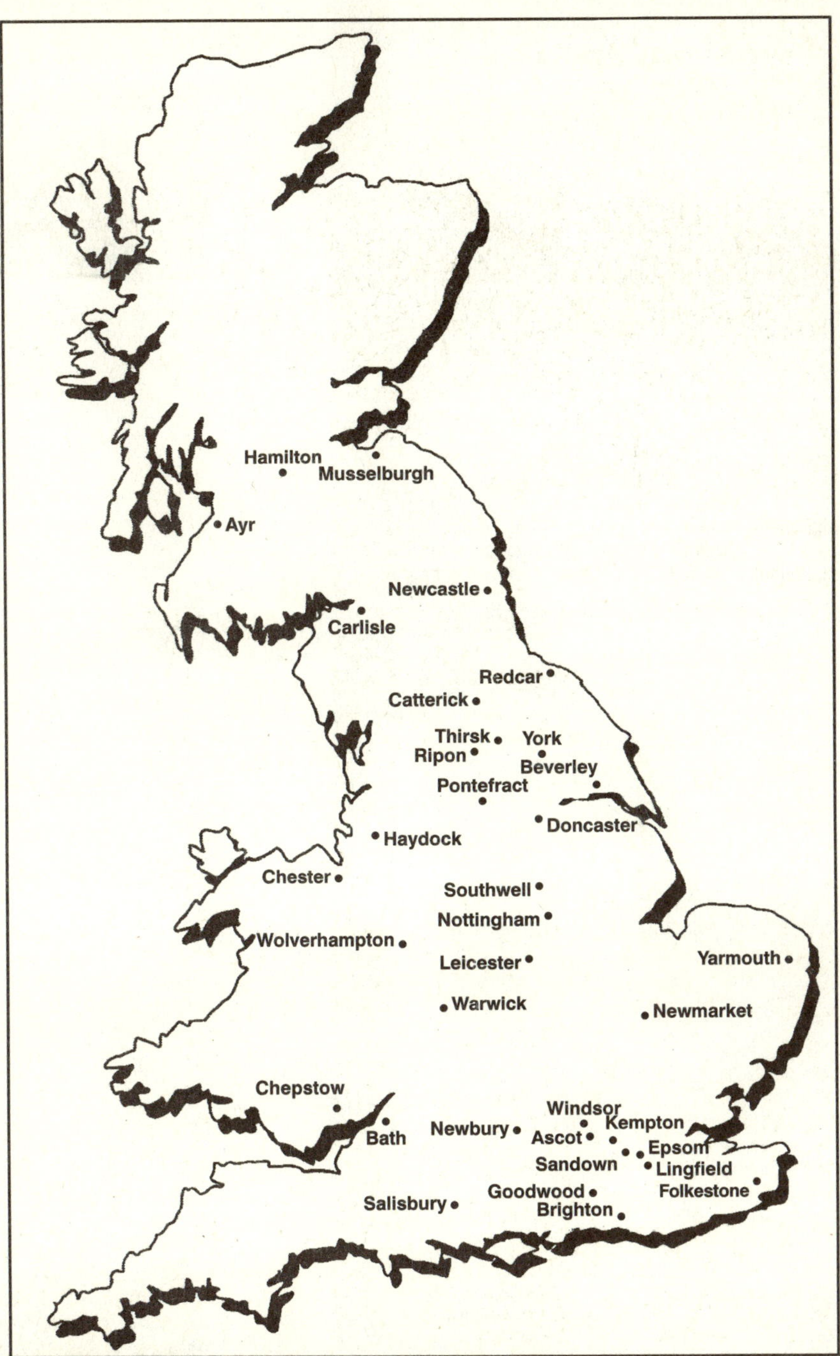

Hamilton
Musselburgh
Ayr
Newcastle
Carlisle
Redcar
Catterick
Thirsk
York
Ripon
Beverley
Pontefract
Doncaster
Haydock
Chester
Southwell
Nottingham
Wolverhampton
Leicester
Yarmouth
Warwick
Newmarket
Chepstow
Windsor
Newbury
Kempton
Bath
Ascot
Epsom
Sandown
Lingfield
Goodwood
Folkestone
Salisbury
Brighton

Fixtures

Key - **Flat**, *Flat evening*, Jumps, *Jumps evening*

March

22 Saturday ....Carlisle, **Doncaster**, Haydock, **Kempton**, Newton Abbot, *Wolverhampton*
23 Sunday..................**Musselburgh**, Plumpton, Towcester
24 Monday ......Chepstow, Fakenham, Huntingdon, Plumpton, **Redcar**, **Warwick**, Yarmouth
25 Tuesday..................Fontwell, **Pontefract**, Sedgefield
26 Wednesday ....Kempton, Newcastle, *Wolverhampton*, **Great Leighs**
27 Thursday ....Ayr, Exeter, **Lingfield**, *Great Leighs*
28 Friday..................*Kempton*, **Lingfield**, Newbury, **Wolverhampton**
29 Saturday..................Bangor-on-dee, **Doncaster**, **Kempton**, Newbury, Stratford-on-avon, *Wolverhampton*
30 Sunday ....Kempton, Wincanton
31 Monday..................**Lingfield**, **Southwell**, Wincanton

April

1 Tuesday..................**Folkestone**, Wetherby, **Great Leighs**
2 Wednesday ....**Catterick**, *Kempton*, **Lingfield**, **Nottingham**
3 Thursday ....**Leicester**, Aintree, Taunton, *Great Leighs*
4 Friday..................Aintree, **Southwell**, *Wolverhampton*, **Great Leighs**
5 Saturday ....Chepstow, *Kempton*, **Lingfield**, Aintree, **Newcastle**
6 Sunday ....Hexham, Market Rasen, Worcester
7 Monday..................Kelso, **Kempton**, Plumpton
8 Tuesday..................**Lingfield**, Sedgefield, **Southwell**
9 Wednesday ....Bath, *Kempton*, Ludlow, Towcester
10 Thursday ....Carlisle, **Folkestone**, Fontwell, Towcester, *Great Leighs*
11 Friday..................Ascot, **Doncaster**, **Musselburgh**, *Wolverhampton*
12 Saturday..................**Doncaster**, **Kempton**, Newbury, Uttoxeter, *Great Leighs*
13 Sunday..................Kelso, Newton Abbot, **Great Leighs**
14 Monday..................Newcastle, **Windsor**, Wolverhampton
15 Tuesday ....Exeter, **Nottingham**, **Warwick**
16 Wednesday..................**Beverley**, Cheltenham, **Newmarket**, *Wolverhampton*
17 Thursday ....Cheltenham, **Newmarket**, Ripon, *Great Leighs*
18 Friday..................Ayr, *Cheltenham*, **Newbury**, *Taunton*, **Thirsk**, *Great Leighs*
19 Saturday..................Ayr, Bangor-on-dee, **Newbury**, *Nottingham*, Thirsk, *Wolverhampton*
20 Sunday ....Stratford-on-avon, Wincanton, **Great Leighs**
21 Monday..................Hexham, Plumpton, **Pontefract**, *Sedgefield*, *Windsor*
22 Tuesday..................*Bath*, **Folkestone**, Kempton, **Southwell**, *Towcester*
23 Wednesday ....**Catterick**, *Kempton*, **Nottingham**, Perth, *Worcester*
24 Thursday ....**Beverley**, Fontwell, Perth, *Southwell*, *Great Leighs*
25 Friday..................*Bangor-on-dee, Chepstow, Newton Abbot*, Perth, **Sandown**, Wolverhampton
26 Saturday ....*Haydock*, **Leicester**, Market Rasen, **Ripon**, **Sandown**, *Wolverhampton*
27 Sunday..................**Brighton**, Ludlow, Wetherby
28 Monday ....**Lingfield**, *Southwell*, Towcester, *Windsor*, Yarmouth
29 Tuesday..................**Bath**, *Sedgefield*, **Southwell**, Wincanton, *Wolverhampton*
30 Wednesday ....**Ascot**, *Kelso*, **Pontefract**, Worcester, *Great Leighs*

May

  1 **Thursday** ....**Folkestone**, Hereford, *Huntingdon*, **Redcar**, *Great Leighs*
  2 **Friday**...............*Bangor-on-dee*, **Musselburgh**, *Fontwell*, **Lingfield**, **Southwell**
  3 **Saturday** ....*Doncaster*, **Goodwood**, *Hexham*, **Newmarket**, **Thirsk**, Uttoxeter
  4 **Sunday**...**Hamilton**, **Newmarket**, **Salisbury**
  5 **Monday**.................................**Kempton**, **Newcastle**, **Warwick**, **Windsor**
  6 **Tuesday** ....*Catterick*, **Chepstow**, *Exeter*, Kelso, **Southwell**
  7 **Wednesday** ....**Beverley**, *Cheltenham*, **Chester**, Fakenham, *Huntingdon*
  8 **Thursday** ....**Chester**, **Goodwood**, Newton Abbot, *Wetherby*, *Wincanton*,
      ....*Great Leighs*
  9 **Friday** ....**Chester**, *Hamilton*, **Lingfield**, *Aintree*, **Nottingham**, *Ripon*
 10 **Saturday**...............**Ascot**, **Haydock**, Hexham, **Lingfield**, **Nottingham**, *Thirsk*,
      ....*Warwick*
 11 **Sunday** ....Plumpton, Uttoxeter, Worcester
 12 **Monday** ....**Redcar**, *Towcester*, **Windsor**, **Wolverhampton**, **Yarmouth**
 13 **Tuesday**.........**Brighton**, *Newton Abbot*, **Southwell**, **Yarmouth**, *Great Leighs*
 14 **Wednesday** ....*Bath*, Exeter, Fontwell, *Perth*, **York**
 15 **Thursday** ....*Folkestone*, *Ludlow*, **Newmarket**, Perth, **Salisbury**, **York**
 16 **Friday** ....*Hamilton*, Aintree, **Newbury**, *Newcastle*, Newmarket, **York**
 17 **Saturday** ....Bangor-on-dee, *Doncaster*, **Newbury**, **Newmarket**, **Thirsk**,
      ....Uttoxeter
 18 **Sunday**...Fakenham, Market Rasen, **Ripon**
 19 **Monday** ....**Bath**, **Musselburgh**, Newton Abbot, *Windsor*, *Wolverhampton*
 20 **Tuesday**.................**Beverley**, **Musselburgh**, *Leicester*, **Southwell**, *Towcester*
 21 **Wednesday**..............................**Ayr**, **Goodwood**, Kelso, *Sandown*, *Sedgefield*
 22 **Thursday** ....**Goodwood**, **Haydock**, *Salisbury*, Wetherby, *Worcester*
 23 **Friday**...................**Brighton**, *Haydock*, **Newcastle**, **Newmarket**, *Pontefract*,
      ....*Stratford-on-avon*
 24 **Saturday**.......................**Beverley**, *Cartmel*, **Catterick**, **Haydock**, **Newmarket**,
      ....*Stratford-on-avon*
 25 **Sunday** ....Fontwell, **Newmarket**, Uttoxeter
 26 **Monday** ....**Carlisle**, Cartmel, **Chepstow**, **Leicester**, **Redcar**
 27 **Tuesday** ....**Chepstow**, *Hexham*, *Huntingdon*, **Leicester**, **Redcar**
 28 **Wednesday** ....*Beverley*, Cartmel, *Southwell*, **Yarmouth**, Great Leighs
 29 **Thursday**.....**Ayr**, *Newcastle*, *Sandown*, *Wetherby*, **Yarmouth**, Great Leighs
 30 **Friday** ....**Brighton**, *Musselburgh*, **Goodwood**, *Haydock*, *Towcester*, **York**
 31 **Saturday**..........**Doncaster**, **Goodwood**, **Haydock**, *Lingfield*, *Newbury*, **York**

June

  1 **Sunday**..**Bath**, Perth, Stratford-on-avon
  2 **Monday**..................................**Carlisle**, **Leicester**, *Thirsk*, *Windsor*
  3 **Tuesday**................................*Folkestone*, **Ripon**, *Sedgefield*, **Southwell**
  4 **Wednesday** ....Fontwell, *Kempton*, **Lingfield**, **Nottingham**, *Ripon*
  5 **Thursday** ....**Hamilton**, **Lingfield**, Newton Abbot, *Sandown*, Uttoxeter,
      ....Wetherby
  6 **Friday** ....*Bath*, **Catterick**, *Doncaster*, **Epsom**, *Goodwood*, **Wolverhampton**
  7 **Saturday**.....................**Doncaster**, **Musselburgh**, **Epsom**, Hexham, *Lingfield*,
      ....*Newcastle*, Worcester
  8 **Sunday** ....**Brighton**, **Southwell**, Worcester
  9 **Monday** ....**Folkestone**, Newton Abbot, *Pontefract*, *Windsor*
 10 **Tuesday**.......................................*Chester*, **Redcar**, **Salisbury**, *Southwell*
 11 **Wednesday**.................**Beverley**, **Brighton**, *Hamilton*, *Kempton*, **Nottingham**
 12 **Thursday** ....*Fontwell*, **Haydock**, **Newbury**, *Uttoxeter*, **Yarmouth**

13	Friday	...........*Chepstow, Goodwood, Aintree*, Market Rasen, **Sandown, York**

13 Friday..........*Chepstow, Goodwood, Aintree*, Market Rasen, **Sandown, York**
14 Saturday......................**Bath**, Hexham, *Leicester, Lingfield*, Sandown, **York**
15 Sunday..**Doncaster, Salisbury**, Stratford-on-avon
16 Monday..**Carlisle**, Sedgefield, *Warwick, Windsor*
17 Tuesday..**Ascot**, *Newton Abbot*, **Thirsk, Yarmouth**
18 Wednesday...............................**Ascot, Hamilton**, *Kempton, Ripon*, Worcester
19 Thursday.........**Ascot**, *Leicester*, **Ripon**, *Towcester*, **Warwick**, *Great Leighs*
20 Friday...............**Ascot**, *Ayr*, **Musselburgh**, *Goodwood, Newmarket*, **Redcar**
21 Saturday...................**Ascot, Ayr**, *Haydock, Lingfield*, **Newmarket, Redcar**
22 Sunday ....**Hereford, Hexham, Pontefract**
23 Monday ....*Chepstow*, **Lingfield**, *Windsor*, **Wolverhampton**
24 Tuesday ....**Beverley, Brighton**, *Newbury*, *Newton Abbot*
25 Wednesday ....*Bath*, **Carlisle**, *Kempton*, **Salisbury**, Worcester
26 Thursday...............*Hamilton, Leicester*, **Newcastle, Warwick, Great Leighs**
27 Friday ....*Chester*, **Doncaster, Folkestone**, Market Rasen, *Newcastle,*
....*Newmarket*
28 Saturday..**Chester**, *Doncaster, Lingfield*, **Newcastle, Newmarket, Windsor**
29 Sunday ....**Salisbury**, Uttoxeter, **Windsor**
30 Monday.........................*Musselburgh*, **Pontefract**, *Windsor*, **Wolverhampton**

July

1 Tuesday..**Brighton, Hamilton**, *Lingfield, Thirsk*
2 Wednesday ....**Catterick**, *Chepstow, Kempton*, Perth, Worcester
3 Thursday................**Haydock**, *Newbury*, Perth, *Redcar, Warwick*, **Yarmouth**
4 Friday...........*Beverley, Haydock, Salisbury*, **Sandown, Southwell, Warwick**
5 Saturday ....**Beverley**, *Carlisle*, **Haydock, Leicester**, *Nottingham*, **Sandown**
6 Sunday ....**Ayr, Brighton**, Market Rasen
7 Monday.................................**Brighton, Musselburgh**, *Ripon, Windsor*
8 Tuesday ....**Pontefract**, *Southwell, Uttoxeter*, **Wolverhampton**
9 Wednesday................**Catterick**, *Kempton*, **Lingfield, Newmarket**, *Worcester*
10 Thursday..........*Doncaster*, **Folkestone, Newmarket**, *Nottingham*, **Warwick**
11 Friday....................**Ascot**, *Chepstow, Chester, Newbury*, **Newmarket, York**
12 Saturday ....**Ascot, Chester**, *Hamilton*, **Nottingham**, *Salisbury*, **York**
13 Sunday...**Haydock**, Perth, Stratford-on-avon
14 Monday...........................**Ayr**, Newton Abbot, *Windsor, Wolverhampton*
15 Tuesday ....**Beverley, Brighton**, *Yarmouth, Great Leighs*
16 Wednesday ....**Catterick**, *Kempton*, **Lingfield**, Uttoxeter, *Worcester*
17 Thursday..............*Bath*, Cartmel, *Doncaster*, **Hamilton, Leicester**, *Sandown*
18 Friday..................*Hamilton*, **Newbury**, *Newmarket*, **Nottingham**, *Pontefract,*
....Southwell
19 Saturday..*Haydock, Lingfield*, Market Rasen, **Newbury, Newmarket, Ripon**
20 Sunday...Newton Abbot, **Redcar**, Stratford-on-avon
21 Monday...**Ayr**, *Beverley, Windsor*, **Yarmouth**
22 Tuesday ....*Bangor-on-dee*, **Salisbury, Yarmouth**, *Great Leighs*
23 Wednesday...................**Catterick**, *Leicester*, **Lingfield**, *Sandown*, Worcester
24 Thursday ....**Bath**, *Doncaster, Folkestone, Kempton*, **Sandown**, Uttoxeter
25 Friday ....**Ascot**, *Chepstow, Newmarket*, **Thirsk, Wolverhampton**, *York*
26 Saturday ....**Ascot**, *Lingfield*, **Newcastle, Newmarket**, *Salisbury*, **York**
27 Sunday...**Ascot, Carlisle, Pontefract**
28 Monday ....**Southwell**, *Uttoxeter, Windsor*, **Yarmouth**
29 Tuesday ....**Beverley, Goodwood**, *Perth, Worcester*
30 Wednesday ....**Goodwood**, *Kempton, Leicester*, Perth, **Redcar**
31 Thursday...................*Musselburgh*, **Goodwood, Nottingham**, *Sandown,*
....Stratford-on-avon

August

1 Friday ......Bangor-on-dee, *Bath*, Goodwood, *Haydock*, *Newmarket*, Thirsk
2 Saturday ..Doncaster, Goodwood, *Hamilton*, *Lingfield*, Newmarket, Thirsk
3 Sunday ....Chester, Market Rasen, **Newbury**
4 Monday.................................*Carlisle*, Newton Abbot, **Ripon**, *Windsor*
5 Tuesday ....Catterick, Chepstow
6 Wednesday..............Brighton, *Kempton*, Newcastle, Pontefract, *Yarmouth*
7 Thursday ....*Bath*, Brighton, *Folkestone*, Haydock, *Sandown*, Yarmouth
8 Friday.........................Brighton, *Haydock*, Lingfield, *Newmarket*, Worcester
9 Saturday ....Ascot, *Ayr*, Haydock, *Lingfield*, Newmarket, Redcar
10 Sunday ....Leicester, Redcar, Windsor
11 Monday...................................Southwell, *Thirsk*, *Windsor*, Wolverhampton
12 Tuesday ....*Musselburgh*, Lingfield, Newton Abbot, *Nottingham*
13 Wednesday.................Beverley, *Hamilton*, Salisbury, *Sandown*, Yarmouth
14 Thursday ....Beverley, *Chepstow*, Salisbury, Sandown, *Stratford-on-avon*,
....*Great Leighs*
15 Friday.*Catterick*, *Kempton*, Newbury, Newcastle, *Newmarket*, Nottingham
16 Saturday ....Bangor-on-dee, *Lingfield*, Market Rasen, **Newbury**, Newmarket,
....**Ripon**
17 Sunday ....Bath, Pontefract, Southwell
18 Monday ....Lingfield, *Windsor*, Wolverhampton, *Yarmouth*
19 Tuesday ....Brighton, *Newton Abbot*, *Worcester*, **York**
20 Wednesday....................Carlisle, *Folkestone*, Hamilton, *Newton Abbot*, **York**
21 Thursday ....*Chester*, Fontwell, Stratford-on-avon, **York**, Great Leighs
22 Friday ....*Bath*, *Hamilton*, Newbury, *Newcastle*, Newmarket, **York**
23 Saturday.......Beverley, Cartmel, **Goodwood**, Newmarket, *Redcar*, *Windsor*
24 Sunday ....Beverley, Goodwood, Yarmouth
25 Monday ....Cartmel, **Chepstow**, Huntingdon, **Kempton**, Newcastle, Ripon,
....**Warwick**
26 Tuesday ....Ripon, Great Leighs
27 Wednesday ....Ayr, Catterick, Great Leighs
28 Thursday ....Ayr, Lingfield, Great Leighs
29 Friday ....Chester, Hamilton, *Salisbury*, Sandown, *Wolverhampton*
30 Saturday ......*Bath*, Chester, *Market Rasen*, Newton Abbot, **Ripon**, Sandown
31 Sunday ....Musselburgh, Folkestone, Newton Abbot

September

1 Monday...Hamilton, Kempton, Lingfield
2 Tuesday ....Goodwood, Sedgefield, **Southwell**
3 Wednesday.................................Brighton, Hereford, *Kempton*, Lingfield
4 Thursday...................................Redcar, Salisbury, Warwick, *Great Leighs*
5 Friday ....Catterick, Chepstow, *Kempton*, Lingfield
6 Saturday ....Haydock, Kempton, Stratford-on-avon, **Thirsk**, *Wolverhampton*
7 Sunday...Fontwell, **Thirsk**, Worcester
8 Monday ....Bath, Folkestone, Newcastle
9 Tuesday ....Beverley, Leicester, Lingfield
10 Wednesday ....Doncaster, *Kempton*, Uttoxeter, **Warwick**
11 Thursday..................Chepstow, Doncaster, Sandown, *Great Leighs*
12 Friday ....Bangor-on-dee, **Doncaster**, Sandown, *Wolverhampton*
13 Saturday...............Chester, Doncaster, Goodwood, *Kempton*, Great Leighs
14 Sunday ....Goodwood, Stratford-on-avon, **Great Leighs**
15 Monday...Musselburgh, Leicester, Redcar
16 Tuesday ....Haydock, Lingfield, Yarmouth
17 Wednesday ....Beverley, *Kempton*, Sandown, Yarmouth
18 Thursday.................................Ayr, Pontefract, Yarmouth, *Great Leighs*

19 Friday..**Ayr, Newbury, Newmarket**, *Wolverhampton*
20 Saturday ....**Ayr, Catterick, Newbury, Newmarket**, *Wolverhampton*
21 Sunday..**Hamilton**, Plumpton, Uttoxeter
22 Monday..**Hamilton, Kempton, Leicester**
23 Tuesday ....**Beverley, Folkestone**, Sedgefield
24 Wednesday ....**Goodwood**, *Kempton*, Perth, **Redcar**
25 Thursday ....Fontwell, Perth, **Pontefract**, *Great Leighs*
26 Friday..............................**Ascot, Haydock**, *Wolverhampton*, Worcester
27 Saturday...................**Ascot, Chester, Haydock**, Market Rasen, *Great Leighs*
28 Sunday ....**Ascot, Musselburgh**, Market Rasen
29 Monday ....**Bath, Brighton, Windsor**
30 Tuesday...Sedgefield, **Southwell, Warwick**

October

1 Wednesday ....*Kempton*, **Newcastle, Nottingham, Salisbury**
2 Thursday ....**Ayr, Goodwood, Newmarket**, *Great Leighs*
3 Friday..............................Hexham, **Lingfield, Newmarket**, *Wolverhampton*
4 Saturday ....Fontwell, **Kempton, Newmarket, Redcar**, *Wolverhampton*
5 Sunday ....Huntingdon, Kelso, Uttoxeter
6 Monday..**Pontefract, Warwick, Windsor**
7 Tuesday..**Catterick, Folkestone, Leicester**
8 Wednesday ....Exeter, *Kempton*, **Nottingham**, Towcester
9 Thursday...............................**Newbury**, Wincanton, Worcester, *Great Leighs*
10 Friday...**Ayr**, Carlisle, **Lingfield**, *Wolverhampton*
11 Saturday ....**Ascot**, Bangor-on-dee, Chepstow, **Musselburgh**, Hexham,
....*Wolverhampton*
12 Sunday ....**Bath, Goodwood**, Great Leighs
13 Monday...**Kempton, Windsor, Wolverhampton**
14 Tuesday ....Huntingdon, **Leicester, Newcastle**
15 Wednesday.............................*Kempton*, **Lingfield**, Uttoxeter, Wetherby
16 Thursday.............................**Brighton**, Ludlow, **Nottingham**, *Great Leighs*
17 Friday ....Cheltenham, *Kempton*, **Newmarket, Redcar**
18 Saturday............**Catterick**, Cheltenham, Kelso, **Newmarket**, *Wolverhampton*
19 Sunday..Fontwell, Kempton, **Southwell**
20 Monday ....Plumpton, **Pontefract, Windsor**
21 Tuesday ....Exeter, **Lingfield**, Yarmouth
22 Wednesday ....**Bath**, *Kempton*, Worcester, **Great Leighs**
23 Thursday..............................**Brighton**, Carlisle, Ludlow, *Great Leighs*
24 Friday ....**Ayr, Doncaster**, Fakenham, *Wolverhampton*
25 Saturday ....Chepstow, **Doncaster**, Aintree, **Newbury**, Stratford-on-avon,
....*Wolverhampton*
26 Sunday...Aintree, Towcester, Wincanton
27 Monday...**Kempton, Leicester, Lingfield**
28 Tuesday ....**Catterick, Southwell**, Yarmouth
29 Wednesday ....Huntingdon, *Kempton*, **Nottingham**, Great Leighs
30 Thursday ....**Lingfield**, Newcastle, Stratford-on-avon, *Great Leighs*
31 Friday ....**Newmarket**, Uttoxeter, Wetherby, *Wolverhampton*

November

1 Saturday......................**Ascot, Ayr, Newmarket**, Wetherby, *Great Leighs*
2 Sunday ....Carlisle, Huntingdon, **Southwell**
3 Monday.....................................Plumpton, Warwick, **Wolverhampton**
4 Tuesday ....**Catterick**, Exeter, **Southwell**
5 Wednesday ....Chepstow, Huntingdon, *Kempton*, **Nottingham**
6 Thursday.............................Haydock, **Lingfield**, Towcester, *Great Leighs*
7 Friday ....**Musselburgh**, Fontwell, Hexham, *Wolverhampton*

8 Saturday ....**Doncaster**, Kelso, Sandown, Wincanton, *Wolverhampton*
9 Sunday...Hereford, **Kempton**, Market Rasen
10 Monday...Carlisle, **Southwell**, Wolverhampton
11 Tuesday ....Exeter, Lingfield, Sedgefield
12 Wednesday................Bangor-on-dee, Kempton, **Southwell**, *Wolverhampton*
13 Thursday....................................**Lingfield**, Ludlow, Taunton, *Great Leighs*
14 Friday.............................Cheltenham, *Kempton*, Newcastle, **Southwell**
15 Saturday ..Cheltenham, Uttoxeter, Wetherby, *Wolverhampton*, Great Leighs
16 Sunday.................................Cheltenham, Fontwell, Stratford-on-avon
17 Monday ....**Kempton**, Leicester, **Wolverhampton**
18 Tuesday ....Fakenham, Folkestone, **Southwell**
19 Wednesday................................Hexham, *Kempton*, **Lingfield**, Warwick
20 Thursday ....Hereford, Market Rasen, Wincanton, *Great Leighs*
21 Friday...................................Ascot, Exeter, Kelso, *Wolverhampton*
22 Saturday ....Ascot, Haydock, Huntingdon, **Lingfield**, *Wolverhampton*
23 Sunday.................................Aintree, Plumpton, Towcester
24 Monday ....Ayr, **Lingfield**, Ludlow
25 Tuesday..................................Lingfield, Sedgefield, **Southwell**
26 Wednesday ....Chepstow, Kempton, Wetherby, *Wolverhampton*
27 Thursday ....Newbury, Taunton, Uttoxeter, *Great Leighs*
28 Friday.............................Musselburgh, *Kempton*, **Lingfield**, Newbury
29 Saturday ....**Kempton**, Newbury, Newcastle, Towcester, *Wolverhampton*
30 Sunday.................................Carlisle, **Kempton**, Leicester

December

1 Monday ....Fakenham, Folkestone, **Wolverhampton**
2 Tuesday ....Hereford, **Lingfield**, **Southwell**
3 Wednesday ....Ayr, Catterick, *Kempton*, Plumpton
4 Thursday.......................Leicester, Market Rasen, Wincanton, *Great Leighs*
5 Friday...........................Exeter, **Lingfield**, Sandown, *Wolverhampton*
6 Saturday .....Chepstow, Sandown, Wetherby, *Wolverhampton*, Great Leighs
7 Sunday.......................................Kelso, **Lingfield**, Warwick
8 Monday ....Musselburgh, **Lingfield**, Wolverhampton
9 Tuesday...Fontwell, Sedgefield, **Southwell**
10 Wednesday...........................Hexham, *Kempton*, Leicester, **Southwell**
11 Thursday ....Huntingdon, Ludlow, Taunton, *Great Leighs*
12 Friday...........................Cheltenham, Doncaster, **Southwell**, *Wolverhampton*
13 Saturday ....Cheltenham, Doncaster, Lingfield, **Southwell**, *Wolverhampton*
14 Sunday.................................Musselburgh, **Lingfield**
15 Monday ....Ayr, Plumpton, **Wolverhampton**
16 Tuesday ....Catterick, Folkestone, **Southwell**
17 Wednesday.............................Bangor-on-dee, *Kempton*, **Lingfield**, Newbury
18 Thursday............................Exeter, Ludlow, **Southwell**, *Great Leighs*
19 Friday..............................Ascot, **Southwell**, Uttoxeter, *Wolverhampton*
20 Saturday ....Ascot, Haydock, **Lingfield**, Newcastle, *Wolverhampton*
21 Sunday ....Carlisle, **Great Leighs**
22 Monday ....Hereford, **Kempton**, Lingfield
23 Tuesday...Fontwell, **Southwell**
26 Friday...............Huntingdon, Kempton, Market Rasen, Sedgefield, Towcester,
....Wetherby, Wincanton, **Wolverhampton**
27 Saturday.................Chepstow, Kempton, **Southwell**, Wetherby, *Great Leighs*
28 Sunday.................................Catterick, Leicester, **Lingfield**
29 Monday ....Musselburgh, Newbury, **Great Leighs**
30 Tuesday ....Haydock, **Lingfield**, Taunton, *Wolverhampton*

Big-race dates

March
29 Mar   Newcastle..William Hill Lincoln (Heritage Handicap)

April
16 Apr   Newmarket...Shadwell Stud Nell Gwyn Stakes (Group 3)
17 Apr   Newmarket.......................................Weatherbys Earl of Sefton Stakes (Group 3)
17 Apr   Newmarket........................banshahousestables.com Craven Stakes (Group 3)
19 Apr   Newbury ....Dubai Duty Free Fred Darling Stakes (Group 3)
19 Apr   Newbury ....Dubai Tennis Championships John Porter Stakes (Group 3)
19 Apr   Newbury...Lane's End Greenham Stakes (Group 3)
25 Apr   Sandown Park ....Betfred Gordon Richards Stakes (Group 3)
26 Apr   Sandown Park...betfred.com Mile Stakes (Group 2)
26 Apr   Sandown Park.......................................Betfred Classic Trial Stakes (Group 3)
30 Apr   Ascot ....Woodcote Stud Sagaro Stakes (Group 3)

May
3 May   Newmarket ....Stan James 2000 Guineas Stakes (Group 1)
3 May   Newmarket..Stan James Dahlia Stakes (Group 3)
4 May   Newmarket ....Stan James Palace House Stakes (Group 3)
4 May   Newmarket ....Stan James 1000 Guineas Stakes (Group 1)
4 May   Newmarket.....................StanJamesUK.com Jockey Club Stakes (Group 2)
7 May   Chester......................................totesport Chester Cup (Heritage Handicap)
8 May   Chester...Akkroball Huxley Stakes Group 3)
8 May   Chester..MBNA Chester Vase Stakes (Group 3)
9 May   Chester ....Blue Square Ormonde Stakes (Group 3)
9 May   Chester ....Aktiv Capital UK Ltd Dee Stakes (Group 3)
10 May   Ascot...totesport Victoria Cup (Heritage Handicap)
10 May   Lingfield Park................................totesport Derby Trial Stakes (Group 3)
14 May   York ....Duke of York Hearthstead Homes Stakes (Group 2)
14 May   York ....Tattersalls Musidora Stakes (Group 3)
15 May   York...totesport Dante Stakes (Group 2)
15 May   York ....totepool Middleton Stakes (Group 3)
16 May   York ....Emirates Airline Yorkshire Cup Stakes (Group 2)
17 May   Newbury...Juddmonte Lockinge Stakes (Group 1)
21 May   Sandown Park...........wbx.com World Bet Exchange Henry II Stakes (Group 2)
24 May   Haydock Park...betfair.com Temple Stakes (Group 2)
29 May   Sandown Park...................betfair.com Brigadier Gerard Stakes (Group 3)

June
6 Jun   Epsom...................................Vodafone Coronation Cup Stakes (Group 1)
6 Jun   Epsom ....Vodafone Oaks Stakes (Group 1)
6 Jun   Epsom ....Princess Elizabeth Stakes (Group 3)
7 Jun   Epsom ....Vodafone Derby Stakes (Group 1)
7 Jun   Epsom ....Vodafone Diomed Stakes (Group 3)
17 Jun   Royal Ascot...Queen Anne Stakes (Group 1)
17 Jun   Royal Ascot ....St James's Palace Stakes (Group 1)
17 Jun   Royal Ascot...Coventry Stakes (Group 2)
17 Jun   Royal Ascot...King's Stand Stakes (Group 2)
18 Jun   Royal Ascot ....Prince of Wales's Stakes (Group 1)
18 Jun   Royal Ascot ....Queen Mary Stakes (Group 2)
18 Jun   Royal Ascot ....Windsor Forest Stakes (Group 2)
18 Jun   Royal Ascot...Jersey Stakes (Group 3)
18 Jun   Royal Ascot ....Royal Hunt Cup (Heritage Handicap)
19 Jun   Royal Ascot ....Gold Cup (Group 1)
19 Jun   Royal Ascot ....Ribblesdale Stakes (Group 2)
19 Jun   Royal Ascot..Norfolk Stakes (Group 2)
20 Jun   Royal Ascot ....Coronation Stakes (Group 1)

20 Jun	Royal Ascot	King Edward VII Stakes (Group 2)
20 Jun	Royal Ascot	Albany Stakes (Group 3)
20 Jun	Royal Ascot	Queen's Vase (Group 3)
21 Jun	Royal Ascot	Golden Jubilee Stakes (Group 1)
21 Jun	Royal Ascot	Hardwicke Stakes (Group 2)
21 Jun	Royal Ascot	Wokingham (Heritage Handicap)
28 Jun	Newcastle	Newcastle Brown Ale Chipchase Stakes (Group 3)
28 Jun	Newcastle	John Smith's Northumberland Plate (Heritage Handicap)
28 Jun	Newmarket	Cheveley Park Stud Criterion Stakes (Group 3)

July

5 Jul	Haydock Park	bet365 Lancashire Oaks (Group 2)
5 Jul	Haydock Park	bet365 Old Newton Cup (Heritage Handicap)
5 Jul	Sandown Park	Coral-Eclipse Stakes (Group 1)
5 Jul	Sandown Park	Laurent-Perrier Champagne Sprint (Group 3)
9 Jul	Newmarket	UAE Hydra Properties Falmouth Stakes (Group 1)
9 Jul	Newmarket	Chippenham Lodge Stud Cherry Hinton Stakes (Group 2)
10 Jul	Newmarket	wbx.com Princess of Wales's Stakes (Group 2)
10 Jul	Newmarket	TNT July Stakes (Group 2)
11 Jul	Newmarket	Bahrain Trophy (Listed)
11 Jul	Newmarket	Darley July Cup (Group 1)
11 Jul	Newmarket	Weatherbys Superlative Stakes (Group 2)
11 Jul	Newmarket	Ladbrokes Bunbury Cup (Heritage Handicap)
11 Jul	York	Cuisine de France Summer Stakes (Group 3)
12 Jul	Ascot	Sony Summer Mile (Group 3)
12 Jul	York	John Smith's Cup (Heritage Handicap)
14 Jul	Ayr	Giles Insurance Brokers (Heritage Handicap)
19 Jul	Newbury	Uplands Racing Hackwood Stakes (Group 3)
19 Jul	Newbury	Weatherbys Super Sprint
26 Jul	Ascot	King George VI and Queen Elizabeth Diamond Stakes (Group 1)
26 Jul	Ascot	totesport International (Heritage Handicap)
26 Jul	York	Skybet York Stakes (Group 2)
27 Jul	Ascot	Princess Margaret Stakes (Group 3)
29 Jul	Goodwood	Betfair Cup (Registered as the Lennox Stakes) (Group 2)
29 Jul	Goodwood	Gordon Stakes (Group 3)
29 Jul	Goodwood	Betfair Molecomb Stakes (Group 3)
30 Jul	Goodwood	BGC Sussex Stakes (Group 1)
30 Jul	Goodwood	Veuve Cliquot Vintage Stakes (Group 2)
31 Jul	Goodwood	ABN AMRO Goodwood Cup (Group 2)
31 Jul	Goodwood	Audi King George Stakes (Group 3)
31 Jul	Goodwood	Lillie Langtry Stakes (Group 3)

August

1 Aug	Goodwood	Sterling Insurance Richmond Stakes (Group 2)
1 Aug	Goodwood	Oak Tree Stakes (Group 3)
1 Aug	Goodwood	totesport Mile (Heritage Handicap)
2 Aug	Goodwood	Blue Square Nassau Stakes (Group 1)
2 Aug	Goodwood	Blue Square Stewards' Cup (Heritage Handicap)
9 Aug	Ascot	Blue Square Shergar Cup Day
9 Aug	Haydock Park	Totepool Rose of Lancaster Stakes (Group 3)
9 Aug	Newmarket	skybet.com Sweet Solera Stakes (Group 3)
14 Aug	Salisbury	totesport Sovereign Stakes (Group 3)
16 Aug	Newbury	Hungerford Stakes (Group 2)
16 Aug	Newbury	Geoffrey Freer Stakes (Group 3)
19 Aug	York	Juddmonte International (Group 1)
19 Aug	York	Ladbrokes Great Voltigeur Stakes (Group 2)
19 Aug	York	Weatherbys Insurance Lonsdale Cup (Group 2)
20 Aug	York	Ireland Gimcrack Stakes (Group 2)
21 Aug	York	Darley Yorkshire Oaks (Group 1)
21 Aug	York	Jaguar Cars Lowther Stakes (Group 2)
22 Aug	York	Acomb Stakes (Group 3)

22 Aug	York	totesport Ebor (Heritage Handicap)
22 Aug	York	Coolmore Nunthorpe Stakes (Group 1)
23 Aug	Windsor	totepool Winter Hill Stakes (Group 3)
23 Aug	Goodwood	totesport Celebration Mile (Group 2)
23 Aug	Goodwood	Prestige Stakes (Group 3)
30 Aug	Sandown Park	Iveco Daily Solario Stakes (Group 3)

September

2 Sep	Goodwood	Charlton Hunt Supreme Stakes (Group 3)
6 Sep	Haydock Park	Betfred Sprint Cup (Group 1)
6 Sep	Kempton Park	totepool Sirenia Stakes (Group 3)
6 Sep	Kempton Park	totesport.com September Stakes (Group 3)
11 Sep	Doncaster	Park Hill Stakes (Group 2)
12 Sep	Doncaster	GNER Doncaster Cup (Group 2)
11 Sep	Doncaster	May Hill Stakes (Group 2)
12 Sep	Doncaster	Flying Childers Stakes (Group 2)
13 Sep	Doncaster	Ladbrokes St Leger (Group 1)
13 Sep	Doncaster	Park Stakes (Group 2)
13 Sep	Doncaster	Champagne Stakes (Group 2)
13 Sep	Doncaster	Strensall Stakes (Group 3)
13 Sep	Doncaster	Ladbrokes Portland (Heritage Handicap)
14 Sep	Goodwood	Select Racing UK on Sky 432 Select Stakes (Group 3)
19 Sep	Newbury	Dubai Duty Free Arc Trial (Group 3)
20 Sep	Ayr	TSG Firth of Clyde Stakes (Group 3)
20 Sep	Ayr	totesport Ayr Gold Cup (Heritage Handicap)
20 Sep	Newbury	Dubai Duty Free Mill Reef Stakes (Group 2)
20 Sep	Newbury	Dubai International Airport World Trophy (Group 3)
26 Sep	Ascot	PricewaterhouseCoopers EBF Harvest Stakes (Group 3)
27 Sep	Ascot	Meon Valley Stud Fillies' Mile (Group 1)
27 Sep	Ascot	Queen Elizabeth II Stakes (Group 1)
27 Sep	Ascot	Juddmonte Royal Lodge Stakes (Group 2)
28 Sep	Ascot	Diadem Stakes (Group 2)
28 Sep	Ascot	Grosvenor Casinos Cumberland Lodge Stakes (Group 3)

October

3 Oct	Newmarket	Cheveley Park Stakes (Group 1)
3 Oct	Newmarket	Shadwell Middle Park Stakes (Group 1)
3 Oct	Newmarket	Somerville Tattersal Stakes (Group 3)
4 Oct	Newmarket	Kingdom of Bahrain Sun Chariot Stakes (Group 1)
4 Oct	Newmarket	Countrywide Steel and Tubes Joel Stakes (Group 3)
4 Oct	Newmarket	totesport Cambridgeshire (Heritage Handicap)
4 Oct	Redcar	totepool Two-Year-Old Trophy (Listed)
11 Oct	Ascot	Deloitte Autumn Stakes (Group 3)
11 Oct	Ascot	Willmott Dixon Cornwallis Stakes (Group 3)
18 Oct	Newmarket	Darley Dewhurst Stakes (Group 1)
18 Oct	Newmarket	Emirates Airline Champion Stakes (Group 1)
18 Oct	Newmarket	Owen Brown Rockfel Stakes (Group 2)
18 Oct	Newmarket	VC Bet Challenge Stakes (Group 2)
18 Oct	Newmarket	Darley Stakes (Group 3)
18 Oct	Newmarket	Jockey Club Cup (Group 3)
18 Oct	Newmarket	totesport Cesarewitch (Heritage Handicap)
25 Oct	Doncaster	Racing Post Trophy (Group 1)
25 Oct	Newbury	Mountgrange Stud Horris Hill Stakes (Group 3)
25 Oct	Newbury	St Simon Stakes (Group 3)

November

| 8 Nov | Doncaster | totesport November (Heritage Handicap) |

Track Facts

WANT TO size up the layout and undulations of the course where your fancy's about to line up? Over the next 30-odd pages, we bring you three-dimensional maps of all Britain's Flat tracks, allowing you to see at a glance task facing your selection. The maps come to you courtesy of the *Racing Post*'s website (www.racingpost.co.uk).

We've listed the top dozen trainers and jockeys at each course, ranked by strike-rate, with a breakdown of their relevant statistics over the last five years. The record of favourites is here as well and underline a basic fact of racing – that favourites generally offer very little in the way of value. Market leaders generated a profit (to level stakes of £1) at only five tracks and run up colossal losses on the All-Weather.

We've included addresses, phone numbers, directions and fixture lists for each track, together with Time Test's standard times for all you clock-watchers.

And Graham Wheldon, whose *Sprintline* column is a popular feature of RFO, has chipped in with his views on the draw at every course – see page 225. As his analysis has repeatedly shown, most tracks feature a bias of some kind, so check whether the beast on your betting slip is running on the right side before you hand it over.

ASCOT	188	**MUSSELBURGH**	207
AYR	189	**NEWBURY**	208
BATH	190	**NEWCASTLE**	209
BEVERLEY	191	**NEWMARKET (ROWLEY)**	210
BRIGHTON	192	**NEWMARKET (JULY)**	211
CARLISLE	193	**NOTTINGHAM**	212
CATTERICK	194	**PONTEFRACT**	213
CHEPSTOW	195	**REDCAR**	214
CHESTER	196	**RIPON**	215
DoncaSTER	197	**SALISBURY**	216
EPSOM	198	**SANDOWN**	217
FOLKESTONE	199	**SOUTHWELL**	218
GOODWOOD	200	**THIRSK**	219
HAMILTON	201	**WARWICK**	220
HAYDOCK	202	**WINDSOR**	221
KEMPTON	203	**WOLVERHAMPTON**	222
LEICESTER	204	**YARMOUTH**	223
LINGFIELD (TURF)	205	**YORK**	224
LINGFIELD (SAND)	206		

ASCOT

Ascot, Berkshire SL5 7JX
0870 7227 227

How to get there – Road: M4 junction 6 or M3 junction 3 on to A332.
Rail: Frequent service from Reading or Waterloo
Features: RH
2008 Flat fixtures: April 30, May 10, June 17-21, July 11-12, 25-27, August 9, September 26-28, October 11
Pointers: Marcus Tregoning has a terrific record at the Berkshire track, as does Roger Charlton, but Saeed bin Suroor's runners are most interesting. Godolphin boast an outstanding 17 out of 62 record when Frankie Dettori is in the saddle – it's none from 39 without the Italian.

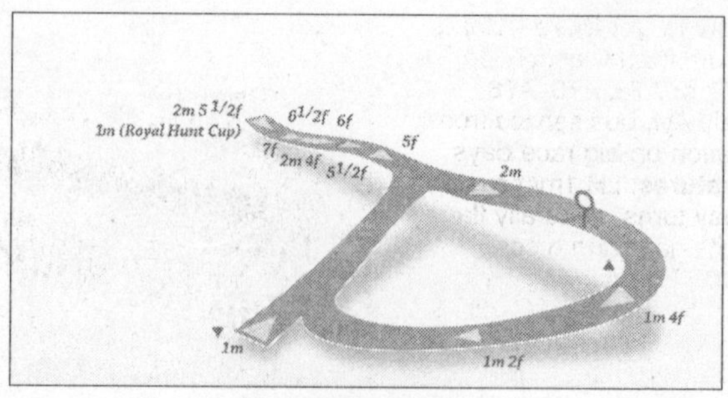

Time Test standard times

5f	58.85	1m (rnd)	1min38.6
6f	1min12.3	1m2f	2min3.2
6f110yds	1min18.7	1m4f	2min27.8
7f	1min25.2	2m	3min23.5
1m (str)	1min37.9	2m4f	4min18.7

Favourites

2-y-o	31.1%	+£0.33
3-y-o+	24.9%	-£47.01
OVERALL	26.2%	-£46.68

Trainers

Trainers	Wins-Runs	%	2yo	3yo+	£1 level stks
G Margarson	4-11	36.4	0-2	4-9	+£36.75
M Tregoning	15-44	34.1	4-7	11-37	+£31.36
Lady Herries	3-10	30.0	0-0	3-10	+£4.75
B Smart	3-13	23.1	3-5	0-8	+£1.75
R Charlton	11-50	22.0	1-6	10-44	+£29.25
Jamie Poulton	3-16	18.8	0-0	3-16	+£86.00
N Callaghan	4-22	18.2	0-8	4-14	+£9.91
S bin Suroor	17-101	16.8	4-11	13-90	-£11.46
Sir M Stoute	26-155	16.8	3-9	23-146	-£31.64
A Jarvis	6-36	16.7	4-16	2-20	+£12.25
J Fanshawe	12-73	16.4	1-4	11-69	-£8.38
J A Osborne	7-43	16.3	4-23	3-20	+£8.63
W Haggas	10-62	16.1	1-10	9-52	+£75.25

Jockeys

Jockeys	Wins-Rides	%	£1 level stks	Best Trainer	W-R
P Dobbs	5-29	17.2	+£3.88	R Hannon	3-16
W Buick	3-18	16.7	+£23.25	J A Osborne	1-1
R Mullen	5-30	16.7	+£25.75	C Wall	2-7
J Murtagh	8-52	15.4	+£79.08	A P O'Brien	2-10
R Ffrench	3-20	15.0	+£2.00	Mrs A Duffield	1-1
J Fortune	22-151	14.6	+£54.50	J Gosden	6-26
K Fallon	23-162	14.2	-£41.53	Sir M Stoute	8-54
L Dettori	33-238	13.9	-£16.71	S bin Suroor	17-62
T P Queally	3-22	13.6	+£73.00	P Grayson	1-1
N Mackay	5-38	13.2	+£13.00	G M Moore	1-1
R Hills	17-129	13.2	-£7.56	M Tregoning	4-14
A Munro	3-23	13.0	-£8.25	J Noseda	1-1
J H Bowman	4-34	11.8	-£3.00	M Channon	2-16

How to get there – Road: south from Glasgow on A77 or A75, A70, A76. Rail: Ayr, bus service from station on big race days

Features: LH 1m4f oval, easy turns, generally flat, suits galloping types

2008 Flat fixtures: May 21, 29, June 20-21, July 6, 14, 21, August 9, 27-28, September 18-20, October 2, 10, 24, November 1

Pointers: When a Newmarket trainer makes the long trip to Ayr it generally pays to take the hint – Luca Cumani, Sir Michael Stoute and Sir Mark Prescott all have excellent strike-rates here, and with a level-stakes profit to boot.

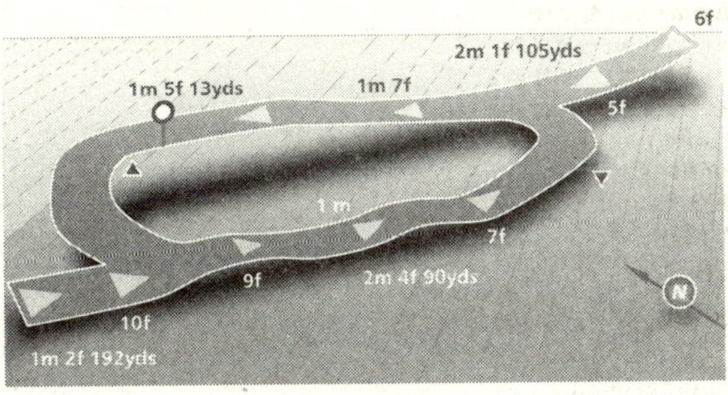

Time Test standard times

5f	57.7	1m2f	2min4.4
6f	1min9.7	1m2f192yds	2min14.3
7f	1min25	1m5f13yds	2min45.4
7f50yds	1min28	1m7f	3min13.2
1m	1min37.7	2m1f105yds	3min46
1m1f20yds	1min50	2m4f90yds	4min25

Favourites

2-y-o	37.5%	-£14.25
3-y-o+	22.7%	-£120.95
OVERALL	26.0%	-£135.20

Trainers	Wins-Runs	%	2yo	3yo+	£1 level stks
L Cumani	7-12	58.3	0-1	7-11	+£19.61
Sir M Stoute	4-11	36.4	0-1	4-10	+£2.45
A Brown	3-9	33.3	0-0	3-9	+£47.60
Sir M Prescott	11-33	33.3	3-13	8-20	+£5.88
Mrs G Rees	3-10	30.0	2-4	1-6	+£15.00
M Jarvis	5-19	26.3	1-5	4-14	-£2.53
B Hills	6-24	25.0	1-9	5-15	+£5.17
E Dunlop	5-22	22.7	4-12	1-10	+£5.31
T Tate	3-14	21.4	0-5	3-9	-£1.12
S bin Suroor	3-15	20.0	1-5	2-10	-£8.89
D Carroll	6-31	19.4	1-2	5-29	+£12.25
W Haggas	4-21	19.0	0-1	4-20	-£2.00
R Hannon	3-16	18.8	2-12	1-4	+£5.00

Jockeys	Wins-Rides	%	£1 level stks	Best Trainer	W-R
S Donohoe	6-18	33.3	+£25.50	D Carroll	1-1
K Fallon	10-33	30.3	-£1.12	Sir M Stoute	3-4
R Hughes	3-11	27.3	+£6.00	R Hannon	2-2
J-P Guillambert	10-37	27.0	+£32.78	Sir M Prescott	1-1
S Golam	5-22	22.7	+£19.50	C Thornton	1-1
K McEvoy	4-18	22.2	-£8.64	S bin Suroor	3-7
S Hitchcott	5-24	20.8	+£23.00	M Channon	2-8
L Dettori	3-15	20.0	-£2.50	B Smart	1-1
J P Spencer	5-25	20.0	+£18.45	K Ryan	2-5
N Mackay	14-76	18.4	+£59.38	J Goldie	6-39
S Sanders	10-57	17.5	-£4.51	Sir M Prescott	5-12
L Jones	4-24	16.7	+£5.08	W Brisbourne	1-6
S De Sousa	5-30	16.7	+£14.35	D Nicholls	1-5

BATH

How to get there – Road: M4, Jctn 18, then A46 south.

Rail: Bath Spa, special bus service to course on race-days

Features: LH oval, uphill straight of 4f.

2008 Flat fixtures: April 9, 22, 29, May 14, 19, June 1, 6, 14, 25, July 17, 24, August 1, 7, 17, 22, 30, September 8, 29, October 12, 22

Pointers: No strong trends to draw upon, apart from Mark Johnston's miserable record with juveniles. He has won with just one of his 16 two-year-old runners at the track in the last five seasons.

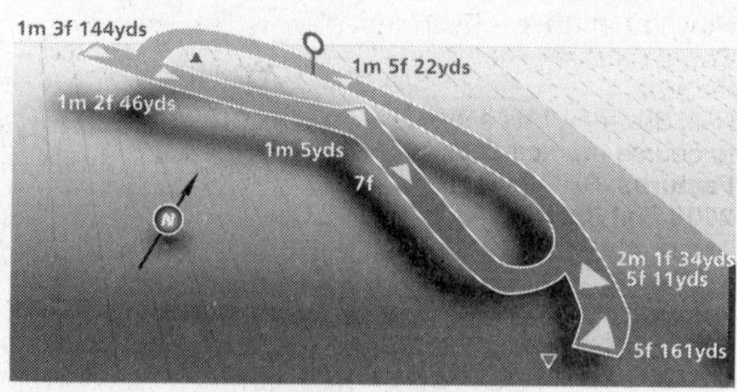

Time Test standard times

5f11yds	1min0.5	1m3f144yds	2min26
5f161yds	1min9	1m5f22yds	2min47.3
1m5yds	1min38	2m1f34yds	3min44
1m2f46yds	2min6.2		

Favourites

2-y-o	37.7%	-£8.85
3-y-o+	30.1%	-£7.62
OVERALL	31.9%	-£16.46

Trainers

Trainers	Wins-Runs	%	2yo	3yo+	£1 level stks
J J Quinn	3-6	50.0	0-0	3-6	+£12.25
J Cullinan	3-8	37.5	0-0	3-8	+£10.83
D Loder	3-10	30.0	1-2	2-8	+£0.50
E S McMahon	4-14	28.6	4-6	0-8	+£11.25
N Callaghan	4-14	28.6	2-6	2-8	+£15.83
L Cumani	11-40	27.5	0-1	11-39	+£4.03
M Tregoning	11-42	26.2	3-12	8-30	-£12.09
M Jarvis	3-12	25.0	2-4	1-8	-£1.27
S bin Suroor	5-20	25.0	3-11	2-9	-£2.33
Sir M Stoute	9-36	25.0	3-7	6-29	-£11.30
R Charlton	16-65	24.6	7-27	9-38	-£5.05
M Johnston	10-43	23.3	1-16	9-27	-£0.30
R Cowell	3-13	23.1	0-0	3-13	+£1.00

Jockeys

Jockeys	Wins-Rides	%	£1 level stks	Best Trainer	W-R
L Fletcher	3-9	33.3	+£19.25	J J Quinn	1-1
S Golam	5-18	27.8	+£40.00	J Boyle	1-1
K Darley	8-29	27.6	-£6.93	M Johnston	5-8
P Robinson	3-11	27.3	-£2.36	C G Cox	1-3
K McEvoy	7-26	26.9	+£25.75	J Spearing	2-3
R Winston	3-12	25.0	+£1.00	P Hiatt	1-1
H Frost	3-13	23.1	+£1.70	M E Hill	2-4
P M Quinn	3-13	23.1	+£57.00	J Spearing	1-1
Pat Eddery	3-13	23.1	-£2.50	J Cullinan	1-1
N Mackay	11-49	22.4	+£15.99	L Cumani	4-16
R Hills	11-51	21.6	+£13.25	M Johnston	2-3
L Dettori	10-52	19.2	-£23.25	B Meehan	3-4
S Sanders	21-121	17.4	+£15.39	R M Beckett	6-22

BEVERLEY

How to get there – Road: Course is signposted from the M62.
Rail: Beverley, bus service to course on race-days
Features: RH, uphill finish
2008 Flat fixtures: April 16, 24, May 7, 20, 24, 28, June 11, 24, July 4-5, 15, 21, 29, August 13-14, 23-24, September 9, 17, 23
Pointers: They may not go off at decent prices, but oppose Saeed bin Suroor's runners here at your peril. He has won with four out of ten since 2003 and shows a small level-stakes profit. Don't be put off by an unusual name in the saddle either – Darryll Holland and Tom Queally both won on their only rides here for the boys in blue.

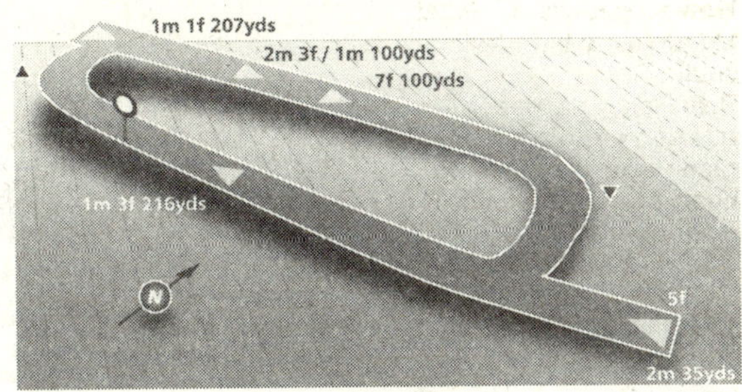

Time Test standard times

5f	1min0.5	1m3f216yds	2min30.6
7f100yds	1min29.5	1m4f16yds	2min32
1m100yds	1min42.4	2m35yds	3min29.5
1m1f207yds	2min0	2m3f100yds	4min16.7

Favourites

2-y-o	36.0%	-£29.51
3-y-o+	29.4%	-£21.71
OVERALL	30.9%	-£51.22

Trainers	Wins-Runs	%	2yo	3yo+	£1 level stks
J Noseda	5-9	55.6	2-2	3-7	+£5.33
R Charlton	4-8	50.0	0-1	4-7	+£16.55
M Wallace	4-9	44.4	4-7	0-2	+£5.87
S bin Suroor	4-10	40.0	2-5	2-5	+£2.00
Mrs A Perrett	6-17	35.3	1-5	5-12	+£0.62
P McBride	3-10	30.0	0-1	3-9	+£7.33
L Cumani	5-18	27.8	0-1	5-17	+£6.91
T Walford	3-11	27.3	0-1	3-10	+£25.00
J Jefferson	3-11	27.3	0-0	3-11	+£9.50
J Spearing	4-15	26.7	0-0	4-15	+£11.88
D Loder	4-16	25.0	2-5	2-11	-£7.87
H Morrison	4-16	25.0	1-2	3-14	+£2.25
A Balding	6-24	25.0	4-5	2-19	-£3.13

Jockeys	Wins-Rides	%	£1 level stks	Best Trainer	W-R
M Dwyer	5-13	38.5	+£6.42	S Gollings	1-1
R Hills	5-16	31.3	+£21.23	M Jarvis	1-1
S Brotherton	3-11	27.3	+£3.25	M W Easterby	1-6
J P Spencer	14-56	25.0	+£15.01	J Fanshawe	3-8
E Ahern	7-30	23.3	+£1.58	J Given	2-2
K Dalgleish	8-35	22.9	+£16.10	M Johnston	7-23
T P Queally	7-38	18.4	+£21.75	S bin Suroor	1-1
N Callan	29-161	18.0	+£19.85	K Ryan	10-44
D Sweeney	3-17	17.6	+£0.75	M Blanshard	1-1
P Robinson	7-41	17.1	-£14.72	M Jarvis	2-13
J Fanning	20-117	17.1	-£19.96	M Johnston	10-38
D Holland	9-53	17.0	-£18.19	S bin Suroor	1-1
S Sanders	13-78	16.7	-£34.48	Sir M Prescott	4-12

BRIGHTON

Freshfield Road, Brighton,
E Sussex BN2 2XZ.
Tel 01273 603 580

How to get there – Road: Signposted from A23 London Road and A27. Rail: Brighton, bus to course on race-days

Features: LH, sharp and undulating, mainly down-hill for last 7f, suitable for handy, speedy types

2008 Flat fixtures: April 27, May 13, 23, 30, June 8, 11, 24, July 1, 6-7, 15, August 6-8, 19, September 3, 29, October 16, 23

Pointers: Certainly a specialists' track as there are some remarkable strike-rates in evidence on the south coast, namely Jeremy Noseda and Sir Michael Stoute on the training side and Frankie Dettori in the saddle. Dettori's two from two record has helped Noseda win with an astonishing 64 per cent of his runners.

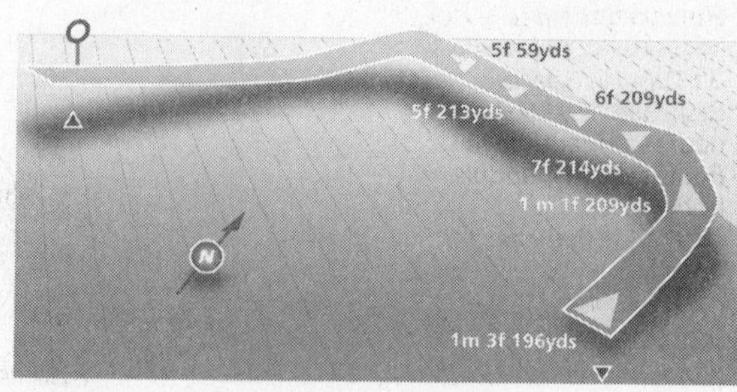

Time Test standard times

5f59yds	59.5	7f214yds	1min32
5f213yds	1min7.5	1m1f209yds	1min57.5
6f209yds	1min19.6	1m3f196yds	2min26

Favourites

2-y-o	42.7%	+£6.87
3-y-o+	27.3%	-£70.45
OVERALL	30.0%	-£63.59

Trainers

Trainers	Wins-Runs	%	2yo	3yo+	£1 level stks
Mrs A Duffield	4-6	66.7	1-1	3-5	+£11.20
J Noseda	9-14	64.3	2-4	7-10	+£13.54
T Dascombe	3-5	60.0	1-3	2-2	+£28.12
Sir M Stoute	12-23	52.2	3-7	9-16	+£26.97
A Stewart	3-6	50.0	0-0	3-6	+£10.13
R Charlton	8-16	50.0	2-5	6-11	+£19.90
C G Cox	4-10	40.0	1-1	3-9	+£19.00
E Vaughan	3-9	33.3	1-1	2-8	+£6.88
H Candy	3-9	33.3	0-0	3-9	+£12.75
Sir M Prescott	15-46	32.6	1-13	14-33	-£10.57
C Wall	5-16	31.3	0-0	5-16	+£2.13
Miss B Sanders	16-53	30.2	0-0	16-53	+£67.50
D Elsworth	3-11	27.3	0-1	3-10	+£17.00

Jockeys

Jockeys	Wins-Rides	%	£1 level stks	Best Trainer	W-R
L Dettori	9-21	42.9	+£16.25	J Noseda	2-2
R Hills	5-13	38.5	+£6.09	M Tregoning	1-1
M Hills	5-13	38.5	+£9.50	J Hills	3-3
W Ryan	3-8	37.5	+£2.88	R Bastiman	1-1
Natalia Gemelova	3-9	33.3	+£27.50	J Long	1-2
G Duffield	5-16	31.3	-£5.22	Sir M Prescott	3-6
T Block	7-24	29.2	+£21.98	H Morrison	2-5
R FitzPatrick	4-15	26.7	+£5.00	E J O'Neill	1-2
K Fallon	6-25	24.0	-£3.40	E Vaughan	1-1
B Doyle	7-32	21.9	+£11.02	Sir M Stoute	5-7
S Sanders	53-248	21.4	-£5.25	Miss B Sanders	8-21
R L Moore	63-300	21.0	+£50.68	G L Moore	10-57
N De Souza	5-24	20.8	+£1.75	P Cole	2-10

Sponsored by Stan James

CARLISLE

How to get there – Road: M6 Jctn 42, follow signs on Dalston Road.
Rail: Carlisle, 66 bus to course on race-days
Features: RH, undulating, uphill finish
2008 Flat fixtures: May 26, June 2, 16, 25, July 5, 27, August 4, 20
Pointers: Mark Johnston is a regular at the Cumbria circuit and local knowledge clearly pays off. He has struck with more than 30 per cent of his runners for a £73 profit to £1 level stakes.

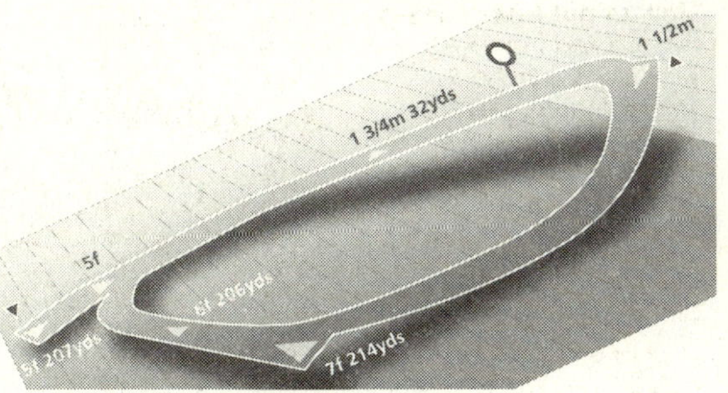

Time Test standard times

5f	59.6	1m1f61yds	1min55
5f193yds	1min11.8	1m3f107yds	2min23
6f192yds	1min24.7	1m6f32yds	2min59.2
7f200yds	1min37.6	2m1f52yds	3min42

Favourites

2-y-o	41.3%	-£1.89
3-y-o+	27.5%	-£25.23
OVERALL	30.0%	-£27.11

Trainers	Wins-Runs	%	2yo	3yo+	£1 level stks
E Dunlop	3-4	75.0	0-0	3-4	+£6.50
L Cumani	3-7	42.9	0-2	3-5	+£5.62
Sir M Prescott	8-19	42.1	0-5	8-14	-£0.16
J R Best	4-10	40.0	2-3	2-7	+£22.70
M Johnston	21-68	30.9	10-21	11-47	+£73.42
J S Moore	3-10	30.0	3-5	0-5	+£9.25
A Balding	3-11	27.3	1-5	2-6	-£0.21
M Channon	7-31	22.6	3-10	4-21	+£4.19
Mrs A Duffield	9-42	21.4	4-11	5-31	+£15.51
P Evans	4-22	18.2	0-4	4-18	+£1.63
B Smart	12-69	17.4	5-28	7-41	+£41.25
Mrs J Ramsden	3-19	15.8	2-9	1-10	-£7.56
H Morrison	3-20	15.0	0-3	3-17	+£1.38

Jockeys	Wins-Rides	%	£1 level stks	Best Trainer	W-R
L Jones	3-9	33.3	+£29.00	Mrs G Rees	1-1
J P Spencer	10-32	31.3	+£3.57	A Jarvis	2-4
E Ahern	3-10	30.0	-£0.05	Mrs A L King	1-1
W Supple	5-18	27.8	+£4.97	E Dunlop	2-2
Alex Greaves	4-16	25.0	+£9.00	D Nicholls	4-16
N Mackay	5-20	25.0	+£13.41	J S Moore	2-2
S Sanders	8-37	21.6	-£11.91	Sir M Prescott	4-11
N Callan	5-24	20.8	-£5.13	K Ryan	3-9
S Donohoe	4-20	20.0	+£1.38	P Evans	1-3
K Darley	13-67	19.4	-£17.22	M Johnston	3-11
M Lawson	4-23	17.4	+£4.00		
J Fanning	13-86	15.1	+£33.07	M Johnston	5-16
M Stainton	3-21	14.3	+£7.25	Miss S Hall	1-1

CATTERICK

Catterick Bridge, Richmond,
N Yorkshire, DL10 7PE.
Tel 01748 811 478

How to get there – Road: A1, exit 5m south of Scotch Corner. Rail: Darlington or Northallerton and bus.

Features: LH, undulating, tight turns, lends itself to course specialists

2008 Flat fixtures: April 2, 23, May 6, 24, June 6, July 2, 9, 16, 23, August 5, 15, 27, September 5, 20, October 7, 18, 28, November 4

Pointers: Another northern track at which Mark Johnston excels, with a great strike-rate and an impressive level-stakes profit. The more selective runners of a clutch of southern handlers are hard to beat but often short prices, which has helped favourites boast a comparatively strong record with just a small overall loss.

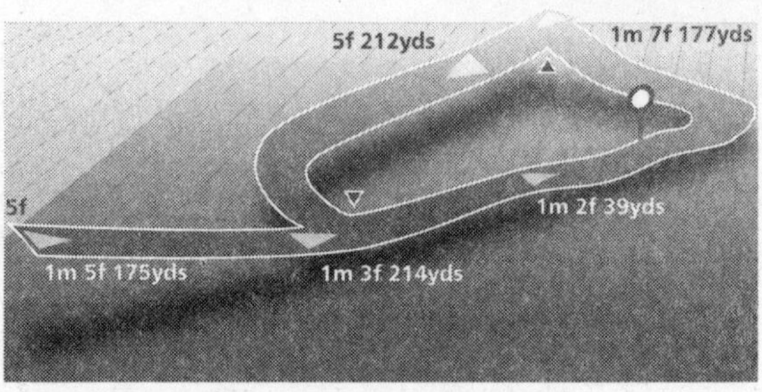

Time Test standard times

5f	57.5	1m3f214yds	2min31
5f212yds	1min10.5	1m5f175yds	2min55.3
7f	1min23.2	1m7f177yds	3min21.2

Favourites

2-y-o	37.7%	+£9.65
3-y-o+	30.6%	-£13.49
OVERALL	32.3%	-£3.84

Trainers

Trainers	Wins-Runs	%	2yo	3yo+	£1 level stks
R Charlton	3-4	75.0	0-0	3-4	+£4.85
J Dunlop	5-12	41.7	0-2	5-10	+£9.44
Sir M Prescott	12-33	36.4	3-14	9-19	-£0.63
E Dunlop	5-15	33.3	3-9	2-6	+£0.68
M Bell	6-19	31.6	1-5	5-14	+£7.60
Sir M Stoute	4-13	30.8	2-6	2-7	-£2.11
M Johnston	41-139	29.5	19-57	22-82	+£62.13
M Tompkins	7-26	26.9	1-7	6-19	-£6.47
W Tinning	3-12	25.0	0-0	3-12	+£20.50
E J O'Neill	4-16	25.0	3-9	1-7	-£1.67
J A Osborne	4-17	23.5	1-7	3-10	+£1.00
M Wallace	4-17	23.5	4-11	0-6	+£1.30
Miss V Haigh	3-14	21.4	0-6	3-8	+£12.50

Jockeys

Jockeys	Wins-Rides	%	£1 level stks	Best Trainer	W-R
Paul Scallan	6-20	30.0	+£70.44	B Smart	3-11
M Geran	4-14	28.6	-£0.17	P Evans	2-4
J Quinn	8-28	28.6	+£4.25	J Dunlop	1-1
N Mackay	3-13	23.1	+£2.00	M Tompkins	1-1
S Golam	6-30	20.0	+£8.58	Mrs A Duffield	3-8
J Fanning	20-102	19.6	+£26.10	M Johnston	12-34
T O'Shea	3-17	17.6	+£41.50	G A Swinbank	1-1
G Duffield	8-46	17.4	+£1.79	Sir M Prescott	4-7
S De Sousa	7-41	17.1	+£27.00	D Nicholls	4-11
S Sanders	10-59	16.9	-£34.92	Sir M Prescott	3-7
D Tudhope	11-65	16.9	+£21.88	D Carroll	3-12
R Winston	28-172	16.3	+£9.55	J Howard Johnson	3-8
L Fletcher	6-37	16.2	+£37.50	H Morrison	2-3

CHEPSTOW

How to get there – Road: M4 Jct 22 on west side of Severn Bridge, A48 north, then A446 Monmouth Rd. Rail: Chepstow, bus to course on race-days

Features: LH, undulating

2008 Flat fixtures: May 6, 26-27, June 13, 23, July 2, 11, 25, August 5, 14, 25, September 5, 11

Pointers: Little stands out in terms of trends, though Roger Charlton has a good strike-rate and it's interesting to note that Ryan Moore's record improves when discounting rides for Richard Hannon, who has supplied more winners for Moore than any other handler but at a rate of one in eight rides.

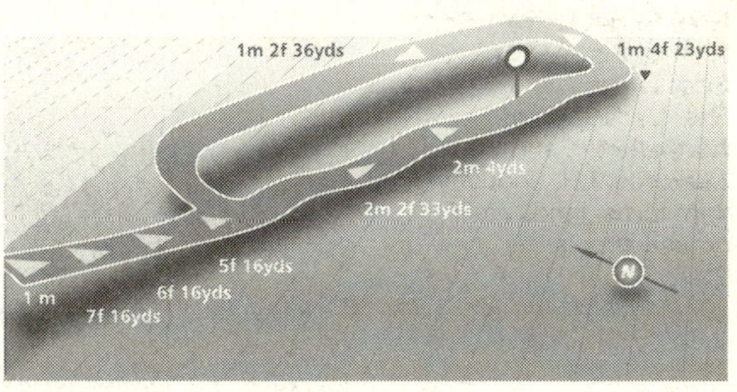

Time Test standard times

5f16yds	57	1m4f23yds	2min31.3
6f16yds	1min8.8	2m49yds	3min28
7f16yds	1min20.5	2m1f40yds	3min41
1m14yds	1min32.6	2m2f	3min52
1m2f36yds	2min4.2		

Favourites

2-y-o	34.9%	-£17.25
3-y-o+	27.6%	-£30.11
OVERALL	29.1%	-£47.35

Trainers	Wins-Runs	%	2yo	3yo+	£1 level stks
N Callaghan	3-8	37.5	3-4	0-4	+£5.29
R Charlton	10-27	37.0	3-7	7-20	+£22.74
H Cecil	3-10	30.0	0-2	3-8	-£2.70
Sir M Stoute	4-14	28.6	1-1	3-13	-£5.85
G L Moore	4-15	26.7	0-2	4-13	+£3.25
J Gosden	7-27	25.9	2-6	5-21	+£3.05
E Dunlop	8-34	23.5	0-8	8-26	+£1.18
W S Kittow	8-36	22.2	1-3	7-33	+£36.95
Sir M Prescott	3-14	21.4	3-11	0-3	-£2.42
R J Price	6-28	21.4	0-0	6-28	+£79.75
B Hills	6-28	21.4	1-7	5-21	-£7.80
H Candy	7-34	20.6	2-8	5-26	-£3.18
M Bell	3-15	20.0	0-5	3-10	-£4.25

Jockeys	Wins-Rides	%	£1 level stks	Best Trainer	W-R
K Fallon	7-26	26.9	-£5.03	B Hanbury	1-1
M Halford	4-16	25.0	+£16.00	J C Poulton	1-1
T Quinn	7-29	24.1	+£19.54	J Dunlop	2-3
M Henry	3-13	23.1	+£49.50	Miss S Wilton	1-1
R L Moore	16-73	21.9	-£19.06	R Hannon	3-24
J P Spencer	3-14	21.4	-£1.75	R Harris	1-1
H Frost	3-15	20.0	+£22.00	R Harris	1-1
G Gibbons	5-25	20.0	+£43.50	P Evans	3-7
N Callan	6-30	20.0	-£0.75	P Evans	2-7
R Hughes	12-60	20.0	-£8.49	R Hannon	4-21
R Kingscote	7-36	19.4	+£14.00	A King	1-1
Lisa Jones	4-22	18.2	+£27.75	J Gallagher	1-2
B Doyle	3-17	17.6	+£12.88	R Charlton	1-1

Sponsored by Stan James

CHESTER

Steam Mill Street,
Chester, CH1 2LY.
Tel 01244 304 600

How to get there – Road: Join Inner Ring Road and A458 Queensferry Road. Rail: Chester General, bus to city centre

Features: LH, flat, almost circular

2008 Flat fixtures: May 7-9, June 10, 27-28, July 11-12, August 3, 21, 29-30, September 13, 27

Pointers: Barry Hills is known as the king of the Cheshire track, but our stats show that too much attention can sometimes be paid to such supposed truisms. Hills has sent out 26 winners here in the last five years, but from 140 runners and shows a significant level-stakes loss. Sir Michael Stoute has quietly built up some more impressive figures.

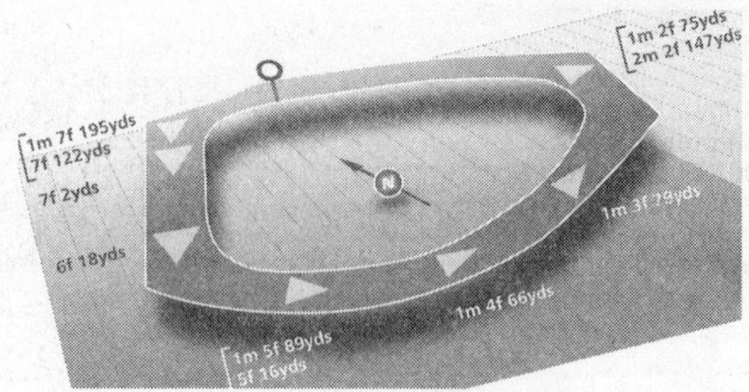

Time Test standard times

5f16yds	59.8	1m3f79yds	2min22.7
6f18yds	1min13	1m4f66yds	2min35
7f2yds	1min24.7	1m5f89yds	2min48.6
7f122yds	1min31.2	1m7f195yds	3min22
1m1f70yds	1min55	2m2f147yds	4min1
1m2f75yds	2min8		

Favourites

2-y-o	43.7%	+£1.80
3-y-o+	29.4%	-£21.32
OVERALL	33.0%	-£19.52

Trainers	Wins-Runs	%	2yo	3yo +	£1 level stks
C G Cox	3-8	37.5	0-0	3-8	+£10.75
A P O'Brien	3-9	33.3	0-0	3-9	-£0.06
W R Swinburn	5-16	31.3	1-1	4-15	+£8.25
M Jarvis	9-31	29.0	0-2	9-29	+£16.26
Sir M Stoute	14-50	28.0	1-4	13-46	+£11.37
T J Pitt	4-17	23.5	1-4	3-13	+£29.75
E S McMahon	3-13	23.1	2-6	1-7	-£2.50
E Dunlop	3-13	23.1	1-1	2-12	+£4.00
J Given	6-27	22.2	3-6	3-21	+£12.13
R Hannon	11-52	21.2	6-26	5-26	+£24.22
Sir M Prescott	4-20	20.0	2-9	2-11	-£10.12
J Gosden	7-35	20.0	0-1	7-34	+£1.01
B Hills	26-140	18.6	12-33	14-107	-£55.61

Jockeys	Wins-Rides	%	£1 level stks	Best Trainer	W-R
M Henry	3-7	42.9	+£22.75	M Jarvis	1-1
W Buick	3-11	27.3	+£16.50	A Balding	2-3
K Fallon	14-58	24.1	-£13.86	Sir M Stoute	6-14
R Hills	9-39	23.1	-£13.65	Sir M Stoute	4-7
M Hills	23-116	19.8	-£42.93	B Hills	15-75
P Robinson	6-31	19.4	+£5.01	M Jarvis	5-19
J-P Guillambert	8-44	18.2	-£8.68	M Johnston	3-10
A Munro	3-17	17.6	+£0.75		
R L Moore	3-17	17.6	+£6.50	E S McMahon	1-1
F P Ferris	3-17	17.6	+£12.25	P Evans	2-12
K Darley	10-57	17.5	-£6.28	M Jarvis	2-2
A Mullen	4-23	17.4	-£4.00	K Ryan	2-5
L Dettori	5-30	16.7	-£2.12	J Dunlop	1-1

Sponsored by Stan James

Grand Stand, Leger Way, Doncaster. DN2 6BB.
Tel 01302 320066/7

How to get there – Road: M18 Jctn 3, A638, A18 to Hull. Rail: Doncaster Central.

Features: LH, flat

2008 Flat fixtures: March 22, 29, April 11-12, May 3, 17, 31, June 6-7, 15, 27-28, July 10, 17, 24, August 2, September 10-13, October 24-25, November 8

Pointers: Last year's return to Doncaster will have pleased Saeed bin Suroor, who is the man to follow here, particularly if Frankie Dettori or Kerrin McEvoy are riding. Bin Suroor has won with 16 out of 50 runners when one of these two are in the saddle, but just four out of 29 when forced to look elsewhere for a jockey.

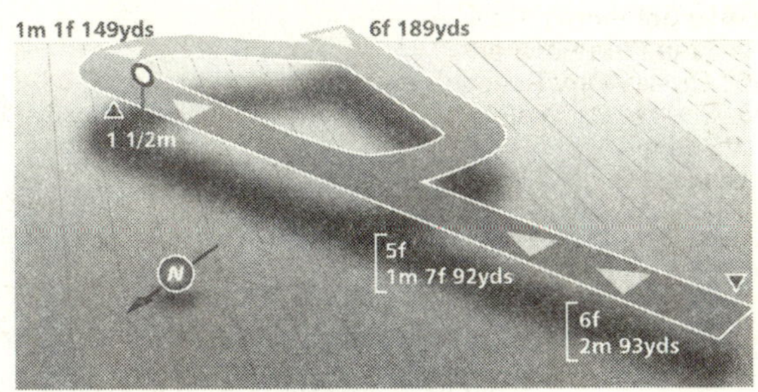

Time Test standard times

5f	58.6	1m1f149yds	2min0.2
6f	1min11	1m4f	2min33.6
6f189yds (Rnd)	1min21.8	1m7f92yds	3min19.4
7f(str)	1min24	2m93yds	3min32.7

Favourites

2-y-o	32.0%	-£17.28
3-y-o+	26.0%	-£53.25
OVERALL	27.8%	-£70.53

Trainers	Wins-Runs	%	2yo	3yo+	£1 level stks
R Johnson Houghton	3-6	50.0	1-2	2-4	+£20.50
S bin Suroor	20-79	25.3	9-27	11-52	+£0.91
G Balding	3-12	25.0	0-0	3-12	+£21.67
G Wragg	5-20	25.0	1-3	4-17	+£18.38
D Loder	7-28	25.0	2-8	5-20	-£2.50
J Fanshawe	11-44	25.0	2-11	9-33	-£4.17
R Charlton	4-17	23.5	3-11	1-6	+£2.88
M Tregoning	4-18	22.2	2-6	2-12	-£7.34
W R Swinburn	3-16	18.8	0-6	3-10	+£0.75
J Noseda	5-28	17.9	2-9	3-19	-£5.85
Sir M Stoute	14-81	17.3	5-36	9-45	-£31.27
C Wall	6-36	16.7	1-5	5-31	+£57.00
M Jarvis	8-49	16.3	6-14	2-35	+£13.53

Jockeys	Wins-Rides	%	£1 level stks	Best Trainer	W-R
O Urbina	4-13	30.8	+£2.13	J Fanshawe	3-9
W Buick	4-16	25.0	-£0.09	B Hills	2-2
S Golam	4-19	21.1	-£0.87	M Tompkins	2-6
L Dettori	24-115	20.9	+£25.72	S bin Suroor	11-32
A Mullen	3-16	18.8	+£8.50	K Ryan	2-8
K McEvoy	8-47	17.0	+£1.23	S bin Suroor	5-18
J P Spencer	21-126	16.7	+£7.53	J Fanshawe	5-16
K Fallon	22-133	16.5	-£35.26	Sir M Stoute	5-21
S Hitchcott	4-25	16.0	+£17.75	M Channon	3-16
G Carter	3-19	15.8	-£6.00	J Akehurst	1-1
R Hills	16-101	15.8	+£13.32	B Hills	5-18
R L Moore	15-96	15.6	+£1.86	R Hannon	8-34
G Baker	4-29	13.8	+£53.50	C Wall	4-10

EPSOM

How to get there – Road: M25 Jctn 8 (A217) or 9 (A24) 2m south of Epsom on B290
Rail: Epsom & raceday bus, Epsom Downs or Tattenham Corner
Features: LH, undulating, downhill 5f is fastest in the world
2008 Flat fixtures: June 6-7
Pointers: Only two days of racing at the Derby venue this year, with May's meeting scrapped. Frankie Dettori blew one theory out of the water last year when he won the Derby on Authorized, putting paid to a view that he couldn't ride the circuit, which had already been shown as nonsense anyway by our figures.

Time Test standard times

5f	53.8	1m114yds	1min41.6
6f	1min8	1m2f18yds	2min3.5
7f	1min20.2	1m4f10yds	2min33.6

Favourites

2-y-o	38.0%	+£2.34
3-y-o+	28.4%	+£19.46
OVERALL	29.8%	+£21.80

Trainers

Trainers	Wins-Runs	%	2yo	3yo+	£1 level stks
P Chapple-Hyam	3-7	42.9	2-3	1-4	+£6.25
S C Williams	8-23	34.8	1-1	7-22	+£18.86
E Vaughan	3-9	33.3	1-1	2-8	+£0.80
A Newcombe	3-9	33.3	0-1	3-8	+£17.50
Miss G Kelleway	3-9	33.3	0-1	3-8	+£17.00
P Cundell	3-9	33.3	1-2	2-7	+£2.75
Mrs J Ramsden	3-10	30.0	0-0	3-10	+£12.00
R Johnson Houghton	3-13	23.1	1-3	2-10	+£12.50
J Dunlop	10-44	22.7	6-8	4-36	-£2.16
Sir M Prescott	4-18	22.2	3-10	1-8	-£7.49
Sir M Stoute	8-40	20.0	0-2	8-38	-£7.13
H Morrison	5-26	19.2	0-4	5-22	+£2.00
J J Quinn	4-22	18.2	0-0	4-22	+£16.50

Jockeys

Jockeys	Wins-Rides	%	£1 level stks	Best Trainer	W-R
R Winston	3-10	30.0	+£17.50	J J Quinn	1-2
K Fallon	17-73	23.3	+£6.01	Sir M Stoute	4-15
T P Queally	9-40	22.5	+£14.98	B Curley	2-2
K Dalgleish	3-15	20.0	+£0.50	M Johnston	3-9
L Dettori	16-84	19.0	-£10.65	S bin Suroor	5-24
S Golam	3-16	18.8	+£2.25	S C Williams	1-1
J P Murtagh	3-18	16.7	+£20.87	J W Payne	1-2
P Dobbs	4-24	16.7	-£0.75	H Morrison	1-1
M Dwyer	15-91	16.5	+£20.85	A Balding	5-22
W Supple	4-25	16.0	+£2.83	B Hills	2-3
S Sanders	17-106	16.0	+£30.11	C Brittain	3-10
R Hills	5-32	15.6	-£16.20	M Jarvis	1-1
J-P Guillambert	4-27	14.8	-£1.25	J Hills	1-1

FOLKESTONE

How to get there – Road: M20 Jctn 11, A20 south. Rail: Westenhanger from Charing Cross or Victoria
Features: RH, sharp turns
2008 Flat fixtures: April 1, 10, 22, May 1, June 3, 9, 27, July 10, 24, August 7, 20, 31, September 8, 23, October 7
Pointers: The combination of Richard Hannon and Richard Hughes are always worth a second look. Both have strong records individually, and have won on nine out of 24 occasions when they teamed up in the last five years. John Gosden and Frankie Dettori are the other men to follow.

Time Test standard times

5f	58.6	1m1f149yds	2min0.2
6f	1min11	1m4f	2min33.6
6f189yds (Rnd)	1min21.8	1m7f92yds	3min19.4
7f(str)	1min24	2m93yds	3min32.7

Favourites

2-y-o	41.4%	+£1.96
3-y-o+	30.1%	-£34.58
OVERALL	32.5%	-£32.61

Trainers

Trainers	Wins-Runs	%	2yo	3yo+	£1 level stks
D Nicholls	3-7	42.9	0-1	3-6	+£23.00
J Gosden	5-15	33.3	1-4	4-11	+£20.00
Sir M Prescott	7-22	31.8	0-8	7-14	-£7.07
R Johnson Houghton	4-13	30.8	2-5	2-8	+£21.23
R Charlton	7-23	30.4	3-8	4-15	-£1.54
D Daly	3-10	30.0	0-2	3-8	+£8.50
Sir M Stoute	5-17	29.4	2-5	3-12	+£11.75
L Cumani	7-25	28.0	1-7	6-18	+£5.07
R Hannon	21-81	25.9	14-44	7-37	+£23.23
P Grayson	3-12	25.0	1-1	2-11	+£20.75
V Smith	3-13	23.1	1-3	2-10	+£7.50
P Evans	7-34	20.6	3-9	4-25	-£3.36
M Saunders	3-15	20.0	0-0	3-15	+£11.75

Jockeys

Jockeys	Wins-Rides	%	£1 level stks	Best Trainer	W-R
L Dettori	16-44	36.4	+£16.76	J Gosden	2-2
R Hughes	17-68	25.0	-£5.48	R Hannon	9-24
J P Spencer	21-85	24.7	+£8.30	J R Best	3-3
K Fallon	4-18	22.2	-£5.49	A Balding	1-1
L Morris	3-14	21.4	+£4.50	A Carroll	1-2
T Quinn	13-61	21.3	-£8.50	J Akehurst	4-7
S Drowne	19-91	20.9	+£36.06	H Morrison	6-15
W Ryan	3-15	20.0	+£12.50	H Cecil	1-2
A Quinn	5-25	20.0	+£22.38	J Boyle	2-8
S Sanders	30-157	19.1	-£24.49	Sir M Prescott	5-17
T Dean	3-16	18.8	+£1.57	R Harris	2-3
N De Souza	3-16	18.8	+£11.75	J R Best	1-1
R L Moore	15-95	15.8	-£13.00	R Hannon	3-10

GOODWOOD

How to get there – Road: signposted from A27 south and A285 north
Rail: Chichester, bus to course on race-days
Features: RH, undulating
2008 Flat fixtures: May 3, 8, 21-22, 30-31, June 6, 13, 20, July 29-31, August 1-2, 23-24, September 2, 13-14, 24, October 2, 12
Pointers: Once again Godolphin are the kings of Goodwood, Saeed bin Suroor's 27 per cent strike-rate helping Frankie Dettori and Kerrin McEvoy to two of the top three places in the jockeys' list as well.

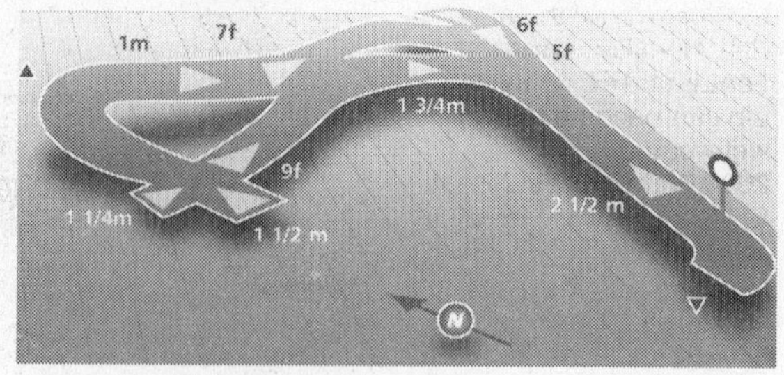

Time Test standard times

5f	56.4	1m3f	2min20
6f	1min10	1m4f	2min32.7
7f	1min24.4	1m6f	2min59
1m	1min36.8	2m	3min22
1m1f	1min52	2m4f	4min13
1m1f192yds	2min2.2	2m5f	4min27.3

Favourites

2-y-o	33.5%	-£14.11
3-y-o+	28.7%	-£5.30
OVERALL	29.7%	-£19.41

Trainers

Trainers	Wins-Runs	%	2yo	3yo+	£1 level stks
P Harris	8-23	34.8	0-1	8-22	+£34.37
S bin Suroor	28-101	27.7	4-13	24-88	+£15.31
Sir M Stoute	28-118	23.7	1-8	27-110	+£12.56
C Wall	5-22	22.7	0-1	5-21	+£10.38
J Noseda	12-53	22.6	4-13	8-40	-£6.33
P Chapple-Hyam	9-41	22.0	4-17	5-24	+£6.83
J Fanshawe	12-58	20.7	0-1	12-57	-£11.50
W J Knight	5-25	20.0	0-6	5-19	+£5.00
Sir M Prescott	6-30	20.0	0-7	6-23	+£7.25
L Cumani	11-56	19.6	0-1	11-55	+£10.03
D Ffrench Davis	3-16	18.8	1-5	2-11	+£15.38
M Tregoning	27-154	17.5	9-49	18-105	-£0.83
D Arbuthnot	3-18	16.7	0-2	3-16	+£12.00

Jockeys

Jockeys	Wins-Rides	%	£1 level stks	Best Trainer	W-R
B Doyle	3-9	33.3	+£7.00	W Musson	1-1
L Dettori	51-215	23.7	-£26.55	S bin Suroor	14-50
K McEvoy	22-109	20.2	+£47.37	S bin Suroor	6-27
T Block	5-26	19.2	+£33.25	J Spearing	1-1
M Tebbutt	3-18	16.7	+£8.50	J Akehurst	2-4
K Fallon	27-166	16.3	-£26.77	Sir M Stoute	12-38
T Quinn	22-145	15.2	+£113.70	D Elsworth	7-31
S Sanders	23-152	15.1	+£85.73	P Makin	4-12
R L Moore	51-342	14.9	+£93.71	R Hannon	12-90
Lisa Jones	4-27	14.8	+£18.00	P Cundell	1-1
J Murtagh	9-62	14.5	-£22.17	J Dunlop	3-3
J Fortune	29-202	14.4	+£18.28	J Gosden	7-53
A Nicholls	9-63	14.3	+£28.13	D Nicholls	7-47

HAMILTON

How to get there – Road:
M74 Jctn 5, off the A74
Rail: Hamilton West
Features: RH, undulating,
dip can become testing in
wet weather
2008 Flat fixtures: May 4,
9, 16, June 5, 11, 18, 26,
July 1, 12, 17-18, August
2, 13, 20, 22, 29,
September 1, 21-22
Pointers: Gerard Butler,
with 31 runners, has been
represented more times
than any other trainer in
our list, underlining the
fact that occasional
raiders tend to make the
long journey back south
with most of the prizes. Jeremy Noseda and Sir Michael
Stoute are the best examples.

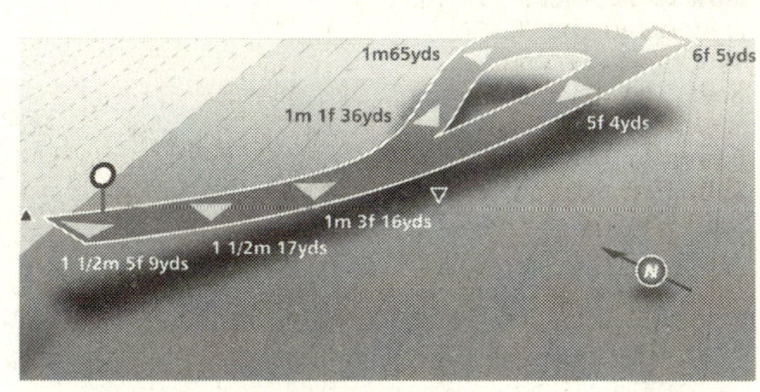

Time Test standard times

5f4yds	58.2	1m1f36yds	1min54.3
5f200yds	1min9.2	1m3f16yds	2min19.2
6f5yds	1min10	1m4f17yds	2min32.2
1m65yds	1min43.5	1m5f9yds	2min45.4

Favourites

2-y-o	43.6%	+£0.34
3-y-o+	30.3%	-£63.73
OVERALL	32.5%	-£63.39

Trainers	Wins-Runs	%	2yo	3yo+	£1 level stks
J Noseda	6-9	66.7	1-2	5-7	+£2.92
Sir M Stoute	9-14	64.3	0-0	9-14	+£13.83
A Balding	4-8	50.0	1-1	3-7	+£8.42
H Morrison	5-10	50.0	0-0	5-10	+£21.00
P Cole	4-10	40.0	1-1	3-9	+£6.13
S bin Suroor	3-9	33.3	0-0	3-9	+£2.23
W Haggas	5-15	33.3	0-0	5-15	+£1.73
Sir M Prescott	9-27	33.3	3-8	6-19	-£11.28
E Dunlop	6-20	30.0	1-1	5-19	-£4.03
G A Butler	9-31	29.0	2-4	7-27	+£25.35
E J O'Neill	7-27	25.9	4-15	3-12	+£22.50
J A Osborne	3-12	25.0	0-4	3-8	-£4.84
M Bell	7-30	23.3	2-8	5-22	-£6.77

Jockeys	Wins-Rides	%	£1 level stks	Best Trainer	W-R
K Fallon	5-12	41.7	+£4.38	R Guest	1-1
R L Moore	6-15	40.0	+£29.75	P Cole	2-2
J Mackay	3-8	37.5	+£3.36	M Bell	2-5
D Heslop	3-9	33.3	+£14.50	W Brisbourne	2-3
W Hogg	3-10	30.0	+£26.50	I Semple	1-3
T E Durcan	5-18	27.8	+£12.17	M Channon	2-6
S W Kelly	4-15	26.7	-£7.55	J A Osborne	2-2
N Callan	10-45	22.2	-£4.44	K Ryan	4-14
K Darley	31-140	22.1	+£2.56	M Johnston	8-28
C Catlin	5-23	21.7	+£18.04	M Channon	2-5
S Sanders	10-46	21.7	-£23.86	Sir M Prescott	5-12
J P Spencer	3-14	21.4	+£4.67	G A Butler	1-1
T P Queally	3-14	21.4	+£30.25	K G Reveley	1-1

Newton-Le-Willows, Merseyside, WA12 0HQ. Tel 01942 725 963

How to get there – Road: M6 Jctn 23, A49 to Wigan
Rail: Wigan & 320 bus or Newton-le-Willows
Features: LH flat track, easy turns, suits the galloping type
2008 Flat fixtures: April 26, May 10, 22-24, 30-31, June 12, 21, July 3-5, 13, 19, August 1, 7-9, September 6, 16, 26-27
Pointers: Without any strong trends, John Gosden is possibly the man to follow here, with a 24 per cent strike-rate significantly improved when Jimmy Fortune – the pair are six from 11 when in tandem.

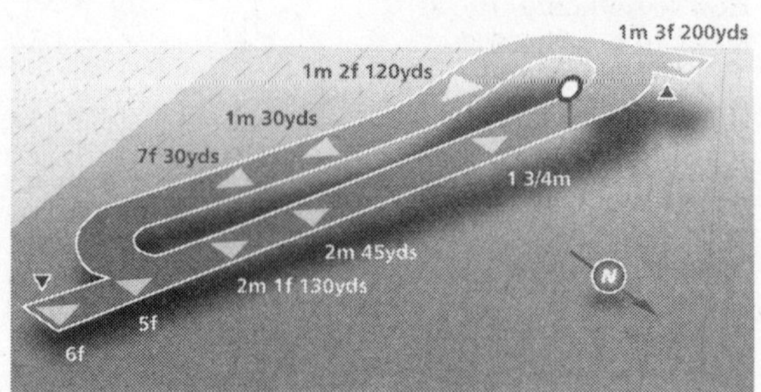

Time Test standard times

5f	59	1m3f200yds	2min28
6f	1min11.3	1m6f	2min54
7f30yds	1min27.4	2m45yds	3min28
1m30yds	1min40.2	2m1f130yds	3min47
1m2f120yds	2min10	2m3f	4min7

Favourites

2-y-o	31.6%	-£18.94
3-y-o+	27.3%	-£66.50
OVERALL	28.2%	-£85.44

Trainers	Wins-Runs	%	2yo	3yo+	£1 level stks
D Loder	4-10	40.0	1-2	3-8	+£19.83
L Lungo	3-9	33.3	0-0	3-9	+£3.00
D Arbuthnot	3-10	30.0	0-1	3-9	+£19.50
H Cecil	6-20	30.0	0-2	6-18	+£7.73
Mrs L Stubbs	7-24	29.2	1-6	6-18	+£29.00
Mrs A Duffield	7-24	29.2	3-15	4-9	+£10.25
Sir M Prescott	8-30	26.7	1-9	7-21	-£4.82
J Gosden	18-73	24.7	3-16	15-57	+£30.84
Mrs J Ramsden	5-21	23.8	0-4	5-17	-£1.62
Sir M Stoute	10-42	23.8	0-3	10-39	+£12.35
W Haggas	13-57	22.8	1-11	12-46	+£27.09
M Jarvis	22-98	22.4	6-21	16-77	+£8.70
L Cumani	14-68	20.6	1-14	13-54	+£4.86

Jockeys	Wins-Rides	%	£1 level stks	Best Trainer	W-R
W Ryan	4-12	33.3	+£13.13	H Cecil	3-5
J P Spencer	14-59	23.7	+£38.34	Seamus G O'Donnell	1-1
T Quinn	11-48	22.9	+£20.72	D Arbuthnot	2-3
R Hughes	18-80	22.5	+£32.25	R Hannon	4-21
R Hills	9-41	22.0	+£4.06	Sir M Stoute	1-1
N De Souza	3-14	21.4	+£1.75	P Cole	1-3
J Fortune	15-71	21.1	+£12.46	J Gosden	6-11
K Fallon	6-33	18.2	-£15.17	W Muir	1-1
M Hills	11-63	17.5	-£25.53	B Hills	8-35
K McEvoy	11-73	15.1	-£21.13	S bin Suroor	5-21
I Mongan	3-21	14.3	-£11.75	Miss G Kelleway	1-1
R L Moore	6-43	14.0	+£17.33	M G Quinlan	2-2
K Darley	32-229	14.0	-£35.85	M Johnston	8-40

Staines Rd East, Sunbury-On-Thames,
Middlesex, TW16 5AQ. Tel 01932 782 292

KEMPTON

How to get there – Road: M3 Jctn 1, A308 towards Kingston-on-Thames
Rail: Kempton Park from Waterloo
Features: Sharp RH track on inside of National Hunt course
2008 Flat fixtures: March 22, 28-29, April 2, 5, 7, 9, 12, 22-23, May 5, June 4, 11, 18, 25, July 2, 9, 16, 23, 30, August 6, 15, 25, September 1, 3, 5-6, 10, 12, 17, 22, 24, October 1, 4, 8, 13, 15, 17, 22, 27, 29, November 5, 9, 14, 17, 19, 28-30, December 3, 10, 17, 22

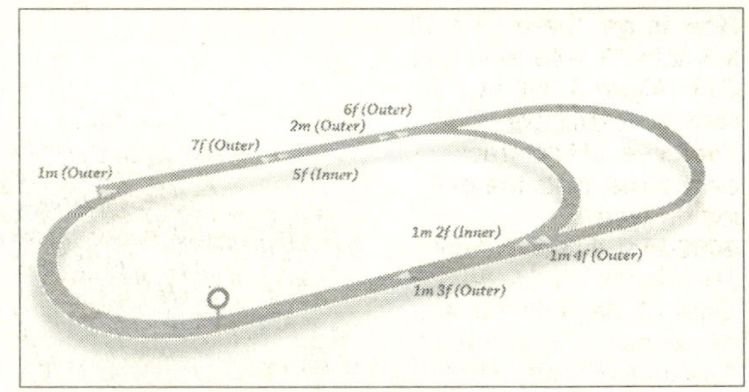

Time Test standard times

5f	59.8	1m2f	2min5.3
6f	1min12.2	1m3f	2min17.8
7f	1min25	1m4f	34.2
1m	1min37.6	2m	3min27

Pointers: Our five-year stats can't really draw much out for punters given the switch to the all-weather. Not surprisingly, Mark Johnston is one of the trainers who figures prominently given his proficiency with horses on all types of surface.

Favourites

2-y-o	33.1%	-£26.04
3-y-o+	25.2%	-£99.81
OVERALL	26.6%	-£125.85

Trainers	Wins-Runs	%	2yo	3yo +	£1 level stks
R A Farrant	3-8	37.5	1-1	2-7	+£23.00
S bin Suroor	7-20	35.0	2-5	5-15	+£1.72
D Coakley	6-22	27.3	0-3	6-19	+£13.75
Jane Chapple-Hyam	8-32	25.0	2-14	6-18	+£5.94
Sir M Stoute	11-44	25.0	3-9	8-35	+£10.33
J Jay	4-18	22.2	0-2	4-16	+£13.51
M Johnston	16-74	21.6	6-31	10-43	+£34.74
B Johnson	6-28	21.4	1-3	5-25	-£2.60
J Gosden	12-56	21.4	7-23	5-33	+£0.92
M W Easterby	4-19	21.1	0-4	4-15	-£7.90
M Botti	8-39	20.5	2-16	6-23	+£40.00
T J Pitt	4-20	20.0	0-2	4-18	-£11.02
G A Butler	9-46	19.6	0-5	9-41	+£11.25

Jockeys	Wins-Rides	%	£1 level stks	Best Trainer	W-R
K McEvoy	5-18	27.8	+£26.75	S bin Suroor	1-1
R Hills	11-46	23.9	+£24.25	B Hills	3-6
J Hamblett	4-17	23.5	+£0.25	Sir M Stoute	1-2
G Fairley	8-39	20.5	+£34.91	M Johnston	3-13
J Fanning	11-58	19.0	+£4.31	M Johnston	5-13
R Hughes	29-156	18.6	+£11.81	R Hannon	10-54
L Dettori	12-67	17.9	-£18.07	S bin Suroor	4-7
N Polli	3-17	17.6	+£6.00		
J De Souza	3-17	17.6	+£9.50	R Brotherton	2-3
R Winston	6-34	17.6	+£15.75	Sir M Stoute	2-2
J P Spencer	25-142	17.6	-£40.43	Jane Chapple-Hyam	2-3
P Hills	11-63	17.5	+£4.00	D Ivory	2-6
D McKeown	6-35	17.1	+£22.00	D Shaw	4-18

Sponsored by Stan James

LEICESTER

London Road, Oadby, Leicester, LE2 4QH. Tel 0116 271 6515

How to get there – Road: M1 Jctn 21, A6, 2m south of city
Rail: Leicester, bus
Features: RH, straight mile is downhill for first 4f, then uphill to finish
2008 Flat fixtures: April 3, 26, May 20, 26-27, June 2, 14, 19, 26, July 5, 17, 23, 30, August 10, September 9, 15, 22, October 7, 14, 27

Pointers: Henry Cecil was back in the Classic winner's enclosure last year, so it may pay to give him close attention at a track where he has long maintained a strong record, boasting a strike-rate of close to 30 per cent from 56 runners in the last five years. Saeed bin Suroor should most often provide the main obstacle.

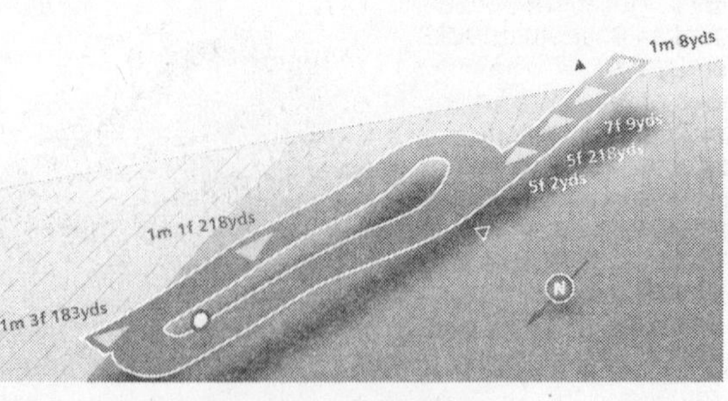

Time Test standard times

5f2yds	58.3	1m (rnd)	1min39.7
5f218yds	1min10.2	1m1f218yds	2min2.7
7f9yds	1min22.3	1m3f183yds	2min28.6
1m60yds	1min41.9		

Favourites

2-y-o	39.0%	-£10.97
3-y-o+	29.5%	-£43.31
OVERALL	31.9%	-£54.28

Trainers

Trainers	Wins-Runs	%	2yo	3yo+	£1 level stks
R Phillips	3-5	60.0	1-1	2-4	+£15.80
S bin Suroor	14-40	35.0	8-29	6-11	-£10.66
P Chapple-Hyam	9-28	32.1	5-18	4-10	+£90.98
R Hodges	4-13	30.8	0-1	4-12	+£10.00
M Tregoning	7-24	29.2	4-12	3-12	+£27.53
J Bethell	9-31	29.0	0-4	9-27	+£39.50
H Cecil	16-56	28.6	3-18	13-38	+£15.57
R Charlton	6-22	27.3	2-10	4-12	-£1.64
M Saunders	3-12	25.0	0-0	3-12	+£32.00
W Jarvis	7-30	23.3	2-8	5-22	+£63.33
N Tinkler	6-26	23.1	1-3	5-23	+£9.58
D Loder	5-22	22.7	3-12	2-10	-£8.91
L Cumani	14-62	22.6	3-19	11-43	-£1.45

Jockeys

Jockeys	Wins-Rides	%	£1 level stks	Best Trainer	W-R
K McEvoy	12-37	32.4	+£17.13	S bin Suroor	3-7
L Dettori	23-81	28.4	-£13.66	S bin Suroor	7-24
J P Murtagh	3-11	27.3	-£5.92	J Fanshawe	2-2
G Fairley	5-19	26.3	+£27.00	M Johnston	3-9
W Woods	3-13	23.1	+£3.25	W Haggas	2-6
J Murtagh	5-22	22.7	+£6.48	J Fanshawe	2-5
K Fallon	15-72	20.8	+£8.32	Sir M Stoute	4-18
J P Spencer	25-120	20.8	-£12.23	E Dunlop	3-5
Pat Eddery	7-35	20.0	-£5.72	J Dunlop	4-12
P Robinson	22-116	19.0	+£30.72	M Jarvis	9-53
N De Souza	6-32	18.8	+£114.00	P Cole	2-5
R Hughes	21-112	18.8	+£21.64	H Cecil	5-9
T Block	4-22	18.2	-£3.00	J A Geake	1-1

LINGFIELD TURF

How to get there – Road: M25 Jctn 6, south on A22, then B2029.

Rail: Lingfield from London Bridge or Victoria

Features: LH, undulating, straight runs downhill

2008 Flat fixtures: May 31, June 7, 14, 21, 28, August 9, 16, 28, September 9

Pointers: Lingfield's summer switch to turf has been particularly kind to Frankie Dettori, who wins with nearly a third of his mounts. Jeremy Noseda just stands out among the trainers.

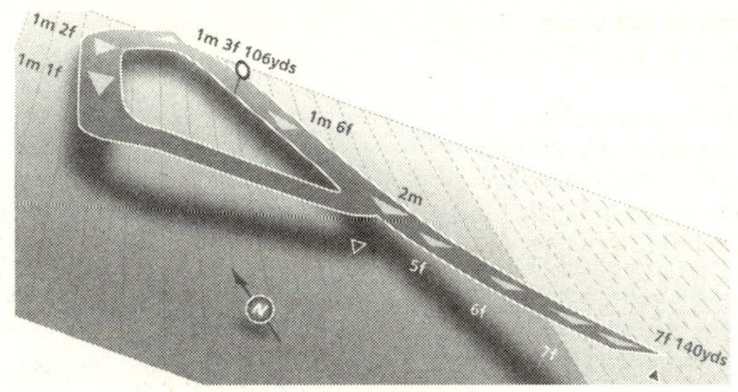

Time Test standard times

5f	56.3	1m2f	2min5.4
6f	1min9	1m3f106yds	2min24.4
7f	1min20.7	1m6f	2min58.6
7f140yds	1min28.2	2m	3min24.6
1m1f	1min52.5		

Favourites

2-y-o	42.1%	+£16.60
3-y-o+	29.2%	-£5.07
OVERALL	32.3%	+£11.53

Trainers	Wins-Runs	%	2yo	3yo+	£1 level stks
M Wigham	4-10	40.0	0-1	4-9	+£10.33
J A Gilbert	3-8	37.5	0-0	3-8	+£56.50
J Noseda	8-23	34.8	2-6	6-17	+£8.47
C Wall	7-22	31.8	1-6	6-16	+£50.13
M Tregoning	3-10	30.0	0-2	3-8	+£19.00
S bin Suroor	5-17	29.4	2-5	3-12	+£5.91
M G Quinlan	4-14	28.6	3-9	1-5	+£11.57
J Gosden	8-29	27.6	2-9	6-20	+£4.97
H Candy	4-15	26.7	1-1	3-14	-£2.62
Sir M Stoute	9-34	26.5	1-3	8-31	-£4.14
Miss S West	3-12	25.0	0-0	3-12	+£3.41
J Given	5-23	21.7	4-8	1-15	+£14.68
E J O'Neill	3-14	21.4	1-4	2-10	-£4.15

Jockeys	Wins-Rides	%	£1 level stks	Best Trainer	W-R
L Dettori	13-40	32.5	+£19.22	S bin Suroor	4-8
T O'Shea	4-14	28.6	+£10.88	M G Quinlan	1-1
K Fallon	10-39	25.6	+£9.92	Sir M Stoute	5-7
P Robinson	5-22	22.7	-£2.75	M Jarvis	5-14
J Murtagh	3-15	20.0	+£9.38	J Given	1-1
R Hughes	14-70	20.0	+£10.60	R Hannon	6-22
S Sanders	26-136	19.1	+£14.61	Miss B Sanders	3-5
K McEvoy	6-34	17.6	-£0.75	Mrs A Perrett	1-1
A Kirby	9-51	17.6	+£16.88	M Wigham	2-2
N De Souza	3-19	15.8	+£8.00	R M Beckett	2-3
W Supple	4-26	15.4	-£11.17	H Howe	1-1
O Urbina	6-42	14.3	+£6.55	J Fanshawe	2-9
S W Kelly	11-79	13.9	-£15.28	J A Osborne	3-15

LINGFIELD SAND

Features: LH, polytrack, tight

2008 Flat fixtures: March 27-28, 31, April 2, 5, 8, 28, May 2, 9-10, June 4-5, 23, July 1, 9, 16, 19, 23, 26, August 2, 8, 12, 18, September 1, 3, 5, 16, October 3, 10, 15, 21, 27, 30, November 6, 13, 19, 22, 24, 28, December 2, 5, 7-8, 14, 17, 22, 28, 30-31

Pointers: Sir Mark Prescott has an excellent strike-rate on the AW track, but his level-stakes loss underlines how hard it is to make money out of this game. That said, Michael Jarvis shows a terrific profit from a similar pool of runners.

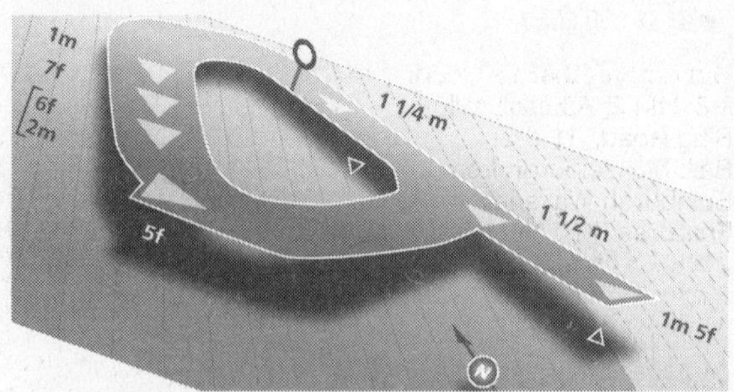

Time Test standard times

5f	58	1m2f	2min3
6f	1min11	1m4f	2min29.6
7f	1min23.2	1m5f	2min43
1m	1min36.6	2m	3min21.5

Favourites

2-y-o	34.0%	-£35.27
3-y-o+	27.5%	-£253.53
OVERALL	28.5%	-£288.80

Trainers

Trainers	Wins-Runs	%	2yo	3yo+	£1 level stks
M W Easterby	4-8	50.0	0-0	4-8	+£7.50
I Semple	3-7	42.9	0-0	3-7	+£14.50
J Wainwright	3-7	42.9	0-0	3-7	+£14.00
Mrs A Duffield	4-12	33.3	2-7	2-5	+£3.75
Miss Tor Sturgis	3-10	30.0	0-1	3-9	+£18.00
J Balding	6-20	30.0	0-0	6-20	+£4.50
C Down	3-11	27.3	0-0	3-11	+£14.50
T Easterby	3-11	27.3	0-1	3-10	+£24.00
S bin Suroor	17-65	26.2	8-27	9-38	+£4.36
E Vaughan	4-16	25.0	1-5	3-11	+£0.50
Sir M Prescott	40-169	23.7	7-66	33-103	-£15.99
M Jarvis	32-142	22.5	10-40	22-102	+£72.27
T Mills	46-204	22.5	12-40	34-164	+£19.45

Jockeys

Jockeys	Wins-Rides	%	£1 level stks	Best Trainer	W-R
D Hutchison	5-14	35.7	+£38.50	G L Moore	2-3
J D O'Reilly	5-16	31.3	+£17.75	T J Pitt	2-6
J Murtagh	4-14	28.6	+£6.67	Mrs A Perrett	2-3
L Dettori	38-138	27.5	+£23.95	S bin Suroor	6-12
Emma Littmoden	3-11	27.3	+£11.75	N Littmoden	3-11
J Edmunds	3-12	25.0	+£2.25	J Balding	2-10
M Worrell	4-16	25.0	+£11.50	Sir M Prescott	3-5
R Hills	15-72	20.8	-£14.79	M Tregoning	5-18
K Fallon	46-228	20.2	-£60.53	P Howling	4-11
J P Spencer	78-397	19.6	-£4.15	M Wallace	6-22
A Munro	12-63	19.0	+£24.71	B Millman	4-15
P J Smullen	3-16	18.8	-£6.56	B Meehan	2-5
G Sparkes	3-16	18.8	+£24.00	J Bridger	3-12

MUSSELBURGH

How to get there – Road: M8 Jctn 2, A8 east, follow Ring Road, A1 east. Rail: Musselburgh from Edinburgh Waverley

Features: RH, flat, tight

2008 Flat fixtures: March 23, April 11, May 2, 19-20, 30, June 7, 20, 30, July 7, 31, August 12, 31, September 15, 28, October 11, November 7

Pointers: Yet another example of Sir Mark Prescott making long trips pay off. He has won with more than 40 per cent of his runners at the Edinburgh track.

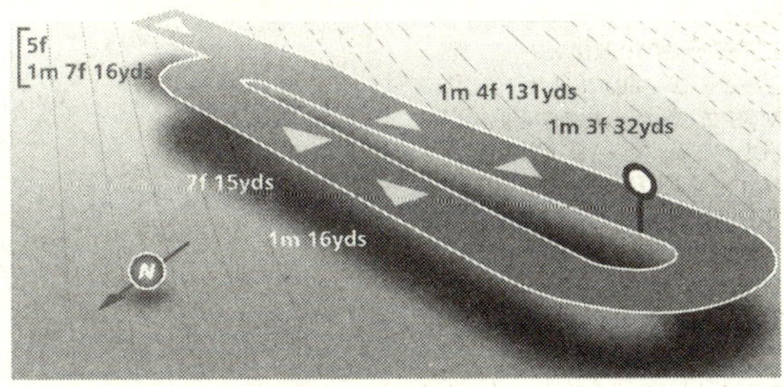

Time Test standard times

5f	57.6	1m4f	2min32.4
7f15yds	1min26.3	1m5f	2min45.3
1m	1min38.3	1m6f	2min58.4
1m1f	1min50.7	1m7f16yds	3min11.3
1m3f32yds	2min20	2m	3min25

Favourites

2-y-o	31.3%	-£35.03
3-y-o+	31.6%	-£1.35
OVERALL	31.5%	-£36.38

Trainers	Wins-Runs	%	2yo	3yo+	£1 level stks
B Meehan	3-6	50.0	3-4	0-2	+£0.75
W Haggas	7-14	50.0	2-6	5-8	+£11.48
M G Quinlan	3-7	42.9	2-4	1-3	+£10.00
Sir M Prescott	15-37	40.5	6-14	9-23	+£12.25
J Balding	4-13	30.8	1-2	3-11	+£24.50
M Todhunter	7-23	30.4	0-2	7-21	+£32.41
E Dunlop	3-11	27.3	0-0	3-11	-£4.00
J R Best	5-21	23.8	0-8	5-13	+£6.75
I A Wood	3-13	23.1	2-4	1-9	-£3.51
M Bell	3-14	21.4	3-5	0-9	-£5.00
J J Quinn	6-28	21.4	2-9	4-19	+£10.25
E J O'Neill	4-19	21.1	2-12	2-7	+£12.50
G A Swinbank	15-71	21.1	4-10	11-61	+£45.94

Jockeys	Wins-Rides	%	£1 level stks	Best Trainer	W-R
R Thomas	3-4	75.0	+£10.50	C Dore	2-3
S Dobson	4-8	50.0	+£33.25	T McLaughlin	1-1
J Edmunds	3-8	37.5	+£24.00	J Balding	3-8
Victoria Behan	3-9	33.3	+£24.50	D Nicholls	1-5
S Hitchcott	5-16	31.3	+£125.10	M Channon	4-12
E Ahern	5-17	29.4	+£4.38	G A Butler	3-5
K Fallon	6-22	27.3	-£9.71	T Hogan	1-1
J Mackay	6-23	26.1	+£21.75	B Meehan	1-1
G Duffield	8-36	22.2	+£10.96	I A Wood	3-5
S Sanders	17-77	22.1	-£27.47	Sir M Prescott	6-17
Alex Greaves	3-16	18.8	+£15.00	D Nicholls	3-16
D Nolan	4-22	18.2	+£3.25	R Fisher	2-8
D Holland	11-61	18.0	-£18.32	Sir M Prescott	2-3

NEWBURY

How to get there – Road: M4 Jctn 13 and A34 south Rail: Newbury racecourse
Features: LH, wide, flat
2008 Flat fixtures: April 18-19, May 16-17, 31, June 12, 24, July 3, 11, 18-19, August 3, 15-16, 22, September 19-20, October 9, 25

Pointers: The track is a real favourite of Sir Michael Stoute, though his impressive record was helped by the expertise of former stable jockey Kieren Fallon around the Berkshire turns. Aidan O'Brien has done well with his few runners.

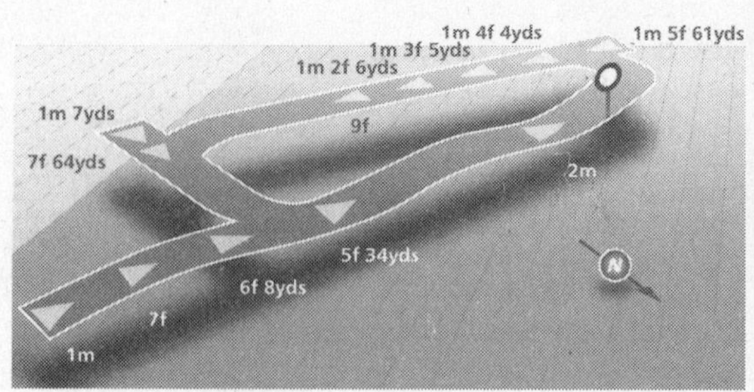

Time Test standard times

5f34yds	1min0	1m1f	1min49.7
6f110yds	1min16.6	1m2f6yds	2min2
7f	1min23	1m3f5yds	2min15.8
7f64yds(round)	1min26.4	1m4f4yds	2min29.3
1m(str)	1min36	1m5f61yds	2min45.8
1m7yds(round)	1min35.3	2m	3min23

Favourites

2-y-o	30.2%	-£25.47
3-y-o+	28.3%	-£10.65
OVERALL	28.8%	-£36.12

Trainers

Trainers	Wins-Runs	%	2yo	3yo+	£1 level stks
T Tate	3-6	50.0	0-2	3-4	+£15.50
E Vaughan	3-7	42.9	1-2	2-5	+£36.38
Mrs A L King	4-13	30.8	0-0	4-13	+£17.75
A P O'Brien	7-23	30.4	4-14	3-9	+£11.57
T Easterby	3-11	27.3	1-3	2-8	+£22.00
T Dascombe	3-12	25.0	1-7	2-5	+£6.00
M Jarvis	14-66	21.2	5-22	9-44	+£10.48
Sir M Stoute	28-132	21.2	5-29	23-103	+£8.50
S bin Suroor	15-72	20.8	6-21	9-51	-£3.65
J R Best	3-15	20.0	0-2	3-13	+£81.00
W Haggas	9-47	19.1	1-11	8-36	+£14.08
J Fanshawe	8-42	19.0	0-2	8-40	-£4.06
L Cumani	10-57	17.5	0-5	10-52	+£8.63

Jockeys

Jockeys	Wins-Rides	%	£1 level stks	Best Trainer	W-R
C O'Donoghue	3-5	60.0	+£18.57	A P O'Brien	1-2
A Rutter	3-8	37.5	+£21.83	B Palling	1-1
M Kinane	7-29	24.1	-£5.50	A P O'Brien	2-3
G Fairley	3-14	21.4	+£3.50	M Johnston	2-9
J P Murtagh	10-47	21.3	+£18.88	Sir M Stoute	3-4
P Robinson	20-103	19.4	+£40.81	M Jarvis	9-40
K Fallon	30-158	19.0	+£29.64	Sir M Stoute	7-28
N De Souza	4-22	18.2	+£6.50	D Ffrench Davis	1-1
R Miles	3-19	15.8	-£1.33	T Mills	2-5
J P Spencer	21-139	15.1	+£28.93	M Bell	3-4
A Kirby	7-49	14.3	+£8.25	C G Cox	4-13
L Dettori	28-196	14.3	-£23.89	S bin Suroor	9-40
N Mackay	6-43	14.0	+£29.00	L Cumani	2-10

Sponsored by Stan James

High Gosforth Park,
Newcastle-Upon-Tyne NE3 5HP.
Tel: 0191 236 2020 or 236 5508

How to get there – Road: Signposted from A1
Rail: Newcastle Central, metro to Regent Centre or Four Lane End & bus

Features: LH, 1m6f round, galloping, half-mile straight is all uphill

2008 Flat fixtures: April 5, May 5, 16, 23, 29, June 7, 26-28, July 26, August 6, 15, 22, 25, September 8, October 1, 14

Pointers: Once again we find a northern track at which an obvious name like Mark Johnston is missing from our list, with occasional visitors like Sir Michael Stoute, Saeed bin Suroor, John Dunlop and Barry Hills proving more solid punting material, even though their runners often aren't great value.

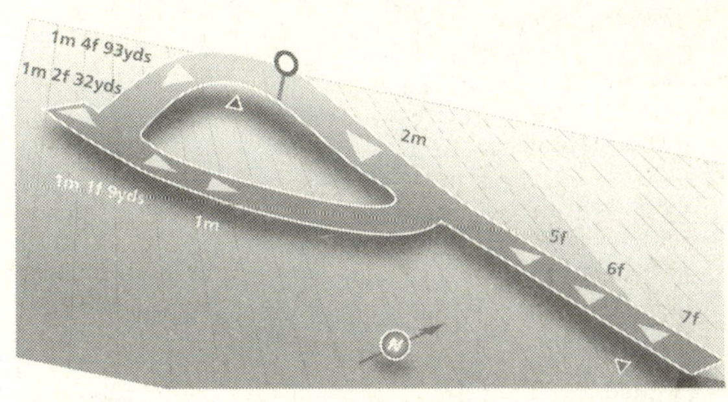

Time Test standard times

5f	59	1m1f9yds	1min52.5
6f	1min11.8	1m2f32yds	2min6.7
7f	1min24.2	1m4f93yds	2min37
1m(round)	1min39.7	1m6f97yds	3min2
1m3yds(str)	1min37.2	2m19yds	3min23.7

Favourites

2-y-o	30.9%	-£18.47
3-y-o+	29.3%	+£2.68
OVERALL	29.6%	-£15.79

Trainers	Wins-Runs	%	2yo	3yo+	£1 level stks
T Walford	3-4	75.0	0-0	3-4	+£41.50
D Loder	4-9	44.4	1-4	3-5	-£0.80
Lady Herries	3-9	33.3	0-0	3-9	+£23.75
Sir M Stoute	3-10	30.0	2-4	1-6	+£1.28
S bin Suroor	7-24	29.2	3-16	4-8	-£7.89
J Dunlop	7-24	29.2	0-3	7-21	-£2.73
B Hills	6-21	28.6	0-3	6-18	+£0.50
L Cumani	5-18	27.8	0-3	5-15	-£5.47
J Noseda	4-16	25.0	0-6	4-10	-£5.07
M Jarvis	5-20	25.0	1-5	4-15	-£2.09
Sir M Prescott	7-29	24.1	2-12	5-17	-£5.82
M Bell	9-39	23.1	4-16	5-23	+£18.00
G A Swinbank	16-72	22.2	4-16	12-56	+£71.58

Jockeys	Wins-Rides	%	£1 level stks	Best Trainer	W-R
M Hills	4-9	44.4	+£6.92	B Hills	4-7
D Kinsella	4-10	40.0	+£35.00	M Bell	1-1
K McEvoy	8-24	33.3	+£5.26	S bin Suroor	2-7
S Drowne	6-22	27.3	-£4.72	M Channon	6-9
J P Spencer	14-58	24.1	+£28.14	S bin Suroor	2-4
D Holland	9-38	23.7	+£20.91	Mrs M Reveley	2-2
D Heslop	3-13	23.1	+£5.00	W Brisbourne	1-1
S Sanders	13-58	22.4	+£1.94	Sir M Prescott	2-10
J Egan	5-23	21.7	+£37.00	J S Moore	1-1
P Robinson	6-30	20.0	+£22.25	M Jarvis	3-12
R Hills	5-26	19.2	-£11.86	J Dunlop	2-5
J-P Guillambert	7-48	14.6	+£63.50	R Whitaker	1-1
R Winston	28-192	14.6	+£51.71	B Ellison	3-10

NEWMARKET

Westfield House, The Links, Newmarket, Suffolk. CB8 0TG

How to get there – Road: from south M11 Jctn 9, then A11, from east or west A45, from north A1 or A45. Rail: Newmarket

Features: RH, wide, galloping, uphill finish

2008 Flat fixtures: April 16-17, May 3-4, 15-17, 23-25, September 19-20, October 2-4, 17-18, 31, November 1

Pointers: The summer nights at the July Course and the abundance of top racing at HQ means punters increasingly need to look beyond the obvious, with the likes of Godolphin finding their runners often overbet and underpriced, even though they have a good record. Roger Charlton is the man to follow as the underrated handler has a strong strike-rate and a decent level-stakes profit from a good sample of runners.

ROWLEY MILE

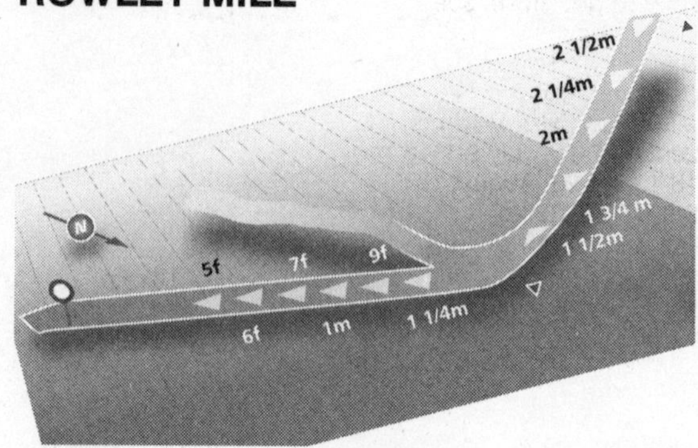

Time Test standard times

5f	57.5	1m2f	2min1.4
6f	1min10.5	1m4f	2min27.7
7f	1min22.7	1m6f	2min54.4
1m	1min35.7	2m	3min20.3
1m1f	1min48.6	2m2f	3min48

Trainer stats below apply for both Newmarket courses.

Trainers	Wins-Runs	%	2yo	3yo+	£1 level stks
P Mitchell	3-7	42.9	0-1	3-6	+£51.00
D Carroll	3-7	42.9	0-1	3-6	+£12.50
J J Quinn	3-9	33.3	0-0	3-9	+£0.63
G A Swinbank	5-18	27.8	0-1	5-17	+£4.95
J Portman	3-11	27.3	3-6	0-5	+£27.50
A P O'Brien	3-11	27.3	3-8	0-3	-£0.75
B Ellison	3-12	25.0	0-1	3-11	+£4.33
R Charlton	19-79	24.1	3-16	16-63	+£20.31
E Vaughan	3-13	23.1	1-2	2-11	+£2.25
D Loder	12-53	22.6	9-38	3-15	-£5.78
Sir M Prescott	4-18	22.2	0-4	4-14	-£6.57
B Smart	3-14	21.4	0-4	3-10	+£0.50
S bin Suroor	22-103	21.4	11-44	11-59	-£42.47
H Cecil	12-59	20.3	4-19	8-40	-£6.03
J R Best	6-30	20.0	2-10	4-20	+£39.50
J Gosden	24-122	19.7	12-55	12-67	+£8.12
J Noseda	21-108	19.4	8-44	13-64	+£1.20
J Boyle	4-23	17.4	0-1	4-22	+£65.63
Sir M Stoute	25-152	16.4	5-60	20-92	-£17.23
D Elsworth	16-98	16.3	0-19	16-79	+£29.87
C Wall	8-52	15.4	0-11	8-41	-£16.12

Westfield House
The Links,
Newmarket, Suffolk
CB8 0TG

How to get there: see facing page
Features: RH, wide, galloping, uphill finish
2008 Flat fixtures: June 20-21, 27-28, July 9-11, 18-19, 25-26, August 1-2, 8-9, 15-16, 22-23
Pointers: See previous page.

NEWMARKET

JULY COURSE

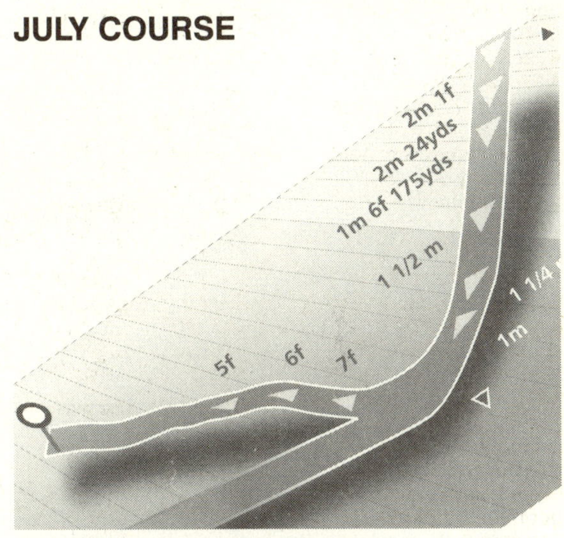

Time Test standard times

5f	57.7	1m2f	2min1
6f	1min10	1m4f	2min26.7
7f	1min22.8	1m6f175yds	3min3
1m	1min35.7	2m24yds	3min21.2
1m110yds	1min42	2m1f65yds	3min36

Favourites

(apply for both courses)

2-y-o	35.7%	-£13.40
3-y-o+	27.1%	-£55.44
OVERALL	29.7%	-£68.84

Jockey stats apply for both Newmarket courses.

Jockeys	Wins-Rides	%	£1 level stks	Best Trainer	W-R
G Fairley	3-6	50.0	+£37.75	M Johnston	2-12
L Dettori	41-157	26.1	-£37.04	S bin Suroor	21-120
R Kingscote	4-17	23.5	+£15.50	T Dascombe	1-3
L Jones	5-26	19.2	+£11.50	W Haggas	5-12
A Culhane	4-21	19.0	+£34.50	M Channon	3-21
K Fallon	26-139	18.7	-£17.50	Sir M Stoute	19-104
T O'Shea	5-31	16.1	+£20.50	M Channon	4-24
S Drowne	24-150	16.0	+£32.48	R Charlton	16-7
K McEvoy	18-115	15.7	+£57.66	S bin Suroor	10-6
J P Murtagh	6-40	15.0	-£5.95	J Fanshawe	3-
R Hughes	35-234	15.0	-£36.37	R Hannon	27-
J Fortune	28-190	14.7	-£0.95	J Gosden	24
M Halford	5-35	14.3	-£10.50	D Elsworth	
J Murtagh	8-57	14.0	-£13.61	Mrs A Perrett	
W Supple	12-88	13.6	+£6.12	T Easterby	
J P Spencer	24-178	13.5	-£5.51	J Fanshawe	
S Carson	4-30	13.3	+£37.00	R Stronge	
R Hills	18-136	13.2	-£23.67	J Dunlop	
W Buick	3-23	13.0	-£2.50	J Fanshawe	

Sponsored by Stan James

NOTTINGHAM

Colwick Park, Colwick Road,
Nottingham, NG2 4BE.
Tel 0115 958 0620

How to get there – Road: M1 Jctn 25, A52 east to B686, signs for Trent Bridge, then Colwick Park Rail: Nottingham

Features: LH, flat, easy turns

2008 Flat fixtures: April 2, 15, 19, 23, May 9-10, June 4,11, July 5, 10, 12, 18, 31, August 12, 15, October 1, 8, 16, 29, November 5

Pointers: Backing Saeed bin Suroor's older runners is a source to riches here – he has won with 15 of his 35 runners aged three or older in the last five years. Having Frankie Dettori or Kerrin McEvoy in the saddle is another big factor.

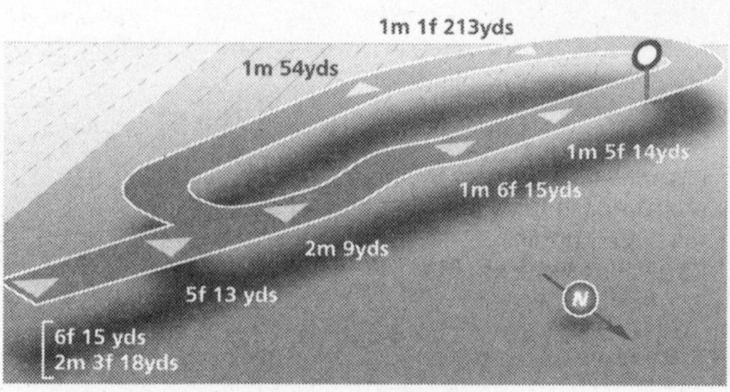

Time Test standard times

5f13yds	58.7	1m6f15yds	2min58.5
6f15yds	1min11.3	2m9yds	3min24.3
1m54yds	1min40.3	2m2f18yds	3min52.3
1m1f213yds	2min2.4		

Favourites

2-y-o	31.6%	-£39.37
3-y-o+	29.9%	-£49.69
OVERALL	30.4%	-£89.06

Trainers	Wins-Runs	%	2yo	3yo+	£1 level stks
Jamie Poulton	3-8	37.5	0-0	3-8	+£51.67
S bin Suroor	23-65	35.4	8-30	15-35	+£14.64
J Noseda	4-13	30.8	1-3	3-10	+£5.75
Mrs A Perrett	14-47	29.8	2-15	12-32	+£36.40
M Jarvis	16-55	29.1	3-20	13-35	+£26.12
B Powell	3-11	27.3	0-2	3-9	+£25.00
D Loder	4-16	25.0	4-7	0-9	-£7.91
E J O'Neill	8-33	24.2	5-15	3-18	+£39.88
Mrs L Stubbs	4-17	23.5	1-6	3-11	+£21.00
N Callaghan	7-30	23.3	6-16	1-14	+£5.67
Sir M Stoute	14-62	22.6	9-31	5-31	-£15.48
E Alston	4-18	22.2	1-3	3-15	+£10.00
G Reveley	5-23	21.7	0-0	5-23	+£37.00

Jockeys	Wins-Rides	%	£1 level stks	Best Trainer	W-R
...ard	3-10	30.0	+£41.00	D Ivory	3-7
	29-97	29.9	+£4.41	S bin Suroor	11-28
	17-59	28.8	+£32.55	S bin Suroor	5-11
	6-23	26.1	+£4.37	J Fanshawe	2-6
	4-16	25.0	+£6.50	P Makin	1-1
	16-77	20.8	+£5.87	M Jarvis	9-25
	17-93	18.3	+£15.57	M Bell	3-3
	21-127	16.5	+£124.94	E Alston	3-5
	3-19	15.8	+£22.50	H Collingridge	1-1
	10-64	15.6	-£10.00	Sir M Stoute	3-10
	53	15.1	-£12.99	B Millman	2-14
	7	14.8	+£23.50	K R Burke	3-12
	-97	14.4	-£22.56	R Charlton	3-8

211

33 Ropergate, Pontefract,
WF8 1LE. Tel 01977 703 224

How to get there – Road: M62 Jctn 32, then A539 Rail: Pontefract Monkhill or Pontefract Baghill from Leeds

Features: LH, undulating, sharp home turn, last half-mile is all uphill

2008 Flat fixtures: March 25, April 21, 30, May 23, June 9, 22, 30, July 8, 18, 27, August 6, 17, September 18, 25, October 6, 20

Pointers: Another track at which Henry Cecil has kept his name in the spotlight, though Sir Michael Stoute and Barry Hills have done well with more ammunition.

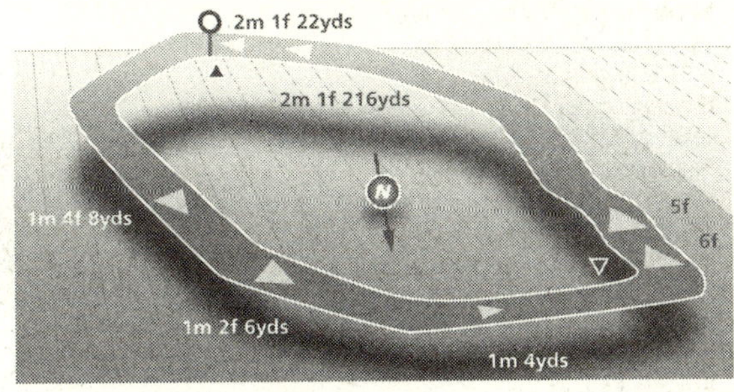

Time Test standard times

5f	1min1.3	1m4f8yds	2min34.5
6f	1min14.2	2m1f22yds	3min42.2
1m4yds	1min41.8	2m1f216yds	3min52
1m2f6yds	2min7.2	2m5f122yds	4min48

Favourites

2-y-o	38.8%	-£12.55
3-y-o+	29.7%	+£1.36
OVERALL	31.5%	-£11.19

Trainers	Wins-Runs	%	2yo	3yo+	£1 level stks
H Cecil	10-23	43.5	0-2	10-21	+£13.91
J A Osborne	3-8	37.5	2-3	1-5	+£2.95
P Cole	5-14	35.7	2-3	3-11	+£9.00
S bin Suroor	6-18	33.3	1-3	5-15	+£2.07
Sir M Stoute	18-54	33.3	3-7	15-47	+£12.14
J Gosden	10-32	31.3	5-12	5-20	+£14.01
M Wallace	3-11	27.3	2-5	1-6	+£8.50
B Hills	17-66	25.8	4-16	13-50	+£1.34
Sir M Prescott	5-21	23.8	1-6	4-15	-£7.20
Mrs P Sly	3-13	23.1	0-2	3-11	+£60.00
A Stewart	3-13	23.1	1-3	2-10	+£1.62
E Dunlop	8-35	22.9	1-6	7-29	+£12.94
W Haggas	10-48	20.8	2-14	8-34	-£3.99

Jockeys	Wins-Rides	%	£1 level stks	Best Trainer	W-R
T Quinn	8-22	36.4	+£51.62	P Cole	1-1
K Fallon	20-57	35.1	+£20.22	Sir M Stoute	6-14
S Carson	4-15	26.7	+£32.50	J A Geake	1-1
R Hills	14-57	24.6	-£6.67	M Johnston	4-5
K McEvoy	7-29	24.1	+£10.63	J Gosden	2-2
R Hughes	6-27	22.2	-£11.35	H Cecil	2-4
L Dettori	9-41	22.0	+£4.64	J Gosden	2-4
R L Moore	5-23	21.7	-£8.22	Sir M Stoute	1-2
S W Kelly	5-23	21.7	-£1.18	J Noseda	1-1
M Hills	10-52	19.2	-£1.91	B Hills	9-32
T O'Shea	3-16	18.8	+£5.75	M Channon	2-6
T P Queally	9-50	18.0	+£33.45	J Given	3-14
J P Spencer	11-62	17.7	-£11.52	Mrs J Ramsden	3-7

REDCAR

How to get there – Road: A1, A168, A19, then A174 Rail: Redcar Central from Darlington

Features: LH, flat, galloping

2008 Flat fixtures: March 24, May 1, 12, 26-27, June 10, 20-21, July 3, 20, 30, August 9-10, 23, September 4, 15, 24, October 4, 17

Pointers: Saeed bin Suroor makes more trips to Redcar than you might expect, but it's no wonder when he is winning with such regularity – a 32 per cent strike-rate has already paid for the petrol money for this year.

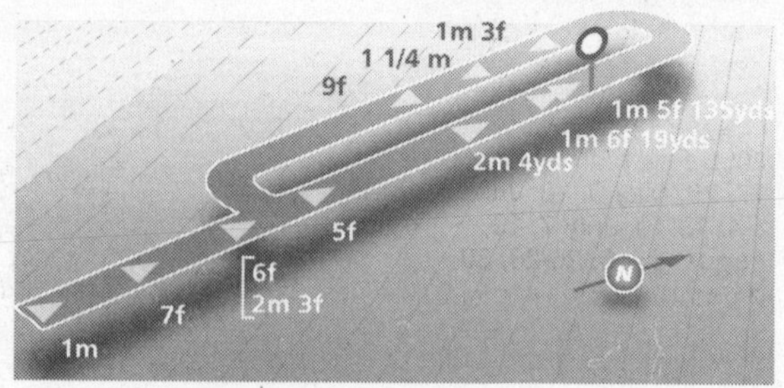

Time Test standard times

5f	56.7	1m3f	2min17
6f	1min9.4	1m4f	2min30
7f	1min22	1m5f135yds	2min54.7
1m	1min34.7	1m6f19yds	3min0
1m1f	1min49.3	2m4yds	3min25
1m2f	2min2.6	2m3f	4min5.3

Favourites

2-y-o	34.9%	-£25.79
3-y-o+	26.4%	-£57.10
OVERALL	28.5%	-£82.90

Trainers	Wins-Runs	%	2yo	3yo+	£1 level stks
P Cole	5-8	62.5	0-1	5-7	+£25.00
D Loder	4-10	40.0	4-7	0-3	-£0.51
P Chapple-Hyam	3-8	37.5	0-2	3-6	+£0.17
Mrs C Dunnett	3-9	33.3	0-2	3-7	+£11.83
J Gosden	7-21	33.3	2-8	5-13	+£4.42
S bin Suroor	10-31	32.3	1-10	9-21	+£2.27
C Brittain	6-19	31.6	3-5	3-14	+£24.75
J Dunlop	8-27	29.6	2-8	6-19	-£0.31
P Harris	5-17	29.4	0-1	5-16	+£16.00
M Bell	10-34	29.4	4-11	6-23	+£4.37
Sir M Stoute	4-14	28.6	1-3	3-11	+£6.87
J Noseda	6-21	28.6	4-9	2-12	+£8.66
Mrs A Perrett	3-13	23.1	2-4	1-9	-£0.33

Jockeys	Wins-Rides	%	£1 level stks	Best Trainer	W-R
S Brotherton	3-9	33.3	+£33.00	M W Easterby	3-6
K McEvoy	13-44	29.5	-£3.06	S bin Suroor	7-11
L Dettori	4-14	28.6	+£1.87	P D'Arcy	1-1
S Drowne	3-12	25.0	+£11.50	Miss E Lavelle	1-1
T P Queally	9-37	24.3	+£41.82	D Loder	1-1
R Hughes	4-17	23.5	-£3.88	H Cecil	2-3
M Dwyer	3-14	21.4	-£2.25	P Harris	1-1
J Egan	3-14	21.4	-£7.21	P L Gilligan	1-1
S Sanders	18-89	20.2	+£23.71	J Dunlop	3-5
J P Spencer	14-72	19.4	-£3.10	J Fanshawe	2-6
N Callan	25-131	19.1	+£67.44	K Ryan	9-49
N Mackay	7-38	18.4	-£1.13	L Cumani	3-15
I Mongan	4-22	18.2	+£21.50	S Gollings	2-4

RIPON

How to get there – Road: A1, then B6265
Rail: Harrogate, bus to Ripon centre, 1m walk
Features: RH, sharp
2008 Flat fixtures: April 17, 26, May 9, 18, June 3-4, 18-19, July 7, 19, August 4, 16, 25-26, 30
Pointers: Barry Hills is a regular visitor to the North Yorkshire track and punters should have learned to pay close attention to his runners – he has won with 20 out of 60 for a £30 level-stakes profit. However, Michael Hills has a comparatively modest record for his father, winning with 23 per cent of his mounts.

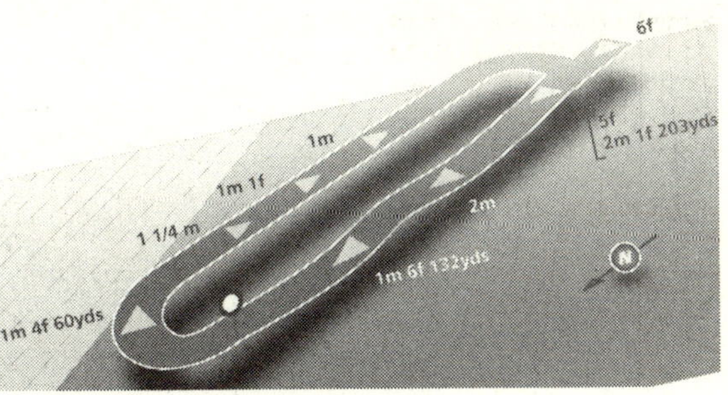

Time Test standard times

5f	57.8	1m2f	2min3.3
6f	1min10.6	1m4f10yds	2min31
1m	1min37.8	2m	3min27
1m1f170yds	2min0.4	2m1f203yds	3min52

Favourites

2-y-o	34.4%	-£4.57
3-y-o+	27.2%	-£63.42
OVERALL	29.1%	-£67.98

Trainers	Wins-Runs	%	2yo	3yo+	£1 level stks
G Wragg	4-11	36.4	0-0	4-11	+£9.40
J Dunlop	9-26	34.6	2-2	7-24	+£0.54
E J O'Neill	4-12	33.3	3-6	1-6	+£7.88
B Hills	20-60	33.3	3-8	17-52	+£30.39
Sir M Stoute	8-26	30.8	1-1	7-25	-£2.69
P Cole	3-10	30.0	0-0	3-10	+£14.63
T Tate	11-38	28.9	1-7	10-31	+£105.75
M Jarvis	8-29	27.6	1-4	7-25	+£8.05
S bin Suroor	3-11	27.3	0-2	3-9	-£0.28
Sir M Prescott	3-12	25.0	1-6	2-6	£0.00
M Tompkins	6-25	24.0	0-0	6-25	+£19.00
R Hannon	4-17	23.5	3-9	1-8	+£10.32
J Gosden	4-18	22.2	0-0	4-18	-£7.83

Jockeys	Wins-Rides	%	£1 level stks	Best Trainer	W-R
Lisa Jones	3-6	50.0	+£70.00	D Chapman	2-2
P Robinson	15-49	30.6	+£33.18	M Jarvis	7-25
R Hills	7-23	30.4	-£3.85	J Dunlop	2-3
M Dwyer	6-23	26.1	+£26.25	B Hills	2-2
J Egan	5-21	23.8	+£20.41	T Easterby	2-3
J P Spencer	9-38	23.7	+£12.36	J Bradley	2-2
M Hills	6-26	23.1	+£0.02	B Hills	4-17
R Hughes	5-22	22.7	-£5.12	R Hannon	2-7
D Holland	12-53	22.6	+£12.96	M Tompkins	3-6
K Dalgleish	4-18	22.2	+£14.55	M Johnston	3-9
S Sanders	14-67	20.9	+£16.10	J Dunlop	2-3
E Ahern	5-24	20.8	-£0.92	E Alston	2-2
N Callan	24-128	18.8	+£111.39	K Ryan	16-54

Sponsored by Stan James

SALISBURY

Netherhampton, Salisbury, Wilts, SP2 8PN. Tel 01722 326 461

How to get there – Road: 2m west of Salisbury on A3094
Rail: Salisbury, bus
Features: RH, uphill finish
2008 Flat fixtures: May 4, 15, 22, June 10, 15, 25, 29, July 4, 12, 22, 26, August 13-14, 29, September 4, October 1
Pointers: Once more it's Saeed bin Suroor who heads the list, and with a small level-stakes profit to boot, though punters may be better served following Sir Michael Stoute.

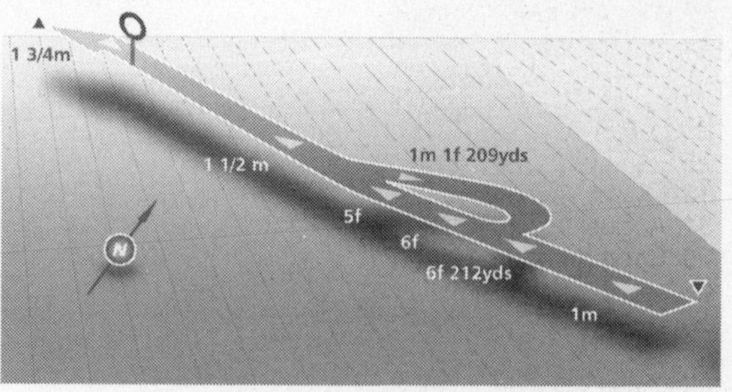

Time Test standard times

5f	59.6	1m1f209yds	2min5
6f	1min12	1m4f	2min32
6f212yds	1min25.2	1m6f15yds	2min58.3
1m	1min39.2		

Favourites

2-y-o	32.6%	-£20.74
3-y-o+	25.8%	-£95.05
OVERALL	27.6%	-£115.79

Trainers

Trainers	Wins-Runs	%	2yo	3yo+	£1 level stks
S bin Suroor	13-40	32.5	4-17	9-23	+£5.38
M Tompkins	4-13	30.8	0-1	4-12	+£7.50
Sir M Stoute	16-56	28.6	4-19	12-37	+£18.56
M Jarvis	6-22	27.3	3-6	3-16	+£3.23
R Harris	6-29	20.7	0-1	6-28	+£17.88
Stef Liddiard	3-15	20.0	0-0	3-15	+£12.00
L Cumani	8-40	20.0	0-0	8-40	-£11.16
W Haggas	4-22	18.2	3-6	1-16	+£0.87
H Candy	11-61	18.0	4-16	7-45	+£15.96
B Meehan	10-56	17.9	7-31	3-25	+£5.50
C G Cox	7-41	17.1	1-9	6-32	+£11.33
J Gosden	14-85	16.5	5-34	9-51	+£2.49
R Charlton	11-68	16.2	2-21	9-47	-£1.35

Jockeys

Jockeys	Wins-Rides	%	£1 level stks	Best Trainer	W-R
S Breux	3-5	60.0	+£25.00	R Hannon	1-1
P Robinson	9-25	36.0	+£6.98	M Jarvis	5-11
K McEvoy	14-51	27.5	+£57.50	S bin Suroor	3-8
J H Bowman	4-16	25.0	+£7.13	B Millman	2-3
K Fallon	15-63	23.8	-£1.70	Sir M Stoute	3-13
L Dettori	21-95	22.1	-£35.74	S bin Suroor	7-25
J P Spencer	9-41	22.0	+£1.82	Jane Chapple-Hyam	1-1
R Hills	14-73	19.2	-£10.15	J Dunlop	3-14
J Murtagh	3-16	18.8	+£0.12	Mrs A Perrett	2-7
S Sanders	16-97	16.5	+£5.12	R M Beckett	6-14
J Egan	20-128	15.6	-£17.61	D Elsworth	6-24
J Fortune	22-143	15.4	-£19.18	J Gosden	7-32
W Supple	4-27	14.8	-£8.00	P Harris	1-3

SANDOWN

How to get there – Road: M25 Jctn 10 then A3
Rail: Esher from Waterloo
Features: RH, last 7f uphill
2008 Flat fixtures: April 25-26, May 21, 29, June 5, 13-14, July 4-5, 17, 23-24, 31, August 7, 13-14, 29-30, September 11-12,17

Pointers: The cream comes to the top at Sandown, so it's no surprise to see Sir Mark Prescott scoring with a shade under 39 per cent of his runners. Michael Jarvis, John Gosden, Mark Johnston and Saeed bin Suroor are other notable names with a strike-rate above 20 per cent.

Time Test standard times

5f6yds	59.2	1m2f7yds	2min5
7f16yds	1min27	1m3f91yds	2min21.7
1m14yds	1min40	1m6f	2min57
1m1f	1min52	2m78yds	3min30.4

Favourites

2-y-o	39.3%	+£8.27
3-y-o+	29.9%	-£4.59
OVERALL	31.9%	+£3.68

Trainers

Trainers	Wins-Runs	%	2yo	3yo+	£1 level stks
Sir M Prescott	7-18	38.9	2-4	5-14	+£12.75
A Coogan	3-8	37.5	0-0	3-8	+£16.58
J Given	5-20	25.0	1-1	4-19	+£28.00
M Jarvis	16-71	22.5	2-11	14-60	+£13.21
J Gosden	23-106	21.7	7-26	16-80	-£2.56
M Johnston	27-125	21.6	11-36	16-89	+£4.79
J Spearing	3-14	21.4	0-0	3-14	+£50.87
M Bell	7-33	21.2	0-9	7-24	+£0.50
S bin Suroor	13-65	20.0	1-12	12-53	+£6.63
S C Williams	3-16	18.8	0-0	3-16	+£1.50
Sir M Stoute	26-141	18.4	4-24	22-117	-£24.41
D Loder	3-17	17.6	1-6	2-11	+£0.50
H Cecil	6-34	17.6	0-5	6-29	+£3.08

Jockeys

Jockeys	Wins-Rides	%	£1 level stks	Best Trainer	W-R
J Millman	5-14	35.7	+£12.50	B Millman	2-5
K Dalgleish	4-16	25.0	-£1.77	M Johnston	3-14
R Hills	31-132	23.5	+£29.13	J Gosden	5-10
R Ffrench	6-26	23.1	+£28.00	J Given	1-1
T P Queally	5-23	21.7	+£12.20	B Curley	1-1
W Ryan	3-14	21.4	+£8.00	N Callaghan	1-1
P Hanagan	3-15	20.0	-£2.42	R Fahey	2-7
L Dettori	29-149	19.5	+£8.05	S bin Suroor	7-34
G Carter	3-16	18.8	+£50.00	Miss D Mountain	2-3
S Sanders	24-130	18.5	+£35.91	Sir M Prescott	7-15
T Block	3-17	17.6	-£3.88	J Spearing	1-1
P Robinson	18-110	16.4	+£18.38	M Jarvis	10-48
W Supple	6-38	15.8	+£14.50	J Gosden	2-4

Sponsored by Stan James

SOUTHWELL

How to get there – Road: A1 to Newark, then A617 or M1 to Nottingham then A612; Rail: Rolleston

Features: LH fibresand, sharp

2008 Flat fixtures: March 31, April 4, 8, 22, 24, 28-29, May 2, 6, 13, 20, June 3, 8, July 4, 8, 28, September 2, 30, October 19, 28, November 2, 4, 10, 12, 14, 18, 25, December 2, 9-10, 12-13, 16, 18-19, 23, 27

Pointers: Following the favourites on the all-weather is always a route to the poor house, but selectively backing them wouldn't be a bad thing here as the losses are astonishingly small compared to the other tracks.

NB: Due to the shortage of meetings on the turf course, our trainer, jockey and favourite stats relate to AW racing only.

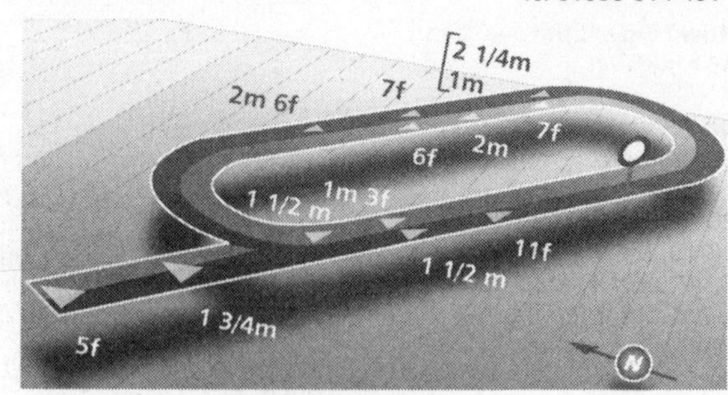

Time Test standard times

5f	57.7	1m4f	2min34
6f	1min13.5	1m5f	2min47.4
7f	1min27	1m6f	3min1.7
1m	1min40	2m	3min30
1m3f	2min21.6	2m2f	3min58

Favourites

2-y-o	36.9%	-£1.40
3-y-o+	29.5%	-£103.26
OVERALL	30.2%	-£104.65

Trainers

Trainers	Wins-Runs	%	2yo	3yo+	£1 level stks
J Noseda	4-8	50.0	0-0	4-8	+£7.60
J Gosden	5-11	45.5	2-4	3-7	+£9.50
J Toller	5-14	35.7	0-0	5-14	+£15.08
W Haggas	20-56	35.7	4-13	16-43	+£14.68
J Fanshawe	5-15	33.3	0-3	5-12	-£3.55
M Bell	8-26	30.8	1-2	7-24	+£6.04
T Dascombe	4-14	28.6	0-2	4-12	+£2.38
D Loder	4-14	28.6	0-0	4-14	-£1.35
M G Quinlan	11-40	27.5	3-10	8-30	+£16.13
G Huffer	4-15	26.7	0-0	4-15	+£4.88
T Mills	4-15	26.7	1-3	3-12	-£1.01
M Jarvis	10-38	26.3	2-10	8-28	+£13.66
W Jarvis	12-46	26.1	5-6	7-40	+£15.06

Jockeys

Jockeys	Wins-Rides	%	£1 level stks	Best Trainer	W-R
T Block	7-21	33.3	+£12.90	H Morrison	5-15
J Fortune	4-13	30.8	+£1.49	J Gosden	3-4
N Brown	4-14	28.6	+£5.91	D Carroll	2-7
R Price	4-14	28.6	+£49.00	M Ryan	2-2
W Woods	4-15	26.7	-£4.64	Sir M Prescott	4-9
L Ellison	3-12	25.0	+£15.50	B Ellison	3-9
J P Spencer	20-83	24.1	-£19.94	T Barron	3-3
S Sanders	26-116	22.4	-£28.89	Sir M Prescott	9-23
P Hills	3-14	21.4	-£3.45	M Usher	1-1
K Darley	4-19	21.1	+£4.00	T Barron	2-4
J Millman	11-54	20.4	+£27.33	B Millman	6-27
J Jones	3-15	20.0	+£15.91	John Joseph Murphy	1-1
L Dettori	3-15	20.0	-£7.40	S bin Suroor	1-1

THIRSK

How to get there – Road: A61 from A1 in the west or A19 in the east
Rail: Thirsk, 10 min walk
Features: LH, sharp, tight turns, drains well
2008 Flat fixtures: April 18-19, May 3, 10, 17, June 2, 17, July 1, 25, August 1-2, 11, September 6-7
Pointers: Little suggests itself from the stats, with John Dunlop, Marcus Tregoning and Saeed bin Suroor dominating the trainers' list but from relatively few runners.

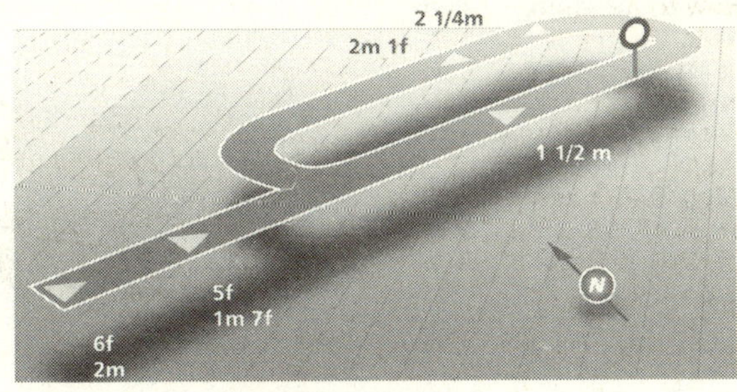

Time Test standard times

5f	57.4	1m	1min35.8
6f	1min9.5	1m4f	2min30
7f	1min23	2m	3min22.6

Favourites

2-y-o	37.6%	-£10.61
3-y-o+	29.0%	-£38.28
OVERALL	31.1%	-£48.89

Trainers	Wins-Runs	%	2yo	3yo+	£1 level stks
J Dunlop	5-11	45.5	0-0	5-11	-£0.06
J A Osborne	5-11	45.5	4-6	1-5	+£22.25
M Tregoning	4-10	40.0	1-1	3-9	+£0.89
S bin Suroor	6-16	37.5	1-3	5-13	+£3.36
P Chapple-Hyam	5-14	35.7	1-4	4-10	+£8.60
J Gosden	3-9	33.3	0-1	3-8	-£2.30
M Tompkins	3-9	33.3	0-1	3-8	+£0.62
Sir M Stoute	8-25	32.0	1-3	7-22	-£2.25
J Fanshawe	4-13	30.8	1-2	3-11	-£0.88
B McMahon	3-10	30.0	1-2	2-8	-£0.15
P Harris	3-10	30.0	0-0	3-10	+£15.00
B Meehan	4-14	28.6	3-11	1-3	+£4.11
L Cumani	4-15	26.7	0-1	4-14	+£1.43

Jockeys	Wins-Rides	%	£1 level stks	Best Trainer	W-R
M Hills	4-7	57.1	+£6.25	B Hills	4-7
C Haddon	5-14	35.7	+£11.75	W G M Turner	4-11
W Ryan	3-9	33.3	+£15.00	J Given	1-1
A Munro	4-13	30.8	+£67.50	J Balding	1-1
N Brown	4-13	30.8	+£10.25	M Dods	2-2
D Corby	3-11	27.3	+£11.67	M Wallace	2-5
L Jones	4-15	26.7	+£0.50	W G M Turner	1-3
P Robinson	5-21	23.8	+£9.35	J Given	1-1
A McCarthy	4-17	23.5	+£6.50	R Harris	1-2
D Holland	3-13	23.1	+£9.00	W Haggas	1-1
J P Spencer	10-45	22.2	-£12.16	J Fanshawe	2-3
K McEvoy	6-29	20.7	-£10.59	S bin Suroor	2-6
N Mackay	8-45	17.8	-£10.33	L Cumani	4-14

Sponsored by Stan James

WARWICK

6 Hampton Street, Warwick
CV34 6HN. Tel 01926 491 553

How to get there – Road: M40 Jctn 14, A429
Rail: Warwick
Features: LH, sharp turns
2008 Flat fixtures: March 24, April 15, May 5, 10, June 16, 19, 26, July 3-4, 10, August 25, September 4, 10, 30, October 6
Pointers: Rising star Kirsty Milczarek has made her mark here, with four winners out of nine rides, though it's hard to better Jamie Spencer's record from a far bigger pool. Peter Chapple-Hyam has done well to show a profit from his visits.

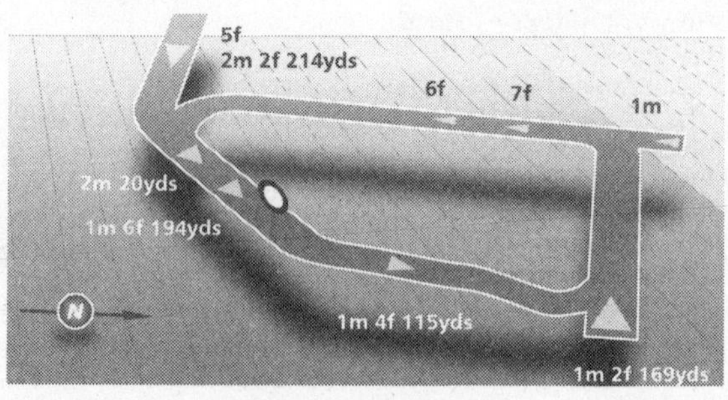

Time Test standard times

5f	58	1m4f115yds	2min34.6
5f110yds	1min4	1m6f194yds	3min6
6f	1min10.6	2m20yds	3min24
7f	1min22.2	2m2f214yds	3min58
1m	1min35.3	2m3f13yds	4min0
1m2f169yds	2min12		

Favourites

2-y-o	35.0%	-£13.20
3-y-o+	27.0%	-£51.42
OVERALL	28.9%	-£64.61

Trainers	Wins-Runs	%	2yo	3yo+	£1 level stks
D Loder	5-13	38.5	3-6	2-7	+£15.38
W Haggas	7-21	33.3	1-4	6-17	+£14.05
John Berry	3-10	30.0	0-0	3-10	+£46.00
P Chapple-Hyam	10-34	29.4	6-19	4-15	+£2.94
M Pipe	3-11	27.3	0-0	3-11	-£0.12
J A Geake	4-16	25.0	0-1	4-15	+£38.75
Miss J Southcombe	3-13	23.1	0-0	3-13	+£14.33
M Quinn	4-18	22.2	1-5	3-13	+£10.00
N Callaghan	3-14	21.4	2-8	1-6	+£3.50
M Dods	6-28	21.4	0-1	6-27	+£19.00
J Fanshawe	9-42	21.4	1-8	8-34	+£16.23
W Jarvis	4-19	21.1	1-7	3-12	-£1.08
T Easterby	4-20	20.0	0-4	4-16	+£13.25

Jockeys	Wins-Rides	%	£1 level stks	Best Trainer	W-R
Kirsty Milczarek	4-9	44.4	+£40.00	D M Simcock	1-1
K Fallon	8-23	34.8	+£3.54	D Cantillon	1-1
J P Spencer	19-68	27.9	+£23.12	P Evans	2-3
S O'Hara	3-11	27.3	+£11.50	Dr J Naylor	2-4
R L Moore	15-64	23.4	+£43.18	R Hannon	5-16
E Ahern	22-99	22.2	+£24.65	J Hills	2-4
R Hills	5-23	21.7	-£12.82	B Hills	1-1
R Hughes	16-76	21.1	+£64.45	B Hills	4-8
N De Souza	4-21	19.0	+£24.00	N Callaghan	1-1
R Miles	4-21	19.0	+£15.50	A Newcombe	1-1
T McLaughlin	4-22	18.2	+£36.25	T Clement	1-2
L Dettori	3-17	17.6	-£6.56	S bin Suroor	2-6
P Robinson	4-23	17.4	-£7.27	M Jarvis	2-7

WINDSOR

How to get there – Road:
M4 Jctn 6, A355, A308
Rail: Windsor Central from
Paddington or Windsor
Riverside from Waterloo
Features: Figure of eight,
flat, easy turns, straight
almost 5f long
2008 Flat fixtures: April
14, 21, 28, May 5, 12, 19,
June 2, 9, 16, 23, 28-30,
July 7, 14, 21, 28, August
4, 10-11, 18, 23,
September 29, October 6,
13, 20

Pointers: Summer
wouldn't be summer
without Monday nights at
Windsor, more often than not featuring winners trained
by Sir Michael Stoute or Saeed bin Suroor. Roger
Charlton also loves to use the track for his juveniles.

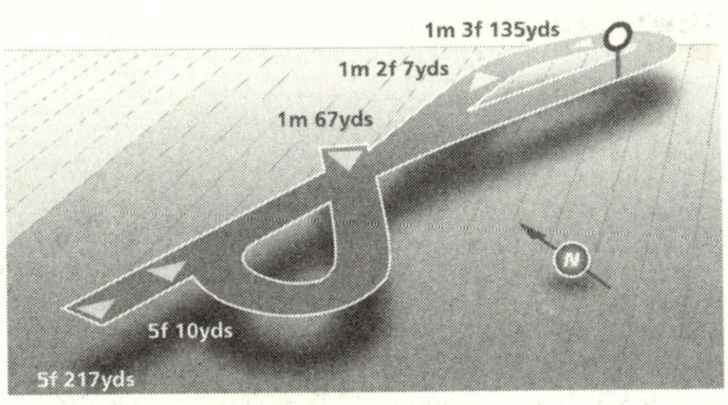

Time Test standard times

5f10yds	58	1m2f7yds	2min3.6
5f217yds	1min10.2	1m3f135yds	2min22.6
1m67yds	1min41.6		

Favourites

2-y-o	37.6%	+£3.39
3-y-o+	30.5%	+£13.12
OVERALL	32.3%	+£16.51

Trainers	Wins-Runs	%	2yo	3yo+	£1 level stks
Sir M Stoute	38-135	28.1	6-23	32-112	-£10.96
E Vaughan	3-12	25.0	0-1	3-11	-£0.50
E S McMahon	6-24	25.0	2-11	4-13	+£13.13
S bin Suroor	19-76	25.0	3-13	16-63	-£2.39
L Cottrell	6-29	20.7	2-5	4-24	+£6.00
G A Butler	8-40	20.0	0-5	8-35	+£44.75
G Margarson	5-26	19.2	1-8	4-18	+£28.50
J Gosden	20-104	19.2	3-8	17-96	-£33.30
R Charlton	18-99	18.2	8-33	10-66	+£8.87
K R Burke	10-57	17.5	2-14	8-43	+£39.50
H Cecil	4-23	17.4	1-2	3-21	-£4.58
M Bell	17-105	16.2	6-40	11-65	+£6.30
M Usher	8-51	15.7	2-16	6-35	+£91.75

Jockeys	Wins-Rides	%	£1 level stks	Best Trainer	W-R
P Cosgrave	3-13	23.1	+£11.70	J Portman	1-1
K Fallon	28-123	22.8	-£9.40	Sir M Stoute	11-29
L Dettori	28-156	17.9	-£33.41	S bin Suroor	5-26
K McEvoy	18-104	17.3	+£34.83	S bin Suroor	8-20
J P Spencer	30-180	16.7	-£55.88	M Bell	6-15
R Hughes	56-344	16.3	-£1.72	R Hannon	27-147
J Murtagh	3-20	15.0	+£14.37	G Margarson	1-1
J Millman	5-34	14.7	+£8.00	B Millman	4-21
J P Murtagh	3-21	14.3	+£34.69	Sir M Stoute	1-1
R L Moore	58-416	13.9	-£122.63	R Hannon	17-99
M Hills	13-96	13.5	-£26.87	B Hills	7-41
J Fortune	30-231	13.0	-£66.59	J Gosden	13-50
A Munro	10-85	11.8	-£12.52	B Millman	5-26

Dunstall Park, Gorsebrook Road, Wolverhampton, West Midlands, WV6 0PE. Tel 08702 202 442

How to get there – Road: of A449, close to M6, M42 and M54
Rail: Wolverhampton, bus
Features: LH, fibresand, very sharp
2008 Flat fixtures: March 22, 26, 28, 30, April 4, 11, 14, 16, 19, 25-26, 29, May 12, 14, June 6, 23, 30, July 8, 14, 25, August 11, 18, 29, September 6, 12, 19-20, 26, October 3-4, 10-11, 13, 18, 24-25, 31, November 3, 7-8, 10, 12, 15, 17, 21-22, 26, 29, December 1, 5-6, 8, 12-13, 15, 19-20, 26, 30

Pointers: The folly of backing favourites on the all-weather cannot be reiterated, emphasised by losses of £379 to £1 level stakes at Wolverhampton. Even Jamie Spencer's 25 per cent strike-rate isn't enough to put him in profit.

Time Test standard times

5f20yds	1min0.2	1m1f103yds	1min57.5
5f216yds	1min13.1	1m4f50yds	2min35.2
7f32yds	1min26.9	1m5f194yds	3min
1m141yds	1min46.7	2m119yds	3min36.6

Favourites

2-y-o	36.1%	-£29.46
3-y-o+	27.2%	-£350.31
OVERALL	28.5%	-£379.76

Trainers

Trainers	Wins-Runs	%	2yo	3yo+	£1 level stks
H Cyzer	4-9	44.4	1-1	3-8	+£15.50
Sir M Stoute	15-42	35.7	4-20	11-22	+£4.11
D Loder	20-58	34.5	6-12	14-46	+£26.89
N J Vaughan	7-22	31.8	4-7	3-15	+£63.91
P Harris	7-23	30.4	1-5	6-18	+£31.00
Mouse Hamilton-Fairl	4-14	28.6	0-0	4-14	+£16.07
L Cumani	19-69	27.5	8-21	11-48	+£15.97
P R Webber	8-32	25.0	0-0	8-32	+£35.50
T Dascombe	9-36	25.0	4-12	5-24	+£17.58
J Noseda	14-56	25.0	5-9	9-47	-£7.98
T J Pitt	13-54	24.1	5-8	8-46	-£6.04
W Haggas	37-170	21.8	15-56	22-114	+£14.12
D Daly	8-37	21.6	3-10	5-27	+£14.95

Jockeys

Jockeys	Wins-Rides	%	£1 level stks	Best Trainer	W-R
L Newnes	6-13	46.2	+£19.25	M Usher	4-6
L Dettori	13-30	43.3	+£22.88	J A Osborne	2-2
L Goncalves	3-9	33.3	+£36.00	Mrs J Ramsden	3-8
G Faulkner	9-29	31.0	+£16.25	P Haslam	4-10
A Ryan	3-10	30.0	+£8.00	K Ryan	2-6
P J McDonald	3-10	30.0	+£6.50	J Wainwright	2-3
P Robinson	6-20	30.0	+£1.42	M Jarvis	5-12
N Jefferson	3-11	27.3	+£25.50	J Jefferson	2-8
L Betts	4-15	26.7	+£6.50	N Wilson	2-10
J P Spencer	80-312	25.6	-£0.48	D Loder	8-21
Marie King	5-20	25.0	+£10.50	P Hiatt	5-18
W Supple	4-18	22.2	+£0.63	D Loder	1-1
J Mitchell	3-14	21.4	+£17.50	P Mitchell	2-4

Jellicoe Road, North Denes, Great Yarmouth, Norfolk, NR30 4AU. Tel 01493 842 527

How to get there – Road: A47 to end, A1064 Rail: Great Yarmouth, bus

Features: LH, flat, drains well

2008 Flat fixtures: March 24, April 28, May 12-13, 28-29, June 12, 17, July 3, 15, 21-22, 28, August 6-7, 13, 18, 24, September 16-18, October 21, 28

Pointers: A favourite track for Sir Michael Stoute and Saeed bin Suroor to run their juveniles, and it pays more to side with Stoute – his one-in-three record is even better with just his two-year-olds and yields a major level-stakes profit.

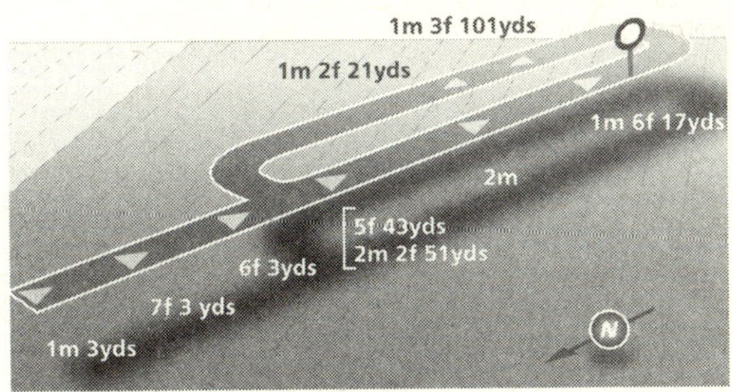

Time Test standard times

5f43yds	1min0.4	1m3f101yds	2min23
6f3yds	1min10.7	1m6f17yds	2min58
7f3yds	1min23	2m	3min25
1m3yds	1min35.5	2m1f170yds	3min48
1m2f21yds	2min3.3	2m2f51yds	3min54

Favourites

2-y-o	36.6%	-£25.08
3-y-o+	30.9%	-£3.81
OVERALL	32.5%	-£28.89

Trainers

Trainers	Wins-Runs	%	2yo	3yo+	£1 level stks
T Dascombe	3-6	50.0	2-5	1-1	+£20.50
A Stewart	3-7	42.9	0-1	3-6	-£0.81
M Tregoning	4-12	33.3	2-2	2-10	+£11.25
Sir M Stoute	28-84	33.3	14-44	14-40	+£40.97
M Jarvis	16-62	25.8	7-28	9-34	-£1.35
J G O'Shea	3-12	25.0	1-4	2-8	+£23.00
Sir M Prescott	12-49	24.5	1-17	11-32	-£9.53
H Cecil	9-39	23.1	0-10	9-29	+£8.54
S bin Suroor	12-53	22.6	7-32	5-21	+£1.98
B Hills	7-32	21.9	4-14	3-18	-£15.72
M Wigham	5-23	21.7	0-0	5-23	+£20.88
D Loder	8-37	21.6	5-19	3-18	+£26.75
S Gollings	3-15	20.0	0-1	3-14	+£29.00

Jockeys

Jockeys	Wins-Rides	%	£1 level stks	Best Trainer	W-R
T Quinn	6-21	28.6	+£9.80	W Haggas	2-2
K Fallon	22-77	28.6	-£2.59	Sir M Stoute	11-24
W Buick	3-13	23.1	-£4.00	M Tregoning	1-1
D Sweeney	3-13	23.1	+£8.75	J G O'Shea	1-2
L Dettori	23-106	21.7	-£2.85	S bin Suroor	5-20
S O'Hara	3-14	21.4	-£1.87	J Wainwright	1-1
J Murtagh	3-15	20.0	-£1.33	G Enright	1-1
Kim Tinkler	3-15	20.0	+£27.00	N Tinkler	3-15
Pat Eddery	3-15	20.0	-£4.05	Sir M Stoute	1-1
J P Spencer	38-192	19.8	-£16.86	M Bell	5-14
S Sanders	38-196	19.4	+£23.09	Sir M Prescott	6-30
D O'Neill	9-49	18.4	+£1.35	M J Attwater	1-1
R Hills	13-71	18.3	-£18.60	M Tregoning	2-4

Sponsored by Stan James

YORK

How to get there – Road: Course south of city on Knavesmire Road. From north, A1, A59 to York, northern bypass from A19 to A64. Otherwise, A64 Rail: York, bus

Features: LH, flat

2008 Flat fixtures: May 14-16, 30-31, June 13-14, July 11-12, 25-26, August 19-22

Pointers: A successful stamping ground for Godolphin, though punters have cottoned on to this and the impressive records of Saeed bin Suroor and Frankie Dettori still show a level-stakes profit. The record of favourites underlines the fact that this is a track for class horses.

Time Test standard times

5f	56.6	1m2f88yds	2min7.2
6f	1min9.2	1m4f	2min27.7
7f	1min22	1m5f197yds	2min53.2
1m	1min36.4	1m7f198yds	3min20.2
1m208yds	1min48.2		

Favourites

2-y-o	33.3%	+£5.51
3-y-o+	28.2%	+£12.78
OVERALL	29.5%	+£18.28

Trainers

Trainers	Wins-Runs	%	2yo	3yo+	£1 level stks
J Oxx	4-9	44.4	0-0	4-9	+£5.88
B Millman	4-11	36.4	0-1	4-10	+£9.08
M Magnusson	3-10	30.0	1-3	2-7	+£19.50
J Spearing	3-11	27.3	1-2	2-9	+£10.75
S bin Suroor	25-99	25.3	3-20	22-79	-£2.67
R Bastiman	3-12	25.0	1-5	2-7	+£25.50
W Jarvis	3-12	25.0	0-1	3-11	-£1.72
E J O'Neill	4-16	25.0	4-11	0-5	+£22.25
J Noseda	15-64	23.4	6-24	9-40	+£52.98
P Chapple-Hyam	4-20	20.0	1-6	3-14	-£11.88
Sir M Prescott	4-21	19.0	1-2	3-19	+£0.25
J Dunlop	10-53	18.9	0-7	10-46	+£36.00
D Loder	7-38	18.4	5-18	2-20	-£6.11

Jockeys

Jockeys	Wins-Rides	%	£1 level stks	Best Trainer	W-R
A McCarthy	5-16	31.3	+£13.21	M Bell	1-1
L Dettori	33-137	24.1	-£26.92	S bin Suroor	14-37
J Mackay	3-13	23.1	+£9.00	M Bell	1-2
Hayley Turner	5-25	20.0	+£36.50	R Whitaker	3-4
K Fallon	38-212	17.9	+£2.77	Sir M Stoute	12-42
R Mullen	7-40	17.5	+£44.00	W Musson	2-8
M Kinane	16-94	17.0	-£1.51	Sir M Stoute	5-24
M Hills	18-122	14.8	+£7.00	B Hills	11-76
N Mackay	9-62	14.5	+£34.13	L Cumani	2-21
S Donohoe	3-21	14.3	+£4.50	W Musson	1-2
J P Spencer	21-163	12.9	-£39.41	D Loder	3-11
G Duffield	4-32	12.5	+£3.25	Sir M Prescott	2-4
Pat Eddery	4-32	12.5	+£28.00	J Noseda	3-3

Sprintline

DRAW ANALYSIS becomes more and more vital in Flat racing with each passing season. Most races (outside Festival meetings) are now restricted to 20 runners, and as many courses can accommodate more than that number the draw plays an increasingly massive part.

It is simply impossible for punters to assess the chances of any runner with any accuracy until they have sized up the effect of the draw. It's fundamental – on some courses, a particular draw is almost impossible to overcome, while on others there are draws that confer a tremendous advantage.

What follows is my outline of the factors you need to consider when betting at Britain's many Flat tracks. During the turf season, I'll be updating these thoughts every week in *Racing & Football Outlook*. I'll also be pointing out horses that have run well from poor draws, so you can back them next time out and turn these biases into profit.

COURSE BY COURSE
YOUR GUIDE TO BRITAIN'S DRAW BIASES

ASCOT (right-handed)

Following extensive redevelopment things have become far less predictable than once was the case and watering seems to have become the deciding factor, with far too much applied on more than one occasion (exaggerated distances between runners have unfortunately become the norm).

It's consequently impossible to predict any draw bias from one meeting to the next.

Stalls: Usually go up the stands' side (low).

Biases: One side or other can be favoured but there's no consistency.

Splits: Are common in big-field handicaps and occasionally will occur on soft ground in round-course races, when some head for the outside rail (covered by trees).

AYR (left)

Throughout the 90s high numbers were massively favoured in the Gold and Silver Cups but things have become less clear-cut since.

Traditionally the centre of the course has ridden slower, meaning low numbers were often favoured over 7f50y and 1m, but this didn't look the case on more than one occasion last year.

Stalls: Usually go up the stands' side (high) in sprints, but occasionally go on the other side. It wasn't uncommon last year for jockeys to switch from the far side to race down the centre or even come right across

and this could well continue in the new season.

Biases: There's ultimately not a lot between the two sides in big fields now.

Splits: Are becoming more common, having only usually occurred in the Silver and Gold Cups in the past.

BATH (left)

The draw is basically of far less importance than the pace at which races are run. In big fields, runners drawn low are often inclined to go off too fast to hold a rail position (the course turns left most of the way, including one major kink) and this can see hold-up horses drawn wide coming through late.

Conversely, in smaller fields containing little pace, up front and on the inside is often the place to be.

Stalls: Always go on the inside (low).

Splits: Fields almost always stick together, but soft ground can see a split, with the outside rail (high) then favoured.

BEVERLEY (right)

A high draw is usually essential on good to soft or faster ground over 5f and also on the round course, particularly in races of 7f100y and 1m100y, although there was a spell last year during which the stands' side (low) was quicker.

In sprints, runners have to negotiate a right-handed jink not long after the start and it seems harder here than at any course for runners drawn low to get over to the favoured rail (there's also a camber).

The course management experimented with moving stalls to the stands' side over 5f in 2002 (unsuccessfully, as it led to a huge low bias) and haven't done so since.

Stalls: Go on the inside (high) at all distances.

Biases: High numbers are massively favoured at 5f on good to soft or faster ground and are also best on the round course.

Splits: Splits are rare and only likely over 5f on soft ground.

BRIGHTON (left)

Much depends on the going and time of year; on good to soft or slower ground runners often head for the outside rail, while in late season it's usually just a case of whichever jockey finds the least cut-up strip of ground.

Otherwise, low-drawn prominent-racers tend to hold sway in fast-ground sprints, with double figures always facing an uphill task over 5f59y.

Stalls: Always go on the inside (low) in sprints.

Splits: These occur frequently, as jockeys look for a fresh strip on ground that seems to churn up easily.

CARLISLE (right)

Runners racing with the pace and hardest against the inside rail (high) do well in big fields on decent ground.

This is largely down to the fact that the Flat course and NH course are one and the same, and that those racing nearest the fence are running where the hurdle wings were positioned, while those wider out are on the raced-on surface.

On soft ground, the bias swings completely, with runners racing widest (low) and grabbing the stands' rail in the straight favoured at all distances.

Stalls: Normally go on the inside (high) but can go down the middle in sprints (usually on slow ground).

Biases: High numbers are best in fast-ground sprints. Look to back low numbers on soft/heavy ground.

Splits: Rarely will two groups form but, on easy ground, runners often spread out.

CATTERICK (left)

When the ground is testing, the stands' rail is definitely the place to be, which suits high numbers in 5f races and high-drawn prominent-racers at all other distances.

However, when the ground is good to firm or faster, horses drawn on the inside (low) often hold the edge and there have been several meetings over the last few seasons in which those racing prominently hardest against the inside rail have dominated (over all distances, presumably as a result of watering).

Stalls: Go on the inside (low) at all distances these days (they often used to go on the outer over 5f212y).

Biases: Low numbers are best in sprints on fast ground (particularly watered firm going) but the stands' rail (high) rides faster under slower conditions.

Splits: Are common over 5f.

CHEPSTOW (left)

High numbers enjoyed a massive advantage in straight-course races in 2000 and the course management duly took steps to eradicate the faster strip, using the same 'earthquake' machine that had been employed at Goodwood in the late 90s.

This has led to little in the way of a draw bias since.

Stalls: Always go on the stands' side (high) on the straight course.

Biases: Have become hard to predict in recent times.

Splits: Splits occasionally happen, when jockeys drawn low in big fields head far side.

CHESTER (left)

It's well known that low numbers are favoured at all distances, even in the 2m2f Chester Cup, and the bias is factored into the prices these days.

That said sprints (and in particular handicaps) are still playable, as it often pays to stick to a runner drawn 1-3.

Stalls: Go on the inside (low) at all distances bar 1m2f75y and 2m2f117y (same starting point) when they go on the outside. Certain starters ask for the stalls to come off the inside rail slightly in sprints.

Biases: Low numbers are favoured at all distances. Soft ground seems to accentuate the bias until a few races have been staged, when a higher draw becomes less of a disadvantage as the ground on the inside becomes chewed up.

DONCASTER (left)

The course has been closed until recently for redevelopment and there wasn't a lot between the two sides upon resumption.

As a rule of thumb in the past, the stands' rail (high) always offered an advantage in sprints when the stalls were on the stands' side, with low numbers best the odd occasions they went on the far side.

Stalls: Can go either side but tend to go up the stands' side (high) whenever possible.

Biases: Runners down the centre are usually worst off. The longer the trip on the straight course the better chance the far side (low) has against the stands' side in big fields.

EPSOM (left)

When the going is on the soft side, jockeys tack over to the stands' side for the better ground (this strip rides quicker in such conditions as the course cambers away from the stands' rail).

In 5f races, the stalls are invariably placed on the stands' side, so when the going is soft the majority of the runners are on the best ground from the outset.

Prominent-racers drawn low in round-course races are able to take the shortest route around Tattenham Corner, and on faster ground have a decisive edge over 6f, 7f and 1m114y.

Over 5f, high numbers used to hold quite an advantage, but the bias is not so great these days.

Stalls: Always go on the outside (high) over 5f and 6f (races over the latter trip start on a chute) and inside

(low) at other distances, bar 1m4f10y (centre).
Biases: Low-drawn prominent racers are favoured at between 6f and 1m114y.
Splits: Good to soft ground often leads to a few trying the stands' side route.

FOLKESTONE (right)

Prior to 1998, Folkestone was never thought to have much in the way of a bias, but nowadays the draw is often crucial on the straight course (up to 7f).

On easy ground, the far rail (high) rides faster than the stands' rail, which in turn rides quicker than the middle of the track.

Runners now often go across to the far side over 6f and 7f (although not as often last year) but over 5f, when the stalls are up the stands' rail, fields don't often split any more (it seems the ground lost by switching across over the minimum trip can't be regained from racing on the faster surface).

Stalls Usually go up the stands' side (low) on the straight track, but occasionally down the centre.
Biases: High numbers are favoured over 6f and 7f, and also over the minimum trip when 14 or more line up. However, very low numbers have a good record in smaller fields over 5f. Front-runners are well worth considering at all distances.
Splits: Often occur.

GOODWOOD (right and left)

The course management took steps to end the major high bias seen in the Stewards' Cup throughout the late 90s by breaking up the ground by machine in 1998.

This led to the stands' side (low) dominating the race in 1999 before the far side gradually took over again. Things weren't as clear cut last year, though, and biases changed frequently.

Stalls: Invariably go on the stands' side (low).
Biases: High numbers are best at between 7f-1m1f, and the faster the ground, the more pronounced the bias (keep an eye out for the rail on the home turn being moved during Glorious week, usually after the Thursday).
Splits: Although fields tend not to break into groups in most sprints, runners often spread out to about two-thirds of the way across in fields of around 20 or more.

HAMILTON (right)

Extensive drainage work was carried out in the winter of 2002 in a bid to level up the two sides of the track but, after encouraging early results, the natural bias in favour of high numbers (far side) seemed to kick in again.

For whatever reason, though, that all changed last year and the stands' side (low) is now best on good or faster ground, especially after watering.

The far side is not even quicker when the going rides soft and, under these circumstances, the middle of the course now seems the place to be.

High numbers are best over 1m65y, thanks to runners encountering a tight right-handed loop soon after the start.
Stalls: It's not uncommon for the ground to become too soft for the use of stalls, but otherwise they go either side.
Biases: High draws are best in soft/heavy-ground sprints, but the bias becomes middle to high otherwise (often switching to low on watered fast ground). Front-runners do particularly well at all distances.
Splits: Look for high numbers to peel off in fields of 8+ when the stalls are stands' side unless the ground is fast.

GLORIOUS: runners head for home at Goodwood where there is a pronounced draw bias

HAYDOCK (left)

High numbers used to enjoy a major advantage in soft-ground sprints, but that seems to have been turned full circle by drainage work carried out in the late 90s, with the far side (low) now best on very bad ground.

Otherwise, runners usually head for the centre these days, the draw rarely making much of a difference (although very high numbers can be worst off in big fields on faster going).

Stalls: Usually go down the centre in the straight.

KEMPTON (right)

The first two years of All-Weather racing in 2006-2007 only showed up draw biases at shorter ditances, with high numbers favoured between 5f and 7f. Nothing stood out over a mile and further.

Stalls: Normally go on the inside.

LEICESTER (right)

There was a four-year spell between 1998-2001 when the centre-to-far-side strip (middle to high) enjoyed a decisive advantage over the stands' rail, jockeys eventually choosing to avoid the near side.

However, that's changed recently, with very low numbers more than holding their own.

Stalls: Invariably go up the stands' side (low).

Splits: Still occur occasionally.

LINGFIELD TURF (left)

The draw advantage is nothing like as defined as in years past, but the stands' rail (high) again went through a good spell in the second half of last season, as was the case the year before.

The one factor that can have a massive effect on the draw is heavy rainfall on to firm ground.

Presumably because of the undulating nature of the track and the fact that the far rail on the straight course is towards the bottom of a slope where it joins the round course, rainfall seems to make the middle and far side ride a deal slower.

In these conditions, the top three or four stalls have a massive edge.

Stalls: Go up the stands' side (high) at between 5f and 7f and down the middle over 7f140y.

Biases: High numbers are massively favoured on fast ground after recent rain, but otherwise the most recent meeting is often the best guide.

Splits: It's unusual to see two distinct groups, but runners often fan out centre to stands' side in big fields.

LINGFIELD ALL-WEATHER

There is little bias over most trips, but it is an advantage to be drawn low over 6f and 1m 2f with both starts being situated very close to the first bend.

A low to middle draw is preferable over 5f even with a safety limit of just ten, though the very inside stall has a poor recent record. No horse managed to win from stall one over that trip in 2004, which suggests the ground right against the inside rail is slower than elsewhere.

Stalls: Are against the outside rail (high) over 5f and 1m, but against the inside rail (low) for all other distances.

Splits: Due to the nature of the circuit, the fields never split though some horses can be forced very wide on the home bend.

MUSSELBURGH (right)

The bias in favour of low numbers over 5f isn't as pronounced as many believe, apart from on soft ground, while the bias in favour of high numbers at 7f and 1m also isn't that great.

Stalls: Usually go up the stands' side (low) over 5f nowadays, but they can be rotated.

Splits: Look out for runners drawn very high in big-field 5f races on fast ground, as they occasionally go right to the far rail.

NEWBURY (left)

There's basically little between the two sides these days, apart from on soft ground, in which case the stands' rail (high) is often the place to be.

When the ground is testing it's not uncommon to see runners race wide down the back straight and down the side at between 1m3f56y and 2m (particularly over 1m5f61y). In such circumstances, a high draw becomes an advantage.

Stalls: Can go anywhere for straight-course races.

Splits: It's not often fields are big enough for a split to occur.

NEWCASTLE (left)

Things occasionally change but it's always been a case of high numbers best at up to and including 7f on good or firmer, and low numbers having the advantage when the ground is good to soft or softer.

Over the straight 1m, the stands' rail (high) is the place to be apart from on very bad ground.

Stalls: Invariably go on the stands' side (high) only being switched to the inside under exceptional circumstances.

Splits: Two groups are usually formed when 14+ go to post, and often when 8-13 line up.

NEWMARKET – JULY COURSE (right)

The major draw biases seen under the former Clerk of the Course have become a thing of the past since Michael Prosser took over and now only the occasional meeting will be affected.

The course is permanently divided into two halves by a rail (the Racing Post now carry information regarding which side is to be used) and, as a rule of thumb, the two outside rails (stands' rail when they're on the stands'-side half, far rail when they're on the far-side half) ride faster than the dividing rail.

Stands'-side half - On fast ground (particularly watered) very high numbers are often favoured at up to 1m, when there's a narrow strip hard against the fence that rides quicker.

However, on good to soft or slower ground, runners racing down the centre are favoured.

Far-side half - There's rarely much in the draw, apart from on slow ground, when the far side (low) rides faster.

Stalls: Can go either side on either half of the track.
Splits: Runners just about tend to form two groups in capacity fields, but are more likely to run to their draw here than at tracks such as Newcastle.

NEWMARKET – ROWLEY MILE

Similarly to the July Course, the draw seems to have been evened out since the clerk of the course changed, although it's still generally a case of the further away from the stands' rail the better.
Stalls: Can go anywhere and are rotated.
Biases: High numbers have dominated the 2m2f Cesarewitch in recent years, the logic here being that those on the inside can be switched off early, while low numbers have to work to get into position before the sole right-handed turn.
Splits: It's not unusual for jockeys to come stands' side on slow ground in round-course races.

NOTTINGHAM (left)

On the straight course, it used to be a case of low numbers being favoured when the stalls were on the far rail and high numbers when they were stands' side, with low being best when the stalls spanned the entire course.

These days, though, it's less clear-cut and the going makes the biggest difference. On soft ground low numbers are usually best but high tend to be favoured on good to firm or faster.
Stalls: Tend to go on the stands' side (high) unless the ground is very soft.
Splits: Fields usually split in sprints when 14+ line up.

PONTEFRACT (left)

Low numbers have always been considered best here for the same reason as at Chester, in that the course has several distinct left-hand turns with a short home straight, but this is not always true.

High numbers at least hold their own over 6f now, whatever the ground, but massively so on soft/heavy.

Drainage work was carried out in the late 90s to try and eradicate the outside-rail bias on slow ground, and this worked immediately afterwards, but during the last few seasons there have been definite signs that it's now riding much faster.
Stalls: Go on the inside (low) unless the ground is very soft, when they're switched to the outside rail.
Splits: Although it's uncommon to see distinct groups, high numbers usually race wide these days on good to soft or slower ground.

REDCAR (left)

It's not unusual to see big fields throughout the season here and, while the draw has rarely played a part in the past, with runners inclined to converge towards the centre, high numbers were definitely best on occasions last year.
Stalls: Go towards the stands' side (high).
Splits: Splits are unusual.

RIPON (right)

The draw is often the sole deciding factor in big-field sprints and watering plays a major part. As a general rule, low numbers are best when the ground is good to firm or faster, while the far side is always best on softer going but, ultimately, the best guide here these days is the most recent meeting.
Stalls: Go on the stands' side (low) apart from under exceptional circumstances.
Biases: Front-runners (particularly from high draws over 1m) have an excellent record, and any horse trying to make ground from behind and out wide is always facing a tough task.
Splits: Fields tend to stay together in races of 12 or fewer, but a split is near guaranteed when 15 or more line up. Look for 'draw' jockeys who might chance going far side in fields of 13-14.

SALISBURY (right)

In the past high numbers have tended to be best on fast ground but this was rarely the case last year and frequently races developed out towards the centre.

The draw is more defined on slower ground, as jockeys invariably head towards the stands' rail (good to soft seems to be the cut-off point).
Stalls: Go on the far side (high) unless the ground is soft, when they're often moved to the near side.
Biases: High numbers are best on the straight course on fast ground, there's not much in it on good to soft, while low take over on soft/heavy.
Splits: Fields only tend to divide on good to soft ground; otherwise they all converge towards either rail, dependant upon going.

SANDOWN (right)

On the 5f chute, when the going is on the soft side and the stalls are on the far side (high), high numbers enjoy a decisive advantage.

On the rare occasions that the stalls are placed on the stands' side, low numbers enjoy a slight advantage when all the runners stay towards the stands' rail, but when a few break off and go to the far side high numbers comfortably hold the upper hand again.

High numbers enjoy a decent advantage in double-figure fields over 7f and 1m on good going or faster, but jockeys invariably head for the stands' side on slow ground.
Stalls: Usually go far side (high) over 5f, as the course is more level that side.
Splits: It's unusual for runners to split over 5f, with capacity fields rare and jockeys all inclined to head for the far rail.

SOUTHWELL ALL-WEATHER (left)

Over most trips on the round track it is preferable to be drawn away from the extreme inside or outside.

The exceptions are over 6f and 1m 3f, which both start close to the first bend and therefore it is better to be drawn low to middle.

At most meetings the centre of the track rides faster than against either rail, though that can change in extreme weather when power-harrowing can even out the bias.

A low to middle draw is preferable over the straight

5f and it is noticeable that even when a high draw wins, the horse concerned almost always gives the stands' rail a wide berth having been angled to its left to race more towards the centre.

Stalls: Are placed next to the inside rail (low), except over 5f where they are placed next to the stands' rail (high).

Splits: The fields do not tend to split into groups as such, but can fan right out and take varied routes once into the home straight. Even in big fields over the straight 5f, the runners basically stick to their draw and race as straight as they can from start to finish.

THIRSK (left)

This used to be the biggest draw course in the country, back in the days of the old watering system (which was badly affected by the wind) but, while biases still often show up, they're not as predictable as used to be the case.

Field sizes, watering and going always have to be taken into account when 12 or more line up (11 or fewer runners and it's rare to see anything bar one group up the stands' rail, with high numbers best).

Otherwise, either rail can enjoy the edge on watered fast ground (the one place not to be under any circumstances is down the middle).

Low-drawn prominent-racers are well worth considering whatever the distance.

Stalls: Always go up the stands' side (high).

Biases High numbers are best in sprints when 11 or fewer line up, but it's hard to know which side is likely to do best in bigger fields on fast ground. The far (inside) rail is always best on slow going (the softer the ground, the greater the advantage).

Splits: Runners invariably stay towards the stands' side in sprints containing 12 or fewer runners (unless the ground is soft) and frequently when 13-14 line up. Any more and it becomes long odds-on two groups.

WARWICK (left)

Low numbers are favoured in fast-ground sprints, but not by as much as many believe, and the prices often over-compensate.

However, when the ground is genuinely soft, high numbers can enjoy an advantage

Stalls: Always go on the inside (low).

WINDSOR (figure of eight)

It's typical to see large fields all season, and the draw almost always plays a part.

In sprints, things are set in stone, with high numbers best on good or faster going (particularly watered fast ground), not much between the two sides on good to soft, and the far side (low) taking over on soft or heavy ground.

It can be difficult for runners who switch off the stands' rail to make up the leeway (because the course turns sharply left soon after the finish, those pulled wide must think they're being asked to quicken up into a dead end).

On slower ground, jockeys head centre to far side, and right over to the far rail on genuine soft/heavy

(again it's difficult to make ground from behind).

Stalls: Can be positioned anywhere for sprints.

Biases: High-drawn prominent-racers are favoured in fast-ground sprints, and also over 1m67y. On good to soft going, there's rarely much between the two sides, but it's a case of nearer to the far rail (low) the better on bad ground.

Splits: Splits only occur on good to soft ground, and even then it's rare to see two defined groups.

WOLVERHAMPTON ALL-WEATHER (left)

The huge bias that used to exist towards those horses that raced away from the inside rail on the old Fibresand is a fading memory, but even though the Polytrack is relatively new (installed October 2004), some biases are emerging.

A low draw is a big advantage over 5f and 6f and low to middle is preferable over 7f. Beyond that it doesn't seem to matter, though it is never a good idea to race too wide on the home bends and those that do so rarely seem to make up the lost ground.

Stalls: Are placed against the outside rail (high) over 7f and against the inside rail (low) at all other distances.

Splits: Do not happen and most of the time the runners stay as close as they can next to the inside rail unless traffic problems force them wide.

YARMOUTH (left)

High numbers enjoyed a major advantage for much of the 90s, but this was put to an end by the course switching from pop-up sprinklers (which were affected by the off-shore breeze) to a Briggs Boom in 1999.

These days a bias will appear occasionally but it's hard to predict, and runners often head for the centre whatever the going.

Stalls: Go one side or the other.

Splits: It's common to see groups form, often including one down the centre, in big fields.

YORK (left)

The draw is nothing like as unpredictable in sprints as many believe, although things are never quite as clear-cut in September/October as earlier in the season.

Essentially, on good or faster ground, the faster strip is to be found centre to far side, which means in capacity fields, the place to be is stall 6-12, while in fields of 12-14 runners drawn low are favoured (the course is only wide enough to house 20 runners).

On soft/heavy ground, the stands' side (high) becomes the place to be, and high numbers often get the rail to themselves, as this is not a bias well known among jockeys.

Low numbers are best on fast ground on the round course, although watering can reduce the bias.

Stalls: Can go anywhere.

Biases: Prominent racers in the centre are favoured in fast-ground sprints, but high numbers take over on genuine soft/heavy ground. Low numbers are best in big fields on the round course, apart from on slower going, when runners leave the inside in the straight.

Splits: Defined groups are rare.

racing & football outlook

HOTLINE

THIS GAME IS EASY

No handicap is too hard for Sprintline.
Stewards' Cup, Wokingham, I've done the lot!
So don't delay.
For more winners call

0906 911 0231

on line 9pm evening before racing Calls cost £1/min . Outlook Press, Compton. RG20 7NL

Win – free form!

THIS YEAR'S QUIZ could hardly be more simple, and the prize should prove invaluable to our lucky winner. We're offering a free subscription to The Form Book Flat, the BHB's official form book – every week from May to November, you could be getting the previous week's results in full, together with note-book comments highlighting future winners, adjusted Official Ratings and Raceform's *Performance* ratings. The winner will also get a copy of last year's complete form book.

All you have to do is this: identify the three horses pictured on the following pages. And here's a clue – they are all French horses who won Group 1 races in Britain last year. If you think you know the answer, write their names in the box below in the order in which they appear.

Send your answers along with your details on the entry form below, to:

**2008 Flat Annual Competition, Racing & Football Outlook,
Floor 23, 1 Canada Square, London, E14 5AP.**

Entries must reach us no later than first post on April 18. The winner's name and the right answers will be printed in the RFO's April 22 edition.

Six runners-up will each receive a copy of last year's form book.

Name

Address

Town

Postcode

In the event of more than one correct entry, the winner will be drawn at random from the correct entries. The Editor's decision is final and no correspondence will be entered into.

   Sponsored by Stan James

ROYAL ASCOT

10
skybet

BETTING CHART

ON	ODDS	AGAINST
50	Evens	50
52.4	11-10	47.6
54.5	6-5	45.5
55.6	5-4	44.4
58	11-8	42
60	6-4	40
62	13-8	38
63.6	7-4	36.4
65.3	15-8	34.7
66.7	2-1	33.3
68	85-40	32
69.2	9-4	30.8
71.4	5-2	28.6
73.4	11-4	26.6
75	3-1	25
76.9	100-30	23.1
77.8	7-2	22.2
80	4-1	20
82	9-2	18
83.3	5-1	16.7
84.6	11-2	15.4
85.7	6-1	14.3
86.7	13-2	13.3
87.5	7-1	12.5
88.2	15-2	11.8
89	8-1	11
89.35	100-12	10.65
89.4	17-2	10.6
90	9-1	10
91	10-1	9
91.8	11-1	8.2
92.6	12-1	7.4
93.5	14-1	6.5
94.4	16-1	5.6
94.7	18-1	5.3
95.2	20-1	4.8
95.7	22-1	4.3
96.2	25-1	3.8
97.2	33-1	2.8
97.6	40-1	2.4
98.1	50-1	1.9
98.5	66-1	1.3
99.0	100-1	0.99

The table above (often known as the 'Field Money Table') shows both bookmakers' margins and how much a backer needs to invest to win £100. To calculate a bookmaker's margin, simply add up the percentages of all the odds on offer. The sum by which the total exceeds 100% gives the 'over-round' on the book. To determine what stake is required to win £100 (includes returned stake) at a particular price, just look at the relevant row, either odds-against or odds-on.

Sponsored by Stan James

RULE 4 DEDUCTIONS

When a horse is withdrawn before coming under starter's orders, but after a market has been formed, bookmakers are entitled to make the following deductions from win and place returns (excluding stakes) in accordance with Tattersalls' Rule 4(c).

	Odds of withdrawn horse	Deduction from winnings
(1)	3-10 or shorter	75p in the £
(2)	2-5 to 1-3	70p in the £
(3)	8-15 to 4-9	65p in the £
(4)	8-13 to 4-7	60p in the £
(5)	4-5 to 4-6	55p in the £
(6)	20-21 to 5-6	50p in the £
(7)	Evens to 6-5	45p in the £
(8)	5-4 to 6-4	40p in the £
(9)	13-8 to 7-4	35p in the £
(10)	15-8 to 9-4	30p in the £
(11)	5-2 to 3-1	25p in the £
(12)	100-30 to 4-1	20p in the £
(13)	9-2 to 11-2	15p in the £
(14)	6-1 to 9-1	10p in the £
(15)	10-1 to 14-1	5p in the £
(16)	longer than 14-1	no deductions

(17) When more than one horse is withdrawn without coming under starter's orders, total deductions shall not exceed 75p in the £.

Starting-price bets are affected only when there was insufficient time to form a new market.

Feedback!

If you have any comments or criticism about this book, or suggestions for future editions, please tell us.

Write

Nick Watts,
2008 Flat Annual
Racing & Football Outlook
Floor 23,
1 Canada Square,
London E14 5AP

email   rfo@racingpost.co.uk

Fax   FAO Nick Watts, 0207 510 6457

Horse Index

All horses discussed, with page numbers, except for references in the Group 1 and two-year-old form sections (pages 87-112), which have their own indexes.

Achill Island 28
Albabilia 25
Alessandro Volta 28
Alexander Castle 29, 58
Alfie Flits 58
Allegretto 45
Alwaabel 65
Amaakin...19
Amylee..9
Anna Pavlova..59
Appointment 66
Arch Swing 51
Atlantic Sport...53
Austintatious 54
Babodana 45
Bahamian Ballet 68
Barricado 55
Beacon Lodge...9, 19
Berbice...62
Bonjour Allure 14
Bruges 19, 29
By Command 65
Calming Influence 19
Campfire Glow.......................................22, 51
Cape Amber 24, 44
Captain Gerrard...60
Cartimandua 67
Cat Junior 19
Celtic Slipper 25
Centennial 30
Chain Of GOld..68
Chartist 62
Cheshire Prince...69
Chinese White 24, 51
City Leader 27, 54
Clowance...55
Collection..30
Conference Call...22
Confront...19, 29
Cruel Sea...25, 54
Cuban Missile 55

Curtain Call 29
Dar Re Mi...25, 70, 71
Dalhaan 66
Dansili Dancer 9
Deer Daylami..53
Den's Gift..9
Dhehdaah 69
Diamond Tycoon 55
Domestic Fund 29
Dona Alba 64
Don't Forget Faith 10
Don't Panic 44
Double Duty...54
Dragon Dancer 46
Dream Desert 53
Drifting Gold 10
Dunelight 10
Edge Of Gold..63
Electrolyser 10
Elmaleeha 64
Endless Luck 57, 77
Excellent Art...49
Exclamation 54
Falcon's Fire 14
Famous Name 51
Fast Company 17, 29, 70
Feared In Flight 54
Festivale...65
Festoso 22
Finsceal Beo 51
Firestreak..62
First Avenue..30
Foolin Myself 29
Foresight 66
Forgotten Voice 19
Francesca D'Gorgio 22
French Riviera 29
Frozen Fire..28
Full Of Gold 30
Gaia Prince 66
Gee Dee Nen...44

Generous Thought 46
Giganticus 53
Goodwood Starlight 65
Gothenburg 19, 30
Grafty Green 69
Gypsy Baby 63
Haatef 51
Halfway To Heaven 22
Haradasun 50
Hello Morning 27
Hellvellyn 60
Henrythenavigator.............18, 28, 49
Highland Daughter 11
Hoh Hoh Hoh 63
Honolulu 50
Hotel Du Cap 47
Hustle......................................62
Hyde Lea Flyer 67
Ibn Khaldun 17, 27, 70, 76
Il Warrd 56
Janina 54
Jimmy Styles 11
Jupiter Pluvius 18, 29, 49
Just Lille..................................14
Just Oscar 69
Kandahar Run 29, 43, 70
Katiyra 24, 51
Kayf Aramis 69
Kingdom Of Naples..............28, 49
King Of Queens........................30
King Of Rome 28
King Supreme 62
King's General 66
Kingsgate Native 66
Kitty Matcham 22, 24
Kostar......................................11
Kotsi..25
Kylayne 46
Lady Rangali 14
Latin Lad 61
Laughter...................................25
Laureldean Gale 22, 25
Lille Ida 56
Listen 20, 23, 48
Lobby.......................................66
Look Here 25

Louis Seffens 58
Luck Money 19
Lush Lashes 21, 23, 51
Mad About You 23, 51
Madame Hoy 53
Mahler 50
Makaaseb 22
Malaaseb 25
Masiyma 25
Massalek 56
McCartney 19, 29
Meydan Dubai 66, 75
Midships 66
Mighty 46
Miracle Seeker 11
Missit 53
Montevetro...............................63
Mount Nelson 49
Mountain Pride 65
Moynahan 19
Multidimensional 44
Mutajarred 46
Muthabara 25
Myboycharlie 50
Mystery Sail 66
Nahoodh 21, 53
Natagora 20, 76
New Approach 17, 26, 51, 76
New Star 69
Nijoom Dubai......................21, 53
Nownownow 51
Oarsman 55
Ovthenight 69
Palace Moon 53
Patkai 29
Pearly Wey 11
Peeping Fawn 49
Perfect Art 11
Perfect Star 11
Perks 65
Phoenix Tower 44
Pipedreamer 47
Pivotal Flame 67
Plan 18, 29
Planetarium 57
Polmailly 54

Pressing 45
Prime Defender 54
Prime Exhibit 55
Prince Namid 15
Proviso 20, 25, 76
Psalm 22
Queen Of Naples 25
Quotation 45
Rajeh 69
Raquel White 63
Raven's Pass 17, 70, 76
Red Rocks 54
Red Somerset 63
Red Twist 53
Regal Best 66
Reel Gift 61
Rinterval 22
Rio De La Plata 17, 27, 70, 76
Robby Bobby 57
Rock Peak 53
Roman Maze 69
Rosa Grace 25
Ruff Diamond 75
Sakhee's Secret 52, 77
Samarinda 69
San Silvestro 15
Saoirse Abu 20
Savethisdanceforme 21, 24, 49
Sawpit Sunshine 69
Scintillo 61
Screen Star 25
Scuffle 55
Secret Asset 68
Sense Of Joy 22, 23, 70
Septimus 50
Shabiba 56
Shandlelight 15
Sharp Nephew 54
Sheekey 58
Silver Suitor 71
Simawa 25
Skadrak 54
Sky Dive 71
Slam 54
Smart Instinct 59
Smokey Oakey 45

Soldier Of Fortune 49
Solent 60
Major Cadeaux 61
Spacious 22
Spinning Lucy 54
Square Eddie 75
Star Of Gibraltar 65
Stimulation 53
Strike The Deal 45
Sugar Mint 54
Tajaaweed 29
Tajdeef 19, 54
Talk Of Saafend 62
Tartan Bearer 29
Terentia 67
Tharawaat 54
The Real Guru 15
Thewayyouare 19, 27
Tiger Dream 59
Time Table 43
Toboggan Lady 15
Tourist 54
Trianon 55
Turbo Linn 58
Twice Over 26, 43, 70
US Ranger 50
Utmost Respect 59
Visit 21
Washington Irving 27, 49
West With The Wind 72
Whiteoak Lady 69
Wi Dud 58
Wing Play 53
Winker Watson 18, 44
Wood Chorus 72
Yankadi 54
Yathreb 65
Yeats 50
Young Pretender 19, 30
You'resothrilling 21
Zaahid 53
Zaham 57
Zarkava 20, 23, 76

Sponsored by Stan James